Theorizing Fieldwork in the Humanities

Shalini Puri • Debra A. Castillo
Editors

Theorizing Fieldwork in the Humanities

Methods, Reflections, and Approaches to the Global South

Editors
Shalini Puri
Department of English
University of Pittsburgh
Pittsburgh, Pennsylvania, USA

Debra A. Castillo
Department of Comparative Literature
Cornell University
Ithaca, New York, USA

ISBN 978-1-137-60331-9   ISBN 978-1-349-92834-7   (eBook)
DOI 10.1057/978-1-349-92834-7

Library of Congress Control Number: 2016958189

Cover illustration: © 2015 Saul Landell

Printed on acid-free paper

This Palgrave Macmillan imprint is published by Springer Nature
The registered company is Nature America Inc. New York

CONTENTS

v

Acknowledgments

Many of the contributors to this volume along with several fellow travelers first gathered as a group in March 2014 at the University of Pittsburgh for a two-day colloquium on "Theorizing Fieldwork in the Humanities" to share our work in progress and talk about its underpinnings. It has been a stimulating and convivial collaboration across disciplines and generations. To all who were present, our thanks. Special thanks to Yveline Alexis, Reid Andrews, Tyler Bickford, Laura Brown, John Frechione, Christine Leuenberger, Neepa Majumdar, Scott Morgenstern, Imani Owens, Mina Rajagopalan, Kirk Savage, Peter Trachtenberg, and the students in Shalini Puri's graduate seminar "Interdisciplinary Methods in the Humanities" (2014, 2015).

We gratefully acknowledge generous support of our efforts by the University of Pittsburgh's Dietrich School of Arts and Sciences Faculty Scholarship and Research Grant, a Humanities Center Faculty Collaborative Research Grant, the Center for Latin American Studies, the English Department, the Charles Crow Fund, and the staff of the Center for Latin American Studies. Shalini was also the grateful recipient of the University of Pittsburgh's University Center for International Studies Faculty Fellowship, which laid the groundwork for this project.

At Cornell University, thanks are due to the Center for Engaged Learning and Research; the Mario Einaudi Center for International Studies, which co-supported many of the students in the study abroad course led by Debra Castillo; and especially International Programs in the College of Agriculture and Life Sciences, the administrators for the field course, and alumni from the International Agriculture and Rural Development course (IARD 401/4010) who did fund-raising to support it.

We are especially grateful to Sara Abraham, Laura Brown, and Lara Putnam for their far-reaching comments on earlier versions of the Introduction.

Thanks to the anonymous press readers and to the editorial team at Palgrave Macmillan—Brigitte Shull and Paloma Yannakakis. Melissa Castillo-Garsow, Jarrell D. Wright, and John Kennedy provided valuable assistance with various aspects of research and manuscript preparation.

Duke University Press kindly granted permission to reprint "Finding the Field: Notes on Caribbean Cultural Criticism, Area Studies, and the Forms of Engagement" by Shalini Puri. It first appeared in *Small Axe* 41 (July 2013): 58–73, a special issue entitled "What Is Caribbean Studies?"

Above all, deep thanks to the many people in our various fields for the conversations and insights that animate the entire project.

About the Contributors

Debra A. Castillo is Stephen H. Weiss Presidential Fellow, Emerson Hinchliff Professor of Hispanic Studies, and Professor of Comparative Literature at Cornell University. She is the past president of the international Latin American Studies Association. Among her most recent books are *Cartographies of Affect: Across Borders in South Asia and the Americas* (with Kavita Panjabi) (2011), *Mexican Public Intellectuals* (with Stuart Day) (2014), and *Despite all Adversities: Spanish American Queer Cinema* (with Andrés Lema Hincapié) (2016).

Naminata Diabate is Assistant Professor of Comparative Literature at Cornell University. A scholar of sexuality, race, biopolitics, and postcoloniality, she researches African, African American, and Afro-Hispanic literatures and film. Her recent writing on these subjects has appeared in journals and collections of essays. One of her forthcoming essays is "Genealogies of Desire, Extravagance, and Radical Queerness in Frieda Ekotto's *Chuchote Pas Trop*" (*Research in African Literatures*). Currently, she is working on two book projects: "Naked Agency: Genital Cursing, Biopolitics, and Africa" and "Same-Sex Sexuality and Digitality in Africa."

Neil Doshi is Assistant Professor of French in the Department of French and Italian at the University of Pittsburgh. He is presently completing a manuscript titled *Staging the Novel: Bodies of Francophone Algerian Culture*, which studies the relationships between theatrical and prose forms in Francophone-Algerian literature.

Tori Holmes is Lecturer in Brazilian Studies at Queen's University Belfast, Northern Ireland. Her main research interests are in digital culture and the texts and practices of urban representation in Brazil, particularly relating to favelas. She has broader interests in digital ethnography and ethical and methodological issues in interdisciplinary research on digital culture. She is a member of the Digital Latin American Cultures Network and one of the founders of REBRAC (European Network of Brazilianists working in Cultural Analysis).

Jennifer Lynn Kelly is a University of California President's Postdoctoral Fellow in the Department of Communication at University of California, San Diego. She received her PhD in American Studies with a Portfolio in Women's and Gender Studies from the University of Texas at Austin. She is currently working on her first book, a multisited ethnographic study of solidarity tourism in Palestine. Publications related to this research appear in *American Quarterly* and are forthcoming in *GLQ: A Journal of Lesbian and Gay Studies.*

Stephanie Newell is Professor of English and Senior Research Fellow in International and Area Studies at Yale University. Her research focuses on the public sphere in colonial West Africa, particularly newspapers and pamphlets. She has published widely on the cultural histories of printing and reading in West Africa, and on the spaces for local creativity and subversive resistance in colonial-era newspapers. Her most recent book is *The Power to Name: A History of Anonymity in Colonial West Africa* (2013).

Kavita Panjabi is Professor of Comparative Literature and Coordinator of the Centre for Studies in Latin American Literatures and Cultures at Jadavpur University, Kolkata. Her book *Unclaimed Harvest: An Oral History of the Tebhaga Women's Movement* is forthcoming with Zubaan and the Indian Institute of Advanced Studies. She has edited *Poetics and Politics of Sufism and Bhakti in South Asia: Love, Loss and Liberation* (2011) and co-edited *Women Contesting Culture: Changing Frames of Gender Politics in India* (with Paromita Chakravarti) (2012) and *Cartographies of Affect: Across Borders in South Asia and the Americas* (with Debra Castillo) (2011).

Shalini Puri is Associate Professor of English at the University of Pittsburgh. She is the author of *The Grenada Revolution in the Caribbean Present: Operation Urgent Memory* (2014) and the award-winning *The Caribbean Postcolonial: Social Equality, Post-Nationalism, and Cultural Hybridity* (2004). Her edited collections include *The Legacies of Caribbean Radical Politics* (2010), *Marginal Migrations: The Circulation of Cultures within the Caribbean* (2003), and *Caribbean Military Encounters* (with Lara Putnam).

Lara Putnam is Professor of History at the University of Pittsburgh. Her publications include *Radical Moves: Caribbean Migrants and the Politics of Race in the Jazz Age* (2013), *The Company They Kept: Migrants and the Politics of Gender in Caribbean Costa Rica, 1870–1960* (2002), and over two dozen articles and chapters. Work in progress uses examples from the history of Venezuela, Trinidad, and Grenada to explore methodological and theoretical dilemmas within history's transnational and digital "turns."

Renato Rosaldo is Professor Emeritus of Anthropology as well as social and cultural analysis at New York University. He is the author of *Ilongot Headhunting, 1883–1974: A Study in Society and History* (1980), *Culture and Truth: The Remaking of Social Analysis* (1989), and *The Day of Shelly's Death: The Poetry and Ethnography of Grief* (2014). He is also the editor of many books, including *Anthropology of Globalization* (with Jon Inda) (2001) and *Cultural Citizenship in Island Southeast Asia: Nation and Belonging in the Hinterlands* (2003).

Rashmi Sadana is Assistant Professor of Anthropology at George Mason University and received her PhD from the University of California, Berkeley. She is the author of *English Heart, Hindi Heartland: The Political Life of Literature in India* (2012) and co-editor (with Vasudha Dalmia) of *The Cambridge Companion to Modern Indian Culture* (2012). She is currently writing an ethnography of Delhi's new metro rail system.

Paul Youngquist teaches English at the University of Colorado Boulder. For several years, he and Professor Frances Botkin of Towson University have helped organize the annual Charles Town International Maroon Conference in conjunction with the Quao Day Celebration held in Charles Town's Asafu Yard. He writes on Jamaican marronage, British Romanticism, contemporary music, and science fiction.

LIST OF FIGURES

CHAPTER 1

Introduction: Conjectures on Undisciplined Research

Debra A. Castillo and Shalini Puri

A number of years ago a comparative literature graduate student came to Debra's office in Cornell University to inquire about possibilities for funding fieldwork she hoped to pursue in Mexico. When asked what specifically she wanted to do there, she said, "Honestly, what I really need to do is to breathe the air and eat the food." Debra told her she needed a more compelling academic justification in order to satisfy the evaluators.

Years later, looking back on this incident, we might well ask if the student had a point, under-theorized but implicit in the blunt statement of her underlying need for something that sounds—on the face of it—all too distant from the objective, academic work we are traditionally taught to aspire to. Perhaps she was reaching for something she could not yet name—something like Renato Rosaldo's invocation of the value of "deep hanging out,"[1] or Rebecca Solnit's account of walking in a place as a valuable kind of "reading with one's feet,"[2] or Michel de Certeau's discussion of the importance of walking in the city,[3] or Stuart Hall's metaphorical direction of cultural studies toward the "dirty crossroads"[4] where popular culture and the high arts meet. All point to the gains of emplaced and embodied cultural encounter, in James Clifford's words: "embodied activities pursued in historically and politically defined places"[5]; or in Anand Pandian's eloquent phrasing: "an enchantment with the unknown promise of worldly circumstance."[6] Such phrases are starting points for our exploration of fieldwork in this volume.

D.A. Castillo (✉)
Department of Comparative Literature, Cornell University, Ithaca, USA

S. Puri
English Department, University of Pittsburgh, Pittsburgh, USA

© The Author(s) 2016
S. Puri, D.A. Castillo (eds.), *Theorizing Fieldwork in the Humanities*,
DOI 10.1057/978-1-349-92834-7_1

1

For there is no institutional consensus in literary studies specifically or in the humanities in general on the value of such work; still less is there institutionalized opportunity for it. In fact, recurrent motifs in the experience of scholars who want to undertake such research have been skepticism, caution, discouragement, deferral (until after the dissertation, after tenure, after...), and an intense sense of constraint. Sometimes the discouragement stems not from skepticism but from a desire to protect fellow scholars from institutional consequences; it recognizes, in other words, that notwithstanding routinized invocations of interdisciplinarity, our disciplines rarely reward such work or make allowances for the time it takes.

Nonetheless, those of us who have found ways to undertake fieldwork have found it an indispensable tool, one that has transformed the practice, goals, and conclusions of our scholarship. In fact, other recurrent motifs in our experience of fieldwork have been gratitude for the richness of ongoing relationships forged in the field, the possibility of collaborative work, invigoration by the felt connection of academia with the world outside it, a sense of our writing as one part of a larger shared project, and intense pleasure at the conjunction of sensory and intellectual cognition.

Doing fieldwork in the humanities thus often involves strangely dissonant experiences of intellectual exhilaration and intersubjective connection on the one hand and disciplinary isolation and professional incomprehension on the other. We are enriched by the knowledge that we gain through place-based research; yet, this knowledge is often largely incompatible with the conventions of scholarship in which we are professionalized. This volume is both for those who are deeply immersed in fieldwork in the humanities and for those of us who would like to be so, such as the graduate student who said to Shalini after hearing a talk she gave at a conference in Essex: "I didn't know you could use material like that as evidence. I went back and rewrote my talk after hearing yours." We hope she will find in this volume an emerging community of scholars with whom to think. For, indeed, when we find others attempting fieldwork in the humanities, it is like finding family one didn't know one had.

In our experience, it is quite typical that the methods that humanities-based fieldwork emerges from and forges, the decision points along the way, remain largely invisible or backstage or appear only in brief allusions onstage. Many of our field-based conversations do not show up explicitly in our writing yet nonetheless infuse and transform the entire project. One goal of this volume is thus simply to launch a public conversation among scholars doing fieldwork in the humanities, to make such methods more widely visible without seeking to standardize them.

Our claim, then, is not that there are no scholars in the humanities doing fieldwork. On the contrary, there are a number of inspiring examples of fieldwork-based humanities study, often located at the fringes of disciplines, or dispersed across the muddled *undisciplines* that may be highly praised but are somewhat institutionally homeless. What we want to do is to articulate, share, and refine our practices; to compare our varying understandings of fieldwork in our different disciplines, most of which have no public discourse on fieldwork and offer no training in how to conduct it.

Cultural studies was an early practitioner of fieldwork when it emerged as an interdiscipline in the 1960s, breaking away from literature in response to massive social upheavals around race and empire, self-consciously an irritant that hoped to produce a pearl in the oyster shell of academic life, as Stuart Hall put it.[7] Cultural studies at that time turned to sociology and a range of ethnographic practices to realize its promise. But even a cursory sampling of recent cultural studies readers reveals that the center of gravity of its canonized versions has long since shifted away from fieldwork.[8] Some of the energy, sense of political urgency, and turn toward fieldwork as a method that characterized early incarnations of cultural studies now also animates the newer field of public humanities (including the work of Brooks, Cooper, Harney and Moten, Jay and Graff, Nussbaum, Sommer, Woodward, and the Critical University Studies series published by Johns Hopkins University Press, to name a few).[9] Unlike cultural studies, however, the public humanities have gained *institutional* currency and legitimation in a technocratic environment where it has become necessary to justify the usefulness of the humanities and where interdisciplinarity is often a form of resource consolidation.

Fieldwork-based projects have also been important in contemporary art history and architecture. Likewise, a handful of historians led the way in making oral histories a recognized and legitimate archive for their discipline; Bourdieu describes his research as "fieldwork in philosophy"; and feminist cultural geography, music and ethnomusicology, scholarship on popular culture and everyday life have all turned to fieldwork. So too have scholars in emergent disciplines and interdisciplines such as sound studies; the movement outward from literary studies to music studies; performance studies at the intersection with literature and theater studies or with ethnography, *testimonio* studies, and subaltern studies.[10]

There is also an emerging group of scholars who explicitly define their projects in the context of literary fieldwork—albeit often by way of references that are as tantalizing as they are brief. We might include Muniza Ahmad (Indian Muslim literature), Lara Maconi (Tibetan oral literature), Emily Lethbridge (Icelandic sagas), Tim Frye (Panama), Béquer Seguín (Cuba), Catalina Neculai (New York). Sean Heuston in his book *Modern Poetry and Ethnography* offers an extended meditation on poetic fieldwork; Renato Rosaldo describes his study of grief in *The Day of Shelly's Death* as ethnographic poetry; and Saidiya Hartman describes her 2008 *Lose Your Mother: A Journey along the Atlantic Slave Route* as an exercise in literary fieldwork.[11]

In his brief article, Seguín acknowledges that fieldwork is "a strange task" for a literary scholar.[12] Ahmad issues a clear call to action: "The role and methodologies of fieldwork in the literary sphere are far less clearly defined than in other disciplines, such as anthropology or history. Yet with the gradual

expansion of literary studies in Europe and North America towards the literatures of Africa, Asia and the Middle East, together with the growing emphasis
on interdisciplinary perspectives, this aspect of our research would surely benefit from collective discussion."[13]

Joan (Colin) Dayan's remarkable study *Haiti, History and the Gods* offers a
relatively early example in this brief genealogy. Dayan uses the term "literary
fieldwork" to describe the novelistic achievement of Marie Chauvet's *Fonds
des nègres*: "using a literary text as data that can test, confirm, or enhance facts
from other sources."[14] Dayan argues that Chauvet's novel offers historical
insights that are lost in empiricist and nationalist records, and provides an
opportunity for questioning generic divisions between fact and fiction. The
term "literary fieldwork" could well be applied also to Dayan's own work and
to name what is at the heart of the richness of that work. In a 2013 interview,
Dayan acknowledges the pivotal role of her time in Haiti: "I traveled to Haiti
for the first time as I worked on the book, met Aubelin Jolicoeur in the lobby
of the Oloffson, discovered vodou and nothing was ever the same again."[15]
Dayan also credits anthropologist Michele-Rolph Trouillot's question "[t]o
what extent do 'local initiative and local response' account for motion in the
system?" as guiding her own work. Paying tribute to the significance of his
work, she observes: "This insistence on the *local* ... set the bar for everything
I wrote, not only my writing about Haitian historiography and literature, but
also my engagement with the practical quandaries of the rapprochement of
anthropology and literary criticism, what I later called 'literary fieldwork.'
What he referred to as a '*methodology for the study of particulars as sources of
change* in their own right,' was for him an enduring bulwark against over-
simplification.... [It] was to engage with details that led to nothing short
of revelation."[16] To our knowledge, the aforementioned essay and interview
are among the few places where Dayan writes about the profound ways in
which the conjunction of literary text, the lens of the local, field exposure in
Haiti, and her own experience of the US south's racial history transformed
her work.

Similarly, Gayatri Spivak in *Death of a Discipline* speaks of her transformation as a scholar associated with French high theory, after she takes on work as a
teacher in rural West Bengal, asking herself of the relationship between her work
as an activist and an academic: "How is it possible to reconcile what I touch in
the field—other people—with what I teach for a living—literary criticism?"[17]
What Spivak calls "open-plan fieldwork" (35, 50), a fieldwork that emerges
from her activist experience and is not standardized into a Euro-US model
academic code (37), becomes integral to the disciplinary alliance she imagines
between area studies and comparative literature. The supplementation of one
with the other would provide a counterpoint to monolingual models of world
literature (global English) that bow out of deep or sustained engagement with
place or history. And it would infuse traditionally social science-heavy models
of area studies with the desires of the humanities. Thus, area studies' deeply
grounded place-based research would be combined with disciplined literary

attention to language as an active cultural medium (9) and to forms of knowledge that do not readily translate into policy—for literature's generalizations are unverifiable (44, 50); it offers prefiguration rather than prediction (48; see also 44). Combined, such practices exemplify and enable "learn[ing] to learn from below" (36) and contribute to the formation of "counterglobalizing networks of people's alliances" (35), indeed to imagining the human itself not in terms of identity categories but rather as an orientation, "intended toward the Other" (73).

In *Learning Zulu*, Mark Sanders explicitly links language learning to such projects. He describes learning Zulu, a language he plots in relations to the dense linguistic histories of power in South Africa, as making reparation toward a language for a crime.[18] This reparative quality directed toward the violent history of colonization, and one that is deeply entangled with missionary practices and policies, is something to which he is acutely attentive as a South African of white descent. And he observes: "A learner of language—any language—always follows a pattern of making mistakes and accepting correction" and "since the native speaker determines what is correct—it is also a perpetual process of reparation, of undoing of error."[19] Learning the languages of the global south, engaging them through fieldwork, thus crucially recalibrates the relations between self and other.

Years earlier, Mary Louise Pratt challenged diffusionist, assimiliationist, and other models of culture and language based on homogeneity by reframing colonization and the Americas as a "contact zone" in which one needed to reckon with the active role of subordinated others in shaping culture. From the discipline of media studies, Wendy Willems more recently called for more ethnographic work as a way of studying the south on its own varied terms rather than through the complacencies of "normative dewesternization," which represents "'the Other,' but from within the prism and norms of 'the Self.'"[20] In her study of minority writers in the Americas, Doris Sommer reads the range of textual mechanisms by which minority writers install difference, distance, delays, and blocks to ready access in their texts; she reads these maneuvers as resistances to being neutralized or assimilated to dominant codes. Comparative literature and anthropology scholar Vincent Crapanzano describes one of his goals in writing his ethnographies thus: "to create … a kind of conceptual turbulence in the reader."[21] Both Doris Sommer's literary examples and Crapanzano's description of fieldwork potentially produce similar kinds of conceptual turbulence, an estrangement and revaluation of the self through an encounter with the Other.

One of the questions at the heart of this book is what happens to literary studies when it shifts the *medium* of its encounter with difference from text to everyday life, or more precisely, when it *doubles* the textual encounter with lived encounter? How does that movement between a bounded text and the unbounded, unfinishedness of life *matter?* At the core of all the foregoing examples is a notion of encounter. What fieldwork in the humanities does is to shift the humanities' medium of encounter.

We do not claim, of course, that humanities fieldwork can only usefully occur in the global south or on subaltern or disenfranchised subjects. Such a suggestion would concede to the universalist pretensions of the north, whereas for us part of the value of fieldwork, whether carried out in the north or the south, is precisely, as Dipesh Chakrabarty put it, to provincialize Europe (and by extension the North more generally).[22] In such a project, fieldwork is valuable whether undertaken in relation to subalterns or elites, and whether these populations are located in the global north or the global south. It could contribute to the renewal of Victorian studies in Britain or urban studies in the contemporary USA or any number of other undertakings.

However, much of the most exciting contemporary work is indeed coming from engagements and entanglements with the south. And this volume is offered also as an intervention in postcolonial studies; it is in relation to this field that we have focused our efforts. We use the term "global south" rather than postcolonial studies or decolonial studies because it has a life outside academia. And unlike the term "third world," it signals the particular transnational reorganization of a still unequal world after the end of the Cold War and after the faltering of anticolonial nationalisms. However, like "third world," it refers to a locus of solidarity and contestation that seeks futures more democratic than those held out by first world capitalism, developmentalism, and sub-imperialisms within the south.[23] Thus, though fieldwork may productively be carried out in any part of the world, many of our preceding examples as well as the essays gathered in this volume have undertaken fieldwork on the global south with the goal of checking and countering material inequalities and epistemic privileging of western/northern and elite southern norms.

Because Shalini and Debra's shared home discipline of literary studies has been one of the most resistant to fieldwork, we emphasize in this collection the work of scholars who are forging theoretical and methodological interventions there. We can imagine another volume that might focus more on music, cinema, and art history. We hope that this one will offer a start at making more readily available to scholars in the humanities an understanding of the rationales, methods, dilemmas, risks, and gains of fieldwork. And we hope that it will contribute to the legibility of fieldwork in our disciplines and to the legitimacy of undertaking it. Every discipline has its preferred scholarly centers of thought and key thinkers, its variation on a citational index. But in that preference it also delegitimizes certain sources and voices. We believe that fieldwork draws on an abundant and too often inadmissible field of knowledge, a vast shadow archive that one might call the MLA Works Uncited.

HUMANITIES FIELDWORK AND ANTHROPOLOGY

Fieldwork in the humanities is often framed by two stammered apologies—"I know I'm not an anthropologist, but…." and "I know I'm supposed to be a literary critic, but…." Thus, a few words are in order about the relationship of fieldwork in the humanities to fieldwork in anthropology. The centrality of fieldwork to anthropology and the latter's long history of self-critique and rethinking of its methods make it an obvious interlocutor for us. Moreover, literature and anthropology share an obvious focus on narrative and representation; much has been written on the poetics of ethnography, including literary components such as setting, point of view, texture, detail, voice, and character. Less commonly noted is that anthropology's historical emphasis on language learning, philology, and folklore also overlaps with literature, and that these emphases have played a crucial role in the division of people into the categories of modern and premodern.[24]

This brings us to both the promise and the problem of anthropology for people working on the global south. On the one hand, it offers a capacious archive on nonwestern/southern cultures and a great deal of self-reflexivity about fieldwork. But on the other are anthropology's inescapable historical associations with the colonial enterprise, its holistic models of culture, its privileging and exoticizing of remote others in enclosed cultures, its frequent misunderstandings of native knowledge, its imbrication with positivist science, and the problems and privileges built into the lone (male) ethnographer model.[25] Already a generation ago, in 1988, Clifford Geertz pithily captured some of those criticisms in a list of fieldwork "don'ts": Don't commit: ethnographic ventriloquism, text positivism, the illusion of dispersed authorship, confessionalism, minimization of the authorial role.[26]

It is precisely such risks that prompt Kofi Agawu, writing out of ethnomusicology, to reject social scientific certainty and to call instead for "an abandonment of ethnography and an embrace of fiction."[27] In fact, he urges "a rejection of all first-level, ostensibly objective descriptions, and a substitution of second- or third-degree suppositions, some of them openly speculative, none of them realist."[28] Indeed, fiction from the global south has often thematized the figure of the anthropologist in critical terms, most famously perhaps in Achebe's conclusion to *Things Fall Apart*, in which the colonial anthropologist's cursory account of the Igbo is given the lie by the entirety of the preceding novel. Similarly, in Jorge Luis Borges' short story "The Ethnographer," the cross-cultural encounter transforms the ethnographer so completely that he altogether abandons the academic ethnographic project and its driving assumptions.

A key figure in the literary turn of anthropology, James Clifford, found in fieldwork a crucial legacy, albeit one in need of reexamination. He expanded the term "fieldwork" to explore something akin to what Mary Louise Pratt calls "contact zones"—systems of interlocking travel, dwelling, and displacement that might include fieldwork in the city where one lives or in virtual spaces. Moreover, in a formulation not unlike Spivak's "learning to learn from below" and counter-globalizing networks, Clifford insisted on the need to rethink the relation between fieldwork and homework[29] and to redirect fieldwork toward different kinds of knowledge practices—in the field and at home—that could better be described as "alliance building" and community collaborative practices.

In 2004, Vincent Crapanzano likened field research to montage, describing anthropology as an "interstitial discipline" with affinities with both literature and philosophy: "less … a social science than … a philosophical discipline—in the Kantian critical tradition but by no means in a Kantian way—in which the limits of human understanding, of our cultural pretense, are laid bare."[30] Such thinking anticipates the controversial decision by the American Anthropological Association in 2010 to remove the word "science" from its mission statement.[31]

Liisa Malkki, too, has an expansive understanding of both ethnography and fieldwork. For her, ethnography is not just a form of writing: "Ethnography, understood here as situated, long-term empirical field research (as opposed to its other meaning as a genre of writing and a practice of representation), is simultaneously *a critical theoretical practice, a quotidian ethical practice,* and *an improvisational practice.*"[32] Malkki points to both the centrality of fieldwork in the discipline and the creativity, flexibility, and variations within it. According to her, there is not and has never been any unified practice designated by the term "fieldwork"; rather, improvisation has been *constitutive* of anthropological fieldwork: "a tradition of improvisation" (180). Ultimately, what defines anthropology is not that it studies culture; so do many other disciplines. What defines it, argues Liisa Malkki, is a sensibility (162–163).

We believe that literature shares this sensibility. For both disciplines explore the embeddedness of everyday life in larger social structures and the embodied experience of macro-events. Both also pay attention to the singularities that *escape* (or are sacrificed to) systemic analysis; they are finely attuned to the static of the local that disturbs the frequencies of the global and betrays the blind spots of many a macro-narrative. Their relationship to culture is not predictive or instrumentalist. Instead, they may dwell in the uncertain possibilities of subjunctive rather than in the declarative or imperative. At their best they enter into dialog in an open spirit that does not insist on first knowing "for what?" or positing in advance the value of the outcome as a condition of conversation. Across all the divergent and sometimes fragmentary practices of fieldwork that contributors to this volume have undertaken, it is perhaps elements of this sensibility rather than any particular practice or method of fieldwork that we share and that we seek to infuse into our disciplines. As Anand Pandian puts it in *Reel World*, "the most crucial significance of the sensory and affective turn that so many disciplines have taken in recent years" is the "chance to confront and engage the open-ended unfinished nature of life, to follow things as they happen, to fold the uncertainty and vulnerability of living relations into the very substance of our intellectual work" (16). One reason we were drawn to the image by Saul Landell on the cover of our book is that it evokes an awareness of partiality, of realities glimpsed or implied beyond our fields of vision, of the labor and lenses involved, of the work of lifting the mirror, of reflection on and of similarity and difference.

There are also elements of anthropology that the humanities often do not share but would benefit from. For example, as Akhil Gupta and James Ferguson observe, anthropology is one of the few disciplines that routinely dialogue with a wide cross section of people rather than only experts and elites.[33] Such extensive dialogue is a necessary but not sufficient condition for relativizing rather than naturalizing one's own cultural norms and values and for understanding one's self in relational terms. Yet while such exchange with a wide range of people in the course of their everyday lives is the stuff of literature, literature as a discipline and literary criticism as a practice have no tradition of exchange with nonexperts. Moreover, the disciplinary rejection of authorial intent, useful for enhancing interpretive autonomy, is significantly more problematic if one thinks of authors, critics, and readers and people outside the academy as having potentially shared projects in a shared world to which we all contribute from our different disciplinary and social locations. It is such questions of collaboration, learning from below, reciprocal translation, and exchange with nonexperts that are beginning to be seriously addressed by public humanities scholars.

There is something else that is appealing and potentially useful about the modesty of scale that immersive methods like those of anthropology and sometimes area studies permit. Literature departments, jobs, and publishers push us to claim ever-larger tracts of land or ocean over which we wield expert command, in what risks becoming a present-day version of Thomas Babbington Macaulay's belief, stated in his 1835 "Minute on Indian Education," that "a single shelf of a good European library was worth the whole native literature of India and Arabia."[34] The logic of the market place and profit is to claim scale; the logic of cost reduction to reduce the number of experts working on the south: "just" one author, "just" Trinidad, "just" the Caribbean, just the Americas, just immigrant literature will not do. In disciplined circles, we are often required to speak in the name of world literature (preferably alongside primary specialization in British and/or American literature). In a technocratic university or a practical skills-ruled university, even literature itself does not do. "Too narrow" is the dismissal that haunts the postcolonialist who tries to dwell in one place for too long, the person who is held responsible for continents, centuries, and entire language families. Insistence on the value of and focus on the local is a useful corrective to such arrogance.

GUIDING QUESTIONS

As we work out the practices and gains of fieldwork in the humanities, anthropology has consistently been a fellow traveler. Yet given our quite different disciplinary histories and trainings, and given the different status of fieldwork in our disciplines, it will not be surprising that "fieldwork" in this volume may also signal practices different from most anthropological understandings, despite their range.

Few of the essays in this volume emerge from year(s)-long fieldwork, which remains a norm or ideal in much anthropology. Indeed, we have deliberately used the term "fieldwork" rather than "ethnography" in this volume to hold open a distance between the two terms, so as to clarify that in our usage a written ethnography may not be the end goal or result of fieldwork. What happens to fieldwork when it shifts discipline, shifts form, shifts audience, shifts medium, shifts end point, and shifts traditions of interaction? When the book is only one possible endpoint? In most of the chapters in this volume, information gleaned from the field is routed back into an undisciplining inquiry rather than into an ethnography per se, though—of course—as a published volume, one route continues to be that of academic exchange.

Alive to the fact that fieldwork looks different in different disciplines, we asked our contributors to reflect on the following questions: What made you turn to fieldwork? How did it extend, shift, or transform your scholarship? How did it change the questions you asked or the answers you arrived at? How did it surprise your expectations and hypotheses? How do the histories and orientations of your discipline in the humanities inflect your visions of fieldwork? In what ways were the questions you asked enabled by, informed by, or grounded in your discipline? In what ways did you break with traditional practices of your discipline? What forms of interdisciplinarity did you practice? How do you understand the relationship of your fieldwork to the practices and questions of social science fieldwork? What are the similarities and differences? What kinds of conversations between social science and the humanities were necessary or enabled by your project? When did you find your disciplinary vocabularies particularly well suited or particularly inadequate for the tasks at hand? What are appropriate terminologies? (For example, "research subject," "informant," "interviewee," "interlocutor," and "collaborator" all encode and distribute power differently.) What counts as data? Most disciplines have some notion of what constitutes precision: Was it relevant to the work you did? What kinds of ethical dilemmas and protocols arose for you in the course of fieldwork? What forms of accountability might fieldwork facilitate that we might ordinarily not develop in the humanities? How can fieldwork contribute to the project and methodologies of a humanities-informed comparative area studies? What have you found to be some of the most powerful examples of humanities-based fieldwork, to which you turned for help? How might fieldwork contribute to the goals of the humanities? How might it expand the topics and scope of humanities inquiry? What are the gains and methods of fieldwork if the topic of investigation is not contemporary? In short: What does it mean to theorize fieldwork in the humanities?

On Theory and Theorizing

In some ways, the term "reflection" carries less baggage than "theory" or "theorizing." But we retained the term "theorizing" in the title of this book because one of our interests is precisely to think about how fieldwork *surprises* theory: How context surprises absolutes, what lives or dies hidden in the folds of macro-explanations, what kinds of generalizations fieldwork yields or refuses, and how daily practices surprise our disciplinary or theoretical models. Such surprises appear as productive dissonances.

There is a certain irony to the fact that the thick description or distilled detail that literary scholars so value in literature—close attention to the manifestations at the micro-level of systemic phenomena; texture, affect, point of view, intensely embodied description, setting; contextual rather than absolute knowledge—is something that we often purge from our criticism.[35] This leaves us in the position of the historians ruefully invoked by the Popular Memory Group: "Hence the feeling not uncommonly experienced in reading secondary interpretations of first accounts: we wish the bloody historian would go away and let us listen to the account itself! It seems more interesting, more nuanced, more complex and actually more explanatory than its secondary appropriation allows."[36]

Colin Dayan, too, notes the *theoretical* power of Truillot's work: it "moves from the ground up, from the little facts or minute incidents that are most often overlooked in favor of sweeping claims or familiar assumptions, to arrive at 'new cultural patterns' that yet preserve the ambiguity and nuance—and, ultimately, the power—of lives lived on the periphery but not outside of what Albert Memmi once dubbed 'the game of history.'"[37] Along similar lines, Anand Pandian describes his anthropological writing as seeking "to lead readers accustomed to looking chiefly for arguments back into the empirical thickets from which these arguments arise."[38] Fieldwork is inseparable from experience, but, as Pandian reminds us, drawing on Raymond Williams' history of the word "experience" in *Keywords*, although one trajectory of the word signals immediacy, authenticity, or absence of reflection, another links it to *experiment*: "Experience is a matter of experiments with life, an arena of conjectures, trials, and difficult lessons."[39] We believe that fieldwork involves the latter sense of experience: not merely travel or presence but also consideration, reflection, analysis, trying, and testing.[40] As Pandian puts it, freshness of insight lies in "travers[ing] the line between empirical life and conceptual possibility."[41]

Thus, the forms that theorizing take in this volume vary dramatically—in their degrees of abstraction, narrative style, and formal experimentation. This range of form can be attributed to many things, including individual stylistic preference; different practices, experiences, and goals of fieldwork; different scholarly conventions of the authors' home disciplines; and the particular traditions of fieldwork that authors are in conversation with. There is no self-evident, recognizable, or preexisting model or genre for theoretical writing on fieldwork in the humanities. Nor should there be. We read, therefore, with an ear for both the harmonies and the dissonances across chapters, and hope that both will be generative. Perhaps under-specifying the terms "theorizing" and "fieldwork" is a virtue at this point—their very fuzziness allows a necessary capaciousness and openness of experience, a recognition of an at least temporarily undisciplined engagement with place.

On Privilege

The hushed archive, the ivory tower, the lettered city—all these are emblems of the privileged separation of researcher or knowledge from that messy thing we called everyday life. They remain the ruling images and the most recognizable models for literary scholarship. But in contrast to the model of the solitary researcher in the isolation of the library, fieldwork depends on immersion. It requires the researcher to navigate a cultural space dense with meanings and to register its resistances, debates, and active subjectivities. Such encounters jolt one out of complacence. Interruption is part of the point.

Literary scholarship (along, perhaps, with philosophy) is one of the disciplines of the humanities to which fieldwork has been most alien. As noted earlier, art history, music, performance studies, and media studies tend to make more provision for travel to sites of cultural production under study, though it is hardly the case that they routinely permit lengthy stays. Moreover, the extent to which their focus is on interactions with the place or its people varies widely. Sometimes our disciplinarily sanctioned trips to archives have the spin-off benefit of allowing an encounter with the place outside the archive at the same time. But for scholars of the global south, it is often the case that the archives are housed in the global north, and so even a tangential practice of fieldwork is elusive.

Yet if the creative space and scholarly solitude of a room of one's own represent privilege, so, very often, does heading to the field. Fieldwork, especially when it involves travel or extended dwelling away, can be expensive; and workloads and institutions often withhold the kind of time it requires. Even so, independent scholars and artists, grassroots intellectuals, and scholars working at less privileged universities in the north or south find ways of undertaking lower-cost fieldwork, for example, drawing on and developing thick associations with local or neighboring rather than distant subjects.

Academic publication in a globally dominant language is itself often both an expression and a measure of privilege. Our volume does not escape this privilege or the risks it entails. One of the structural risks of publication on fieldwork is that it will disproportionately involve research by scholars based in elite institutions in the global north. This volume consists mostly of contributors based in the global north who work on the global south.[42] Yet, we believe the structural risk is worth taking, especially since our disciplines in their more conventional forms are hardly innocent of power. Publication of scholarship on the global south, whether fieldwork derived or not, is already skewed by location—and no less consequentially so. The risk of northern scholars (mis) representing the global south needs to be weighed against the possibilities that fieldwork offers to counter erasures of the global south.

At the same time, fieldworkers located in the south publish work which may or may not be in dialogue with the northern theory du jour, may be written in languages other than English, and may be read in different print circuits from English-dominant or international scholarly circles. And scholars involved in fieldwork may also choose to direct their fieldwork not toward academic publication but toward the arts, social policy, teaching, or community activism. We would thus like to think the academically oriented forms of fieldwork represented in this volume alongside a range of other fieldwork-based projects. To note just a few examples: 1998 Fest'Africa project brought ten African writers to Kigali to facilitate an organized, collective, artistic commemoration of the genocide through the lenses of fiction.[43] The Jamaican theater group Sistren has for decades now created fieldwork-based theater, involving writing and acting by community members. Marlon James' novel *A Brief History of Seven Killings* undertakes a literary fieldwork akin to that which Dayan saw in Marie Chauvet's novels; it offers a kind of literary ethnography of Kingston's gang culture, an anthropology of violence, as it were. Field-based progressive responses to the 1984 anti-Sikh riots in Delhi after the assassination of Indira Gandhi included street theater across Delhi that sought to build solidarity across warring communities; other forms of solidarity work such as helping victims file compensation claims and publishing an investigative report which was distributed in the immediate aftermath of the riots and was based on interviews carried out by the People's Union for Democratic Rights and the People's Union for Civil Liberties[44]; and anthropologist Veena Das' study *Life and Words*.[45]

We hope that this volume and related undertakings will be of use to collaborative efforts in the humanities, ranging from co-authorship to north-south alliances and projects, to south-south collaborations and the public humanities more generally. We invite you to walk with us through the chapters that follow, which navigate a range of disciplinary, historical, and cultural landscapes.

CHAPTER SUMMARIES

The chapters in this volume involve various forms of emplaced cultural communications and share insights gleaned from the interactions of everyday life and cultural texts. Without exception they are in dialogue with nonacademic spaces and people. The book is divided into four sections representing strands in this dialogue with fieldwork.

The first section, "Memory, Conflict, Contestation," includes chapters by Shalini Puri, Naminata Diabate, and Kavita Panjabi. Puri's chapter leads the volume, not only for its relevance to this section but also because it was the text that launched our collaborative project and was shared reading for the participants; it is the only chapter that has been previously published. Puri's chapter reflects on how fieldwork, her encounter with the physical space of Grenada, transformed her approach to the memory of the Grenada Revolution, enabling her to dwell on artistic production in relation to the cultural geography of Grenada and to everyday utterances and practices. Thus, she shows how her fieldwork on memory of the Grenada Revolution both originated in and extended literary studies, and how it enabled alternatives to psychoanalytic approaches in memory and trauma studies. Moreover, it changed her sense of who her interlocutors were.

Diabate's inquiry began as a conundrum. As a woman from Côte d'Ivoire, she was astounded that African and African American Studies in the USA did not register most of the women from the continent or the rich range of agency and response she had seen in them. Diabate uses what she calls "retrospective observation" to draw on cultural experience acquired and events witnessed when she lived in Côte d'Ivoire; she combines this with fieldwork she undertook after the place became an object of intellectual inquiry. This reencounter as an academic with the place where she grew up included discussing with women their understanding of their practices of genital cursing, contesting literary silences, and reading the discrepancies among literary, journalistic, and anthropological accounts of women's agency. For example, she opens up the theoretical discussions of scholars like Giorgio Agamben to supplements that their Euro-American-based grounding has ignored. And she calls to account critics who lavish care on the women protagonists of the novels they read, yet ignore entirely the women whose lives in some mediated way the literature represents. Retrospective observation and fieldwork were crucial not only to her being able to answer her questions but to ask them in the first place.

For Panjabi, fieldwork enables a rethinking of philosophical understandings of aesthetics. Her chapter is grounded in an oral history project in which she interviewed women participants in Bengal's Tebhaga movement in the late 1940s. She explores how the affective impact of witnessing the starvation of peasants in the Bengal famine became a critical mobilizing force for the urban activists she interviewed. Those interviews, the affect and recalled excitement of the women, the recurrent tropes in their accounts lead Panjabi to argue for restoring to aesthetics its lost currency as a mode of "sensuous cognition" and prompt insight into the ways that poetic truths and historical activism may reinforce one another.

The second section, "Place, Performance, Practices," includes chapters by Jennifer Kelly, Neil Doshi, Tori Holmes, and Rashmi Sadana. Each of these scholars uses fieldwork methodologies to shake up theoretical and disciplinary understandings of core concepts from post/colonial studies, performance studies, or presumptions about "the literary" itself.

Kelly undertook fieldwork on anticolonial Palestinian tourism in response to the numerous Christian, Zionist, birthright, and diplomatic tours of Israel that shape Israel's place in American imagination and policy. Prior to her fieldwork, she thought of the tours of Palestine as "justice tourism," but as a result of fieldwork she came to think of them as "solidarity tourism," a less resounding term that better captured the flawed but necessary practice structured by the demand of the privileged that Palestinians provide evidentiary weight for their claims. In the course of explaining how she navigated institutional constraints and how those constraints shaped the particular fieldwork methods she developed, Kelly also offers us detailed glimpses of and insights from her field notebooks, including observations about the expressions of shop owners when tourists promised they would "come back later"; the ways Palestinian tour guides corrected Israeli tour guides' narratives; the shared pedagogical labor that tour guides and teaching assistants both perform; the tour guides' boredom with the repetitive nature of their work even as they recognized it as politically and economically necessary; and a running account of Kelly's and others' expectations and the disruption of those expectations. She traces how her training in American Studies enabled her to frame the topic in terms of US militarism and empire; how coursework in anthropology enabled her to trace the daily effects of empire, militarism, and colonialism; and how her literary training enabled her to refuse evaluative approaches to solidarity tourism.

Doshi's fieldwork ranges across Algeria and India. He explores the spaces where Algerian playwright Abdelkader Alloula's controversial plays were once performed—disenfranchised city spaces that remain urgently present, though the performances themselves have been largely silenced. He combines an encounter with that space with what he calls "distant fieldwork" as a participant observer in JANAM, an Indian street theater group in New Delhi that shared many aspects of Alloula's political vision and formal techniques. Putting together the space of Algeria with the performances Doshi participates in with the JANAM theater group, he imagines the contours of Alloula's absent play.

Holmes focuses on the ethical implications of fieldwork. Her project combines study of web-based communities with place-based communities and fieldwork, including extended interviews with bloggers. She explores blogs produced by favela dwellers in Rio, raising questions about the relationship between literature and literacy and between cultural works and the human practices surrounding them. The choice to treat web producers as "research subjects" or "authors" involves a series of other considerations that need to be weighed—the risks of erasure, the protections of invisibility, the gains of recognition, the implicit allocation of more or less authority in each term.

Sadana's experience as an intern at *Granta* (where she helped determine which essays would be selected for publication) made her a participant observer in a center of Anglophone publishing.[46] Her subsequent immersion in Delhi as an insider/outsider decentered *Granta*'s model of "many Englishes" and became instead a study of English as one of India's many literary languages. She reflects here on her book *English Heart, Hindi Heartland: The Political Life of Literature in India*, which studied the literary life of Delhi and the multilingual circuits of publication, sale, and recognition that are embedded in the geography of the city and its neighborhoods. Her newer project explores the remaking of circuits of mobility and sociality by Delhi's metro rail. Sadana thus traces the logic of her movement from being a student of literature in Britain to an anthropologist researching the literary in Delhi. Throughout the chapter, Sadana explores the ways in which while doing fieldwork "you are your method, and you are part of your research, and yet it is not about you."

"Medium and Form" includes discipline-interrogating meditations by historian Lara Putnam and anthropologist Renato Rosaldo. Putnam notes that historians' expanding access to digitized sources means that international research now requires less and less international residence. This has been an unacknowledged driver of history's "transnational" turn. She explores the gains, risks, and trade-offs of the digital turn in the discipline of history, urging that digital research be undertaken in conjunction with place-based research that has been a foundation of historical method. What, she asks, might the new digital technologies drive into the shadows?

Rosaldo's chapter may be thought of as a companion piece to his essay "Notes on Poetry and Ethnography" (which appears in his much-lauded sui generis book, *The Day of Shelly's Death*), where he devises the term "antropoesis" or ethnographic poetry to describe the poetry in which he weaves together his own grief at the death of his wife, his family's grief, and Ilongot practices of grieving; his experience of grief transformed his understanding of the Ilongot and of the very project of anthropology. In the chapter at hand, he comments on the ethnographic poetry of Yusef Komunyakaa and Naomi Shihab Nye, addressing not only cultural translation but also linguistic translation. As someone familiar with the American racial field, who weighed in on the translation of Komunyakaa's poem on Vietnam into Spanish, he reads Komunyakaa's poem as a continuation of the civil rights struggle by other means. His chapter in this volume is a meditation on what a poet, translator, and ethnographer may have in common.

The final section—"Institutions, Organizations, Collaborations"—with chapters by Stephanie Newell, Paul Youngquist, and Debra Castillo, offers examples of ways that engaged scholarship can shake up institutional practices or redefine hierarchical assumptions about collaboration.

Newell's chapter centers on the ubiquitous presence of dirt in discourses about urban Africa and notes its crucial role in the ideological work of othering. Through a collaborative and comparative study of Nairobi and Lagos, she draws attention to alternative, cosmopolitan, and vernacular discourses of dirt that surfaced in fieldwork and in social media in a polylinguistic context. Newell explores methodological questions that arose out of her collaborative and comparative multisited fieldwork, including the limits of comparing different colonial histories and natural resources of structurally similar African cities; the coincidental but highly consequential outbreak of Ebola in West Africa in 2014, which rendered her planned comparisons between Lagos and Nairobi infeasible by literally changing daily interactions; and the gaps between protocols prescribed by the project's international funding agency and what material conditions on the ground permitted.

Youngquist explains the circuitous route by which a Romanticist interrupted his archival musings on Marcus Rainsford's account of the Haitian Revolution, to follow up on a hint about Jamaica, and ended up collaborating on a regular basis with Charles Town maroons on their annual conference. In the course of his often playful narrative, he describes the importance of "lateral listening" for his method; he also describes fieldwork as "collaborative, immersive, multiple, and inconclusive," involving both the systematic study dear to his archival roots and the illuminating, often maddening, negotiations of knowledge held in the ambient oral histories that contradict and supplement the sparse and biased archival record.

Finally, Castillo addresses fieldwork as a practice of engaged pedagogy in the Study Abroad course she often teaches in Chiapas. She explores the encounter between privileged Cornell students and underprivileged indigenous people in Mexico, looking for practices of cultural translation as well as incommensurability, and explores the opportunities the course offers to learn on and in different cultural terms. Castillo draws on the Zapatistas' understanding of "*acompañamiento*"—the practice of walking with someone—a word that suggests collaboration, proximity, and a slowed pace as crucial elements in learning. She proposes it as a model for our own scholarly practice.

Coda

We share our experiences of fieldwork here without wishing them to become standardized, prescriptive, or paradigmatic. Fieldwork is not the only route to knowledge. Its insights come with no stamp of assurance or authenticity. Our own knowledge is vulnerable and our interlocutors in the field have no special or privileged knowledge. Everyday life is no more transparent than literary texts. But fieldwork offers different archives, different media of encounter, different methods of engagement, different interlocutors—and thus potentially different insights—that can deepen our understanding of others in a way that also involves an estrangement and reassessment of the self. To return to Clifford's term, this is the "homework" that fieldwork makes possible.

The Cuban author Alejo Carpentier provides a context for the student who needed to go to Mexico to eat the food. According to Carpentier, to understand the Nanjing massacre, one needs to breathe the air of that city; to understand Mexican literature, one needs a basic grasp of that nation's philosophy of cooking.[47] Carpentier elaborates on why this in-country fieldwork is even more crucial in the global south than it is in the north: He argues that the "universal" images of the pine and palm so familiar in poetic texts need to be set against the *ceiba* and the papaya, which he describes with a lush barroquism. In his paired juxtaposition of the pine and palm versus the *ceiba* and papaya tree, in each case the first tree of the pair represents a symbol linked to primordial sacred practices, while the second tree provides exotic or everyday fruit, depending on the geography—dates, perhaps, or papayas. How does one talk about the *ceiba*, without telling the story of Africans in the Caribbean, or of the deep Mayan respect for the world tree, now hybridized with European Christian overtones in "traditional Catholic" practices?

Global markets now make papayas available to consumers across the globe, but they cannot speak to the conjunction of the *ceiba* and the papaya, or capture the fragrance of the *selva*, or the taste of freshly picked fruit in the mouth. The same cultural observation can go in the opposite direction, though Carpentier does not speak of this aspect; a Puerto Rican student once observed that she never understood the attraction of eating an apple until she came to the

USA. How does a North American explain cranberries to someone from other latitudes without talking about Thanksgiving and the history of that maligned, celebrated holiday in the USA? When does a mango eaten far from the tropics materialize nostalgia or desire—in a tropical immigrant or London dweller who has never left home? When does it become a mouthful of stereotypes of tropicality or mischievous counter-stereotypes?[48] Such interactions with everyday life, of which fieldwork is a sustained practice, in which we encounter facts folded into their intricately textured lived experience are also an inoculation against cultural laziness and intellectual shortcuts.

Similarly, it is one thing to know that Afghanistan has more people maimed by land mines than any other country in the world and quite another to grasp, as we did from Nadeem Aslam's novel *The Wasted Vigil*, that in bazaars in Afghanistan shoes may be bought not in pairs but singly. Aslam reminds us, too, that there is no reason to fetishize fieldwork. Fieldwork is neither a requirement for nor a guarantee of insight. Indeed, Aslam wrote a first draft of his brilliant novel without ever setting foot in Afghanistan. And then he went there.[49]

NOTES

1. Clifford Geertz credits the phrase to James Clifford in "Deep Hanging Out," 69–72, 69. James Clifford credits it to Rosaldo. *Routes: Travel and Translation in the Twentieth Century*, 56.
2. Solnit, *Wanderlust: A History of Walking*, 70.
3. Certeau, "Walking in the City," 91–110.
4. Hall, "Race, Culture, and Communications," 336.
5. Clifford, *Routes*, 8.
6. Pandian, *Reel World: An Anthropology of Creation*, 280.
7. Hall, "Race, Culture, and Communications," 337.
8. In fact, Angela McRobbie noted this trend as early as 1994, calling for a return to analysis of the terrain of lived experience in conjunction with Gramscian cultural analysis. *Postmodernism and Popular Culture*, 39–41. Ann Gray's *Research Practice for Cultural Studies: Ethnographic Methods and Lived Cultures* is an important correction to this trend. It understands itself as an effort to answer the questions "What is cultural studies?" and "How does cultural studies understand culture?" and to study its ethnographic methods and aid the development of research projects. It is no coincidence that Gray herself is trained in the tradition of the Birmingham School of Cultural Studies, where ethnography was a particularly significant method. The closure of Birmingham's Department of Cultural Studies in 2002 as part of a top-down "restructuring" speaks to the precariousness of institutional space for such work.
9. Harney and Moten's work is a radical iteration of the public humanities imagined as fugitive undercommons within a largely corporate university;

they would see their work as being at odds with the project of remaking the American university that is the goal of many of the other public humanities scholars named here.

10. For examples, see Bibliography and Further Reading. Interestingly, several humanities projects in such disciplines have gained funding through the National Science Foundation, which has been more ready to institutionalize fieldwork, given the sciences' privileging of empirical data collection.

11. Sean Heuston, *Modern Poetry and Ethnography: Yeats, Frost, Warren, Heaney, and the Poet as Anthropologist*; Renato Rosaldo, *The Day of Shelly's Death: The Poetry and Ethnography of Grief*; and Hartman, "Across the Atlantic Slave Route."

12. Seguín, "The Texture of Literary Fieldwork," 9.

13. Ahmad, "Notes on Fieldwork."

14. Dayan, *Haiti, History and the Gods*, xviii.

15. "Dread and Dispossession: An Interview with Colin Dayan."

16. Dayan, "And Then Came Culture," 141.

17. Spivak, *Death of a Discipline*, 36. Subsequent citations appear as parenthetical references in the main text.

18. Sanders, *Learning Zulu: A Secret History of Language in South Africa*, 7.

19. Sanders, 12–13.

20. "Beyond Normative Dewesternization," 8.

21. Crapanzano, *Imaginative Horizons: An Essay in Literary-Philosophical Anthropology*, 3.

22. Dipesh Chakrabarty, *Provincializing Europe: Postcolonial Thought and Historical Difference*. Several of the aforementioned cultural studies scholars in fact undertook fieldwork in Britain. See Bauman and Briggs for an elaboration of Chakrabarty's ideas in relation to anthropology.

23. Aside from the innumerable critiques that accompanied the institutionalization of postcolonial studies in the US, for later redirections of the field, see the literature on the global south and decolonial studies, for example: Shu-mei Shih and Francoise Lionnet, eds., *Minor Transnationalism*, especially the essays by Koshy and Behdad; Walter Mignolo, *The Darker Side of Western Modernity: Global Futures, Decolonial Options*; Ramón Grosfoguel, "Decolonizing Post-colonial Studies and Paradigms of Political Economy: Transmodernity, Decolonial Thinking, and Global Coloniality," 1–37; and the journal *Global South*.

24. See Richard Bauman and Charles Briggs, *Voices of Modernity: Language Ideologies and the Politics of Inequality*.

25. For a brief history of paradigms and traditions in anthropology, see George W. Stocking, "Paradigmatic Traditions in the History of Anthropology," 712–27.

26. Geertz, *Works and Lives*, 145. Subsequent citations appear as parenthetical references in the main text.

27. Agawu, *Representing African Music: Postcolonial Notes, Queries, Positions*, 170.
28. Agawu.
29. Clifford, *Routes*, 85.
30. Crapanzano, *Imaginative Horizons*, 5, 11.
31. See Nicholas Wade, "Anthropology a Science? Statement Deepens a Rift."
32. Malkki, "Tradition and Improvisation in Ethnographic Field Research," 164. Subsequent citations appear as parenthetical references in the main text.
33. Gupta and Ferguson, *Anthropological Locations*, 36.
34. Macaulay, "Minute on Indian Education."
35. An extreme example of this is the model of "distant reading" that scholars like Franco Moretti have undertaken, a systematizing project for understanding world literature, in which distance and the omission of the rich details of reality and close reading are conditions of both inclusion in the canon and theoretical knowledge. *Distant Reading*, 48–49. Data-driven digital analysis is key to his method. See also Stephen Best and Sharon Marcus' claims for "surface reading," which also contest close reading practices. "Surface Reading: An Introduction," in "The Way We Read Now," 1–21.
36. Popular Memory Group, "Popular Memory: Theory, Politics, Method," 228.
37. Dayan, "And Then Came Culture," 142.
38. Pandian, *Reel World*, 280.
39. Pandian, 16, 293.
40. Williams, *Keywords: A Vocabulary of Culture and Society. Revised Edition*, 126–29.
41. Pandian, "The Time of Anthropology," 566.
42. However, see the chapter by Kavita Panjabi for an account of fieldwork by a scholar located in the global south; and see the chapters by Stephanie Newell and Paul Youngquist for examples of fieldwork that involve significant collaboration with southern academic researchers or grassroots intellectuals. Examples of such collaborations beyond our volume include the University of Pittsburgh's Center for Latin American Studies' 2015 theme, "Leading from the South," the Latin American Studies Association's "Otros saberes" initiative, and numerous other engaged learning projects involving collaborations with southern-based intellectuals, artists, and activists. Humanities-informed centers of study located largely in the global south include transnational research and collaborations such as the Inter-Asia Cultural Studies Society, the Johannesburg Workshop in Theory and Criticism which is "an exploration of global conversation based in the south" (http://www.jwtc.org.za/), and the Center for the Study of Developing Studies in New Delhi. See also the collaborative and interdisciplinary "Planned Violence: Postcolonial Urban Infrastructures and Literature" project convened by Elleke Boehmer at Oxford University that studies London, Delhi, and Johannesburg (http://plannedviolence.org/).

43. See Nicki Hitchcott, "A Global African Commemoration: *Rwanda: Écrire par devoir de mémoire*," 151–61.
44. People's Union for Democratic Rights and the People's Union for Civil Liberties, *Who are the Guilty? Report of a joint inquiry into the causes and impact of the riots in Delhi from 31 October to 10 November 1984.*
45. Veena Das, *Life and Words: Violence and the Descent into the Ordinary.*
46. Reading Sadana's book in conjunction with Diabate's chapter, one cannot help but wonder how many fictional African women languished in the reject bins of other publishers, unfit for marketing needs driven by sensationalist depictions of victimization and niche readerships.
47. Carpentier, *Tientos y diferencias*, 30.
48. See John Agard, "English Girl Eats Her First Mango," 39; and Mohsin Hamid, et al., "How to Write About Pakistan."
49. Interview by Harriett Gilbert, *The Word*, BBC Radio World Service, October 14, 2008, http://www.bbc.co.uk/worldservice/programmes/the_word.shtml.

BIBLIOGRAPHY AND FURTHER READING

Agard, John. 1985. English Girl Eats Her First Mango. In *Mangoes and Bullets: Selected and New Poems, 1972–84,* 39. London: Pluto Press.

Agawu, Kofi. 2003. *Representing African Music: Postcolonial Notes, Queries, Positions.* New York: Routledge.

Ahmad, Munizha. n.d. Notes on Fieldwork. School of Oriental and African Studies, University of London. http://www.soas.ac.uk/soaslit/issue1/AHMAD.PDF. Accessed 30 November 2015.

Aslam, Nadeem. 2008. Interview by Harriett Gilbert. *The Word.* BBC Radio World Service. October 14. http://www.bbc.co.uk/worldservice/programmes/the_word.shtml.

———. 2009. *The Wasted Vigil.* New York: Vintage.

Barz, Gregory F., and Timothy J. Cooley. 2008. *Shadows in the Field: New Perspectives for Fieldwork in Ethnomusicology.* New York: Oxford University Press.

Bauman, Richard, and Charles Briggs. 2003. *Voices of Modernity: Language Ideologies and the Politics of Inequality.* Cambridge: Cambridge University Press.

Behar, Ruth, and Deborah A. Gordon. 1996. *Women Writing Culture.* Berkeley, CA: University of California Press.

Best, Stephen, and Sharon Marcus. 2009. Surface Reading: An Introduction. In *The Way We Read Now,* ed. Sharon Marcus and Stephen Best, with Emily Apter and Elaine Freedgood. Special issue. *Representations* 108(1): 1–21.

Beverley, John. 2004. *Testimonio: On the Politics of Truth.* Minneapolis, MN: University of Minnesota Press.

Boehmer, Elleke. n.d. Planned Violence: Post/Colonial Urban Infrastructures and Literature. http://plannedviolence.org. Accessed 30 November 2015.

Borges, Jorge Luis. 1998. The Ethnographer. In *Collected Fictions,* trans. Andrew Hurley, 334–335. New York: Viking.

Bourdieu, Pierre. 1990. Fieldwork in Philosophy. In *In Other Words: Essays Towards a Reflexive Sociology,* 3–33. Stanford, CA: Stanford University Press.

Boyd, Douglas A., and Mary A. Larson, eds. 2014. *Oral History and Digital Humanities: Voice, Access, and Engagement*. New York: Palgrave.

Brooks, Peter, and Hilary Jewitt, eds. 2014. *The Humanities and Public Life*. New York: Fordham University Press.

Brown, Nicholas, and Imre Szeman, eds. 2015. *Pierre Bourdieu: Fieldwork in Culture*. New York: Palgrave.

Burton, Antoinette. 2006. *Archive Stories: Facts, Fictions, and the Writing of History*. Durham, NC: Duke University Press.

Cárcamo-Huechante, Luis. 2013. Indigenous Interference: Mapuche Use of Radio in Times of Acoustic Colonialism. In *Políticas y mercados culturales en América Latina*, ed. Víctor Vich and José Ramón Jouve-Martín. Special issue. *Latin American Research Review* 48: 50–68.

Carpentier, Alejo. 1967. *Tientos y diferencias*. Buenos Aires: Arca.

de Certeau, Michel. 2011. *The Practice of Everyday Life*. 3rd ed. Berkeley, CA: University of California Press.

Chakrabarty, Dipesh. 2000. *Provincializing Europe: Postcolonial Thought and Historical Difference*. Princeton, NJ: Princeton University Press.

Charlton, Thomas L., Lois E. Myers, and Rebecca Sharpless. 2008. *Thinking about Oral History: Theories and Applications*. New York: Altamira Press (Division of Rowman and Littlefield).

Clifford, James. 1988. *The Predicament of Culture*. Cambridge, MA: Harvard University Press.

———. 1997. *Routes: Travel and Translation in the Twentieth Century*. Cambridge, MA: Harvard University Press.

Clifford, James, and George E. Marcus, eds. 1986. *Writing Culture*. Berkeley, CA: University of California Press.

Coombes, Annie. 2003. *History After Apartheid: Visual Culture and Public Memory in a Democratic South Africa*. Durham, NC: Duke University Press.

Cooper, David. 2014. *Learning in the Plural: Essays on the Humanities and Public Life*. East Lansing, MI: Michigan State University Press.

Crapanzano, Vincent. 2004. *Imaginative Horizons: An Essay in Literary-Philosophical Anthropology*. Chicago, MA: University of Chicago Press.

Das, Veena. 2007. *Life and Words: Violence and the Descent into the Ordinary*. Berkeley, CA: University of California Press.

Daughtry, Martin J. 2015. *Listening to War: Sound, Music, Trauma, and Survival in Wartime Iraq*. 1st ed. Oxford: Oxford University Press.

Dayan, Joan. 1998. *Haiti, History and the Gods*. Berkeley, CA: University of California Press.

Dayan, Colin. 2013. Dread and Dispossession: An Interview with Colin Dayan. *The Public Archive*, September 23. http://thepublicarchive.com/?p=3988.

———. 2013. *The Law is a White Dog*. Princeton, NJ: Princeton University Press.

———. 2014. And Then Came Culture. Special issue in honor of Michel Rolph Trouillot. *Cultural Dynamics* 26(2): 137–148.

Ewing, Suzanne, Jeremie Michael McGowan, Chris Speed, and Victoria Clare Bernie, eds. 2011. *Architecture and Field/Work*. London: Routledge.

Faubion, James D., and George E. Marcus. 2011. *Fieldwork is Not What It Used to Be: Learning Anthropology's Method in a Time of Transition*. Ithaca, NY: Cornell University Press.

Fusco, Coco. 2008. *A Field Guide for Female Interrogators*. New York: Seven Stories Press.

Gautier, Ochoa, and Ana María. 2014. *Aurality: Listening and Knowledge in Nineteenth-Century Colombia*. Durham, NC: Duke University Press.

Geertz, Clifford. 1988. *Works and Lives*. Stanford, CA: Stanford University Press.

———. 1998. Deep Hanging Out. *New York Review of Books* 22: 69–72.

Glazener, Nancy. 2016. *Literature in the Making: A History of U.S. Literary Culture in the Long Nineteenth Century*. Oxford: Oxford University Press.

Gray, Ann. 2003. *Research Practice for Cultural Studies: Ethnographic Methods and Lived Cultures*. London: Sage Publications.

Grosfoguel, Ramón. 2011. Decolonizing Post-colonial Studies and Paradigms of Political Economy: Transmodernity, Decolonial Thinking, and Global Coloniality. *Transmodernity: Journal of Peripheral Cultural Production of the Luso-Hispanic World* 1(1): 1–37.

Grossberg, Lawrence, Cary Nelson, and Paula Treichler, eds. 1992. *Cultural Studies*. New York: Routledge.

Guha, Ranajit, and Gayatri Spivak, eds. 1988. *Selected Subaltern Studies*. Oxford: Oxford University Press.

Gupta, Akhil, and James Ferguson. 1997. *Anthropological Locations: Boundaries and Grounds of a Field Science*. Berkeley, CA: University of California Press.

Hall, Stuart. 1996. Race, Culture, and Communications: Looking Backward and Forward at Cultural Studies. In *What Is Cultural Studies?* ed. John Storey, 336–343.

Hall, Stuart, Dorothy Hobson, Andrew Lowe, and Paul Willis, eds. 1980. *Culture, Media, Language: Working Papers in Cultural Studies, 1972–79*. London: Unwin Hyman.

Hamid, Mohsin, Mohammed Hanif, Daniyal Mueenuddin, and Kamila Shamsie. 2010. How to Write About Pakistan. *Granta: The Magazine of New Writing*. 112, September 28. Web: 9 February 2016. http://granta.com/How-to-write-about-Pakistan.

Harney, Stefan, and Fred Moten. 2013. *The Undercommons: Fugitive Planning and Black Study*. New York: Autonomedia.

Harrison, Faye, ed. 1991. *Decolonizing Anthropology: Moving Further Toward and Anthropology for Liberation*. Washington, DC: American Anthropological Association.

Hartman, Saidiya. 2007. *Lose Your Mother: A Journey along the Atlantic Slave Route*. New York: Farrar, Strauss and Giroux.

———. 2016. Across the Atlantic Slave Route. http://library.fora.tv/speaker/1667/Saidiya_Hartman. Accessed 11 April 2016.

Heuston, Sean. 2011. *Modern Poetry and Ethnography: Yeats, Frost, Warren, Heaney, and the Poet as Anthropologist*. New York: Palgrave Macmillan.

Hitchcott, Nicki. 2009. A Global African Commemoration. *Rwanda: Écrire par devoir de mémoire. Forum for Modern Language Studies* 45(2): 151–161.

Jain, Kajri. 2007. *Gods in the Bazaar: The Economies of Indian "Calendar Art"*. Durham, NC: Duke University Press.

Jaji, Tsitsi. 2014. *Africa in Stereo: Modernism, Music, and Pan-African Solidarity*. Oxford: Oxford University Press.

James, Marlon. 2014. *A Brief History of Seven Killings: A Novel*. New York: Riverhead Books.

Jay, Paul, and Gerald Graff. 2012. Fear of Being Useful. *Inside Higher Ed*, January 5. https://www.insidehighered.com/views/2012/01/05/essay-new-approach-defend-value-humanities.

Johannesburg Workshop in Theory and Criticism. http://www.jwtc.org.za/. Accessed 30 November 2015.

Knudsen, Britta Timm, and Carsten Stage. 2015. *Affective Methodologies*. New York: Palgrave.

Lethbridge, Emily. n.d. The Saga-Steads of Iceland: A 21st-Century Pilgrimage. http://sagasteads.blogspot.com. Accessed 30 November 2015.

van Maanen, John. 2011. *Tales of the Field: On Writing Ethnography*. Chicago, MA: University of Chicago Press.

Macaulay, Thomas Babbington. 1920. Minute on Indian Education. In *Selections from Educational Records, Part I (1781–1839)*, ed. H. Sharp, 107–117. Calcutta: Superintendent, Government Printing.

Macfarlane, Alan, and Mark Turin. 2015. The Digital Himalaya Project. Last modified 16 November 2015. http://www.digitalhimalaya.com.

Maconi, Lara. 2008. One Nation, Two Discourses: Tibetan New Era Literature and the Language Debate. In *Modern Tibetan Literature and Social Change*, eds. Lauran R. Hartley, and Patricia Schiaffini-Vedani, 173–201. Durham, NC: Duke University Press.

Madison, Soyini. 2005. *Critical Ethnography: Methods, Ethics, and Performance*. London: Sage Publications.

———. 2010. *Acts of Activism: Human Rights as Radical Performance*. Cambridge: Cambridge University Press.

Malkki, Liisa. 2007. Tradition and Improvisation in Ethnographic Field Research. In *Improvising Theory: Process and Temporality in Ethnographic Fieldwork*, eds. Allaine Cerwonka, and Liisa Malkki, 162–187. Chicago, MA: University of Chicago Press.

Mallon, Florencia. 1994. The Promise and Dilemma of Subaltern Studies: Perspectives from Latin American History. *American Historical Review* 99(5): 491–515.

McRobbie, Angela. 1994. *Postmodernism and Popular Culture*. London: Routledge.

Mignolo, Walter. 2011. *The Darker Side of Western Modernity: Global Futures, Decolonial Options*. Durham, NC: Duke University Press.

Moretti, Franco. 2013. *Distant Reading*. New York: Verso.

Mowitt, John. 1992. *Text: The Genealogy of an Antidisciplinary Object*. Durham, NC: Duke University Press.

Narayan, Kirin. 2012. *Alive in the Writing: Crafting Ethnography in the Company of Chekhov*. Chicago, MA: University of Chicago Press.

Neculai, Catalina. 2014. *Urban Space and Late Twentieth-Century New York Literature: Reformed Geographies*. New York: Palgrave.

Newell, Stephanie. n.d. DirtPol. http://www.sussex.ac.uk/dirtpol/. Accessed 15 November 2015.

Newell, Stephanie, and Onookome Okome, eds. 2013. *Popular Culture in Africa*. New York: Routledge.

Nimis, John. 2010. Literary Listening: Readings in Congolese Popular Music. PhD diss., New York University. ProQuest (UMI 3427959).

Nussbaum, Martha. 2012. *Not For Profit: Why Democracy Needs the Humanities*. Princeton, NJ: Princeton University Press.

Olaniyan, Tejumola. 2004. *Arrest the Music! Fela and His Rebel Art and Politics*. Bloomington, IN: Indiana University Press.

Pandian, Anand. 2012. The Time of Anthropology: Notes from a Field of Contemporary Experience. *Cultural Anthropology* 27(4): 547–571.

———. 2015. *Reel World: An Anthropology of Creation.* Durham, NC: Duke University Press.

Papastergiadis, Nikos. 2004. South-South-South: An Introduction. In *Complex Entanglements: Art, Globalisation and Cultural Difference*, ed. Nikos Papastergiadis, 156–177. London: Rivers Oram Press.

People's Union for Democratic Rights and the People's Union for Civil Liberties. 1984. *Who are the Guilty? Report of a joint inquiry into the causes and impact of the riots in Delhi from 31 October to 10 November 1984.* New Delhi: PUDR and PUCL.

Perks, Robert, and Alistair Thomson, eds. 1988. *The Oral History Reader.* New York: Routledge.

Popular Memory Group. 1982. Popular Memory: Theory, Politics, Method. In *Making Histories: Studies in History-writing and Politics*, eds. Richard Johnson, Gregor McLennan, Bill Schwarz, and David Sutton, 205–252. Minneapolis, MN: University of Minnesota Press.

Pratt, Mary Louise. 1991. Arts of the Contact Zone. *Profession* 91: 33–40.

———. 1992. *Imperial Eyes: Travel Writing and Transculturation.* London: Routledge.

Quayson, Ato. 2014. *Oxford Street, Accra: City Life and the Itineraries of Transnationalism.* Durham, NC: Duke University Press.

Rabinow, Paul. 2007. Preface to *Reflections on Fieldwork in Morocco*, xi–xxviii. 30th Anniversary ed. Berkeley, CA: University of California Press.

Rabinow, Paul, and George Marcus. 2008. *Designs for an Anthropology of the Contemporary.* Durham, NC: Duke University Press.

Radano, Ronald, and Tejumola Olaniyan. 2016. *Audible Empire: Music, Global Politics, Critique.* Durham, NC: Duke University Press.

Roach, Joseph. 1996. *Cities of the Dead: Circum-Atlantic Performance.* New York: Columbia University Press.

Rodríguez, Ileana, ed. 2001. *The Latin American Subaltern Studies Reader.* Durham, NC: Duke University Press.

Rosaldo, Renato. 2014. *The Day of Shelly's Death: The Poetry and Ethnography of Grief.* Durham, NC: Duke University Press.

Sadana, Rashmi. 2012. *English Heart, Hindi Heartland: The Political Life of Literature in India.* Berkeley, CA: University of California Press.

Sanders, Mark. 2016. *Learning Zulu: A Secret History of Language in South Africa.* Princeton, NJ: Princeton University Press.

Seguín, Bécquer. 2014. The Texture of Literary Fieldwork. *LASA Forum* 45(2): 9–10.

Shih, Shu-mei, and Françoise Lionnet, eds. 2005. *Minor Transnationalism.* Durham, NC: Duke University Press.

Small, Helen. 2014. *The Value of the Humanities.* Oxford: Oxford University Press.

Solnit, Rebecca. 2001. *Wanderlust: A History of Walking.* New York: Penguin.

Sommer, Doris. 1999. *Proceed with Caution, When Engaged by Minority Writers in the Americas.* Cambridge, MA: Harvard University Press.

———. 2013. *The Work of Art in the World.* Durham, NC: Duke University Press.

Spivak, Gayatri Chakravorty. 1988. Can the Subaltern Speak? In *Marxism and the Interpretation of Culture*, eds. C. Nelson, and L. Grossberg, 271–313. London: Macmillan.

———. 2005. *Death of a Discipline.* New York: Columbia University Press.

Stewart, Kathleen. 2007. *Ordinary Affects.* Durham, NC: Duke University Press.

Stocking, George W. 1996. Paradigmatic Traditions in the History of Anthropology. In *Companion to the History of Modern Science*, eds. R.C. Olby, G.N. Cantor, J.R.R. Christie, and M.J.S. Hodge, 712–727. London: Routledge.

Stoler, Ann. 2015. Of Critique, Philosophy, and Anthropology: An Interview with Ann Stoler. *Allegra Lab*. September 29. http://allegralaboratory.net/of-critique-philosophy-and-anthropology-an-interview-with-ann-stoler/.

Storey, John. 1996. Cultural Studies: An Introduction. In *What Is Cultural Studies?* 1–13.

———. 1996. *What Is Cultural Studies? A Reader*. London: Arnold.

Taylor, Diane. 2003. *The Archive and the Repertoire. Performing Cultural Memory in the Americas*. Durham, NC: Duke University Press.

Thompson, Paul. 1978. *The Voice of the Past: Oral History*. Oxford: Oxford University Press.

Wade, Nicholas. 2010. Anthropology a Science? Statement Deepens a Rift. *New York Times*. December 9. http://www.nytimes.com/2010/12/10/science/10anthropology.html. Accessed 11 April 2016.

Wagner, Roy. 1981. *The Invention of Culture*. Chicago, MA: University of Chicago Press.

Waterson, Alisse, and Maria D. Vesperi. 2011. *Anthropology off the Shelf*. New York: Wiley Blackwell.

White, Luise, Stephan A. Miescher, and David William Cohen, eds. 2001. *African Words, African Voices: Critical Practices in Oral History*. Bloomington, IL: Indiana UP.

Willems, Wendy. 2014. Beyond Normative Dewesternization: Examining Media Culture from the Vantage Point of the Global South. In *New Media and Mass/Popular Culture in the Global South*, ed. John Nimis. Special issue. *Global South* 8(1): 7–23.

Williams, Raymond. 1983. *Keywords: A Vocabulary of Culture and Society*. Rev. ed. New York: Oxford University Press.

Wolf, Diane, ed. 1996. *Feminist Dilemmas in Fieldwork*. Boulder, CO: Westview Press.

Woodward, Kathleen. 2009. The Future of the Humanities in the Present and in Public. *Daedalus* 138(1): 110–123.

Wright, Melissa W. 2006. *Disposable Women and Other Myths of Global Capitalism*. New York: Routledge.

Wright, Handel Kashope, and Meaghan Morris, eds. 2013. *Cultural Studies of Transnationalism*. New York: Routledge.

PART I

Memory, Conflict, Contestation

Finding the Field: Notes on Caribbean Cultural Criticism, Area Studies, and the Forms of Engagement

Shalini Puri

This is how she would come to know a place, listening for its four o'clock in the morning.

—*Dionne Brand, In Another Place, Not Here*

When I think back to the work I have done that has been most satisfying to me and that has had a vigorous life both inside and outside the academy, I think of my study of *dougla* identities and poetics in Trinidad in the 1990s (where

This essay first appeared in *Small Axe* 41 (July 2013): 58–73. Copyright 2013. Small Axe, Inc. All rights reserved. It is republished here by permission of the present publisher Duke University Press, www.dukeupress.edu. Versions of sections of this chapter have appeared in Shalini Puri, "Memory-Work, Field-Work: Reading Merle Collins and the Poetics of Place," in *The Routledge Companion to Anglophone Caribbean Literature*, edited by Michael Bucknor and Alison Donnell, 490–498 (London: Routledge, 2011). I am grateful to audiences and interlocutors at various venues in the Caribbean, the USA, Canada, and the UK for their feedback on presentations I made on this material, and to participants at the "What Is Caribbean Studies? Prisms, Paradigms, Practices," held at Yale University, on 1–2 April 2011, for which I wrote a draft of this essay. Special thanks to Deborah Thomas, Lara Putnam, Nancy Glazener, Thora Brylowe, and the reviewer for *Small Axe* for their suggestions on an earlier draft.

S. Puri (✉)
English Departmtent, University of Pittsburgh, Pittsburgh, USA

© The Author(s) 2016
S. Puri, D.A. Castillo (eds.), *Theorizing Fieldwork in the Humanities*,
DOI 10.1057/978-1-349-92834-7_2

dougla refers to the mixed descendants of Afro- and Indo-Caribbean people) and of my research on cultural memory of the Grenada Revolution.[1] Both projects began as explorations of literary silences or archival absences. It was these absences in what Cecilia Green once referred to as "undocumented societies" that impelled me to the field.[2] Part of the project became to help *assemble* an archive and to witness in the one case, the lived experience of dougla identities, and, in the other case, the subterranean memories of the Grenada Revolution. In the former instance, a complex overlay of accreted race-color hierarchies, racialized electoral politics, and cultural nationalist control over women's sexuality colluded to silence dougla experience yet also to construct dougla identities as potential sites of resistance. In the case of Grenada, the problems of slender resources for archiving that are faced by any small and impoverished nation of the global south were compounded by the destructive forces of hurricanes, state censorship, and the bombing of the country by the USA. (When the USA bombed the radio station, for example, the nation's radio news and calypso archives were destroyed.) For both research projects, then, I turned to a kind of improvised fieldwork, one that offers an important route to knowledge and expression unavailable in print; to disallowed or delegitimized knowledges; to localized or vernacular rather than globalized knowledge and memory; to transient expressions of popular opinion; and to exploration of controversial issues about which people were not willing to speak publicly. Common to both research contexts was that my encounter with the "field" in question—Trinidad and Grenada, respectively—and with its inhabitants transformed the study.

In this chapter, I will focus on the Grenada project to explain how and why a literary critic began to practice fieldwork; address the need to carve a space for fieldwork in literary-critical practice; and contribute to the development of a shared public discourse about fieldwork in the humanities. In the process, I will comment, from my home discipline of literature, on the relationship of my work on Grenada to various other fields, disciplines, methodologies, and practices—to cultural studies, area studies, anthropology, cultural geography, and memory and trauma studies.

A brief note on the Grenada Revolution and its fall may be useful to contextualize the project: the Grenada Revolution was the first and only socialist revolution in the Anglophone Caribbean; it also drew on various Black Power and other regional radical movements. Lasting from 1979 to1983, the revolution made significant gains in such areas as mass political participation, employment, housing, health, education, and workers' and women's rights. Although Maurice Bishop, the prime minister, remained a highly popular figure, the revolution was justly criticized for its intransigent suppression of dissent, overcentralization of power, and failure to hold elections. In October 1983, a split surfaced in the party leadership on the issue of whether there should be joint leadership between Prime Minister Bishop and Finance Minister Bernard Coard. In a series of events too complex to summarize here, the crisis escalated, and on 19 October 1983, Bishop and several of his closest comrades were executed. A "Revolutionary Military Council" took over and placed the island under shoot-on-sight curfew. On October 25, the USA invaded, ending any remaining chance that popular revolutionary forces might regroup. The imprisonment, trials, and appeals of the "Grenada 17" (those convicted for the executions, including Bernard Coard) stretched from 1983 through 2007. The last of the Grenada 17 were released from prison in 2009. The bodies of their slain comrades have not been recovered or given proper burial. The Grenada Revolution has remained an organizing fracture in the national memory—not just along the lines of Right versus Left but within the Left itself. It has also cast a long shadow on leftist political organizing and imagination in the region, making an engagement with its legacies all the more urgent.

The project I had originally planned was a literary close reading of a few novels, essays, and poems about the Grenada Revolution. It was to have been a fairly recognizable literary-critical project, in which my inquiry into the pasts and futures of leftist politics in the region would be disciplinarily mediated through close readings of literary form. When I actually went to Grenada in 1998, it rapidly became clear to me that my planned approach was not tenable. I came to believe that place was not accidental or extraneous to the memory of the Grenada Revolution but fundamental to the very *structure* of that memory, deeply linked to the topography and scale of the island. There is of course a well-established tradition of scholarship that theorizes the links between memory and place.[3] But Grenada presents a particularly compelling and unusual instance. The *contrast* between the public discursive silence on the subject of the revolution and the visual presence and rumbling subterranean memory of the revolution was so striking that it was an almost physical shock. How did Grenadians live with that contradiction—between the visual and the written, between the publicly (un)spoken and the whispered word? In the context of the massive silencing of the Grenada Revolution, landscape emerged as the site of traces of the revolution and of negotiations over its memory: the bombed-out People's Revolutionary Government headquarters at Butler House (ironically, demolished in 2007 to make way for a new hotel); Fort Rupert (now restored to its colonial name, Fort George), where one side of the revolutionary leadership executed the other and where both the bullet holes and the cement that attempts to cover them up are still visible; the ruins of a mental asylum that the USA bombed; and abandoned Cuban and Soviet planes on the old airfield. Such visible material residues of the revolution meet one everywhere.

The landscape is also dotted with memorials—memorials to fallen US soldiers, a modest sign pointing the way to the "Maurice Bishop Highway," the recently renamed Maurice Bishop International Airport, the plaque to those executed at the fort. There are also plans for memorials to Cubans who died during the invasion. Such memorials represent both state-choreographed memory and the results of sustained and organized pressures on the state to honor the revolution's memory. The landscape also features eruptions of popular memory in the form of graffiti and murals: "Grenada-Cuba Friends Forever" or "Maurice Bishop Lives" or "March 13 is our history." (The revolution came to power on 13 March 1979.)

Moreover, the land holds not only material historical traces of the revolution but also powerful emotional geographies.[4] The very topography and scale of Grenada are linked to people's memories of events in 1983: thousands of people stormed security barricades to release Prime Minister Maurice Bishop from house arrest and swelled the streets in broad daylight as they went to Fort Rupert. Even if one was not among those thousands, one could still hear the sounds of gunfire across the island, see columns of smoke rising, and scramble up on a hill and see the crowds as panic overtook them. It was a highly public, highly spectacular moment of collective euphoria that quickly turned into equally spectacular trauma. The sheer sensory immediacy of it all is heightened by a scale that prevents violence from being experienced as distant, abstract, or anonymous.

Caribbean literature and painting have a long tradition of preoccupation with place and landscape. From colonial and tourist representations of the landscape, and refutations of such representations, to laying claim to a land to which the majority of its inhabitants came in chains or servitude, to ecological efforts toward a sustainable future, landscape has had such prominence in the literature that Glissant refers to it not merely as setting but as a *character* implicated in the action.[5] Moreover, given that landscape is an emblem of the local and the particular, it offers a metaphor for a locally *grounded* politics. Representations of Grenadian landscape often urge the translation of Marxist theory into local terms, or imagine an indigenized or vernacular Marxism. They have also thus functioned as an argument for political accountability to the local. The local idiom of landscape also offers a *vernacular* memory; in this sense, landscape is the visual equivalent of Creole. Finally, in a context of both the self-imposed repression of traumatic memory and a state-led punitive apparatus for sympathy with the revolution and its memory, landscape and its representations become a way of visually asserting that which has been verbally silenced. It also offers a way of situating memory *outside the body*, thereby both sparing the body punishment, and locating memory in a public and accessible space. In literature about Grenada, from Merle Collins's poem "Shame Bush" to V.S. Naipaul's essay "An Island Betrayed" and beyond,[6] as well as in the conversations I had with many Grenadians, the poetics of land are so strong, and make such powerful arguments for the *analytical* importance of place and locality, that it seemed to me misguided to study the poetics on the page without engaging the place off the page. To understand a Caribbean poetics and a cultural memory that is so thoroughly mediated by place, fieldwork offers a barely tapped resource for Caribbean literary criticism.

One aspect of my project developed by reading literary and extraliterary landscape in Grenada *alongside each other* as sites of memory; another read literature in relation to other arts; a third developed by reading literary narratives alongside nonliterary narratives by Grenadians with whom I was in conversation. Interaction with a range of Caribbean people other than scholars, artists, and experts became integral to the project. It is largely as a result of moving outward from the page to include the other forms of engagement that fieldwork involves that my project became one of witnessing: to study the visual traces of the revolution in the landscape; to study the agonic silences, both state- and self-imposed; to locate fragments of memory, to listen for its murmuring; and to contribute to the creation of spaces for public speech on the topic.[7]

Perhaps an example would help. It is one that concentrates many of the foregoing claims. In the north of the island, at the old airfield at Pearls, which the revolution sought to replace with a new international airport at Point Salines (the airport the USA claimed was being built for military purposes), lie two abandoned planes, one Cubana and one Aeroflot. For 25 years they have remained on the runway of the old airport. In a state and public discourse where memory of the Grenada Revolution remains largely repressed, these planes are neither official commemoration nor popular remembrance. They are in fact the very *antithesis* of an official commemoration. There is nothing in them of the sentimentality that surrounds ruins. Birds perch on the propeller; goats graze in their shadow; weekend car races take place on the old runway. One entrepreneurial Grenadian has floated the idea (thus far unsuccessfully) of moving the planes to make them a crowd-drawing prop in a restaurant he hopes to open. Left as debris or garbage, more eloquent in their materiality than any commentary, resistant to interpretation as any kind of "message," their persistent presence is a powerful provocation. To see them is to confront the stubborn residue of history.

Fig. 2.1   Cubana and Aeroflot planes at the abandoned Pearls Airport, Grenada. *Source*: Puri 2007

Fig. 2.2   Planes at Pearls Airport, rainy season. *Source*: Puri 2007

One rainy season when I was there, the planes were partially submerged, so overgrown that from certain angles they appeared to merge with the hills. The two planes raised several of the questions that were to become the focus of my book: the question of submerged but residual memory, the question of the relationship of the Grenada Revolution to the rest of the Caribbean (here embodied by the Cuban plane), and the vexed question of how Marxist theory inhabited the local landscape. How does the language of revolution and of working-class consciousness inhabit (and transform) a geography that is imagined and lived in terms of parishes—St. George, St. David, St. Andrew, and so on? Does the very distance of these planes from the center of memory and censorship, the capital of St. George's, protect them from removal? What other discreet residues of the revolution might exist in Grenada, notwithstanding the repression or demonization of the revolution's memory? And where should one look for them? How is the memory trace represented by those planes on the old airfield different from the commemorative function (carried out by the state under popular pressure) of the 2009 renaming of the Point Salines International Airport as the Maurice Bishop International Airport?

I arrived at my sense of the urgency of studying place not via theory but because of my own physical encounter with Grenada and because of the prominence of place in discursive accounts of the revolution. But it also fit with my developing theoretical dissatisfaction with dominant cultural studies accounts of globalization, which seemed to me to be privileging space over place with considerable loss of analytical insight.[8] My research on cultural memory in Grenada in the period 1979–1983 sharply brought home the fact that all memories do not cross borders with equal facility; not all memories are internationalized or globalized. For example, if one looks at the images from that place that is so often hailed as placeless or as the highway that connects all places—the Internet—one finds that four days of the US invasion of Grenada are documented over 100 times more than four *years* of the Grenada Revolution. Where, then, are those memories of the revolution, memories that have been *rendered* local? Where can one find such vernacular memory? How does the Grenada Revolution surface in the *commonplaces*, as it were, of everyday Grenadian life? And how does "everyday Grenadian life" surface in other parts of the globe—in diasporas to London, Toronto, New York; in its regional diasporas, to Trinidad and Venezuela; in places to which solidarity workers returned, such as Jamaica and Cuba? Surprisingly, Angola, too, turned out to be a scene of memory of the Grenada Revolution, for many Cubans who served in Grenada were sent to Angola after the fall of the revolution and their return to Cuba. If Grenada was the "place" I was most immediately studying, all these other sites were part of the "area" of study.

My decision to go to Grenada was simultaneously one person's effort to practice a cultural studies redirected toward "place" over "space" and an effort to both claim and contribute to a reimagined area studies, which, for all the legitimate critiques that have been levied against it, remains a rubric for academic study that takes place, fieldwork, and language study seriously. The funding for the project came almost entirely from area studies centers, which remain the primary funded source of support for research involving travel that is available to me as someone who works in an English department. Any insights—either about Grenada or about methodologies for humanities-based inquiry into the Caribbean—that might derive from my attempt to synthesize literary-critical training and field-based inquiry thus owe a tremendous debt to area studies.

At a moment when area studies programs are being aggressively defunded in favor of global studies programs in the name of fiscal efficiency and a transformed geopolitics, it is worth remembering the *risks* of jettisoning area studies and the gains of reimagining it.[9] For both practices and critiques of area studies are themselves *placed*. In its search for vernacular rather than global memory, area studies fieldwork can seek out Gikuyu or Urdu or Creole, not just Global English. Fieldwork may, in fact, be no more and no less than the equivalent of immersion for foreign language learning. Area studies enables scholarship that "dwells" on the nonmetropolitan places of the global south and that focuses on not only metropolitan migrants but also peripheral subalterns.[10] It was in fact the founder of the largest area studies exchange program in the world, Senator William Fulbright, who remarked: "Most Americans can never remember what most people can never forget." Imaginative practices of area studies can be crucial allies in the battle against such forgetfulness.

It was with a discomfiting awareness of my lack of training in field-based inquiry that I embarked upon this project, which an anthropologist colleague informed me consisted of "mixed methods qualitative research." Even such a rudimentary summary characterization of what I was attempting was unavailable in my discipline. Fieldwork-based practices in literature and the humanities more generally have much to learn from anthropology's own self-critique, rejection, and reinventions of practices of fieldwork and ethnography.[11] The twin risks of populism and paternalism are never far from any practice of fieldwork. Certainly, to represent a culture is to exercise power, yet it would be a grave mistake to think that literary critics and the keepers of the canon are innocent of power.[12] In fact, all academic credentialing or "expertise" is by definition a claim of power/knowledge. As Akhil Gupta and James Ferguson remind us, however, "Anthropology departments continue to be among the few places in the Western academy not devoted exclusively or largely to the studies of the lives and policies of elites."[13] My fieldwork was animated by a paucity of documentary resources, an overrepresentation of elite documents among them, and a desire to put existing archives into dialog with the spoken narratives of uncredentialed Grenadians.

For the most part, the humanities simply have no public discourse at all about fieldwork; those of us who undertake it, do so without training and mostly in isolation, improvising our own rough tools as we stumble along. This chapter is both an argument for the importance of fieldwork in a Caribbean literary and cultural studies and a modest effort toward articulating and refining the humanities' own untheorized practices of fieldwork.[14]

My own working-through of how to approach the project necessarily involved trying to articulate the relationship of my practices to those of anthropology, the discipline that has the longest standing and most clearly articulated practices and theorizations of fieldwork. What could we learn from anthropology, and what could we contribute? Given that fieldwork is marginal to one discipline and foundational to another and that social-scientific inquiries and humanities inquiries into culture have substantially different disciplinary histories, are the possibilities and problems of fieldwork different for literature and anthropology? Since many of us in the humanities who do fieldwork do so without models or training or the benefit of a public discourse on the subject, let me briefly outline how I went about it: I had no training in interview methods or data collection; I made no claims to be engaged in a "scientific" study of culture or of an event; given the marginality and even *unintelligibility* of fieldwork-based scholarship in literature, there was no chance that I could find institutional support to undertake fieldwork for the lengths of time supported in anthropology departments. Repeated shorter stays over a span of 11 years, but concentrated in 3 years, would be the best I could manage. Studying a migratory society such as Grenada's, and the aftermath of a traumatic transnational event, also required travel to England, Toronto, New York, Barbados, and Jamaica for the purposes of interviewing. For lack of time and funding, I was unable to travel to Dominica, Cuba, or Guyana for the purposes of research, though I was able to be in conversation with diasporic Dominicans and Cubans who had been involved with the revolution and with others at community or scholarly gatherings outside the region.

I prepared for the study in a fairly typical fashion: reading all that I could find on the topic of the revolution in every discipline; reading newspapers and primary documents (such as minutes of party meetings, stamps released in the revolutionary and postrevolutionary period, etc.); studying monuments, memorials, and exhibits in Grenada and at a US military base, the struggles over them, and what they chose to remember and to disavow. I followed the continually updated and truly remarkable website Grenada Revolution Online (and learned much from the very fact that it needed to be continually updated, for it indicated that in many ways, the Grenada Revolution is a still-unfolding event). I followed recent eBay trades of the spoils of the 1983 war against Grenada; I watched YouTube posts by US combatants in the invasion and studied the ways they understood the relationship of Grenada to other US wars; I participated in a call-in radio show. Through the Grenada Broadcast Network archives and personal contacts, I tracked calypsos that commented on the revolution. I photographed the landscape. In the course of fieldwork, I did over 40 interviews, ranging from a half-hour single interview to repeat interviews that ran up to three hours. Some were planned and prepared, where I went in with a list of questions; others were entirely fortuitous conversations that were sparked not by my questions but by unsolicited comments by people with whom I was in conversation. (Indeed, the very fact that the revolution might surface at surprising moments in conversations about other things was itself illuminating to me.) My interviews almost certainly did not fit any model of a scientific sample, but equally certainly I sought out a wide cross section of people. Among those I spoke with were the surviving political leadership of the revolution, people who had been supporters of the revolution but subsequently broke with it, members of opposing political parties, dissidents who were imprisoned by the revolution, union leaders, actors, playwrights, poets, novelists, painters, calypsonians, current politicians, historians of Grenada, members of the National Youth Organization, church groups, journalists, members of cooperatives, members of the People's Revolutionary Army, members of left groups from elsewhere in the region, travel guides, rastas, schoolteachers, students, and African American and English solidarity workers. I began with the names that appeared in the documentary records—those who had held public office, for example—and slowly formed networks that led me to other more grassroots participants in or dissidents from the revolution. As the project developed, I became increasingly interested in forging a relationship with people beyond the length of an interview, in understanding their wide-ranging desires in telling me a story, and in writing a book that was sensitive to those desires. If there was a thoroughness to the method, it emerged in a fairly haphazard and unschooled way.

Though the methods of anthropology and literature have historically been quite different, a basic affinity between them lies in their interest in micro-processes, in how the "big events" of history are experienced by ordinary people in daily life. It is perhaps not coincidental that the Haitian novelist Jean Price Mars was an ethnologist or that the Caribbeanist anthropologist Richard Price has also written a novel. There are several other such examples of overlaps between social-scientific and literary projects, both in their witnessing and documentary impulses and in their inquiries into representation itself. There is thus, for example, a resonance between Dionne Brand's coming "to know a place, listening for its four o'clock in the morning," and Clifford Geertz's notion of "thick description."[15] Similarly, the sociologist and novelist Erna Brodber observed that she wrote her first novel, *Jane and Louisa Will Soon Come Home*, as a fictional case study because no formal academic case study or sociological data existed.[16] Merle Collins's novel *Angel* sought to record and reclaim the expressions and beliefs of the many Grenadians whose opinions were not considered legitimate academic sources for inclusion in her dissertation.[17] Whether as object of anticolonial satire (Chinua Achebe's *Things Fall Apart*) or interrogation (Michael Ondaatje's *Anil's Ghost*), or as fellow traveler (someone also interested in the lived experience of nonelites), the anthropologist is often an interlocutor in postcolonial literature.[18] Such examples predate and develop independently of both the "literary turn" in anthropology in the 1980s and the move of literature toward cultural studies at around the same time. These shifts in the 1980s represented critical experiments and practices of interdisciplinarity.

This interdisciplinarity is by no means an abandoning of one's discipline. Thus, my fieldwork was deeply informed by my literary commitments. It was by centering subjective narratives that I hoped to understand the long shadow of the Grenada Revolution and its fall. This is literature's strength. For though there are several excellent social-scientific studies of the Grenada Revolution, many of them *motivated* by solidarity with Grenada and an investment in democratic leftist politics, the disciplinary demands of objectivity in the social sciences have sometimes limited their ability to explicitly address the subjective dimensions of the Grenada experience. Let me offer some examples of the discipline-specific questions with which I went to Grenada and that I continued to develop and revise: Why is so little literature written in Grenada *set* in the period after 1983 (i.e., after the fall of the revolution)? What is the relationship between the political ending of the revolution and the failure of new narrative beginnings? What were the favored genres for telling the story of the Grenada Revolution? Epic? Tragedy? Romance? Why did the defeat of the Grenada Revolution not generate a literary form like the *testimonio* that was so common in neighboring Latin American revolutionary politics of the same period? Why was it that in several texts that were clearly and centrally motivated by a desire to work through the legacy of the revolution, to house its memory adequately, and to make peace in a restless, numbed, or divided nation, the revolution's entry into the texts was markedly delayed? How did the small scale of Grenada surface as a consideration in the literature and in the calypso—variously as material fact, political constraint, ethic, poetics, and shaper of genre?

Fieldwork and literature enable forms of experiential and imaginative engagement, respectively, that are crucial for any far-reaching solidarity. A particular form of cultural studies, fieldwork can exceed discourse analysis-based forms of cultural studies, engaging with the *people* who utter texts and with the contexts that move them. Fieldwork invites us to achieve a textured and embodied knowledge of place. Gayatri Spivak faults the complacencies and blind spots of some varieties of global feminism on grounds that "they cannot imagine what they know."[19] It was by experiencing the scale of Grenada outside the realm of the book that I better grasped the impact of scale on poetics, ethics, the distinctiveness of Grenada's political sensorium, and the forms that conflict and reconciliation took there. In my previous research on Grenada, for example, I "knew" that the island was small; I "knew" that this had consequences for kinship, for the practice of politics, and for the long-lasting trauma of the fall of the revolution (for the dead were neighbors, family, members of the same church—they were not anonymous people). It took the experience of fieldwork for me to able to *imagine* the scale as lived reality and to at least begin to subjectively understand it. It was also critical to my resisting the ways in which the small size of Grenada and many Caribbean nations is pathologized and their histories are trivialized. The scale of Grenada makes it all the more important to think through such questions as, How does a revolution that claims world historical significance and ambition *fit* into 12 by 21 miles? How does one understand the role of small islands in global histories of revolutionary politics? Can Grenada illuminate such histories in significant ways? How do human agency and material landscape limit and define each other? How does scale shape a political sensorium? Can Grenada call us to other abandoned memories of violence? Instead of focusing on scale primarily as disability or constraint, could one not ask if it enables particular forms of insight or forgiveness? What has and what might an aesthetics based on a particularly small-island Grenadian poetics of place play in achieving reconciliation and resolution? How have aesthetic and everyday practices outside the grand gestures of epic and tragedy offered ways to lay claim to a collective in which there are deep conflicts?

Without question, my fieldwork was thoroughly grounded in literary training. Yet, how might fieldwork *break with* or refashion literary study? For I believe that humanities fieldwork and its attendant methodologies have the ability to transform and expand the very objects of our disciplinary inquiry. If anthropology has been criticized for fetishizing the "remote local village," then cultural studies—at least as it has been housed in English departments—has historically focused on easily accessible urban populations to the exclusion of analysis of the globe's large rural populations. Fieldwork could serve as a useful corrective. At the most basic level, fieldwork in Caribbean studies also bears on what forms of cultural production we are able to study. For example, it is an important means of correcting our disproportionate study of and reliance on print, film, and other mass media (a disproportion which my own work has certainly not escaped). In the absence of fieldwork, the medium-specific insights of drama, dance, and the embodied practices and performances of everyday life are lost to us and do not feed into our "general" knowledge about a region. (To draw on metaphors of migrancy, we might say that drama and performance are the stay-at-home country cousins of the novel or cinema; they are unable to cross borders with the same ease. Fieldwork makes the effort to travel to them.)[20] Fieldwork is also better able to understand not only spectacularly transgressive cultural practices (like dancehall or carnival) but also the quieter everyday. In doing so, fieldwork makes scholars better able to connect the print or verbal text with its contexts. In Grenada, when I ask people to share their memories, I am able to listen not only to the content of their words, but equally to the pauses, to the lowering of a voice, to the fact that the memory of the killings over 25 years ago still make someone's hair stand on end. Fieldwork thus enables one to study literary texts as part of a wider ensemble of embodied resources and practices. It also remains one of the most important academic models we have for speaking to ordinary people. In the case of Grenada, it is a form of political witnessing. *Literary* fieldwork invites us to put two questions into dialogue, to treat the question "What did people write?" as a subset of the broader question: "What did people do?"

My experiments in literary fieldwork made clear that they held in tension at least two models of literary reading: a New Critical model, which emphasizes the text as a complete system or an artistic totality, and an alternative model which emphasizes the *porosity* of literary texts. Literary fieldwork is interested in the multiple forms of traffic (and roadblocks) between the literary arts, the other arts (such as calypso and visual arts), and the *placed* everyday. It recalibrates the relationship between the literary, the historical, and the everyday. For example, one thing that emerged from numerous conversations was that when working-class people spoke to me, they often used the *same* motifs, dwelled on the *same* places, expressed the *same* incomprehensions and incredulities that I might otherwise have regarded as elements of more exclusively literary or novelistic form. Combined with fieldwork, the discipline-specific form of close reading that I practiced resulted in the de-privileging of literature by understanding it in relation to other artistic and everyday practices. My fieldwork thus addressed not only the exceptionality of literature but also the *ordinariness* of literature—an ordinariness which in this case might be understood as something to celebrate rather than lament.

Moreover, the value of fieldwork lies not least in the way that it renders the researcher vulnerable to history. When a researcher reads in a library, nobody is reading her back. When one reads in the field, one is constantly being scripted, being made the object of a counter-gaze, and is thereby forced to confront not only one's geographical but also one's historical location. This is one sense to which one might apply Gupta and Ferguson's argument that fieldwork should be understood not so much as a study of the local, in traditional terms, but rather as a study of location.[21]

Fieldwork in Grenada also offered important supplements to dominant trauma studies models, which in my view do not fit the particularities of the

Grenadian experience of revolution. One obvious reason is that, unlike the more-analyzed cases of collective trauma—the Holocaust, slavery, the genocides and massacres in Rwanda, Guatemala, Argentina, and El Salvador—the *numbers* of the dead in Grenada were relatively small: 14 people murdered, some others killed trying to escape, some dissidents held and tortured, nothing like the tens of thousands or millions in the cases upon which trauma studies most often focuses. The predicament of Grenada could not be understood and would likely not be approached at all if one thought of it in terms of numerical scale. Similarly, the Truth and Reconciliation Commission (TRC) in Grenada was much less significant than in South Africa's much-studied example; hopes for genuine resolution and reconciliation in Grenada have been much less likely to be routed through the TRC or other state-led efforts than through artistic and other daily practices. Moreover, the state played a different role in the Holocaust or apartheid or slavery from that which it did in the Grenada Revolution. The Grenada Revolution was in many ways a joyous, egalitarian, and emancipatory project. The revolution expanded some democratic processes, even as it curtailed other freedoms. I did not find in most trauma studies accounts ways to understand the particular experience of betrayal grappled with by Grenadians who had invested their hopes in the revolutionary state or to grasp the fundamentally *mixed* legacies of the Grenada Revolution and the profound tension at its heart: a conflict between its democratizing and its authoritarian impulses.[22] This misfit of available theoretical models forced me to the field.

In my own practice, I de-emphasized one of the key resources of trauma studies: psychoanalysis. The medicalized discourse of psychoanalysis places the analyst in a different relationship of authority with respect to the patient or client or text than the one I as a fieldworker wished to occupy. As the anthropologist Veena Das eloquently puts it in her study of Partition and communal riots, implicitly contrasting anthropology to psychoanalysis, "I do not break through the resistance of the other…. I allow the knowledge of the other to mark me."[23] When I have heard resonances between Grenadian poetics and psychoanalytic theory, I have deliberately delayed recourse to the psychoanalytic "version" or translation, so that (to draw a lesson from Merle Collins's story "The Walk") psychoanalysis—and theory more generally—cannot be used as a *shortcut* or a replacement for the walker's knowledge and for the forms of engagement it enables.[24] It is via the aesthetic and vernacular theorizing that I have encountered through fieldwork that I have sought to give Grenadian experience priority, registering its autonomy from the weight and models of two paradigmatic models of trauma—the Holocaust and New World slavery— so that it does not sink under the scale of those global tragedies or the scholarship they have generated. Fieldwork in Grenada has for me been a practice of listening to the local refrain, as Merle Collins urged, and of learning to think with the land. It is thus perhaps better thought of as a practice of *apprenticeship* than a form of expertise.

This also raises the question of how for us, as literary critics, the very *forms* of our arguments and their composition might be marked by that encounter.

Anthropological fieldwork has traditionally involved explicit reflection on process, something that is notably absent in most literary criticism. How a reflection on process might shift the forms and thus the "content of the form"[25] of
literary criticism remains to be seen. As Paul Thompson observes of oral history interviews, "The nature of the interview implies a breaking of the bound-
ary between the educational institution and world, between the professional
and the ordinary public....The reconstruction of history itself becomes a much
more widely collaborative process, in which nonprofessionals must play a critical part."[26] What imprint might such an engagement with nonspecialists leave
on the form of our writing and scholarship? What invitations to translation
might it make? Approaching fieldwork as apprenticeship and witnessing has
fundamentally changed my sense of who my interlocutors are as a literary critic
and to whom I am accountable: not only to fellow critics, or to writers like
Ramabai Espinet or Erna Brodber or Merle Collins, or to other Caribbean
intellectuals, but also to a host of Grenadians who will in all likelihood never
read my book: the lady who runs the roti and take-out shop in Excel Plaza,
the guard at Richmond Hill prison, the librarian who guided me through the
Grenada Broadcast Network's music archives, the calypsonian who hummed
out fragments of calypso recordings that were destroyed or calypsos that were
never recorded in the first place, or the Bishopite taxi driver who mistook me
for CIA. With each of these people I have engaged in the richness of conversation. They have led me to think that perhaps my task is not literary criticism but
literary conversation, a more dialogic project.

Their insights, observations, advice, and cautions transformed my research
agenda. I explicitly asked many of these interlocutors what they would like to
be known about the Grenada Revolution, what they wanted my study to do,
what advice they had for me. As in any conversation, there is plenty of scope for
disagreement. A situation as fraught with conflicting memories as in Grenada
leaves no room for the illusion that experience is necessarily authentic or that
fieldwork grants unmediated access to it or that by speaking to such people
epistemological privilege is assured; no such populism need be involved in the
practice of fieldwork. But thinking through the intensity of conflicting memories and toward a project of reconciliation also clarifies that *the object of scholarship cannot merely be to be right.*

What I am trying to get at is that literary fieldwork can ground a form
of subjective engagement and political solidarity with people as they navigate
forms of power to which fieldworkers also have a relationship. For me, literary fieldwork as an element of a humanities-based area studies is one way of
contributing to what Rob Nixon has called a "transnational ethics of place."[27]
Perhaps the disciplinary sensibilities of the humanities can help to insist on the
value of fieldwork even though it is by no means a rapidly convertible hard
currency. An overwhelming fraction of knowledge I have gained through fieldwork can never be "cashed" to explicitly appear in my book (not least because
some of the most important parts of the conversations were entrusted to me in

confidence), but it nonetheless forms the spine of the entire project and trans-forms its entire sensibility.

Perhaps these arguments for fieldwork in the humanities are belabored articulations of what should be common sense. My hope is that fieldwork will become common *practice*.

***

In a wonderful response to a talk I gave in Toronto in 2006, where I insisted upon the particularities of the Caribbean as a region, the Jamaican playwright and scholar Honor Ford-Smith remarked:

> But what place? Havana or Santiago, Kingston or Accompong, Ponce or Fort-de-France, Pétionville or Cité Soleil in Haiti, in Roseau or Bassetere, Brooklyn or Brixton or Port Limón, Costa Rica? This litany of names imposes a kaleidoscopic awareness of the complexity of a region which only becomes a region when one is outside it, as Rinaldo Walcott is fond of pointing out.

What I want to take from Ford-Smith's irreducibly particular incantation of Caribbean places is this: "space" is not nearly as messy, does not trip one up nearly as much as place does—with its contradictions, its conflicts, its incom-prehensions, its confounding of still necessary generalizations, and its challenge to find generalizations that work. And that is why I keep returning to this dif-ficult, difficult list of places, which continues to humble and inspire me. They remind me that I call myself a Caribbeanist only at my peril (what do I know of Blanchisseuse or Port-au-Prince or Brokopondo?); they chastise me with a map of my ignorance. I approach this map sometimes through fieldwork, some-times through analogy, and sometimes through an act of faith in the glimpsed regional integrity of the Caribbean. It is to these heterogeneous places and the people whose hopes they shape and hold that I dedicate my efforts.

NOTES

1. See Shalini Puri, *The Caribbean Postcolonial: Social Equality, Post-Nationalism, and Cultural Hybridity*, Chaps. 6 and 7, and earlier confer-ence papers in Trinidad on the subject; and *The Grenada Revolution in the Caribbean Present: Operation Urgent Memory*.
2. Cecilia Green, in conversation with the author.
3. To name but a few, see Gaston Bachelard, *The Poetics of Space*; Edward Casey, *Remembering: A Phenomenological Study*, 2nd ed. and Edward Casey, *The Fate of Place: A Philosophical History*; Joel Sternfeld, *On this Site*; Tim Cresswell, *Place: A Short Introduction*; Pierre Nora, *Realms of Memory*, vols. 1–3; Stephen Legg, "Reviewing Geographies of Memory/Forgetting," 456–66; Steven Hoelscher and Derek H. Alderman, eds., "Memory and Place: Geographies of a Critical Relationship,"; and Simon Schama, *Landscape and Memory*.

4. For a theoretical account and diverse set of case studies, see Mick Smith, et al., eds., *Emotion, Place and Culture*.
5. Edouard Glissant, *Poetics of Relation*, 71. For other examples that address the significance of landscape in the Caribbean, see Wilson Harris, *Palace of the Peacock* (1960); Derek Walcott, *The Antilles: Fragments of Epic Memory*; Olive Senior, *Gardening in the Tropics*; Jean Rhys, *Wide Sargasso Sea*; Krista A. Thompson, *An Eye for the Tropics*; Elizabeth M. de Loughrey, et al, eds., *Caribbean Literature and the Environment*; and Maria Cristina Fumagalli, et al., eds., *Surveying the American Tropics*.
6. Collins, "Shame Bush," 50–52; Naipaul, "An Island Betrayed," 61–72.
7. The National Democratic Congress, which held power from 2008 through 2013, created more space for public reflection on and commemoration of revolution than previous governments did.
8. See Casey, *The Fate of Place*, for the argument that after Aristotle, and particularly with Husserl, philosophy increasingly came to treat place as a mere modification of space to its detriment.
9. Several works are particularly illuminating of some significant recent debates that touch upon these concerns. Masao Miyoshi and Harry Harootunian, eds., *Learning Places: The Afterlives of Area Studies*, at the theoretical level is largely critical of area studies, and focuses mainly on Japan and Asian Studies. Some of the best essays in the book, however, practice precisely the kind of revised and reflective area studies that I think we need. Ali Mirsepassi, Amrita Basu, and Frederick Weaver, eds., *Localizing Knowledge in a Globalizing World: Recasting the Area Studies Debate*, is both critical and reconstructive of area studies. Gayatri C. Spivak, *Death of a Discipline*, provides a compelling argument for comparative literature and area studies to transform one another. Her argument focuses on the importance of studying the languages of the global South and on comparative literature as one form of practicing area studies. Paul Zeleza, "African Studies: A Global Perspective" (paper presented at the conference on Area Studies, Diaspora Studies, and Critical Pedagogies, University of Toronto, 30 March–2 April 2006), reminds us of those histories of area studies, particularly African Studies, that predate the Cold War and its imperatives. Dipesh Chakrabarty, "Reconstructing Liberalism? Notes toward a Conversation between Area Studies and Diaspora Studies," 457–82, specifically addresses the role of diasporic scholars in reformulating the relationship and practices of area studies and diaspora studies. And Karla Slocum and Deborah Thomas, "Caribbean Studies, Anthropology, and US Academic Realignments: Insights from Caribbeanist Anthropology," 553–565; and Sidney Mintz, "The Localization of Anthropological Practice: From Area Studies to Transnationalism," 117–33, defend area studies over global studies.
10. This was the motivating sentiment behind Shalini Puri, ed., *Marginal Migrations: The Circulation of Culture within the Caribbean*. Even a cursory sample of scholarship on Caribbean migration reveals that in scholarly practice Caribbean migrations to North America and Europe

(and usually to their largest cities) often stand in for Caribbean migrations to other places.

11. See, for a small set of examples, Ruth Behar, *The Vulnerable Observer: Anthropology that Breaks your Heart*; James Clifford and George Marcus, eds., *Writing Culture: The Poetics and Politics of Ethnography*; Arturo Escobar, *Territories of Difference: Place, Movements, Life*, Redes; Gustavo Lins Ribeiro and Arturo Escobar, eds., *World Anthropologies: Disciplinary Transformations in Systems of Power*; Clifford Geertz, *The Interpretation of Cultures* and *Works and Lives: The Anthropologist as Author*; Akhil Gupta and James Ferguson, eds., *Anthropological Locations: Boundaries and Grounds of a Field Science*; Faye Harrison, *Decolonizing Anthropology: Moving Further Toward an Anthropology for Liberation*; George E. Marcus and Michael M.J. Fisher, *Anthropology as Cultural Critique: An Experimental Moment in the Human Sciences*; Richard Price, *Travels with Tooy: History, Memory, and the African American Imagination*; David Scott, *Refashioning Futures*; George Stocking, *The Ethnographer's Magic and Other Essays in the History of Anthropology* and *Observers Observed: Essays on Ethnographic Fieldwork*; Michael Taussig, *The Magic of the State* and *I Swear I Saw This: Drawings in Fieldwork Notebooks, Namely My Own*; as well as the aforementioned Clifford, Mintz, and Slocum and Thomas. Oral history and cultural geography might be considered sister disciplines to literature, in terms of the marginal status fieldwork has in relation to the mainstream of their disciplines. For a small set of examples of a now substantial body of literature on oral history and its relationship to the discipline of history, to which it has been a not always welcome latecomer, see: Thomas L. Charlton, et al, eds., *Thinking about Oral History*; Robert Perks and Alistair Thomson, eds., *The Oral History Reader*; Alessandro Portelli, *The Death of Luigi Trastulli and Other Stories*; Paul Thompson, *The Voice of the Past: Oral History*, 3rd ed.; Elizabeth Tonkin, *Narrating Our Pasts: The Social Construction of Oral History*; and the journal *Oral History*. Key axes of debate about the status and legitimacy of oral history sources have been whether those sources are as reliable as traditional documentary sources; whether their divergences from fact might be a source of insight rather than error, allowing one to glimpse social desire, imagination, and symbolism; and how to properly interpret narratives through adequate attention to their structuring forms and genres. See Alessandro Portelli, "What Makes Oral History Different?" in Perks and Thomson, *Oral History Reader*, 63–74, esp. 68.

12. While the position of the ethnographer and the complicity of anthropology in imperial and colonial enterprises have received much comment, one might well recall that William Shakespeare didn't exactly arrive in the colonies with no strings attached; Thomas Babbington Macaulay wrote his 1835 "Minute on Indian Education" advocating that English be used specifically to create a governing "class of persons, Indian in blood and color, but English in taste, in opinions, in morals, and in intellect"; the rise of the novel in India is intimately tied to a history of prizes offered by the

Crown; T.S. Eliot and Ezra Pound continue to provide cultural capital; and the Nobel Prize for Literature continues to be an arbiter of literary value and indeed of what political questions and responses may be rewarded in literature.

13. Gupta and Ferguson, *Anthropological Locations*, 36.
14. It is part of a larger collaborative project.
15. Dionne Brand, *In Another Place, Not Here*, 68; Clifford Geertz, "Thick Description": 3–30.
16. See Erna Brodber, "Fiction in the Scientific Procedure," in Selwyn Cudjoe, ed., *Caribbean Women Writers: Essays from the First International Conference*, 165.
17. Merle Collins, in conversation at my graduate seminar on Literature and Revolution, 31 January 2008.
18. Chinua Achebe, *Things Fall Apart*; and Michael Ondaatje, *Anil's Ghost*.
19. Spivak, *Death of a Discipline*, 50.
20. The annual conference of the Caribbean Studies Association in 2009 began a new performance track that serves a valuable function in enabling the circulation of nonprint texts and enabling interaction between critics and performers and artists.
21. Gupta and Ferguson, *Anthropological Locations*, 5.
22. For an extended and insightful treatment of this claim, see Didacus Jules, "Education and Social Transformation in Grenada, 1979–1983."
23. Das, *Life and Words*, 17.
24. Collins, "The Walk," 86–93.
25. Hayden White, *The Content of the Form: Narrative Discourse and Historical Representation*.
26. Thompson, *Voice of the Past*, 12.
27. Nixon, "Environmentalism and Postcolonialism," 239.

BIBLIOGRAPHY

Achebe, Chinua. 1994. *Things Fall Apart*. New York: Anchor Books.

Bachelard, Gaston, M. Jolas, and John R. Stilgoe. 1994. *The Poetics of Space*. Boston, MA: Beacon Press.

Behar, Ruth. 1997. *The Vulnerable Observer: Anthropology That Breaks Your Heart*. Boston, MA: Beacon Press.

Brand, Dionne. 1996. *In Another Place, Not Here*. New York: Grove.

Brodber, Erna. 1990. Fiction in the Scientific Procedure. In *Caribbean Women Writers: Essays from the First International Conference*, ed. Selwyn Cudjoe, 164–168. Wellesley, MA: Calaloux.

Casey, Edward. 1998. *The Fate of Place: A Philosophical History*. Berkeley, CA: University of California Press.

———. 2000. *Remembering: A Phenomenological Study*. 2nd ed. Bloomington, IL: Indiana University Press.

Chakrabarty, Dipesh. 1998. Reconstructing Liberalism? Notes Toward a Conversation Between Area Studies and Diaspora Studies. *Public Culture* 10(3): 457–482.

Charlton, Thomas L., Lois E. Myers, and Rebecca Sharpless. 2007. *Thinking about Oral History: Theories and Applications*. Lanham, MD: AltaMira Press.

Clifford, James, and George Marcus, eds. 1986. *Writing Culture: The Poetics and Politics of Ethnography*. Berkeley, CA: University of California Press.

Collins, Merle. 1990. The Walk. In *Rain Darling*, 86–93. London: Women's Press.

———. 2003. Shame Bush. In *Lady in a Boat*, 50–52. Leeds: Peepal Tree.

Cresswell, Tim. 2004. *Place: A Short Introduction*. Oxford: Blackwell.

Das, Veena. 2006. *Life and Words: Violence and the Descent into the Ordinary*. Berkeley, CA: University of California Press.

DeLoughrey, Elizabeth M., Renée K. Gosson, and George B. Handley, eds. 2005. *Caribbean Literature and the Environment: Between Nature and Culture*. Charlottesville, VA: University of Virginia Press.

Escobar, Arturo. 2008. *Territories of Difference: Place, Movements, Life, Redes*. Durham, NC: Duke University Press.

Fumagalli, Maria Cristina, Peter Hulme, Owen Robinson, and Lesley Wylie, eds. 2013. *Surveying the American Tropics: A Literary Geography from New York to Rio*. Liverpool: Liverpool University Press.

Geertz, Clifford. 1973. Thick Description: Toward an Interpretive Theory of Culture. In *The Interpretation of Cultures: Selected Essays*, 3–30. New York: Basic.

———. 1977. *The Interpretation of Cultures*. New York: Basic.

———. 1988. *Works and Lives: The Anthropologist as Author*. Stanford, CA: Stanford University Press.

Glissant, Édouard. 1997. *Poetics of Relation*. Trans. Betsy Wing. Ann Arbor, MI: University of Michigan Press.

Gupta, Akhil, and James Ferguson, eds. 1997. *Anthropological Locations: Boundaries and Grounds of a Field Science*. Berkeley, CA: University of California Press.

Harris, Wilson. 2010. *Palace of the Peacock*. 1960. Reprint. London: Faber and Faber.

Harrison, Faye. 1997. *Decolonizing Anthropology: Moving Further toward an Anthropology for Liberation*. 2nd ed. Arlington, VA: American Anthropological Association.

Hoelscher, Steven, and Derek H. Alderman. 2004. Memory and Place: Geographies of a Critical Relationship. *Social & Cultural Geography* 5(3): 347–355.

Jules, Didacus. 1992. Education and Social Transformation in Grenada, 1979–1983. PhD diss., University of Wisconsin at Madison.

Legg, Stephen. 2007. Reviewing Geographies of Memory/Forgetting. *Environment and Planning* 39(2): 456–466.

Macaulay, Thomas Babbington. 1920. Minute on Indian Education. In *Selections from Educational Records, Part I (1781–1839)*, ed. H. Sharp, 107–117. Calcutta: Superintendent, Government Printing.

Marcus, George E., and Michael M.J. Fisher. 1999. *Anthropology as Cultural Critique: An Experimental Moment in the Human Sciences*. Chicago, MA: University of Chicago Press.

Mintz, Sidney. 1998. The Localization of Anthropological Practice: From Area Studies to Transnationalism. *Critique of Anthropology* 18(2): 117–133.

Mirsepassi, Ali, Amrita Basu, and Frederick Weaver, eds. 2003. *Localizing Knowledge in a Globalizing World: Recasting the Area Studies Debate*. Syracuse, NY: Syracuse University Press.

Miyoshi, Masao, and Harry Harootunian, eds. 2002. *Learning Places: The Afterlives of Area Studies*. Durham, NC: Duke University Press.

Naipaul, V. S. 1984. An Island Betrayed. *Harper's Magazine* 268 (March): 61–72.

Nixon, Robert. 2005. Environmentalism and Postcolonialism. In *Postcolonial Studies and Beyond*, eds. Ania Loomba, Suvir Kaul, Matti Bunzl, Antoinette Burton, and Jed Esty, 233–251. Durham, NC: Duke University Press.

Nora, Pierre. 1996–1998. *Realms of Memory*. Vols. 1–3. New York: Columbia University Press.

Ondaatje, Michael. 2001. *Anil's Ghost*. New York: Vintage.

Perks, Robert, and Alistair Thomson, eds. 1998. *The Oral History Reader*. New York: Routledge.

Portelli, Alessandro. 1990. *The Death of Luigi Trastulli and Other Stories*. Binghamton, NY: SUNY Press.

———. 1998. What Makes Oral History Different? In *The Oral History Reader*, eds. Robert Perks, and Alistair Thompson, 63–74. New York: Routledge.

Price, Richard. 2007. *Travels with Tooy: History, Memory, and the African American Imagination*. Chicago, MA: University of Chicago Press.

Puri, Shalini, ed. 2003. *Marginal Migrations: The Circulation of Culture within the Caribbean*. Oxford: Macmillan.

———. 2004. *The Caribbean Postcolonial: Social Equality, Post-nationalism, and Cultural Hybridity*. New York: Palgrave Macmillan.

———. 2014. *The Grenada Revolution in the Caribbean Present: Operation Urgent Memory*. New York: Palgrave Macmillan.

Rhys, Jean. 1998. In *Wide Sargasso Sea*, ed. Judith L. Raiskin. New York: W.W. Norton.

Ribeiro, Gustavo Lins, and Arturo Escobar, eds. 2006. *World Anthropologies: Disciplinary Transformations in Systems of Power*. London: Berg.

Schama, Simon. 1995. *Landscape and Memory*. New York: A. A. Knopf.

Scott, David. 1999. *Refashioning Futures: Criticism after Postcoloniality*. Princeton, NJ: Princeton University Press.

Senior, Olive. 1994. *Gardening in the Tropics*. Toronto: McClelland and Stewart.

Slocum, Karla, and Deborah Thomas. 2003. Caribbean Studies, Anthropology, and US Academic Realignments: Insights from Caribbeanist Anthropology. *American Anthropologist* 105(3): 553–565.

Smith, Mick, Joyce Davidson, Laura Cameron, and Liz Bondi, eds. 2009. *Emotion, Place and Culture*. Surrey, England: Ashgate Publishing.

Spivak, Gayatri C. 2003. *Death of a Discipline*. New York: Columbia University Press.

Sternfeld, Joel. 1997. *On This Site: Landscape in Memoriam*. San Francisco, CA: Chronicle.

Stocking, George. 1985. *Observers Observed: Essays on Ethnographic Fieldwork*. Madison, WI: University of Wisconsin Press.

———. 1992. *The Ethnographer's Magic and Other Essays in the History of Anthropology*. Madison, WI: University of Wisconsin Press.

Taussig, Michael. 1997. *The Magic of the State*. New York: Routledge.

———. 2011. *I Swear I Saw This: Drawings in Fieldwork Notebooks, Namely, My Own*. Chicago, MA: University of Chicago Press.

Thompson, Paul. 2000. *The Voice of the Past: Oral History*. 3rd ed. Oxford: Oxford University Press.

Thompson, Krista A. 2006. *An Eye for the Tropics: Tourism, Photography, and Framing the Caribbean Picturesque*. Durham, NC: Duke University Press.

Tonkin, Elizabeth. 1995. *Narrating Our Pasts: The Social Construction of Oral History*. Cambridge: Cambridge University Press.

Walcott, Derek. 1993. *The Antilles: Fragments of Epic Memory.* New York: Farrar, Straus, and Giroux.

White, Hayden. 1990. *The Content of the Form: Narrative Discourse and Historical Representation.* Baltimore, MD: Johns Hopkins University Press.

Zeleza, Paul. 2006. African Studies: A Global Perspective. Paper presented at the International Colloquium on Area Studies, Diaspora Studies, and Critical Pedagogies, University of Toronto, 30 March–2 April 2006.

CHAPTER 3

Women's Naked Protest in Africa: Comparative Literature and Its Futures

Naminata Diabate

Authentic thinking, thinking that is concerned about reality, does not take place in ivory tower isolation, but only in communication.

—*Paulo Freire, Pedagogy of the Oppressed, 1970*

You didn't pick your battles, your battles picked you. Don't sweat it. The challenge will be figuring out how you are going to be responsible to them.

—*Neville Hoad, 2011*

The publication of *The Report on the State of the Discipline* by the American Comparative Literature Association, which explores the direction that the field might take in the future, constitutes a prime opportunity for new concepts, theories, interpretive frameworks, and methods. I highlight the importance of fieldwork for Comparative Literature based on two interrelated claims: one, that fieldwork offers us the opportunity to make contact with certain marginalized groups, those with no access to the conventional channels of knowledge production, but whose lives get impacted (in)directly by our academic initiatives; and two, that given disciplinary specificities such as language abilities and international experiences, Comparative Literature offers uniquely promising possibilities for developing a theory of fieldwork in the Humanities at this time.

I make these arguments in relation to my investigation of women's naked protests in several African societies, where female genitals are considered

N. Diabate (✉)
Department of Comparative Literature, Cornell University, Ithaca, USA

S. Puri, D.A. Castillo (eds.), *Theorizing Fieldwork in the Humanities*,
DOI 10.1057/978-1-349-92834-7_3

dangerous, and their threatening exhibition constitutes the ultimate weapon mature women wield in desperate circumstances to punish their male targets just like warriors wielding their deadliest weapons. Given its cultural potency, this most dangerous female-gendered act has been documented since the fourteenth century but not analyzed. And despite its proliferation in contemporary Africa, the meaning of this retributive act is misunderstood.

My forthcoming book, *Naked Agency: Genital Cursing, Biopolitics, and Africa*, explores the differing and conflicting meanings that genital cursing encounters in Africa (African Studies). The exploration of the unrecognized history of women and their potent forms of political intervention also contributes to two other fields: biopolitics and (postcolonial) feminism. The relatively recent conversations on nudity by Jacques Derrida, Elizabeth Grosz, Jean-Luc Nancy, and Giorgio Agamben frame nudity outside of Judeo-Christian dominant accounts of the state of innocence, truth, and vulnerability in order to highlight its subversive aspects. These subversive aspects reside in the proliferating meanings attached to the event of nudity, especially in its biopolitical configurations (exposure for political dissent). Expanding these accounts, my book argues that genital cursing (literal and biological death of the target of female nudity) revises current theorizations of biopolitics by foregrounding the agentive possibilities that may inhere in vulnerability and precarity. The new theoretical framework that emerges from this study is "naked agency," which names a space between nakedness and power, and a reading praxis that privileges the dialectical movement between positions of victimhood and power. The concept alludes to the unsolicited, yet generative, encounter between African local cosmologies about exposed tabooed skin, Africanized political institutions, and dominant accounts of nakedness as a state of vulnerability, truth, and innocence. Additionally, I seek to disturb the commonplace images of rape, mutilation, and pathology associated with women's bodies in Africa and also to fundamentally reframe the approach to the difficult question of sexuality and power in studies of women by offering a way out of the facile opposition between mere victims and sovereign subjects that informs much of that field.

Given this new account of the kind of social and political work that specific exposed skins can do, the reflections by Derrida, Grosz, and Nancy scream for specifications. These specifications are useful because what I term "the secularization of nudity," thinking of it outside the Judeo-Christian tradition, takes the North Atlantic world as empirical data for conceptualizations whose applications will be universalized. Thus, my contribution is to enrich these reflections on the exposed skin of genitals drawing on data from Africa. To do so, I draw on African visual art, film, novels, medieval oral stories, and journalistic coverage of protests and activism—alongside fieldwork. This chapter explores the place of fieldwork in my project, how and why fieldwork became a necessary part of the book's inquiry.

"You Didn't Pick Your Battles, Your Battles Picked You"

Naked Agency: Genital Cursing, Biopolitics, and Africa evolves out of frustration and hope. The seeds of my frustration were sown when I began studying African literature in the USA. To my initial amazement, the stereotypical images of women I encountered, especially in fictional texts that were published, circulated internationally, and counted as world literature,[1] were radically unlike the women I knew in my neighborhood in Côte d'Ivoire, West Africa. My critique of the pressures and rewards of the international market extends to both African and non-African writers. Given the nature of available images in literature, literary critical work was limited to problematics and approaches that lack variety, thereby strengthening the commonplace narrative accounts of victimized female bodies. It is in the constriction of range that resides the symbolic violence at work in literature and literary criticism.

Having moved from Côte d'Ivoire to the USA to pursue my doctorate, I was especially sensitive to the images of wounded and violated women's bodies. As a Malinké woman whose local culture was shaped by a misinterpretation of Islamic doctrines, I became convinced that my body was and always would be the locus of my subjection to the Malinké patriarchy, its erroneous versions of Islam, the heteropatriarchal modern state, and global configurations of discursive and material powers. In more concrete terms, how was I supposed to feel reading the sobering story of Salimata, the childless, tormented, circumcised wife of Fama, the protagonist of Ahmadou Kourouma's *The Suns of Independence* (1968)? The answer is "depressed." Just like Nnu Ego, the protagonist of Buchi Emecheta's *The Joys of Motherhood* (1979), I considered myself a "prisoner of my own flesh" (187).

In the majority of internationally circulating fictional narratives from and about Africa, two major trends emerged. First, images of women's sexuality were shaped primarily by the rhetoric of cutting (clitoridectomy and infibulation), violation ("corrective rape," rape as war weapon, marital rape), overreproduction, and pathology (HIV/AIDS, prostitution).[2] All are images I have come to call collectively the pervasive picture of negative sexualities. These texts feature a wide spectrum of violence enacted on female bodies, thereby "restaging" the paradigm of victimization. The result is the relative absence of "sexually" powerful and inspiring female characters. The problem is not that the literature depicts violence against women or the victimization of women. The problem is that it does not depict enough else: the ways in which women resist, defy, inspire, risk, wield power, negotiate, are complicit, and much, much more. Such commonplace depictions arguably emerge from and certainly contribute to the politics of what Nigerian novelist Teju Cole has called in 2012 "the White-Savior Industrial Complex."[3] Hence, the postcolonial reimaginings of lives in Africa and the theorizing to which they gave birth were at odds with the world I grew up in and with.

The frustration turned delight that led to the book, which Neville Hoad, my dissertation codirector, framed as "You Didn't Pick Your Battles, Your Battles Picked You," involved a lengthy process of archival work (excavation) and selection. Like Toni Morrison's epiphany about the ways in which blackness heavily impacted form in American literature, and which led to her *Playing in the Dark: Whiteness and the Literary Imagination* (1992), my chapter about how fieldwork broadens the scope of literary criticism "rises from delight, not disappointment" (4). It emerges from what I know about which forms of subjective embodiment defy our liberalism-informed ways of reading and what counts as politics and as agency. It arises from insights that are not acquired through conventional sites in the humanities such as books, lectures, and courses, but from life experiences, smells, and scenes, what Martin Bulmer in Sociology has called "experience recollected in academia" (254), or retrospective observation, or the native-as-stranger approach. Bringing these insights to bear on women and their embodied forms of contestation has the potential to enrich conventional literary criticism.

My focus in this chapter is the scarcity of fictional narratives that offer a wide range of perspectives, and the dearth of problematics that explore ritual nakedness. I am not arguing against the transformative power of fiction or that dominant narrative accounts and analyses contain no hint of reality. My point is that the constant discursive restaging of oppressive violence against female characters and the problematics of victimhood and empowerment in existing investigations affect how female readers view themselves. Amidst this limited problematic of victimhood and these images, female characters were often denied the possibility of "performing the roles" of "'survivor,' 'fighter,' and 'community member,'" a point similar to that which Kimberly Wedeven Segall made in the context of South Africa's Truth and Reconciliation Commission (619).

In order to deepen our understanding of the way nakedness can be read as forms of punishment and an index of precarity in Africa, it is essential to explore multiple perspectives that are unsanitized and unsubordinated to ideological investments.[4] Given the scarcity of fictional narratives and social science research on female exposure for purposes of cursing, informal interviews with ritual activists and other scholars should become part of Comparative Literature's method. We need to explore such questions as: What drives one to disrobe in defiance? What subjective states does it generate? What does it mean to resort to one's last "weapon"? How is one perceived in the community of peers for disrobing against a male family member?

I read the literature against other practices to which I had been exposed, particularly ones in which the power of the female body and motherhood could be mobilized to curtail the prerogatives of patriarchal and state stylistics of domination. Of course, women also found other routes to resistance and self-empowerment. In my childhood neighborhood in the capital city of Abidjan in Côte d'Ivoire, in order to resist verbal and physical abuse and to punish outrageous male family members, the nonliterate and economically disenfranchised women resorted to using their bodies, capitalizing on the fear that men in the community have of female sexuality, which they have been taught to regard as dangerous. Flashing taboo body parts, threatening a man with menstrual cloths, or touching men's food or clothing with secretions considered repugnantly sexual often made men listen or comply in instances where other mechanisms of resistance had failed. Similarly, as a Malinké and Muslim, I had learned that I should not challenge my mother. In my community, the prevailing belief posits that mothers are endowed with a specific form of power, the ability to invoke a curse with their genitals and breasts, which could materialize in the form of a ruined future, insanity, or death.[5]

This threat was actualized in a neighborhood incident that I witnessed 15 years ago. The incident, drawn from my retrospective observation is important for its qualitative nature.[6] A young man, in his twenties, was in an argument with his mother; it became heated. Against all expectations, the man refused to concede to his mother, who declared in anger: "The child that I could have washed down the drain and which I decided to keep is not respecting me." She continued to explain her shame of being disrespected by the fruit of her own womb. So extreme was her experience of shame that the mother ran out of their house with her uncovered breasts which she held, screaming: "If I did not get on my knees to push out of my womb, if these breasts did not feed you, if I did not go into labor for hours in order to give you birth, you would fail in life!"[7] The mother proceeded to recite a litany of other survival challenges that they faced as a working-class family. Her litany, anger, and, most importantly, the resolution in her voice terrified the neighborhood that had gathered, and the community was stunned that a mother had reacted with this ritual curse. The young man's father was equally dumbfounded as he explained to my father later that week that he could not fathom why his wife decided to "spoil the harvest that she has worked so hard to secure" and why "she has cancelled her life insurance on her deathbed." When almost a decade later the young man passed away after an illness, leaving behind a widow and two daughters, rumors circulated that his mother's curse had materialized. It remains unclear to me if the mother was to blame for the young man's death.

The beliefs undergirding the rumors regarding the man's death were disseminated by word of mouth, evening storytelling, but most importantly by several cassettes of recorded versions of the *Epic of Sunjata* by popular Malinké performers known as Djeliw and which constituted the main source of entertainment in the neighborhood.[8]

The most widespread piece of oral literature in Francophone Africa, *The Epic of Sunjata* is also the oldest recorded example of genital cursing in Africa. Part history, part legend, the *Epic* recounts the titular character's ascension in 1235 to the throne of the Mande empire which, at its peak, stretched from the Atlantic coast south of the Senegal River to Gao on the east of the middle Niger bend, making it the most important empire in West Africa at the time. Popular oral versions as well as Djibril Tamsir Niane's 1965 *Sundiata: An Epic of Old Mali* consign female characters to their roles as mothers and sisters, downplaying their political impact in the Mande Empire and their contribution to Sunjata's success during the epic battle between him and his nemesis, King Soumaoro Kanté. However, other versions, Aliou Diabate's and Jeli Mori Kouyate's, in recorded cassettes highlight women's contribution through genital cursing to the building of the Mali empire.

I incorporate these cassette-recorded versions of the epic into my analysis of genital cursing for two main reasons, topical and formal. Topical reasons include the contributions of women that they highlight. On the formal level, attention to their texts in their improvisations, variations, and performances deepens our understanding of how literary texts absorb and contribute to contemporary street and public cultures. This kind of attention reveals forms of cultural productions that traditional Comparative Literature does not usually explore. In order to contextualize them, I draw on exchanges I have had with anthropologists such as David Conrad,[9] Kassim Koné, Ryan Skinner, and Barbara Hoffman[10] in the USA who work on Malinké societies, and on my relationships with Malinké people living in the United States to substantiate and interpret the dynamics of such moments in my neighborhood. For instance, Kassim Koné comments on genital curses among the Malinké:

> A woman's use or threat to use her genitalia to curse a male relative or any male falls into the category of danka but there is no special term for this except descriptive expressions such: *ka i julankolon bila ka X danka* (to strip one's private parts and curse X); or *ka fini bila ka X danka* (to get out of clothes to curse X). Any woman may threaten any man to curse them this way if there is ground for it. Any senior woman may use this threat to curse anybody on the proper grounds.... Mande males are socialized to fear/respect female genitalia for socio-cultural reasons.[11]

As Koné and others suggest, the mother's act and the reactions that it engendered correspond to the belief in many rural and/or working-class Malinké communities that mature women and mothers have the authority and status to mobilize their anger for purposes of punishment or resistance. By baring their nether parts, wielding menstrual cloths, and invoking their wombs and the pains of childbirth, these women can use their bodies and their symbolic positions as their weapons against individual and collective acts of violence and violation. When all else fails, these culturally sanctioned modes of speech and action are the kinds of power that women reach down for, seize, and wield like warriors who reach down for their deadliest weapon. And so I wonder, "Why can't I read, even intermittently, about echoes of my life in narratives that purport to depict African women?"

Back in 2008, I was frustrated by the seeming invisibility of the cultural practice of genital cursing in fiction and in theorizing of agency and subjectivity in African literary studies. Like Limatkazo Kendall, who went to Lesotho looking for her "kind" [lesbians], I went on a "mission" to locate echoes, glimpses, and parallels of my lived experiences in fictional narratives from and about Africa.

My goal was multipronged; first, I wanted to uncover these other stories, the stories of women who live in crippling material realities, those without access to the conventional channels of knowledge production, and who often use these modes of contestation. Their experiences, I thought and still think, may teach us important aspects of what it means to be a resistant subject in spaces that Achille Mbembe compellingly calls "deathscapes." By exploring their forms of contestation, I sought to reflect on the significations of disrobing that are not readily accounted for in dominant liberal definitions of victimhood and agency. Second, I sought to complicate the pervasive pictures of negative sexualities.

My chapter is not prescriptive about the kinds of fieldwork appropriate for Comparative Literature. But my own practice of fieldwork draws heavily on information recollected as retrospective observer and native-as-observer, in conjunction with online exchanges and informal interviews. I argue for the need for such steps and methodologies to be acknowledged as part and parcel of literary criticism.

Hunting and Uncovering

Unable to locate literary fiction on genital cursing in my immediate environment, in 2008, I submitted inquiries to multiple academic listservs, including H-Africa, H-Français, H-French Colonial, H-Minerva, H-West Africa, H-Caribbean, H-African American, H-Women, H-MedAnthro, and H-History of Sexuality, with the title: "Fictional Texts on Genital and Menstrual Curses." The response to my query was encouraging. Given the number of emails, it appears that list members were aware of the practice and that my experiences and assumptions were not isolated. Several emails referred me to texts that did not in fact represent genital cursing. It seems that given the familiarity with the topic, members thought that they had read about it. These false leads and mistaken referrals explain the divide between the scarcity of literary fiction on naked protest and its widespread use on the continent, hence the necessity of fieldwork to expand our understanding of the few precious texts that depict them. This scarcity somewhat confirmed my observations that for understandable reasons, novelistic representations and most critical scholarly inquiries have been apprehensive of theorizing the ways in which women have shown to be powerful in their use of ritualized nudity. For instance, several suggested Sembene Ousmane's *Bouts de Bois de Dieu* (1960, *God's Bits of Wood*), Ngugi wa Thiong'o's *The River Between* (1965), Buchi Emecheta's *The Slave Girl* (1977), and Francis Bebey's *La poupée ashanti* (1973, *The Ashanti Doll* [1977]). French historian of women in Africa, Catherine Coquery-Vidrovitch, emerita of Université Diderot Paris 7, wrote: "When political riots flourished in Côte d'Ivoire, at the beginning of the 1950s (there was a published French parliamentary report on the question), I remember that women demonstrated their nudity in the countryside to express their discontent." Coquery-Vidrovitch was referring to the anticolonial collective genital cursing which is studied in both Henriette Dagri Diabate's historical monograph, *La Marche des Femmes sur Grand-Bassam* (1975), and N'dri Assie-Lumumba's *Les Africaines dans la politique: Femmes Baoulé de Côte d'Ivoire* (1996).

However, from an unlikely place, H-net MedAnthro, I found two precious texts, Obinkaram Echewa's *I Saw the Sky Catch Fire* (1992) and American psychologist Clarissa Pinkola Estes's vignette "Rwandan Women" in *Women Who Run with the Wolves: Myths and Stories of the Wild Woman Archetype* (1992). Estes's work is a collection of reinterpreted folklore: mythical stories and fairy tales, whereas Echewa's novel remains the most iconic representation of naked protest in postcolonial Africa. Published in the USA, Echewa's novel includes a fictional reconstruction of an actual event, the 1929 Women's War, in which thousands of Igbo women in a collective genital shaming gesture showed their naked buttocks to horrified soldiers and British colonial administrators in protest against female taxation and the colonial incursion in Igboland. Further inquiries to Stephen Belcher, through H-net West Africa, combined with my knowledge of the aforementioned *Epic of Sunjata*, led me to American anthropologist David Conrad's compilation, transcription, translation, and publication of Aliou Diabate's and Jeli Mori Kouyate's versions of the oral literature.

Popular oral versions as well as Djibril Tamsir Niane's 1965 *Sundiata: An Epic of Old Mali* consign female characters to their roles as mothers and sisters, dismissing their political impact in the Mande Empire, while Diabate's and Kouyate's versions highlight women's contribution through genital cursing to the building of the Mali Empire. With the help of Conrad's materials, I argue for a longer history of genital shaming in political settings, dating from medieval West Africa, and am therefore able to contest the claim that dates the politicization of female bodies to the colonial era. In these ways, I sense that my insider's knowledge of Malinké society allows me to retrieve more ethnographic data than I could have otherwise done. At play here is the valuable interaction of inside/native knowledges, ethnographic data, research, and textual training, which provides a deeper understanding of certain phenomena while bringing in the women who deploy their nakedness and their lifeworlds to enrich our picture of Mande society.

Although I found only two fictional texts, historians and anthropologists suggested several relevant sources. A new question emerged as a result: How does one account for the divide between the plethora of anthropological sources and the scarcity of fictional narratives on women's genital cursing? Based on my research in the history of publishing in Africa, I propose that factors contributing to the scarcity of fiction on the subject include secrecy around questions of sexuality, the late development of women's formal education and fiction writing, the long-standing masculinist tradition of the publishing industry, the fragility of published fiction (the books go out of print), and the need to "sanitize" the pathologized image of the female body.

My efforts in hunting for and uncovering these sources, with the stumbling blocks, false leads, and mistaken referrals to texts that in fact did not depict genital cursing, should be understood as part of literary analysis and not be ghettoized in the preface. Typically conceived, the affects involved in producing archival work often get relegated to sections of the books that often do not count as rigorous and compelling literary criticism. This is unfortunate because (a) the initial frustration launched the search and (b) the affect sustains one and enables completion. The literary critical project from start to finish was thus framed by ethnographic experience.

Literary criticism and archival work are crucial avenues for preserving cultural records about African societies. Although those activities do not necessarily involve perusing library shelves and leafing through boxes of books, they are important to African Studies, given the fragile nature of published fiction in and about Africa. Aware of the challenges of locating my sources, literary critic Lisa Moore observed during my dissertation defense, "Your work underlines the importance of archival work. Books and film were hard to get a copy of. Even though these texts are recent, they're ephemeral. You're both identifying a tradition and creating it" (2011). In other words, literary criticism becomes a way to preserve these emerging but fragile archives.

Literature Programs have not formalized sources of funding and the time to conduct specific forms of fieldwork, as Shalini Puri accurately argues in her chapter on the subject, "Finding the Field: Notes on Caribbean Cultural Criticism, Area Studies, and the Forms of Engagement" (2013). But, perhaps Comparative Literature may consider forms of the field that involve the Internet and the ease and connections it enables. It could certainly give greater recognition and legitimacy to the significant role that resources such as H-net provide. Indeed, without resources such as the H-net listservs and the kinds of connections that they provide, my book project would have been harder to conceive. Moreover, methodological innovations in the social sciences in recent decades, their questioning of objectivity and the neutrality of ethnographers, and their turn toward the literary should surely increase the affinities between Comparative Literature and the social sciences.

EXISTING ARCHIVES AND THEIR LIMITS

The plethora of anthropological and historical materials on naked protest remained fundamentally unsatisfying, given their etiolated accounts of ritual nudity, and their negation of a crucial aspect of states of resistance and victimhood and their temporariness. So in my attempt to move beyond what Chimamanda Adichie calls the "single story," the single story that seems to stage *ad eternam* women's bodies as overworked, cut, raped, and diseased, I uncovered two other single stories that feature in disciplines other than Literature: on the one hand, the tendency to romanticize ritual nudity, and on the other, to read defiant nudity as backward and immoral. I was then productively caught up in multiple stories that pulled in different directions.

The romanticizing trend, with its triumphalist rhetoric, may be classified under what Lila Abu-Lughod has called in her study of the Bedouin of Egypt, "The Romance of Resistance" (1990), or what Amanda Anderson, speaking of the Victorian-era scholarship, has termed "Aggrandized Agency" (2011). These empowering yet problematic analyses are especially visible in several studies as scholars, male and female, African and American, uncritically rescue from oblivion these female-gendered forms of contestation.[12] In their accounts, they bring to the fore a submerged image of women in Africa and considerably complicate the conventional images that portray women as victimized by their tradition. These critics displace these ubiquitous images by showing that the convergence of new public politics and old traditions produces a distinctive subject position that writes African women into the new political configurations of their respective countries.

For example, using the Igbo cosmogony and the figure of *Aje* to read Echewa's novel, Teresa Washington celebrates the women's use of the divine powers of their bodies in their resistance against British colonialists. Washington's approach, which sheds much-needed light on Igbo society, seeks to critique patronizing Euro-American feminist attitudes toward "victimized" African women. Most importantly, by rejecting Western epistemologies, it aims to showcase a supposed African authenticity: "Although condemned to eternal victimhood by some feminists and international organizations, Africana women possess abundant revolutionary skills and abilities, and they have used them against slavers, colonizers, and their oppressors. The tools they brandish to obtain their goals, however, may vary depending on circumstance and locale" (Washington 134). In the process of retrieving and "brandishing" authentic African women's powers, what disappear are the limitations of their weapons.[13] Indeed, obsessive writing back to and answering the wrong done by the West, as Achille Mbembe would call it,[14] often results in equally sweeping counter-generalizations rather than in a rich description of African women and their diversity.

Using cosmological frameworks to explain contemporary ritual nakedness is just as problematic as reliance on dated anthropological sources. In his analysis of the Nigerian women's 2002 threat to strip in protest of multinational oil companies in Nigeria, Philips Stevens explains the potency of their act, relying heavily on anthropological sources with ethnographic data produced primarily during colonial and postindependence eras by psychiatrist Raymond Prince (1961) and anthropologists Robert Ritzenthaler (1960), Mary Douglas (1966), Caroline Ifeka-Moller (1975), and Shirley Ardener (1973). His resultant analysis frames genital cursing as endlessly powerful and self-empowering.

Although colonialism and neocolonialism cannot have completely erased century-old beliefs, to use colonial and precolonial anthropological data to explain present-day women's deployments of their ritualized nakedness is a questionable methodological approach. It is equally problematic, given the work of detraditionalization in societies that are becoming increasingly precarious, and in a time when women and men are experiencing the effects of processes of gender restructuring. In that space, a precolonial and nativist explanatory matrix that relies essentially on the historical importance and mystical values of "genital power," itself predicated upon reified gender norms, does not offer a broad and complex enough understanding of the dynamics of victimhood and contestation.

Opposed to those social scientists who celebrate the protesters as self-determining subjects are zealous religious leaders, postcolonial statesmen, radical journalists, and bloggers who castigate them for their inability to speak the language of modernity and frame their modes of contestation as immoral and backward. For example, on September 24, 2001, during the presidential electoral campaigns in the Gambia, about 30 "starkly naked" women performed a ritual to denounce "what they claimed was a distasteful ritual by [sic] opposition to 'sacrifice' a dog for election purposes." The ritual participants carried empty calabashes, cursed, swore, prayed, and dug a hole over which some sat while the rest continued to chant in anger. Days after the protest, reacting to the women's ritual, and as the journalist accurately predicted, leaders from multiple religious denominations vehemently condemned the women and their ritual. Their condemnatory terms included "irreligious," "public indecency," "vile and repugnant," "anti-Islamic, antisociety and anticultural," and they called on the government to take tough measures against the protesters to prevent this kind of action from taking hold in the Gambia. That these religious leaders conflate this mode of political participation with backwardness and immorality reflects their rejection of long-sanctioned cultural practices and their aim to manage unruly subjects, those whose supposed unbridled traditionalism holds the power to misdirect the postcolonial state from its well-oiled march toward economic development. The aforementioned examples reveal both the pressure to write the story of African women into frames of tradition and modernity and the inadequacy of doing so.

Moreover, how can one explain the divide between academic discourses in the Humanities and news reports? This question refers to the proliferation of worldwide news reporting about female protesters' uses of ritual forms of exposure in Africa. The late 1990s onward saw a wave of news about genital flashing and other rituals during national political crises. This recent wave follows its mobilization in Africa's past, especially during the anticolonial struggles. With the resurgence of democratic aspirations and growing precarity due to neoliberalization, several parts of sub-Saharan Africa have experienced this massive politicization and weaponization of naked female bodies. In 2012, these forms exceeded the boundaries of the African postcolonial nation-state, when Ivorian women in France demonstrated, using stained menstrual cloths, to protest against the neocolonialist practices of France and the United Nations in Côte d'Ivoire.

Existing studies also tend not to consider the backlash that the women experienced. These backlashes can take quite drastic forms, from desecration to arrest to murder (Côte d'Ivoire 2002, 2011, Nigeria 2002, Ghana 2008). In 2002, at the outbreak of the civil war in Côte d'Ivoire, elderly women of the female society, *Adjanou*, who were performing their purifying ritual in order to bring peace to the country, were kidnapped and killed by alleged rebel soldiers. In March 2008, hundreds of Liberian women war refugees in Ghana staged month-long demonstrations and even publicly exposed their genitals to demand that they either be sent back to Liberia with $1000 instead of $100 or be resettled in the West (Essuman-Johnson 2011; Omata 2012). Reacting to the Liberian women war refugees' nudity, Ghanaian authorities arrested and drove them away from the refugee camp.

The Ghanaian interior minister, Kwamena Bartels, on the *BBC News Africa* program, even threatened to forcibly repatriate the protesters to Liberia, because, he said, "When women strip themselves naked and stand by a major highway that is not a peaceful demonstration."[15] Several observers established a connection between this case and the women of the Niger Delta's threat to disrobe in 2002. Yet despite these useful speculations, no interviews of the Liberian women war refugees exist to refute or confirm these claims. Attention to the women's living conditions in a refugee camp might yield a reading that differs from existing analyses. For instance, what does it mean to demand legal recognition using nonlegally recognizable forms of claims making? What happens when one inscribes agency while sharing similarities with the Agambenian naked life, a body denied legal and political rights?

Genital Power or Naked Agency?

These various situations, the diversity of the continent, and the changing gender norms behoove us to avoid monolithic frameworks as reading lenses. Often, "symbolic" and cosmological paradigms function as metanarratives that obfuscate local voices and intentions. As Max Weber, drawing on Kant, observes: "concepts are primarily analytical instruments for the intellectual mastery of empirical data and can be only that" (106). He goes on to posit that reality is markedly rich and that concepts are abstract and poor. More importantly for my point, Weber analyzes the relationship between reality and concepts and highlights "the danger that the ideal type and reality will be confused with one another" (101). Overgeneralizations erase women's lived experiences which seem to elude scholars' and observers' mode of recognition. Framing corporeal modes of contestation such as genital cursing as endlessly powerful or eternally victimizing ends up replicating the sterile methodology of unitary reading.

My own opinion is that dire material conditions and the lack of options weighed more heavily in women's decision to disrobe than did their innate beliefs in the mystical power of their bodies, as symbolic and anthropological readings would assume. Attention to lived experiences and the affective states that prompt women to mobilize these practices in public would yield more nuanced and supple theorizing. Interviews with the Liberian women war refugees after their protest might have shed light on their intentions and choice of defiant exposure. Their status as refugees akin to the Agambenian *homo sacer* is informative as well. Their narratives, along with those of the Gambian ritual participants, would have been useful in producing a more accurate reading of their ritual nakedness, or whether or not they themselves would view their actions in this context.

As things now stand, there are materially exposed bodies with inaudible voices, for nowhere do the voices of these participants get heard. They move from invisibility to spectacularized visibility and spectacular silence/ing. One reason for this is the women's refusal to engage verbally with journalists, given their understanding of their ritual and the possible language barriers between them and journalists. The implications of their rituals are thus articulated by the commentators through their own background knowledge. For instance, in the Gambian women's case, according to reporter Lamin Dibba, when he attempted to interview one of the women, he was "flatly rebuffed, with an excuse that he was too young to even witness what they were doing." A decade later, in Côte d'Ivoire, when women of the female secret society—the *Adjanou*—refused to speak with journalists during their standoff with Laurent Gbagbo's government about the desecration of their ritual, journalists were left to speculate on the message of the women's curse. For instance, the reporter of the newspaper *Le Mandat* filled in the blanks for the reader:

> These are very serious hours; a spiritual warfare is taking place. This warfare is waged exclusively by a few well-versed women. This is not a war for men and they have to keep away for this is off limits to them. We are in the spiritual realm here; (according to the African tradition, most specifically the Ivorian), power and dominion (strength) belong to women.[16] (my translation)

Reporters often assign meanings to these threatening exhibitions of bodies that are utterly at odds with the meanings that the women may give to their acts. They may frame ritual nakedness as protest, whereas participants may see their actions as cursing. Or observers may present the act as peaceful forms of action *sensu* Gandhi or Martin Luther King, whereas participants hope to highlight violent aspects of their action by wishing a myriad of misfortunes on the targeted males—impotence, infertility, incurable diseases, and death.

Women's refusal to engage verbally with journalists and commentators leaves a void that the rhetoric of the exposed body may fail to fill. Yet their refusal demonstrates the distinction between silent and silenced and powerfully connects to what Doris Sommer has called in Rigoberta Menchu's withholding of information "the audible protests of silence" (32).

The dearth of material exploring women's emotions, strategies, and rationales increases the possibility of their being ventriloquized or misread. Here is what the mother who disrobed 15 years ago said in an informal conversation with me in 2010: "I was in pain beyond words, and I needed to teach him a lesson." She traded her position of victim and wounded to that of agent and teacher in the sense of teaching her son a lesson. Given these fluctuating positions of wounded and teacher, of one both pained and inflicting pain, protest nudity and its various manifestations need to be more subtly theorized, and lived experiences may provide the most promising avenues for such an endeavor.

Working through these materials, sources, and dilemmas has led me to think of ritual nudity more in terms of naked agency than genital power. Naked agency names a space between nakedness and power, and a reading praxis that privileges the dialectical movement between positions of victimhood and power. The concept alludes to the unsolicited yet generative encounter between African local cosmologies about exposed tabooed skin, Africanized political institutions, and dominant accounts of nakedness as a state of vulnerability, truth, and innocence. More specifically, the overdetermination of women's bodies on which the putative power of genital shaming is predicated may be eroded in certain spaces. Kinship structures and family-based networks, with their enforced accountability and responsibility, are also eroded with rapid urbanization and individualization. While ritual disrobing elicits fear and shame in men in a rural area, or in family settings, in urban spaces genital shaming may fail, for there anonymity and tenuous kinship bonds confer a certain kind of agency on individuals and postcolonial authorities. Thus, the idea of naked agency, a phrase that holds in tension two putatively dichotomous states. One has to continually maintain the delicate balance between acknowledging the courage necessary to mobilize these forms of contestation and the possible backlash (arrest and physical violation) that the women may face. Attention to the complex meanings of female bodies holds the possibility of a broad theorization of female sexuality in Africa. But, until we recognize these body-centered forms with their limitations, we will continually theorize no more than our own critical fantasies, anxieties, and projections.

Each individual anecdote or incident I have recounted also raises the question of scale and in/commensurability—in the movement from one woman (in incident in the neighborhood) to the collective (women in Ghana and the Gambia). How does the kinship setting relate to the national setting? How does one transition from a familial involving a mother in pain in a familial setting to a national context in which women activists display outrage?

Hospitality in Comparative Literature

One could argue that literary criticism needs no interviews with ritual participants in order to arrive at more nuanced and accurate readings of ritual genital exposure. Fictional texts, research in the social sciences, and newspaper articles can produce what literary critics need should they prefer historical, sociological, or gender critical approaches to formalist and deconstructive reading praxes because of certain ideas that they seek to bring to the forefront.

But, to read Echewa's *I Saw the Sky Catch Fire* for what it can tell us about our contemporary world may not suffice. In this case, despite its dense textuality, the narrative reimagines a colonial setting with its attendant beliefs and gender norms that may not help make sense of contemporary deployments of ritual exposure. The historical and cultural contexts operative in the narrative—men's violent reaction to female genitals, the power of kinship networks—might not find their equivalences in the postcolonial city. I would even argue that precarity in the postcolonial city with necropolitics as a normalized governmental rationality creates a sense of danger that people living in the colonial era could not imagine. Indeed, in the postcolonial city, the population becomes the surplus and is left prey to multiple forces, including corrupt postcolonial bureaucrats, multinational companies, war machines, evangelists of all stripes, and the Bretton Woods institutions with their Structural Adjustments Programs (Mbembe 2003).

Yet similarities do exist between the two worlds, the rural colonial village setting of the novel and the postcolonial city, and comparison is the work of my discipline. For instance, the killing of more than 100 Igbo women following their genital shaming act by soldiers recruited by the British colonial administration in 1929 could productively be compared to the 2002 killing of the Adjanou performers in 2002. Moreover, the rhetoric of the "spirit-induced madness" and of "a sudden overflow of premenstrual or postpartum hormones" or "spontaneous combustion" that the colonial administration uses to dismiss women's political rationality parallels the vitriolic rhetoric that religious leaders used in the Gambian case. In that sense, there are few differences between the women; they converged in oppositional terrains with regimes of power that refuse to share in their epistemes. The feelings and strategies of the characters may enable the reader to imaginatively engage with the Liberian women war refugees. So the conventional approach of reading novels to make mediated sense of reality can potentially yield powerful insights. However, such an approach has limitations that can potentially be avoided if one makes contact with women activists.[17] As Paolo Freire argues in *Pedagogy of the Oppressed*, "Authentic thinking, thinking that is concerned about reality, does not take place in ivory tower isolation, but only in communication" (64). I thus propose that we consider the other direction, in which an analysis of interviews with women can help illuminate other aspects of the novel that may not otherwise be available.

With time, resources, and institutional blessing, I will analyze Echewa's novel in light of interviews with the women, rather than try to understand the Liberian women war refugees solely through *I Saw the Sky Catch Fire*. Relying exclusively on the novel to make sense of living beings when one has the ability to approach them constitutes an ethics of detachment (with its agentive possibilities for the reader).[18] I would like to see Comparative Literature practice a more humane ethics of hospitality. It is in that sense that literary critic Neville Hoad's insight, "The challenge will be figuring out how are you going to be responsible to them (The battles that picked me) (2011)," continues to shape my connection to the topic and to the agents who collectively mobilize naked protest on the continent. I doubt that Hoad meant "being responsible to them" in the material sense of feeling responsible for ritual participants. What I think he meant was to be mindful of the impact of my readings on the ways in which the topic will be received in the future. In this essay, I try to push further his invitation.

An example of such an effort might be to join David Conrad in his compilation, transcription, translation, and publication of several recorded

Malinké oral studies. Conrad's research made possible my book project, and given the precarious nature of these emerging archives, I am convinced of the importance of his transcription and translation projects. An investment in these kinds of projects or in contemporary ritual participants as living beings, an attempt to understand them, to validate in a way their intentions and emotions is an urgent enterprise—and one to which Comparative Literature can contribute. Just as importantly, the actors' thoughts, regrets, or sense of triumph following their ritual exposure might prove illuminating for the field of Comparative Literature. Ultimately, if the novel and its imagined people give us the latitude of detachment because the stakes are low, how accountable do I feel to the activists whose actions my scholarship is supposed to explain?

In a recent lecture about her much-discussed essay, "Is It Ethical to Study Africa?" (2007), Amina Mama offers compelling ways to engage the women that she features in her documentary, *The Witches of Gambaga* (Fadoa Films 2010). Among her actions was maintaining a relationship with the women by returning to screen the film, even years after the shooting of the documentary. Similarly, American anthropologist Elizabeth Povinelli has provided expert assistance to the aboriginal communities in their land claims against the Australian government. Povinelli has analyzed the lives of these communities in books such as *Economies of Abandonment* (2011) and *The Empire of Love: Toward a Theory of Intimacy, Genealogy, and Carnality* (2006). These examples demonstrate how one can engage with "ordinary" peoples in an ethical way.

As a discipline that understands itself as cross-cultural, transnational, transmedial, and interdisciplinary, and with its emphases on multisided narratives, cosmopolitanism, translation, and postcoloniality (Melas 2007; Apter, 2006; Damrosch, 2003; Spivak 2003), comparativists should be readily equipped to adapt specific methodological practices that do not necessarily get accounted for using conventional disciplinary perspectives and assumptions. Thus, practitioners of Comparative Literature may be able to formulate a powerful theory of fieldwork in the humanities. The high-theory and Euro/US-centric Comparative Literature that Gayatri Spivak critiques and worked to change in the *Death of A Discipline* (2003) is slowly giving way to a revised and more hospitable discipline. That hospitable discipline is what Rey Chow invokes in "The Discipline of Tolerance" (2011). In calling for opening the already-permeable borders of the discipline, I encourage fieldwork that will increase its investment in marginalized people and voices, sources of wisdom, and topics for the continued relevance of Comparative Literature. Given the long history of silencing marginalized groups, those with no access to the dominant channels of knowledge production, given the ease of mobility and the greater access to information enabled by digital technologies, and given the rethinking of what constitutes knowledge in the social sciences, it seems to me that the Humanities should make contact, encounter the subjects whose lives are impacted (in)directly by our academic initiatives.

Notes

1. Examples of childless and psychologically tormented female characters include Buchi Emecheta, *The Joys of Motherhood* (1979), Ahmadou Kourouma, *The Suns of Independence* (1968), Aminata Sow Fall's *L'appel des Arènes* (*The Call of the Wrestling Arenas*) (1982); prostitution in the works of Wole Soyinka, Nuruddin Farah, Cyprian Ekwensi, Mongo Beti, and Sembène Ousmane; female genital surgeries in Frieda Ekotto's *Chuchote pas trop* (2001), Ngugi Wa Thiong'o's *The River Between* (1965), Waris Dirie's *Desert Flower* (1998), Nurrudin Farrah's *From A Crooked Rib* (1970), Evelyn Accad's *The Excision* (1994); HIV/AIDS: Phaswane Mpe's *Welcome to Our Hillbrow* (2001), Carolyne Adalla, *Confessions of an AIDS Victim* (1996), Viola Kala's *Waste Not Your Tears* (1994), Bento Sitoe's *Zabela, My Wasted Life* (1996).
2. The larger framework of postcolonial feminism to which this chapter contributes has produced a number of excellent works on the constricted range within which women from the Global South have been produced. These texts include Gayatri Spivak's foundational 1985 essay, "Can the Subaltern Speak?," Gloria Wekker's *The Politics of Passion: Women's Sexual Culture in the Afro-Surinamese Diaspora* (2006), Saba Mahmood's *Politics of Piety: The Islamic Revival and the Feminist Subject* (2005), and Lila Abu-Lughod's *Writing Women's Worlds: Bedouin Stories* (1993).
3. In a series of tweets and later in an article "The White-Savior Industrial Complex" (2012), Teju Cole reanimated centuries-old debate around the stereotypical images of the continent and its peoples in the west. These depictions and the interventionist and "making a difference" politics they give rise to satisfy American sentimentality without critiquing the geopolitical and structural systems that create the images in the first place.
4. In "Finding the Field: Notes on Caribbean Cultural Criticism, Area Studies, and the Forms of Engagement," Shalini Puri carves out a space of possible conversation between literary criticism and fieldwork with reasons similar to mine and which include the "paucity of documentary resources, an over representation of elite documents among them, and a desire to put existing archives into dialogue with the spoken narratives of un-credentialed Grenadians" (66).
5. This account of the effects of defiant women's bodies is not specific to African contexts as countless historical and anthropological sources, too many to list here, suggest. *La Guerra de las Gordas* by the Mexican writer Salvador Novo, translated into English as *The War of the Fatties and Other Stories from Aztec History* (1994), is an important literary text. In this play, Novo dramatizes how during the war with the Mexicas the battalion of armed men of the Aztec army was defeated by naked women and their milk: "the most hair-raising battalion bursts into our ranks. They came up shouting and slapping themselves on the belly. We were so shocked we couldn't move. And when they got close to us, they squeezed their *chichis*

and bathed our faces with squirts of warm, thick milk!" "The secret weapon! The atomizing pump!" added Axayacatl (54).

6. Given the setup of the neighborhood which functions more like an extended family compound than a conventional one, joys and traditions are communally shared. In this sense, for better or for worse, children are more often than not exposed to adult conversations.

7. Such cultural expressions of counter-shaming are not unique to the Malinké or Agni of Côte d'Ivoire. For example, among the Yoruba, Chief Ọlajubu recounts that the threat may go: "Except it were not I that gave birth to you from my womb/Except it were not I that fed you from my breasts/That so and so would befall you" ("References to Sex," 156).

8. The *Jeliw* or *djeli* (women and men) specialize as oral historians and entertainers; see Conrad, *Sunjata* and Koné, "When Male Becomes Female."

9. David Conrad, email message to author. November 20, 2012.

10. Barbara Hoffman, email message to author. February 25, 2013.

11. In an email communication with Kassim Kone, associate professor at SUNY-Cortland. Quoted with his permission.

12. See Laura Grillo, "Catachresis in Côte d'Ivoire"; Phillips Stevens, "Women's Aggressive Use"; Teresa Washington, *Our Mothers*; Susanna Awason, "Anlu and Takubeng"; Susan Diduk, "The Civility of Incivility"; and Paul Nkwi, "Traditional Female Militancy."

13. The celebration of public undressing has the potential to be empowering, and yet it can also misrepresent the experiences of the embodied subjects. (See "Yorubas Don't Do Gender: A Critical Review of Oyeronké Oyewumi's *The Invention of Women*: Making an African Sense of Western Gender Discourses" [2003]). Bibi Bakare-Yusuf critiques similar authenticity-construction scholarship in Oyeronké Oyewumi's *The Invention of Women* (1997).

14. In "African Modes of Self-Writing," Achille Mbembe describes such intellectual practices as Afro radicalism and nativism or the metaphysics of difference (2002).

15. "Ghana to expel female protesters" *BBC News Africa*. 18 March 2008. http://news.bbc.co.uk/2/hi/africa/7302243.stm. Accessed 15 October 2015.

16. "L'heure est très grave; un véritable combat spirituel se déroule. Ce combat spirituel est mené exclusivement par des femmes averties et bien triées. Ce n'est donc pas une affaire d'hommes qui, d'ailleurs, doivent se tenir loin. Nous sommes dans le domaine spirituel et ici, (selon la tradition africaine, surtout ivoirienne) la force et la puissance appartiennent à la femme'" (K.A).

17. According to Gayatri Spivak, "literature remains singular and unverifiable" despite the legalistic work of literary criticism. *A Critique of Postcolonial Reason*, 175.

18. In *African Intimacies* (2007), Neville Hoad argues for the value of fiction and literary criticism in entering the painful terrains of the questions of sexuality and race in that "the stakes become lower. And mistakes need not be fatal" (22).

BIBLIOGRAPHY

Abu-Lughod, Lila. 1990. The Romance of Resistance: Tracing Transformations of Power through Bedouin Women. *American Ethnologist* 17(1): 41–55.

Adichie, Chimamanda. 2009. The Danger of a Single Story. *TED Ideas worth spreading.* Last modified June 2009. https://www.ted.com/talks/chimamanda_adichie_the_danger_of_a_single_story?language=en

Agamben, Giorgio. 1998. *Homo Sacer: The Sovereign Power and Bare Life.* Trans. Heller-Roazen. Stanford, CA: Stanford University Press.

Altorki, Soraya, and Camillia Fawzi El-Solh, eds. 1988. *Arab Women in the Field: Studying Your Own Society.* Syracuse, NY: Syracuse University Press.

Anderson, Amanda. 2000. The Temptations of Aggrandized Agency: Feminist Histories and the Horizon of Modernity. *Victorian Studies* 43(1): 43–65.

Apter, Emily. 2006. *The Translation Zone: A New Comparative Literature.* Princeton, NJ: Princeton University Press.

Assie-Lumumba, Ndri. 1996. *Les Africaines dans la politique: Femmes Baoulé de Côte d'Ivoire.* Paris: L'Harmattan.

Awasom, Susanna Yene. 2003. Anlu and Takubeng: The Adaptation of Traditional Female Political Institutions to the Exigencies of Modern Politics in Cameroon. In *Indigenous Political Structures and Governance in Africa*, ed. Olufemi Vaughan, 353–363. Lagos: Sefer Press.

Bastian, Misty. 2005. The Naked and the Nude: Historically Multiple Meanings of Oto (Undress) in Southeastern Nigeria. In *Dirt, Undress, and Difference: Critical Perspectives on the Body's Surface*, ed. Adeline Masquelier, 34–60. Bloomington, IN: Indiana University Press.

BBC News. 2008. Ghana to Expel Female Protesters. *BBC News, Africa.* Last modified March 18. http://news.bbc.co.uk/2/hi/africa/7302243.stm

Brett-Smith, Sarah C. 1994. *The Making of Bamana Sculpture Creativity and Gender.* Cambridge: Cambridge University Press.

Bulmer, Martin. 1982. When Is Disguise Justified? Alternatives to Covert Participant Observation. *Qualitative Sociology* 5(4): 251–264.

Cole, Teju. 2012. The White-Savior Industrial Complex. The Atlantic.com. Last modified March 12. http://www.theatlantic.com/international/archive/2012/03/the-white-savior-industrial-complex/254843/

Conrad, David C. 1999a. Mooning Armies and Mothering Heroes: Female Power in the Manden Epic Tradition. In *In Search of Sunjata: The Mande Oral Epic as History, Literature and Performance*, ed. Ralph A. Austen, 189–230. Bloomington, IN: Indiana University Press.

——— 1999b. *Epic Ancestors of the Sunjata Era: Oral Tradition from the Maninka of Guinea.* Madison, WI: University of Wisconsin.

Conrad, David C., and Djanka Tassey Conde. 2004. *Sunjata: A West African Epic of the Mande Peoples.* Indianapolis, IN: Hackett Pub Co.

Chow, Rey. 2011. A Discipline of Tolerance. In *A Companion to Comparative Literature*, ed. Ali Behdad and Dominic Thomas, 13–27. Hoboken, NJ: Wiley-Blackwell.

Damrosch, David. 2003. *What is World Literature?* Princeton, NJ: Princeton University Press.

Diabaté, Henriette. 1975. *La marche des femmes sur Grand-Bassam.* Abidjan: Nouvelles Editions Africaines.

Dibba, Lamine. 2001. In Election Ritual Saga Naked Women Protest in Brikama. *The Independent* (Banjul). Last modified September 28. http://allafrica.com/stories/200109280014.html

Diduk, Susan. 2004. The Civility of Incivility: Grassroots Political Activism, Female Farmers, and the Cameroon State. *African Studies Review* 47(2): 27–54.

Douglas, Mary. 1984. *Purity and Danger: An Analysis of the Concepts of Pollution and Taboo* (1966). London: Ark.

Echewa, Obinkaram T. 1993. *I Saw the Sky Catch Fire* (1992). New York: Plume.

Emecheta, Buchi. 1979. *The Joys of Motherhood*. New York: G. Braziller.

Essuman-Johnson, Abeeku. 2011. When Refugees Don't Go Home: The Situation of Liberian Refugees in Ghana. *Journal of Immigrant & Refugee Studies* 9: 105–126.

Estes, Clarissa Pinkola. 1996. *Women Who Run With the Wolves: Myths and Stories of the Wild Woman Archetype* (1992). New York: Ballantine Books.

Evans-Pritchard, E.E. 1965. *Theories of Primitive Religion*. Oxford: Clarendon Press.

Freire, Paulo. 1970. *Pedagogy of the Oppressed*. New York: Herder & Herder.

Grillo, Laura. 2013. Catachresis in Côte d'Ivoire: Female Genital Power in Religious Ritual and Political Resistance. *Religion and Gender* 3(2): 188–206. doi http://doi.org/10.18352/rg.8329.

Hoad, Neville. 2007. *African Intimacies: Race, Homosexuality, and Globalization*. Minneapolis, MN: The University of Minnesota Press.

———. 2011, March 28. *Genital Power: Female Sexuality in West African Literature and Film*. Final Oral Examination (Naminata Diabate). Austin, Texas.

Hoffman, Barbara E. 2002. Gender Ideology and Practice in Mande Societies and in Mande Studies. *Mande Studies* 4: 1–20.

Ifeka-Moller, Catherine. 1975. Female Militancy and Colonial Revolt: The Women's War of 1929, Eastern Nigeria. In *Perceiving Women*, ed. Shirley Ardener, 127–157. London: Malaby Press.

K.A. 2011. Yamoussoukro/Usurpation de pouvoir: La révolte des femmes de la cité et des villages. *Le Mandat* (Cote d'Ivoire). Last modified 17 February 2011. http://news.abidjan.net/h/391509.html

Koné, Kassim. 2004. When Male Becomes Female and Female Becomes Male in Mande. *Wagadu* 1: 1–10.

Kourouma, Ahmadou. 1970. *Les soleils des indépendances* (*The Suns of Independences*) (1968). Paris: Éditions du Seuil.

Mama, Amina. 2007. Is It Ethical to Study Africa? Preliminary Thoughts on Scholarship and Freedom. *African Studies Review* 50(1): 1–26.

———. 2013, November 7. *Is It Ethical to Study Africa?* Lecture organized by The Minority, Indigenous, and Third World Studies Research Group (MITWS-RG). Cornell University, Ithaca, New York.

Mbembe, Achille. 2003. Necropolitics. Trans. Libby Meintjes. *Public Culture* 15(1): 25–40.

Mbembe, J.-A., and Steven Rendall. 2002. African Modes of Self-writing. *Public Culture* 14(1): 239–273.

Melas, Natalie. 2007. *All the Difference in the World: Postcoloniality and the Ends of Comparison*. Stanford, CA: Stanford University Press.

Moore, Lisa. 2011, March 28. *Genital Power: Female Sexuality in West African Literature and Film*. Final Oral Examination (Naminata Diabate). Austin, Texas.

Morrison, Toni. 1992. *Playing in the Dark: Whiteness and the Literary Imagination*. Cambridge: Harvard University Press.

Nkwi, Paul Nchoji. 1985. Traditional Female Militancy in a Modern Context. In *Femmes du Cameroun: Meres Pacifiques Femmes Rebelles*, ed. Jean-Claude Barbier, 181–193. Paris: Orstom-Karthala.

Niane, Djibril Tamsir. 1960. *Soundjata, ou, L'épopée mandingue*. Paris: Présence Africaine.

Novo, Salvador. 1994. *The War of the Fatties and Other Stories from Aztec History (La Guerra de las Gordas)*. Trans. Michael Alderson. Austin: The University of Texas Press.

Ọlajubu, Chief Oludare. 1972. References to Sex in Yoruba Oral Literature. *The Journal of American Folklore* 85: 152–166.

Omata, Naohiko. 2012. Repatriation and Integration of Liberian Refugees from Ghana: The Importance of Personal Networks in the Country of Origin. *Journal of Refugee Studies* 10: 1–18.

Prince, Raymond. 1961. The Yoruba Image of the Witch. *Journal of Mental Science* 107: 795–805.

Povinelli, Elizabeth. 2011. *Economies of Abandonment: Social Longing and Endurance in Late Liberalism*. Durham: Duke University Press.

Puri, Shalini. 2013. Finding the Field: Notes on Caribbean Cultural Criticism, Area Studies, and the Forms of Engagement. *Small Axe* 41: 58–73.

Segall, Kimberly Wedeven. 2002. Postcolonial Performatives of Victimization. *Public Culture* 14(3): 617–619.

Spivak, Gayatri Chakravorty. 2003. *Death of a Discipline*. New York: Columbia University Press.

Stevens, Phillips, Jr. 2006. Women's Aggressive Use of Genital Power in Africa. *Transcultural Psychiatry* 43(3): 592–599.

Summer, Doris. 1991. Rigoberta's Secrets. *Latin American Perspectives* 18: 32–50.

Van Allen, Judith. 1975. Aba Riots or the Igbo Women's War? Ideology, Stratification, and the Invisibility of Women. *Ufahamu: A Journal of African Studies* 6(1): 11–39.

Washington, Teresa. 2004. *Our Mothers, Our Powers, Our Texts: Manifestations of Aje in Africana Literature*. Bloomington, IN: Indiana University Press.

Weber, Max. 1949. 'Objectivity' in Social Science and Social Policy. *The Methodology of the Social Sciences* 78: 50–51.

The Witches of Gambaga. 2010. Directed by Yaba Badoe. DVD, 55mn. Fadoa Films.

Zahan, Dominique. 1960. Ataraxie et silence chez les Bambara. *Zaire* 14: 491–454.

CHAPTER 4

Aesthetics in the Making of History: The Tebhaga Women's Movement in Bengal

Kavita Panjabi

During the Bengal famine of 1943, there was an unprecedented explosion of women's activism. The membership of the Women's Self-Defence League, or the Mahila Atma Raksha Samiti (MARS), shot up from about 500 members in 1942 to 43,500 in 1943. This additional number of 43,000 included young college-going women, largely first-generation literates, rural and urban home-makers, as well as peasant women themselves, most of whom had never been part of any movement ever before. The MARS had been established in 1942 to co-ordinate the self-defence activities of several women's groups that had sprung up right across Bengal in response to the threats of sexual attacks by the British and US soldiers flooding the cities during World War II and the Japanese soldiers in the far-eastern parts of the state. Within a year of its initiation, which was marked by the onset of the "man-made" Bengal famine, the MARS expanded unpredictably, in both size and nature of work.[1] What was it about the famine that had caused such a massive upsurge in women's political participation in Bengal?

I have shown elsewhere how the solidarities of care that urban women forged during the famine were transformed into a politics of care with thousands of women confronting the government, demanding redress.[2] The reason that I cite my earlier work on the famine and MARS here at some length is because it serves as a concrete launching pad for an elaboration of the ways in which emotional affect actually mobilizes history. The kind of engagement with history that the women cited involved the move from a factual "knowing" of events to a concretized "understanding" of them, that is, from the generally epistemological to the more specifically hermeneutic. Explaining the dynamics of such "understanding," Gertrud Koch asserts that "whatever knowledge we

K. Panjabi (✉)
Department of Comparative Literature, Jadavpur University, Kolkata, India

© The Author(s) 2016
S. Puri, D.A. Castillo (eds.), *Theorizing Fieldwork in the Humanities*,
DOI 10.1057/978-1-349-92834-7_4

have in terms of facts that we believe to be true remains 'dead' as long as we fail to make use of it to interpret, communicate and mediate those facts. The real 'life' of knowledge, which goes beyond mere factual information, in this sense then is that which enables us to understand or explain meaning, intentions, personal acts, emotions and reasons" (395).

In the context of the urban MARS women, I had realized that the knowledge of the famine too had come to them as a "dead" fact, till such a time that personal acts of witnessing the suffering of the peasant women and children, and the emotional impact it had made on them, had brought it to "life." The urban women were deeply disturbed by its impact; and their affective response to it, of distress and outrage, propelled them into political activism and dreams of a just future. The scenario, as I have described it earlier, was thus:

> In 1943 the streets and by lanes of Kolkata resounded with the haunting cry of "Ektu *phayn* de ma" ("Mother give me some rice water"), as thousands of starving peasants streamed in from the villages, all in search of food. Urban women did not even have to step out of their homes to witness this hunger, for often emaciated peasant women would turn up at the kitchen window, desperate to save a dying child. This was the condition in the other towns and cities of Bengal too ... 3 million people had died due to starvation and the epidemics that followed the famine; ... 4.8 million of the rural poor had turned destitute; 6 million were affected in all; families had sold their children, husbands their wives, and women and girls had taken to prostitution to raise money for food.[3]

Urban women talked of the impact of seeing skeletal corpses literally littering the roads and lanes of Kolkata and women carrying bodies of dead children, as well as of having peasant women and children die before their very eyes. The witnessing of such suffering led to a grim determination to combat it, and urban activists of the time whom I interviewed talked about how it was not mere knowledge of the devastation of the famine, but the deep affective impact of it that finally drove thousands of them to join the *langarkhanas*—soup kitchens—set up by the Communist Party (in the absence of adequate response from the British government) and run largely by the MARS to aid in the relief work. Renu Chakravartty, an Oxford-educated woman who became one of the most prominent activists in Bengal and a leader of the MARS, narrated her experience thus: "Their heart rending cry 'Give us the rice water you throw away' still rings in the ears of those who witnessed the nightmare of those days. Women were just skin and bone and their children gasping for their last breath."[4]

Likewise, Ila Mitra, an urban middle-class woman from Calcutta, who went on to become one of the legendary leaders of the Tebhaga peasant women's movement, explained her reasons for joining the MARS, emphasizing that:

> The source of my inspiration was the famine. I learnt to understand that it was a man made famine and I could see helpless people die in thousands. *Actually I did not have any plans to join politics.* I used to be busy with my music, drama,

sports etc. But then I saw the famine, and heard their cry for *phayn*. Once I gave a woman *phayn* and she died the instant she had it. I saw it. Actually after one has starved for many days, even a little food is dangerous. I experienced this when I was in jail myself. There we went on a number of hunger-strikes, and when we had to break one, we never did so with solid food. We used to take liquid for seven days and then gradually move to solid food. But at that time I knew nothing. *I saw her die with my own eyes.* …Gradually I had come to know that this was all created by the English people. They had large amounts of rice but they were sending it to soldiers and creating the famine. Then I saw that the women of the Mahila Atmaraksha Samiti were serving these poverty stricken people in Bidhan Sarani and other places. *I joined them spontaneously.* (Emphases mine)

Further, the deep sorrow and horror of witnessing such suffering also led to a questioning of the reasons for it. Women, young and old, went on from the experience of the *langarkhanas* to join study groups—often clandestine—set up by the Communist Party (CP) in schools, colleges and local clubs, and thus began to develop a systematic understanding of political economy, class relations and imperialism. The *langarkhanas* thus became the sites for the affective and subjective transformation of urban women; they became launching pads for the awakening of political consciousness; and thousands of women who had initially come to lend a hand in relief work began to join the MARS and the CP. The women's movement that ensued within MARS during the famine years constituted a powerful and moving pre-history of the Tebhaga women's movement of the late 1940s and 1950s, and I have elaborated upon it at much greater length in my oral history of the latter—what I wish to share here is the power of the exciting and vital relations between aesthetics and lived history that gradually dawned upon me as I continued, across 15 years, to delve into and put together an oral history of the Tebhaga women.[5]

Moved by what they saw, women like Ila Mitra,[6] who had "no plans to join politics," joined the famine relief work "spontaneously." Yet, clearly, this was not merely a spontaneous affective response, because it translated into actions that went beyond the immediate famine relief work and continued for decades; the memory of the famine also led large numbers of women to join the Tebhaga movement in 1946, and fed into other post-Tebhaga movements too, shaping decades of history. After the immediate pity and fear of the devastation had been purged, something had become clear to these women, something that had had endured and motivated them into continued action across entire lifetimes, as their recollections even 50 years later demonstrated; it was not only their consequent intellectual understanding of the political economy of imperialism and feudalism, and it was something more lasting than affective impact.

A subjective and poetic process of affective response to the Bengal famine lay at the core of consequent historical transformations, and I claim it to be a "poetic truth" of history, for, notwithstanding all the post-structuralist critiques of "Truth," that which transforms history cannot but be a part of the "truth" of that history. Such "truth" originates in individual subjectivity, but transcends it to shape historical change in entire populations.

Such poetic truth of history is premised on subjectivity in the sense of the affective, aesthetic response to events; yet the mobilizing force of history to which it gives us access does not inhabit the shaky ground of individualized subjectivity. For when such poetic truth animates an individual and mobilizes her into historical action, it is an event of an order that has the capacity to animate entire populations; and the factity of such poetic truth resides in the impact of history on the future, in the concrete mobilization of acts, be they of leadership, resistance or survival.[7]

Aesthetics is pervasively central to everyday living, so why is it limited to the arts? Historical events, political upheavals and human actions impact individuals and societies with affective force, we respond with joy, exhilaration, determination, anxiety or fear. Further, such impact is not limited merely to our affective responses; it inspires resistance or transformative action, motivates competition or revenge, results in mass dislocations, or causes withdrawal or resigned submission. In December 2013, the sorrow and fury against the rape and brutalization of a young woman on a bus in Delhi sparked off nationwide protests across India and led to major reformulations of law and policy; during the 1947 partition of India, actual widespread communal violence was the reason for the massive dislocations in the western part of the subcontinent, but on the eastern side it was largely the disproportionate *fear* of such violence that led to the exodus of 3.5 million Hindus from East Pakistan to India; and during the freedom struggle that led to the independence of India and Pakistan in 1947, oral legends of the courageous battle of the Queen of Jhansi against the British in the First War of Independence in 1857 found their way into one of the most popular nationalist poems that inspired resistance, against colonialism, that was born out of a joyous pride in thousands of Indians.

As such, aesthetic response serves as a springboard and catalyst for subsequent actions and, hence, actually shapes future history too. These dimensions and dynamics of lived experience, such as may be revealed through analyses of the aesthetic impact of historical events, are not normally accessed by mainstream historiography; for they can be gleaned only from attentive listening and sensitive questioning in lived interactions "on the field" with the subjects of the history, and through close textual analyses of subjective accounts, drawing upon the approaches of literary as well as sometimes performance studies to bring to the surface the powerful but subterranean currents of aesthetic processes that catalyze future histories.

It is curious indeed that our focus on aesthetics sidesteps the affective power at work in everyday life and remains restricted to "the arts." Aesthetics has been extended from the domains of literature, music, performance and the visual arts to the material, audiovisual and cinematic arts, and even gourmet cooking and embroidery, but has then been kept confined to them, while daily living and labor, production and consumption, commerce, governance, political movements and, of course, war are relegated to the social sciences. The separation of "art" and living is so entrenched that it is almost as if there were nothing artistic, beautiful or affective about our everyday actions or lived relationships and negotiations. The compartmentalization of scholarship into the humanities and the social sciences is certainly one of the basic factors that has kept aesthetics in the realm of the humanities, yet it has to be acknowledged that this compartmentalization has not been as effective the other way around—for we certainly have trained the lenses of history, politics and economics on the arts and humanities. So the question as to why we have refrained from taking the lens of aesthetics to history and other social science practices still remains a confounding one, and perhaps the answer to this lies in a much-elided dimension of the notion of aesthetics that I will address in a later section.

In order to comprehend why we have arrived at such a limiting compartmentalization of our conceptual approaches to knowledge, and to begin to redress the losses incurred in our comprehension of historical transformations, one would need to step across not just disciplinary boundaries but also the borders we have drawn between our notions of "art" and "life." I began to do this inadvertently, in my search for an understanding of the Tebhaga women's movement that had taken place amongst the peasants of undivided Bengal in the late forties and early fifties of the twentieth century, and of which we had no written history.

The fact that I could actually arrive at this understanding of the ways in which such borders between "art" and "life" impoverish our understanding of history, and also move on to develop some understanding of the dynamics of history from the vantage point of a researcher in the humanities, was because of the availability of grants for fieldwork in oral history. The Sephis Grants Programme of The Netherlands was one such rare funding agency that had begun to support South-South research and was open to interdisciplinary research across the humanities and social sciences too, and it was this programme that supported my research. There is of course a significant body of fieldwork-based research done by scholars in the humanities in India, largely in the areas of linguistic surveys and analyses, oral epic traditions, folklore and performance, and much of it is in Indian languages. Much of it has been done without any funding, largely in the areas inhabited by the researchers, as a sheer labor of love. There is also some funding available for teachers for interdisciplinary research in the form of major and minor research grants, from the University Grants Commission, the funding body for public universities in India. So it is not impossible to find proposals, sent in by teachers of literature departments such as English, titled *A Feminist Ethnography of Banjara [Gypsy] Women* on the UGC shortlist[8] or another titled *Documentation and Deciphering of the Traditional Medicinal Folklore of Tribes in Southern Western Ghats* on its final list.[9] By and large, however, most of the projects sent in by teachers of literature relate to literary texts, or to enhancement of language and communication skills. The UGC, however, has also set up a Special Assistance Programme (SAP) for departments of repute in every field in the humanities and social sciences, and interdisciplinary research is encouraged in these. So if I were to start work of this kind today, I could actually get funding for it in the Centre for Advanced Study under the UGC's SAP in my own department (albeit not for international research as yet).[10] Funding is now possible, albeit in limited realms, for interdisciplinary fieldwork such as this in India. It is the conceptual borders dividing disciplines that have yet to be dismantled.

ORAL HISTORY AND SUBJECTIVITY

Oral history comes to us structured in gestural and verbally articulated language as well as in narratives. Straddling both academic faculties, the humanities and the social sciences, oral history is also unique in its critical focus on subjectivity, for it is the analyses of subjectivities—that structure and inform oral narratives—that yield the insights to which the purportedly "objective" historiography, sourced from archival records has no access. It is also no wonder that it is from the late 1960s, when a critical focus on subjectivity began to inflect academic research in the social sciences[11] that most of the groundbreaking oral histories, and holocaust histories based on survivor narratives, began to make their mark.[12] The attention to subjectivity transformed and expanded the realm and signification of historiography, bringing the focus back on to the dynamics of lived realities. This pivotal focusing of oral history on subjectivity in a large body of works, including those just cited, is unique because it combines close textual literary and aesthetic analyses of narrative representation and enactment with the insights of memory studies, historiography, and critical theory harnessed into analyses of the lived history narrated. As the dynamics of human subjectivity became a focal point of oral history, issues of representation also began to occupy center stage in the readings of oral narratives.

The term "subjectivity," as I have used it in my own research, relates to a historically and socially constituted subject, and specifically to the embodied female subject of history, hence also one constituted materially.[13] Further, this subject of history is not just subject to, and thus constituted by the forces of history, but also one capable of agency. In addition, I realized that the activists whose narratives I documented were subjects constituted not just by "subjectification" to the current forces of inequity and oppression, or a party ideology, but also by actual "practices of liberation."[14] The subject of history is subject to the forces of history, but is also simultaneously an active subject that mobilizes future history. It thus stands as a thinking, knowing, affective subject, that in turn shapes history. Hence, subjectivity also connotes the area of *symbolic* activity that "includes cognitive, cultural and psychological aspects ... [and] *forms of awareness such as the sense of identity and consciousness of oneself...*" [italics mine].[15] In this, subjectivity serves as a prism of history via the *dynamics of interiority* catalyzed by the impact of historical events. For, as Portelli asserts, "Subjectivity is as much the business of history as are the more visible 'facts.' What informants believe is indeed a historical fact (that is, the fact that they believe it), as much as what really happened."[16]

Central to oral history are memories of lived history, and memories, like everyday life, accrue complexity infused with subjectivity, aesthetics and affect. Memory is a selective process contingent upon the subjectivity of both the time and the force of the event memorized and the time and conditions of recall. In this, it links the subjectivity of the past which recorded certain memories selectively for posterity and the subjectivity of the present which chooses only certain selections of these memories for reclaiming. Why did certain memories stay with us and not others? Why do they speak to us now? These are telling questions that simmer beneath the surface of history.

Memory also safeguards the aesthetic dimensions of life and their mobilizing power—of that which is unspeakable, of love that transforms, and of affective transformations. Celebrated since time immemorial in poetry, these have, curiously, found little place in what we call history today. Thus, there are bound to be contrasts, even tensions, between readings of memory and readings of history.

Far from sharing history's claims of objectivity, memory is in fact extremely slippery—for it is mediated through affect; it is shaped by desire or fear, by joy or apprehension or even a sense of loss. The useful question then is not about the accuracy of memory, but actually about how its mediations articulate a relationship to the past in the present. Why is memory catalyzed in certain situations and not in others? Why is it suppressed, or even non-existent in some cases? These are critical questions: for fragmented, discontinuous memories, or an absence of memory may well be telling of the violence and silences of lived histories that fall out of the pages of historiography.

Analyses of narrativizations of memory then enable us to comprehend the impact of historical events on subjectivity; and the *aesthetic response* of individuals and communities subject to the affective impact of historical events is what mobilizes history—this is where aesthetics plays a pivotal role in the shaping of history. The lens of subjectivity is invaluable in that it provides access to both epistemological and political standpoints, and this became evident specially in the accounts of women activists; this is because their narrative subjectivities were layered both with the affective impact of historical events as they unfolded for them in their politicized realities and with the ways in which politics was in turn textured by their standpoints and agency. Predicated thus, subjectivity then "embraces not only the *epistemological* dimension but also that concerned with the nature and significance of the *political*" (emphases mine).[17] Subjectivity hence offers itself as a link between the *aesthetic workings of interiority* and the *external workings of politics*; it is on such grounds of subjectivity that both the humanities and the social sciences become indispensable—even as they both stand to benefit from it.

In the logic of the above-mentioned arguments that are built upon my own experience of "fieldwork" across years, but also substantiated by pioneering scholars in oral history such as Passerini and Portelli, there is one missing link. This link has to do with the connection between affective response and knowledge and between aesthetic dynamics and epistemological standpoints.

For while the urban women's actions were of course informed by a powerful rational response to the oppression of the times, further buttressed by their theoretical training, the affective impact of the suffering was the mobilizing factor. How then does affective impact, that has to do with the emotions, translate into the epistemological standpoint from which history is mobilized? The answer to this critical question eluded me for more than a decade, but it was finally with close, sustained reflection upon the verbal—and facial—articulations of the *peasant* women I had interviewed, and my own engagement with aesthetics in literary studies that the connections between affective impact and an epistemological standpoint powerful enough to mobilize thousands of women into political activism across decades began to dawn upon me.

There was a persistent refrain that had echoed across my conversations with most of the peasant women. When I asked them what the experience of being part of the Tebhaga movement was like for them, their eyes would light up, a joyous smile would appear on their faces, and while one would describe it as an experience of *ananda* (profound joy) and another as *mazaa* (fun or pleasure to the point of contentment), yet another would say it brought her *shanti* (peace). It was too persistent a refrain to be ignored—for refrain it was, of a sense of deep enjoyment and rich satisfaction, echoing across this variety of words they used to describe what it was about that lived history that had stayed with them. What also struck me was that this was not of the order of a spontaneous emotional response, for it was more than 50 years since they had participated in the movement, this seemed to be more of the order of an *aesthetic* quality, replete with spirit, yet possessing a quiet, honed confidence.

It was thus that I began to train the lens of aesthetics onto subjectivity—and history. This process was reinforced by the acknowledgement, by oral historians to whom I am deeply indebted for my understanding of the role of subjectivity in the making of history, of the connections between aesthetics and knowledge. Portelli does observe that "aesthetics is a form of knowledge,"[18] and Passerini elaborates that subjectivity connotes the area of *symbolic* activity that "includes cognitive … aspects."[19] I realized that the emergence of the contemporary engagement with subjectivity, which has also become a bedrock of oral history scholarship, has made it imperative for us to reassess the role of aesthetics—and of the relationship between affect, cognition and agency—in the making of history. The argument I wish to make here then is about the critical role of aesthetics in the workings of subjectivity—and hence in the transformation of history.

AESTHETICS, SENSUOUS COGNITION, AND THE CONSTITUTION OF SUBJECTIVITY

This question of aesthetics in the workings of subjectivity brings us to the other, more pervasive reason for the absence of aesthetic study in the "social science" fields—of lived realities, political movements and oral history. The contemporary focus of aesthetics on *perfection* of sensitive cognition and beauty elides the much wider scope of aesthetics that relates to the *process* of cognition through affect. As Marcuse has observed, "The basic experience in the aesthetic dimension is of sensuousness, not of sensuality (appetitive), but of sensuousness (sensitive cognition), the nature of which is 'receptivity', of cognition through being *affected* by given objects."[20] More recently, Simon Gikandi, in his insightful study of the problematic relationship between slavery and eighteenth-century aesthetic culture, has described sensuousness as a "singular investment in the senses as a mode of understanding human experience."[21] Bowie too relocates aesthetics within the larger field of processes of sensuous perception and its role in the constitution of subjectivity: "From being a part of philosophy concerned with the senses, and not necessarily with beauty—the word derives from the Greek 'aisthánesthai,' 'perceive sensuously'—the new subject of 'aesthetics' now focuses on the significance of natural beauty and of art.... The crucial new departure lies in the way aesthetics is connected to the emergence of subjectivity as the central issue in modern philosophy, and this is where the relevance of this topic to contemporary concerns becomes apparent."[22] In the humanities today, it is this much narrowed concern of aesthetics with beauty and perfection of sensitive cognition in what is perceived as art (which narratives of political movements are not), that has resulted in the virtual elision of the affective constitution of subjectivity in lived realities. I hope to show how vital it is to restore the larger concerns of aesthetics, and its role in the constitution of subjectivity, not just to the "humanities" but also to the "social sciences"—if we must continue to insist on such divisive categorizations.

Aesthetics was not always limited to its contemporary concern with the appreciation and criticism of beauty, or with the study of artistic perfection. The eighteenth century witnessed the recognition of a valuable mode of accessing knowledge in human life that was formulated as a critical element of aesthetics, and this was the process of "sensuous cognition." The very term *aesthetics* was coined in 1735 by Alexander Gottlieb Baumgarten (from the Greek *aisthanesthai*, "to perceive") in his dissertation *Meditationes philosophicae*[23]; and in the first of his major two-volume work *Aesthetica* (1750, 1758), he framed his aesthetics as a theory of cognition, that even as it constituted the "art of beautiful cognition" was simultaneously also the "art of the analog of reason" and thus also a "science of sensuous cognition": "Aesthetics (theory of the liberal arts, lower doctrine of cognition, the art of beautiful cognition, the art of the analog of reason), is the science of sensuous cognition."[24]

This sensuous cognition was the "missing link," between affective response and knowledge, that I refer to above. Baumgarten delineated the term to mean "a science of how things are to be known by means of the senses."[25] In his analysis, "18th Century German Aesthetics," Paul Gruyer highlights that Baumgarten also introduced "an emphasis on the emotional impact of art" even as he defined aesthetics conceptually as an "analogue of reason," and in doing so, "open[ed] the way for much more radical reconceptions of aesthetic experience in Germany."[26] He also draws attention to Baumgarten's delineation of aesthetics as an episteme, and retraces its philosophical journey thus:

> Baumgarten's *Meditations on Poetry* conclude with his famous introduction of the term "aesthetics": "The Greek philosophers and the Church fathers have always carefully distinguished between the aistheta and the noeta," that is, between objects of sense and objects of thought, and while the latter, that is, "what can be cognized through the higher faculty" of mind, are "the object of logic, the aistheta are the subject of the episteme aisthetike or AESTHETICS," the science of perception. (*Meditations*, §CXVI, p. 86)

As Moore observes, Baumgarten introduced aesthetics "as an independent sphere of philosophical inquiry, cognate with, but separate from, the truths of logic and morality" (1).

The same century that witnessed the emergence of this critical awareness of the connection between aesthetics and epistemology, however, also created the ground for the eclipse of all but rational modes of cognition, and aesthetics lost currency as a mode of cognition. Herder was one of the few to recognize the dangers of such an eclipse of affect:

> Though many *Aufklärer* were prepared to accept the dissociation of the intellect and emotions as the price of progress, Herder most certainly was not. He strove to bridge the growing gap between the affective and rational sides of our nature, keep in check the enlightened despotism of Reason, and unleash the full potential of the human spirit. Herder was one of the few contemporaries who seemed to grasp the revolutionary implications of Baumgarten's enterprise. For aesthetics, according to Baumgarten's understanding, is not just a philosophy of art but also—indeed, primarily—the "science of sensuous cognition."[27]

Thus a critical casualty on the eighteenth-century checklist of damage done by the deification of reason was the recognition of sensuous modes of cognition, and in this elision was obscured a critical mode of non-conceptual forms of human access to knowledge.[28] If Herder was critical of the dissociation of intellect and emotions, of the rational and affective dimensions of life, Marcuse was even more trenchant in his appraisal—terming this to be a "subjugation" of sensuous faculties by reason and "their repressive utilization" in the utilitarian project of "progress":

> To Kant the aesthetic dimension is the medium in which the senses and the intellect meet.... [T]his mediation is necessitated by the pervasive conflict between the lower and the higher faculties of man generated by the progress of civilization—progress achieved through the subjugation of the sensuous faculties to reason, and through their repressive utilization for social needs.[29]

What is absolutely fascinating is that both Greek tragedy and Sanskrit aesthetic theory focus on the opposite—they elaborate the ways in which processes of the sensuous faculties, affect and emotion respectively, lead not to their "repressive utilization" but to "intellectual clarification" and "heightened states of cognition."

Since the late twentieth century, catharsis has also been interpreted as "intellectual clarification."[30] *The Princeton Encyclopedia of Poetry and Poetics*[31] further identifies two significant variations on "intellectual clarification" that have been suggested: "emotional (as well as intellectual) clarification (Nussbaum) and ethical clarification (Wagner)." In fact, in consideration of these strands, it categorically emphasizes the emergence of a "new intellectual vision" from the new emotional perspective that arises from the witnessing of tragedy:

> Since the new blending that is attained in the cathartic process is psychic, it must involve a new emotional perspective and even, arising from that, a new intellectual vision. A wisdom is distilled from tragic suffering, and the person is *pathei mathos* (taught by suffering) as the chorus in Agamemnon sings. The tragic suffering, and the ensuing intellectual calm have produced in the spectator a new insight into what the plot of the drama, its action—which is to say, its meaning in motion—most essentially represents.[32]

Closely relevant to the urban women's response to the suffering during the famine is Nussbaum's explication of catharsis as "clarification,"[33] which is not necessarily intellectual, but can also take place independently through emotional responses; furthermore, this emotional response itself is capable of facilitating an understanding of our values:

> I have argued that, in his [Aristotle's] view, tragedy contributes to human self-understanding precisely through its exploration of the pitiable and the fearful. The way it carries out this exploratory task is by moving us to respond with these very emotions. For these emotional responses are themselves pieces of recognition or acknowledgment of the worldly conditions upon our aspirations to goodness. Golden's view of clarification is that it is a purely intellectual matter.... This interpretation ... is unnecessarily Platonic. Katharsis does not mean 'intellectual clarification'. It means 'clarification'—and it happens to be Plato's view that all clarification is an intellectual matter. We can ascribe to Aristotle a more generous view of the ways in which we come to know ourselves. First of all, *clarification, for him, can certainly take place through emotional responses*, as the definition states. Just as, inside the *Antigone*, Creon's learning came by way of the grief he felt for his son's death, so, as we watch a tragic character, it is frequently *not thought but the emotional response itself that leads us to understand what our values are.* Emotions can sometimes mislead and distort judgment; Aristotle is aware of this. But they can also, as was true in Creon's case, give us access to a truer and deeper level of ourselves, to values and commitments that have been concealed beneath defensive ambition or rationalization.[34]

The connection that Nussbaum, interpreting Aristotle, draws between emotional response and our understanding of value is extremely critical for oral history—for it provides access to modes of historical mobilization that take place beneath the surface of dominant rationalism, and sometimes even against the direction of its flow.[35]

This sense of clarification, distilled from an emotional experience, or *bhava*, of insight into the core signification, or *rasa*, of a representation, forms the backbone of Sanskrit aesthetic theory too. However, the range of affects that comes under the purview of Bharata's *Natyashastra* is not limited to pity or fear; it is far more encompassing of human experience and includes *rati* (love), *utsaha* (heroism), *krodha* (anger), *jugupsa* (disgust), *hasya* (laughter), *vismaya* (wonder), *soka* (sorrow) and *bhaya* (fear). The corresponding *rasas* are *sringara* (erotic), *virya* (heroic), *raudra* (furious), *bibhitsa* (disgusting), *hasya* (comic), *adbhuta* (marvellous), *karuna* (sadness/compassion) and *bhayanaka* (terrible).[36] Referring to both Sanskrit aesthetic theory and bhakti theology, William M. Reddy elaborates:

> Both ... insist on the difference between everyday particular emotions, called *bhava*, and the refined, generalised moods created by poetry, drama or ritual, called *rasa*, literally nectar or extract.... This distinction parallels the Greek distinction between passion and reason. *Rasa* generalises in the same way that reason does .... just as reason is the tool by which Westerners suppose that they abstract generalized types and conditions from specific circumstances. The passion that unites Krishna and Radha is a form of *rasa*. It is therefore a mistake to call it 'passion', insofar as the Western concept of passion has to do with the appetites, affects or obsessions of specific persons locked into this-worldly action settings, that is, to what in Sanskrit are called *bhava*. *Rasa* is no delusion; it is a *heightened form of cognition*, a means of apprehending a higher reality.[37] (emphasis mine)

The transition from *bhava* to *rasa* then is one from individualized emotional affect and passion driven by personal desire, to a refined, abstracted mood, or rather disposition,[38] that is not only a heightened form of cognition but also a means of apprehending a higher reality that transcends the individualized sensuous experience. It is thus the sensuous experience of *bhava* that leads to its own transcendence; this transcendence takes place through the cognitive element of sensuousness, to the philosophical realization of the *rasa*, literally the juice or the quintessential flow of meaning that lies at the core of the experience of *bhava*. The *rasanispatti* or the "realization of *rasa*"[39] is the realization of the abstracted knowledge that transcends the individualized affect of the *bhava* and leads to the abstracted philosophical wisdom garnered through sensuous cognition. The state of attainment of rasa thus amounts to the attainment of a disposition, an enhanced or refined quality of mind and character.

The attainment of a disposition, involving the realization of abstracted knowledge or philosophical wisdom, is thus also simultaneously the attainment of a standpoint. This standpoint thus may be arrived at through a process born out of sensuous cognition independent of rational modes of cognition, but may also combine with rational thought in further enhancements of perspective. The affective impact of the suffering of the famine, and the emotional sorrow and pity that would have been the spontaneous responses to it, had translated into the heightened form of cognition of *karuna*, or sadness and compassion, that was simultaneously a disposition that constituted character, and that had become the springboard for political action.

When the MARS and Tebhaga leader Manikuntala Sen recollects the "magic of the times" or says "The dream of socialism was in the air and the young shared it," there is a resonance with Passerini, who, referring to the transcendental quality of a certain kind of Italian politics in the 1960s, terms it as "a way of recognizing transcendence in the secular sense." What is significant here is that Passerini explains this to be a "shared project of ... forcing the march of history by means of a participation capable of interpreting it and restoring objectivity to it thanks to an affirmation of extreme subjectivity."[40] How can an affirmation of extreme subjectivity restore objectivity to a march of history? In the context of Sanskrit aesthetic theory, Reddy draws upon the insights of Siegel[41] to explain how the aesthetic theory of universalization gives meaning to individual acts wherein an individual, emotional, sexual experience, that perpetuates entanglement in the everyday world of pain and pleasure, can become a means of transcendence through aesthetic appreciation or the poetic act:

> Contrasting *rati* (everyday sexual love) and *srngara rasa* (spiritual eroticism), Siegel remarks, *Rati* is the basic emotion which in literature crystallizes into the aesthetic experience of love the *srngara-rasa*. It is the feeling of love that Radha experiences in relation to Krishna; the *rasika's* potential for that feeling enables him to empathize with Radha (or Krishna) and through that empathy to experience *rasa* as a literary connoisseur or as a Vaisnava devotee or as both. The rasika's own experience of love, or rati, enables him to perceive the *rasa* in the literary or devotional work and thereby to move from the immanent delight of his own experience, Radha's or Krishna's experience, to the transcendent joy of the universal experience. (57)

Such transcendence and aesthetic universalization are of course not limited to literature or religion alone, for they inform the appreciation of all forms of art; the point, as may well be evident by now, is that the human faculty of aesthetic appreciation is not limited to the arts; it is at work in the daily dynamics of lived history and in political struggle too. Thus, one way of understanding the significance of Passerini's description of secular transcendence as that "shared project of ... forcing the march of history by means of a participation capable of interpreting it and restoring objectivity to it thanks to an affirmation of extreme subjectivity" is through the process of aesthetic universalization, in which the deeply subjective experience facilitates an objective understanding of history.

There also seem to have been interesting modes of gendering at work both in the recollections of the Tebhaga movement and in its lived realities. Women, especially peasant women, in contrast to all men, showed no hesitation articulating an aesthetics of joy that is evident in their articulations of *mazaa*, *shanti* and *ananda*, for they were completely at ease narrating subjective experiences and relatively freer than the men of the pressures of narrating a rational "objective" history, yet, what their tones and laughs signified was that at the core of their deeply subjective articulations of joy was an unshakeable sense of defiance and triumph. The expressions of joy were simultaneously also expressions of victory over oppression, of the thrill of solidarities that had actually succeeded in curtailing the sexual and the economic exploitations of the feudal lords. Embedded deep in the expressions of aesthetic joy was a confident, objective understanding of history, of not just a recognition of the power their collective solidarities had wielded but also of the power within themselves that they had realized in the process. The aesthetic universalization of their intense individual subjective experiences of joy and triumph had led to an objective understanding of the deep interconnections between personal power within and collective political power wielded against their oppressors. And closely linked to this understanding was a critical facet of their lived realities—while the men had been busy analyzing, strategizing, and projecting into the future, focusing on the efficacy of their political strategies and the economic goal of the Tebhaga movement, the women had quite unobtrusively been structuring social relations of bonding, aesthetic pleasure, and caregiving amidst the extreme hardships and violence that governed their lives. The objective knowledge would of course not have bypassed them that these nurturing, intersubjective social relations eventually became the political bulwark of the Tebhaga movement.[42]

Given the resonances of Sen's recollections of the "magic of the times" and "the dream of socialism [that] was in the air," and Passerini's observation about a "way of recognizing transcendence in the secular sense" that was a "shared project of ... forcing the march of history," one is tempted to ask what the nature would be of an aesthetics of liberation. Ironically, it is Foucault himself who has not only acknowledged the aesthetics of existence, drawn our attention to new, emergent forms of subjectivity, and thus prepared the field for a re-examination of the relationship between aesthetics of subjectivity, but also drawn attention to a subject constituted by liberation:

> It is notable that towards the end of his life Foucault himself, who had been one of the main sources of the idea of the death of the subject, became concerned with an "aesthetics of existence' and with the invention of 'new forms of subjectivity"—something which, of course, already requires an inventor that would itself seem to have to be some kind of subject. In an interview in 1983 Foucault suggests that the "transformation of one's self by one's own knowledge is, I think, something rather close to the aesthetic experience,"[43] and in 1984 he states: "I do indeed believe that there is no sovereign, founding subject, a universal form of subject to be found everywhere... I believe, on the contrary, that the subject is constituted through practices of subjectification, or, in a more autonomous way, through practices of liberation."[44] If the subject can be constituted by 'liberation' there must, though, be some way in which one can conceive of what a free subject might be.[45]

If the subject may be constituted by liberation, then one of the tasks of aesthetic theory would be to elaborate what the aesthetics of liberation may be.

This chapter is a sequel to and an attempt to return to and explore the issues of aesthetics I had raised in my book *Unclaimed Harvest*. There, I had explained how the song—"In the Fragrance of the Wet Earth We Dance in Joy"—that they would dance to in ever-widening circles of solidarity during the Tebhaga movement, evoked, in full sensuousness, the dance of the crops and the love of the earth that they tilled. It was far from the traditional language of politics, and actually touched upon the core of their lives, the core that was threatened.

Discussing subjectivity and the workings of aesthetics, Bowie asserts: "The aesthetic object affects the subject without the subject wishing to determine the object. Neither are the subjects slaves to language: the capacity for situated linguistic innovation will be fundamental to the subject"[46] I have shown in the above-mentioned chapter the workings of some of the aesthetics of liberation that transcend traditional political discourse in the women's song and dance and in the vocabulary too that describes their experience of being in the movement; for the words they use—*ananda* (joy), *mazaa* (enjoyment), *nasha* (intoxication), *shanti* (peace)—are all indicative of a powerful affective experience of liberation. These expressions mark linguistic shifts in the conventional vocabulary of political struggle, as do other vocabularies that they forged for other experiences, such as the deep connections between *antorikota o andolon* (inwardness and the movement); or the coming together of love of beloved and love of people in joint struggle with the man one loved, in a *premer jomir khoj* (a search for the terrain of love). All these are expressive of linguistic innovations in the making of new political subjectivities. For them, it was an aesthetic of subjects constituted through practices of liberation.

This understanding of the Tebhaga women's movement is but a drop in the ocean; there is much to be done to make up for all the opportunities for understanding the historical transformations of human culture that we have lost in the centuries in which we have turned away from the play of aesthetics in enriching our lived realities.

NOTES

1. The Bengal famine is often referred to as the "manmade famine" because it was due not to a scarcity of crop but to the British imperial diversion of rice for the war effort and consequent "mismanagement"—the feudal landowners controlling release of production, and the class traders hoarding crop in the face of scarcity. For more on the famine, see Mukerjee, *Churchill's Secret War: The British Empire and the Ravaging of India during World War II.* See also Jean Dreze and A. Sen. *Hunger and Public Action*, 46.

2. Panjabi, *Unclaimed Harvest: An Oral History of the Tebhaga Women's Movement.*
3. Panjabi.
4. Chakravartty, *Communists in the Indian Women's Movement*, 27.
5. The Tebhaga peasants' movement, spearheaded by the Communist Party of India, was launched by landless sharecroppers against feudal lords right across undivided Bengal in 1946. It was marked by the participation of over 50,000 women, both rural and urban. See Kavita Panjabi's, *Unclaimed Harvest* for a detailed oral history of the Tebhaga women's movement that ensued within the context of this peasant movement, and specifically Chap. 3 for an elaboration of the history of MARS.
6. Ila Mitra, Personal interviews by Author (Kolkata: February 12, 1997, March 11, 97, Sept. 17, 97).
7. See Kavita Panjabi, *Unclaimed Harvest*. This is not, however, a claim for the ethical value of such poetic truth, for the power of affect of course applies to all social movements, not just progressive ones. As I had asserted in the very following paragraph of *Unclaimed Harvest*, "The poetic truth of historical mobilization is not ethically value laden in itself, it only bears an explanation of mobilization on the basis of a perception of an event and its affective impact, and there is every likelihood of a clash of poetic truths occurring in volatile, contested contexts, especially where the social, political or economic stakes are high" (np).
8. See http://www.ugc.ac.in/pdfnews/2313343_English.pdf.
9. See http://www.ugc.ac.in/pdfnews/8448621_mrprecommendedcaseslist.pdf.
10. An example of a unique space created for interdisciplinary, fieldwork-based research in the humanities is in the realm of non-governmental organizations (NGO). The People's Linguistic Survey of India, conceived as a radical movement, was launched in 2010 by Professor Ganesh Devy to update the existing knowledge of the languages spoken in India, especially the tribal and the dying languages. It also involves documentation of oral stories and songs in these languages, and the research is being conducted under the aegis of the NGO Bhasha Research and Publication Trust.
11. Blackman, Cromby, Hook, Papadopoulos and Walkerdine, "Creating Subjectivities," 1–27.
12. See Bibliography for examples specifically in the work of Passerini, Butalia, Menon, Bhasian, Portelli, Laub, Young and Koch.
13. See Chap. 2, 'The Retroactive Force of Interiority: The Conscience of Oral History' of *Unclaimed Harvest*.
14. Foucault, *Politics, Philosophy, Culture*, 50.
15. Passerini, "Work, Ideology and Consensus under Italian Fascism," 54.
16. Portelli, *The Death of Luigi Trastulli and Other. Stories: Form and Meaning in Oral History*, 50.
17. Passerini, "Work, Ideology and Consensus under Italian Fascism," 54.
18. Portelli, *The Death of Luigi Trastulli*, x.

19. Passerini, "Work, Ideology and Consensus under Italian Fascism," 54.
20. Marcuse, *Eros and Civilization*, 176.
21. Gikandi, *Slavery and the Culture of Taste*, 222.
22. Bowie, *Aesthetics and Subjectivity from Kant to Nietzsche*, 2.
23. Gregory Moore. Introduction to *Selected Writings on Aesthetics*, by Johann Gottfried Herder, 1.
24. As translated by Andrew G Cooper and Matthew McAndrew in *The Bloomsbury Anthology of Aesthetics*, 158.
25. Guyer, "The Origins of Modern Aesthetics," 15.
26. http://plato.stanford.edu/archives/spr2014/entries/aesthetics-18th-german/.
27. Moore, 3.
28. This elision is of the extent that Baumgarten's *Aesthetica*, written in Latin in 1735, has, to my knowledge, never been translated in the full into English. Sections 1–27 of a total of 613 sections have been translated into English by Andrew G Cooper and Matthew McAndrew in The Bloomsbury Anthology of Aesthetics (2012) cited in this essay. The first complete translation into German (Mirbach) too became available only in 2007.
29. Marcuse, 179.
30. See Leon Golden, *Aristotle on Tragic and Comic Mimesis*; Stephen Halliwell, *Aristotle's Poetics*; Donald Keesey, "On Some Recent Interpretations of Catharsis": 193–205.
31. Greene et al., editors, *The Princeton Encyclopedia of Poetry and Poetics*, 215.
32. Greene et al..
33. See Martha Nussbaum, *The Fragility of Goodness Luck and Ethics in Greek Tragedy and Philosophy*.
34. Nussbaum, 390.
35. Values thus derived may of course be based on misleading emotions or distorted judgements, as may be the case with members of fundamentalist movements the world over; this makes it all the more important for us to recognize the connections between emotional response and commitments, as well as the misleading emotions and distorted judgments that may shape commitments by which human beings choose to wreak havoc on the world.
36. Sujit Mukherjee, *A Dictionary of Indian Literature: Beginnings-1850*, 325.
37. Reddy, "The Rule of Love," 50
38. I am grateful to Tridip Suhrud for drawing my attention to the significance of this dimension of being—and of course becoming—in the transition from the experience of bhava to rasa.
39. Mukherjee, *A Dictionary of Indian Literature: Beginnings-1850*, 265.
40. Passerini, *Autobiography of a Generation: Italy*, 132.
41. Lee Siegel, *Sacred and Profane Dimensions of Love in Indian traditions, as Exemplified in the Gītagovinda of Jayadeva*, 58.

42. Cf Chap. 4 of *Unclaimed Harvest*, "'Meyera Andolone Antorikota Aanlo—Women brought an Inwardness to the Movement': Redefining Political Agency, Creating Affective Solidarities" for a detailed exposition of this process.
43. Foucault, *Politics, Philosophy, Culture*, 14.
44. Foucault, 50.
45. Bowie, *Aesthetics and Subjectivity from Kant to Nietzsche*, 12–13.
46. Bowie, 12.

BIBLIOGRAPHY

Baumgarten A.G. 2007. *Ästhetik*. Latin-German edition. 2 vols. Translation, Preface, Notes, Indexes by Dagmar Mirbach. Hamburg: Felix Meiner Verlag.

Baumgarten, A.G. 2012. Aesthetica. Trans. Andrew G. Cooper and Matthew McAndrew. In *The Bloomsbury Anthology of Aesthetics*, eds. Colin McQuillan, and Joseph J. Tanke, 158–162. London: Bloomsbury Academic.

Blackman, Lisa, J. Cromby, D. Hook, D. Papadopoulos, and V. Walkerdine. 2008. Creating Subjectivities. *Subjectivity* 22: 1–27.

Bowie, Andrew. 1990. *Aesthetics and Subjectivity from Kant to Nietzsche*. New York: Manchester University Press.

Butalia, Urvashi. 1998. *The Other Side of Silence: Voices from the Partition of India*. Viking: New Delhi.

Chakravartty, Renu. 1980. *Communists in the Indian Women's Movement*. New Delhi: People's Publishing House.

Dreze, Jean, and A. Sen. 1993. *Hunger and Public Action*. New Delhi: Oxford University Press.

Foucault, Michel. 1988. *Politics, Philosophy, Culture: Interviews and Other Writings 1977–84*. New York: Routledge.

Gikandi, Simon. 2011. *Slavery and the Culture of Taste*. Princeton, NJ: Princeton University Press.

Golden, Leon. 1992. *Aristotle on Tragic and Comic Mimesis*. Atlanta, GA: Georgia Scholars Press.

Greene, Ronald, S. Cushman, C. Cavanagh, J. Ramazani, P.F. Rouzer, H. Feinsod, D. Marno, and A. Slessarev, eds. 2012. *The Princeton Encyclopedia of Poetry and Poetics*. Princeton, NJ: Princeton University Press.

Gruyer, Paul. 2014. 18th Century German Aesthetics. In *The Stanford Encyclopedia of Philosophy*, ed. Edward N. Zalta. http://plato.stanford.edu/archives/spr2014/entries/aesthetics-18th-german/

Guyer, Paul. 2004. The Origins of Modern Aesthetics. In *The Blackwell Guide to Aesthetics*, ed. Peter Kivy, 15–44. Oxford: Blackwell Publishing.

Halliwell, Stephen. 1986. *Aristotle's Poetics*. London: Duckworth.

Kant, Immanuel. 2010. Transition from Popular Moral Philosophy to the Metaphysic of Morals. In *Fundamental Principles of the Metaphysic of Morals*, trans. Thomas Kingsmill Abbott. http://creativecommons.org/licenses/by-nc-sa/2.5/au/. Accessed 28 August 2010.

Keesey, Donald. 1978–1979. On Some Recent Interpretations of Catharsis. *The Classical World* 72(4) (December 1978–January 1979): 193–205.

Koch, Gertrud. 1997. 'Against All Odds' or the Will to Survive: Moral Conclusions from Narrative Closure. *History and Memory*, 9(1/2): 393–408.

Laub, Dori. 1992. Bearing Witness, or the Viccissitudes of Listening. In *Testimony: Crisis of Witnessing in Literature Psychoanalysis, History*, eds. Soshana Felman, and Dori Laub, 57–74. New York: Routledge.

Marcuse, Herbert. 1987. *Eros and Civilization: A Philosophical Inquiry into Freud*. London: Ark Paperbacks.

Menon, Ritu, and K. Bhasin. 1998. *Borders and Boundaries: Women in India's Partition*. New Delhi: Kali for Women.

Moore, Gregory. 2006. Introduction. In *Selected Writings on Aesthetics*, ed. Johann Gottfried Herder, trans. and ed. Gregory Moore, 1–30. Princeton, NJ: Princeton University Press.

Mukerjee, Madhushree. 2010. *Churchill's Secret War: The British Empire and the Ravaging of India during World War II*. New Delhi: Tranquebar Press.

Mukherjee, Sujit. 1998. *A Dictionary of Indian Literature: Beginnings-1850*. Delhi: Orient Longman.

Nussbaum, Martha. 2001. *The Fragility of Goodness Luck and Ethics in Greek Tragedy and Philosophy*. Rev. ed. Cambridge: Cambridge University Press.

Panjabi, Kavita. 2015. *Unclaimed Harvest: An Oral History of the Tebhaga Women's Movement*. Delhi: Zubaan Books.

Passerini, Luisa. 1989. Women's Personal Narratives: Myths, Experiences and Emotions. In *Interpreting Women's Lives: Feminist Theory and Personal Narratives*, ed. The Personal Narratives Group, 189–200. Bloomington, IN: Indiana University Press.

———. ed. 1992. *International Yearbook of Oral History and Life Stories*. Vol. 1, *Memory and Totalitarianism*. Oxford: Oxford University Press.

———. 1996. *Autobiography of a Generation: Italy*. Trans. Lisa Erdberg. Hanover and London: Wesleyan University Press.

———. 1998. Work, Ideology and Consensus under Italian Fascism. In *The Oral History Reader*, ed. Robert Perks and A. Thomson, 53–63. New York: Routledge.

Portelli, Alessandro. 1990. *The Death of Luigi Trastulli and Other. Stories: Form and Meaning in Oral History*. Albany, NY: State University of New York Press.

———. 1998. What makes Oral History Different? In *The Oral History Reader*, ed. Robert Perks and A. Thomson, 63–75. New York: Routledge.

———. 2003. *The Order Has Been Carried Out: History, Memory, and Meaning of a Nazi Massacre in Rome*. New York: Palgrave Macmillan.

Reddy, William M. 2010. The Rule of Love: The History of Western Romantic Love in Comparative Perspective. In *New Dangerous Liaisons: Discourses on Europe and Love in the Twentieth Century*, ed. Luisa Passerini, L. Ellena, and A.C.T. Geppert, 33–57. New York: Berghahn Books.

Sen, Manikuntala. 2001. *In Search of Freedom*. Translation of Sediner Katha by Stree Publishers. Calcutta: Stree Publishers.

Siegel, Lee. 1978. *Sacred and Profane Dimensions of Love in Indian Traditions, as Exemplified in the Gītagovinda of Jayadeva*. Delhi: Oxford University Press.

Woodhead, John. 1984. *Famine Inquiry Commission Report on Bengal*. New Delhi: Usha Publications.

Young, James E. 1997. Between History and Memory: The Uncanny Voices of Historian and Survivor. *History and Memory* 9(1/2): 47–58.

PART II

Place, Performance, Practices

CHAPTER 5

Locating Palestine Within American Studies: Transitory Field Sites and Borrowed Methods

Jennifer Lynn Kelly

My route to studying solidarity tourism in Palestine was a relatively circuitous one. I came to my master's degree coursework from an undergraduate background in feminist studies and literature with an emphasis, in both, on comparative colonial studies. During those undergraduate years, I appreciated the inclusion of work like Edward Said's, but wondered why so little of his work on Palestine (or, often, any work on Palestine) ever entered into the syllabi I encountered. As I began my graduate work, I charted a course of Middle East studies and American studies, where I grew increasingly confused by American Studies' focus on US empire and interest in detailing US foreign policy in the Middle East, combined with what I saw as its relative unwillingness to broach the subject of Israel/Palestine in any sort of sustained way.[1] I wrote my master's thesis on the representational practice and political economy of US Christian Zionism as a small contribution toward centralizing Palestine within American studies. I understood US Christian Zionism as an infrequently discussed, yet hugely influential, bloc of US support for both Israeli occupation and aggressive US foreign policy in the region. A large part of my research for this project detailed the use of "tours" of the West Bank by Christian diplomats, senators, and pastors in the USA. I traced the import and implications of those Christian Zionist senators who made proclamations, like Senator James Inhofe did on the House floor in 2002, that Israel should keep the West Bank because "God said so," or statements like those of the then House majority leader Tom DeLay when he declared that he "toured Judea and Samaria and stood on the Golan Heights" but "didn't see any occupied territory." "I saw Israel," he explained.[2]

J.L. Kelly (✉)
Department of Communication, University of California, San Diego, USA

© The Author(s) 2016
S. Puri, D.A. Castillo (eds.), *Theorizing Fieldwork in the Humanities*,
DOI 10.1057/978-1-349-92834-7_5

Because tourism, Christian Zionist and otherwise, has been so central to bolstering the narrative that Israel "made the deserts bloom," during my PhD work I wanted to turn to Palestinian organizers to understand how they negotiated and responded to these Zionist forms of travel. I began to research Palestinian anti-occupation and anticolonial forms of tourism: what, in my early graduate work, I called "justice tourism," but what I came to call solidarity tourism, a description less laden with moral certainty. In my subsequent writings on solidarity tourism, I have come to understand the phenomenon as a far more uncertain venture: one that cannot be dismissed as either "disaster tourism" or "occupation voyeurism," nor one that can be hailed as justice in and of itself.

Further, because I took forms of Zionist tourism like birthright tours and Christian Zionist senators' post-tour proclamations as the starting points for my inquiry, I initially positioned Palestinian solidarity tourism as a "response" to Zionist tourist itineraries. For this reason, before I began my fieldwork, I intended to structure my dissertation as a series of snapshots of "Palestinian responses." I planned to write one chapter on Christian anti-Zionist pilgrimage as a *response* to Christian Zionist tourism; one chapter on Palestinian olive-planting tourist initiatives *in response to* Israel's uprooting of Palestinian olive trees and its widespread practice of having tourists plant a tree in Israel before they leave the country; one chapter on Jewish awareness-raising trips on the occupation *in response to* Birthright Israel; and one chapter on queer Palestine solidarity tours as *responses* to Israeli "pink-washing" campaigns in the form of LGBTQ birthright trips. My dissertation proposal detailed this approach, outlining an agenda predicated on the assumption that I could look at these tourist initiatives both as responses and as separate from one another. However, since dissertation proposals are, as I heard one advisor describe them, elaborate works of fiction, this is not the research project I ended up writing.

My study of solidarity tourism in Palestine, by default, necessitated fieldwork. I couldn't talk about Palestinian tourism without talking to tour guides, in the same way that I couldn't talk about solidarity tourism without talking to the tourists themselves. As an American studies scholar, with a capacious approach to method understood as a given, but with no training in those methodological potentialities, I turned to anthropology as a way to learn how to answer the questions I wanted to ask. I emailed anthropology professors to petition for spots in their classes, doing the explanatory work of describing my project and the promissory work of explaining that I made sense in their seminar even though I came from an interdisciplinary field with an unruly approach to method. I culled the study of empire and the inquiry into its taxonomies from the texts on comparative colonialisms I encountered as an interloper in those anthropology classes. The questions I learned to ask, and the way I learned to find answers to them, are approaches I learned from reading ethnographies in anthropology courses, from reading my colleagues' ethnographic work, and from hearing about their fieldwork experiences in our shared classes. These are methods and questions I borrowed, essentially, from a practice of listening, which was as voracious as it was disciplined, to carefully crafted ethnographic research. In many ways, then, I credit American studies with teaching me how to ask questions that centralize the structuring forces of US militarism, empire, and war making, and anthropology with teaching me how to see the daily machinations of these processes and listen to the contours of their effects. As such, ethnography became my method not because it was predetermined by my field, but because the questions I asked and the answers I sought required ethnography as a tool.

In the spring of 2012, I took a preliminary dissertation trip to parse out how solidarity tours to Palestine took shape, who went on them, and what role they played in anticolonial movement building. As an unfunded doctoral student in what is itself an underfunded American studies department, I was only able to make this initial trip after being awarded a small university research grant, which, after paying for tour fees and airfare, left me with enough money to conduct only three weeks worth of preliminary research. On this short research trip, I went on several tours: one weeklong itinerary, many guided city walks, and various day trips. I spoke with tour guides, volunteers, local participants, cooks, bus drivers, and international tourists. I went to Palestine with questions like *why tourism?* and *why now?* The answers I received reshaped the questions I asked. I began to ask what solidarity tourism felt like, what its organizers believed it did, and what strategies they used in their work. I asked how long they had been doing this work and why, when its effects were difficult to discern and when the labor itself was, as they often reminded me, either tirelessly repetitive or, if some new interruption broke the repetition, dishearteningly worse: more roadblocks, more checkpoints, more military zones.

The questions I brought to my research were formed, in large part, by my training in American studies. The questions American studies taught me to ask centered on US foreign policy in Israel/Palestine: how solidarity tourism took shape when it did and why it took shape in the way it did. On this early dissertation research trip, I sat in an East Jerusalem café after an alternative tour of the nearby Israeli settlements with Abu Hassan, an independent tour guide out of Jerusalem. He explained his own arrival at solidarity tourism as a useful, if transient, strategy. "It's the only thing left," he almost shrugged. "We've tried violent resistance. We've tried negotiations; we've tried peace talks; we've tried complying with what the U.S. told us to do by working toward a two-state solution. The only thing left is to *show* the international community what is happening and compel them to do something." My training in American studies taught me to hear his assessment as a description of a historical trajectory of multiple, shifting iterations of Palestinian struggles for freedom from occupation. My background in Palestinian Studies allowed me to hear, in his words, a growing cynicism and disillusionment with the US-led peace process.[3] "Showing the situation on the ground," he suggested, had become an unlikely last-ditch effort to end the occupation. His matter-of-fact assessment, underscoring the deception inherent in positioning the USA as an "honest broker" in what far too many call the "Israeli-Palestinian Conflict," was a narrative thread I learned to focus on as a student of US empire.

At the same time, the questions I brought to my research, and the way my research questions changed shape in the field, were indebted to the time I spent in anthropology classes. "For every hour of participant-observation, write for four," one of my committee members who did ethnography advised me before I left for fieldwork.[4] I tried, and failed, to write that much, given the rushed, frenetic way I ended up having to do fieldwork, but I did write—a lot. When I went on a tour, I took pages and pages of notes. In Field Notebook 1, there are descriptions of the weather on the day of the first tour, notes on the questions tourists asked, notes on their expressions, their surprise, their frustration as they attempted to understand what they were witnessing. Scrawled across the pages of multiple notebooks are notes on how tourists described what they saw; one tourist marveled at the settlements scattered across the hills of the West Bank as the first day turned to dusk, and mused, "They look just like honeycomb!" There are notes on how they understood their presence in Palestine and notes on how they rationalized their inaction before this moment. I took notes on tour guides' repeated refrains, the things I knew, as someone who also lectures before a sometimes recalcitrant audience, that they wanted their audience to remember, the things they honed in on and overemphasized, the concepts and histories they needed the tourists to take home with them. I took notes on the expressions of shop owners when tourists promised they would "come back later"; I took notes on the youth selling bracelets in the streets of Hebron and on the way tourists ignored them, at best, and berated them, at worst. I took notes on the words of shop owners and farmers as they welcomed tourists into their homes, the stories they told, the food they served, the evidentiary weight of occupation they presented to tourists via their narratives, their merchandise, their olive trees. During tours and after, in poring over these notes and stacks of others, in sitting through and listening to interviews, in writing through the process, I came to understand what *else* these moments reveal. I began to articulate the ways in which solidarity tours are organized around the demand to provide evidentiary weight, how tourists wait for Palestinians to provide them with *evidence* of their displacement—both for tourists themselves and for their awaiting audiences back home. What is crystalized in moments like these are the historical ways in which Palestinians have not been constructed as truth-telling subjects and the resultant privilege that inheres in the *demand* for Palestinians to provide evidentiary weight of their own, extremely well-documented, dispossession.

My field notes go on to trace the asymmetries of power and privilege that animate tourists' travels. In Field Notebook 3, there are snapshots of scenes like the one in Nablus when a tourist asked, eagerly, what happened to a wall that had been blackened by some unknown event. "Oh that?" the guide shrugged. "Someone was just spray-painting their bedframe against the wall." The tourist, visibly disenchanted, resumed the walking tour, mumbling, "Oh, I thought it was like a bomb or something." In Field Notebook 5, there are descriptions of walking tours of depopulated spaces inside Israel's 1948 borders, of the passages from Palestinian refugees' memoirs that Israeli tour guides read aloud to tourists, of the neighborhood tour guides led tourists through, describing expulsions of Palestinian residents and showing tourists the outsides of their former homes. There are notes on how long tourists lingered at which houses, the fragments of what they said to each other, the ways Palestinian tour guides corrected Israeli tour guides' narratives, and the political and emotional stakes of each correction. In Field Notebook 7, there are descriptions of what tourists asked each other on olive-picking programs, how they introduced themselves, what constituted their ice breakers, and how they made sense of occupying space and sharing experiences with people they would otherwise likely never meet. There are notes about how tour guides answered the same questions multiple different tourists asked them, the questions they, in turn, asked tourists, the assumptions tourists held about Palestine—and about their role in Palestine solidarity movements—that tour guides worked consistently to redirect.

My notebooks are filled, too, with the themes that cropped up in my interviews with tour guides, the surprising ways they described their labor, the ways they heard my questions, the ways they envisioned their pedagogy, and what else took shape in the space of the interview: who interrupted the interview and for what, what jokes were told, what insights emerged over scores of cigarettes and endless tiny cups of strong coffee. These field notes, I think, were made possible by my years of eavesdropping in anthropology courses: my years of reading and re-reading the intimate writings of my friends and colleagues in ethnography courses that were structured, thankfully, like writing workshops; my semesters of wading happily through thick descriptions; the studying I did in my living room, in coffee shops, and in campus libraries about the significance of the descriptions of details from interviews—not of the "interview material," but of the space of the interview itself, like in Susan Harding's descriptions of the nuances, and invasiveness, of evangelical witnessing, or Veena Das' descriptions of children playing under the table during recitations of the violence of partition.[5]

But neither American Studies nor my pilfered anthropological training prepared me, formally, for fieldwork.[6] I traveled to Palestine for my "official fieldwork" during the fourth year of my PhD program. In my program in American Studies, however, there was no space written into either our timeline or our teaching requirements for fieldwork.[7] Because our stipends were so directly sutured to our teaching responsibilities, there was no space or expectation that PhD candidates in American studies would spend *any* time during the PhD not on campus teaching. In order for fieldwork to emerge as a possibility, in addition to the methodological training—or modeling—I borrowed from anthropology; I also looked outside not only my department but also my institution for fieldwork funding. And, unlike my colleagues in anthropology, the time and space, and even community, for learning the formulas and processes for applying to grants such as the Wenner-Gren Foundation and the National

Science Foundation were not institutionalized in my department. While I applied for grants like these that were, quite literally, outside my field, I also applied for, and received, the Palestinian American Research Center (PARC)'s field-based research grant, which provided the generous funding for the entire duration of my dissertation research in Palestine.

Because PARC grants do not cover a full year of fieldwork, I stretched my fellowship to cover the cost of the tours I went on, transportation to and from my interviews in the West Bank, East Jerusalem, and inside Israel's 1948 borders, and my living arrangements over the summer and fall of 2012. In the spring of 2013, I would have to return to Austin to teach the courses that enabled my funding for the rest of that year. In addition, I conducted my research while on a tourist visa, which expires every three months, so I both exited and reentered Israel/Palestine during my fieldwork in order to (try to) renew my visa. My ability, moreover, to enter, exit, and reenter Israel/Palestine has everything to do with my legibility, to Israeli authorities at checkpoints and in passport control booths, as solely a "tourist" and not as someone with familial ties to Palestine.[8] Had they assumed that I was in "Israel" to go to "Palestine," my experience at passport control would have been very different.[9] Every entry and exit was haunted by the anxiety that they might Google my name, read my work, see that I am a signatory to the boycott of Israeli academic and cultural institutions, deny me entry (or reentry), and foreclose (the rest of) my research.

Because of the size of my research grant and because a potential denial to reenter Israel loomed on the horizon of my three-month tourist visa, I tried to condense a year's worth of research into a four-month period, completing 35 interviews and researching 35 tours during my cumulative time in Palestine. When I wasn't on a tour, I was traveling to and from interviews, charging my phone to record conversations, printing Institutional Review Board (IRB) consent forms, chatting with tourists on worn bus seats, sending emails to set up subsequent interviews, or sitting in offices and on picnic benches asking tour guides about their work. The frenetic pace of my fieldwork, coupled with the slow pace of my interviews themselves, was laden with the anxiety to learn as much as I could during the first three months in case those three months were the only ones I had. The slow ethnography of the texts I love was, in some ways, not available to me with the piecing together of external grants, the small departmental funds, and the teaching stipends that made up what was supposed to be my "fieldwork year." But I tried to make up for this deficit with the slowness of my interviews, each one lingering with the tangents inherent to tour guides venting about their work, each one drawing out connections between the entitlement of the demand for evidentiary weight, the redirection of the impulse to volunteer, the boredom of repetition, and, yet, the imperative of narration.

As my fieldwork began, the more I sat with the knowledge my interlocutors shared with me, the less I began to position these forms of tourism as "responses" and the more I began to understand solidarity tourism as part of a longer trajectory of varying and varied forms of Palestinian resistance to Israeli settler colonial expansion. For example, in a follow-up interview during my fieldwork year, the year after our first meeting, Abu Hassan qualified his initial assertion. Rather than positioning solidarity tourism as a last resort for Palestinian sovereignty struggles, he described that solidarity tourism is "part of the struggle now."[10] "If the third intifada happened tomorrow," he explained, "our strategies would change."[11] Abu Hassan's efforts to clarify the place of solidarity tourism within a larger context of contemporary Palestinian resistance demonstrated, for me, how some Palestinian tour guides and organizers have embraced, consistently, albeit ambivalently, a wholly imperfect strategy. Solidarity tourism is, as guides are often the first to admit, a strategy that is both flawed and temporary. For Abu Hassan and many of the other guides and organizers I spoke to, it is a strategy that both negotiates and narrates the confines of colonial rule at the same time that it enumerates and works to circumvent the manifold Israeli (and US-backed) strategies of containment that fracture the landscape of Palestine. It is a strategy, and also a business, that is as provisional as it is malleable.

This understanding of solidarity tourism as a transient and flawed, yet politically important, strategy echoed across many of my interviews and has subsequently shaped my conclusions and restructured my questions. For this reason, in ways that I think have often frustrated some audiences, I have refused an evaluative approach to solidarity tourism in Palestine. Learning from the work of scholars across the humanities and social sciences who question the certainty of evaluative approaches, I have refrained from positioning solidarity tourism as either "good" or "bad," as either voyeuristic and exploitative or, alternatively, liberatory and redemptive. I have instead sat with the ambivalence of the practice and I have explored how it is both embedded in and working against histories of sustained displacement in Palestine. This approach exceeds the disciplinary boundaries of my training; this refusal to "choose" is one I learned from literature, from feminist studies, from postcolonial studies, from cultural studies, from anthropology, from American studies, from critical tourism studies, from critical ethnic studies. It is one I have learned from reading ethnographies with an American studies perspective, from learning how to study US empire and Israeli settler colonialism without predetermining the answers to my research questions by, in the words of Ann Stoler and Karen Strassler, "casting for the colonial."[12]

This approach, this non-choosing, also required that I follow the afterlife of the tours not to find out "if they work," but to ascertain what kinds of questions, restructuring, or inertia they may have engendered. Because of the truncated amount of time I had to spend in Palestine, and the potentiality that I wouldn't be allowed back in upon renewing my tourist visa, I interviewed tour guides and organizers in Palestine with an urgency that didn't, in turn, translate to the tourists. With the tourists, I instead made the time to do interviews, via Skype, both in between and around my other obligations, my teaching, and my travel to conferences. These interviews, too, were slow, but simultaneously animated by the slow time of technology, the gaps and lulls after each sentence, the frozen screens, the failed attempts at reconnecting. My field notes from my Skype interviews are peppered with question marks. My voice on the recordings repeatedly urges interlocutors to start over: "The last thing I heard was…." The questions I asked centered on the themes that surfaced: their feelings of shame and guilt, the extent to which their feelings enabled their action and/or inaction, what they learned, what they forgot, what they couldn't forget, what resonated, how their time was spent before, during, after the tour.

My fieldwork, across all sites, surprised me. I listened for the latent assumptions, looking to document the voyeurism of tourism, for descriptions of "disaster tourism," for evidence of disregard. With my interviews with tour guides, when I asked them what it felt like to repeat these narratives of displacement for rotating audiences, when I expected them to talk about the difficulty in consistently narrating and renarrating their dispossession, they answered with descriptions of how they negotiated the *boredom* of repetition. This revealed the many ways in which solidarity tourism is, among other things, a job, and a job that can, as jobs are wont to do, be boring. With tourists, when I expected them to describe how they "experienced" occupation, how they "saw what it was like," they instead talked about their awareness of their *distance* from the occupation while they were in Palestine, the racialized privilege that enabled their movement and foreclosed the very same movement of Palestinians in the West Bank, the apartheid practices they not only witnessed but actively embodied. There were moments like the time I sat in a loud café with an Israeli anti-Zionist activist, hoping the recording app on my phone was documenting her voice over all the noise, when I asked her if she ever got irritated with having to repeat things to American audiences that they should already know. Taken aback, she looked at me: "Why should they already know? Their media tells them nothing." The generosity in this assessment startled me as much as my question had startled her. At the same time, I watched tourists predictably gawking at checkpoints, slowing the line, making people late to work; I watched tourists disappointed that spray paint wasn't the remnants of a bomb; I watched tourists scream at street kids trying to sell them trinkets; I heard US tourists describe, in interviews, Israel/Palestine as, somehow, "the first place they ever saw racism." The content of my interviews thus refused the expectations I brought to my fieldwork and simultaneously refused a linear, straightforward, uncomplicated, evaluative assessment.

I also brought to my fieldwork not only my own expectations but also those of all the many other activists and scholars who have rolled their eyes knowingly when I explained that I work on solidarity tourism in Palestine. I carried with me the expectations of those who assume an inherent difference between the "political work" of delegations and the exploitations of its crass cousin *tourism*, or those who think there is a world of difference between the work of weekly anti-occupation protests and the work of leading tourists through the West Bank. Instead, I found tour guides who lead protests on Fridays, delegates on Tuesdays, and tourist groups on Wednesdays. I found a practice of narrative labor that is deeply interconnected with other forms of protest in Palestine, but simultaneously aware of itself as a job, a business, and a site, if only aspirational, of anticolonial strategizing.

My fieldwork was also scripted by my interdisciplinarity and the questions my undisciplined training has taught me to ask. I followed threads of narrative tangents in ways that I can only attribute to my interdisciplinary training. When tour guides paused to read from memoirs, I refrained from treating those pauses as solely the "material" of the tour. Instead, I followed those moments of the tour—like when Israeli tour guides described the theft of books in 1948, for example—to ask more about what these moments reveal about the *processes* of settler colonialism in Israel/Palestine. I detailed what was emphasized from each memoir on the tour, what went missing in translation, what libraries were looted, what books ended up where, and what the theft of books, or as documentary artist Benny Brunner has called it, *The Great Book Robbery* (2012), says about dispossession. I wrote about photography exhibits like Emily Jacir's *Ex Libris*, which documents the 30,000 books appropriated by the Israeli state in 1948 from Palestinian homes, libraries, and institutions, to show how these fragments from the tour do not occur in a cultural vacuum, but exist alongside a constellation of cultural productions, films, and art installations on the looting of Palestinian libraries.[13] When I described how tour guides across the West Bank invite tourists to help plant olive trees on land threatened by Israeli settlement expansion, I followed tour guides' allusions to trace a much longer history of dispossession; in doing so, I worked to provide, for readers, a history of Zionist afforestation—the punitive uprooting of Palestinian olive trees and the deliberate planting of cypress and fir to cover up the destruction of Palestinian villages—that has accompanied Israeli statecraft and began even before the establishment of the state.[14] History and literature and film and art do not form the backdrop for my interviews and participant observation on tours, but, in fact, complete them. In this way, my fieldwork was, itself, a practice of interdisciplinarity.

As a whole, however, my project is incomplete. It is incomplete, literally, in its shifting transition from a dissertation to a book. But it is permanently incomplete, in that my fieldwork, perhaps like all fieldwork, wasn't as long as it could or should have been, I didn't get to ask everything I wanted to, or include everything I imagined, and it was stitched together through only fragments of training, time, space, and funds. In my particularly compressed version of fieldwork, and precisely because I take up the study of mobility, travel, tourism, and the racially structured access to all of above, I didn't "stay in the field," but traveled, with the mobility of a tourist, back and forth, on multiple tours, with multiple guides, in multiple spaces. Because my movement was not policed, I was able to take tours in Tel Aviv, Jerusalem, Nablus, Ramallah, Bethlehem, Hebron, Beit Sahour, and Al Khader. Because I was not surveilled, I was able to do interviews in cafés and offices on both sides of the Green Line. And, because of my passport, I could follow the tourists home. I did interviews in Texas, New York, Pennsylvania, and California. I did interviews from my living room, over the phone, over Skype, and over email. The multisited nature of my fieldwork was thus not only predetermined by my discipline(s), my department(s), and my institution(s) but also made possible by my own expansive mobility in a field site structured by the colonial logics of racialized containment.

Fieldwork in Palestine enabled me to analyze solidarity tourism in a way that troubles how we understand "solidarity" and how we understand "tourism," looking not only at the limitations of each, nor only at their radical potential, but at the uneven and asymmetrical ways they take shape in colonial contexts. Interdisciplinarity, and particularly interdisciplinary American studies, allowed me to understand solidarity tourism as a shifting and transient strategy now—a strategy that, however inadequate, refuses to treat the USA as a honest broker and refuses to treat settler colonialism in Palestine either as "intractable" or as a "conflict," two designations that are too easily and too frequently assigned to Israel/Palestine in the contemporary lexicon of occupation. Fieldwork *as* interdisciplinarity has structured my questions, and continues to shape my study, as I work toward not the "completion" of this project, but the necessarily, and perhaps productively, incomplete analysis that will emerge from these borrowed methods and transitory field sites.

Notes

1. It's worth noting that this was in 2006–2008, and thus far before the American Studies Association's 2013 endorsement of the Palestinian call for a boycott of Israeli academic institutions. The field's relationship to Palestine, thankfully, changed significantly in the intervening years.
2. James Inhofe's statement is referenced in Melani McAlister's "Prophecy, Politics, and the Popular," 781, and also cited in Jane Lampman, "Mixing Prophecy and Politics," 4. See also Lawrence Davidson, "Christian Zionism as a Representation of American Manifest Destiny." It is important to also bear in mind that James Inhofe is the same senator who, upon release of the Abu Ghraib photos, said he was "more outraged by the outrage" (Gregory Hooks and Clayton James Mosher, "Outrages against Personal Dignity: Rationalizing Abuse and Torture in the War on Terror," 1630) and who, notwithstanding the Red Cross Report, which maintained that "between 70 percent and 90 percent of the persons deprived of their liberty in Iraq had been arrested by mistake" (Red Cross Report, in Mark Danner: *Torture and Truth: America, Abu Ghraib, and the War on Terror*, 3), exclaimed, "[T]hese prisoners, they're not here for traffic violations. If they're in Cell Block 1-A or 1-B, these prisoners, they're murderers, they're terrorists, they're insurgents. Most of them probably have American blood on their hands, and we're so concerned about the treatment of these individuals" (Hooks and Mosher, 1628). Tom DeLay's statement is referenced in Barbara Slavin, "Don't Give up 1967 lands, DeLay Tells Israel Lobby."

3. Work on disillusionment with and/or disdain for the US-brokered Oslo Accords is as voluminous as it is varied. For some examples, see Edward Said, *Peace and Its Discontents: Essays on Palestine in the Middle East Peace Process*; Raja Shehadeh, *Palestinian Walks: Forays into a Vanishing Landscape*; Saree Makdisi, *Palestine Inside Out: an Everyday Occupation*; Rashid Khalidi, *Brokers of Deceit: How the U.S. has Undermined Peace in the Middle East*; and articles like Ilan Pappe's "More Oslos: The Two-State Solution Died Over a Decade Ago." For an extended meditation on the potentially generative politics of cynicism in Palestine, see: Lori Allen, *The Rise and Fall of Human Rights: Cynicism and Politics in Occupied Palestine*.

4. My other committee members—from disciplined and undisciplined fields across the humanities—weren't quite sure how I intended to incorporate interviews and participant observation into my research, but trusted that I would figure it out.

5. Susan Harding, *The Book of Jerry Falwell: Fundamentalist Language and Politics*; Veena Das, *Life and Words: Violence and the Descent into the Ordinary*. I have endless gratitude to Ann Laura Stoler for assigning ethnographic work that changed the way I understood colonial rule, and the detritus it leaves in its wake, and Kathleen Stewart for running her classes like writing workshops, which changed the way I wrote about what I was trying to understand.

6. Though conversations with my colleagues in anthropology have, more than once, confirmed that their "formal training," too, consisted solely of *reading ethnographies* rather than being taught how to *do* ethnography. Modeling our work on the ethnographies we read has emerged often as a shared strategy in these conversations across disciplines.

7. In fact, with the increasing neoliberalization of the public university in the USA, even shorter timelines have been introduced across campuses, including at University of Texas at Austin, where I received my PhD. At UT Austin, university officials have recently mandated a six-year cap on the PhD in American Studies even though the majority of its PhD students have to teach or serve as teaching assistants for one to two classes during every semester in order to receive their stipends and many American Studies PhD candidates do archival or ethnographic work, necessitating more time spent researching before writing.

8. I detail this racialized policing of mobility in the book when I talk about the vastly different experiences at Ben Gurion International Airport of white participants on solidarity tours and Palestinian American participants on solidarity tours, who are often detained before they are allowed entry or deported and denied entry to their homeland altogether. See also: Jennifer Lynn Kelly, "Asymmetrical Itineraries: Militarism, Tourism, and Solidarity in Occupied Palestine."

9. For more on the policing of Palestine solidarity at Israel's borders, see, for example, Robert Naiman, citing campaign organizer Mazin Qumsiyeh in

"Welcome to Palestine: 'Even Prisoners Are Allowed Visits,'" *Al Jazeera* (April 14, 2012). The article details the "Welcome to Palestine" campaign, or the Flytilla (referencing the Flotillas that have attempted to break the siege on Gaza), wherein international activists flew to Ben Gurion and declared that they were going to Palestine instead of the usual performance of "passing" as a tourist to Israel in order to get to the West Bank. These activists were not let in the country, and, often, were not even allowed to board Israel-bound planes in their home countries, evidencing not only Israeli restrictions on Palestinian movement but also Israeli restrictions on Palestinian movement building.

10. Abu Hassan, interview with author, Jerusalem, August 30, 2012.
11. Abu Hassan.
12. Stoler and Strassler, "Casting for the Colonial: Memory Work in 'New Order' Java," 4–48.
13. Cynthia Cruz, "Silence is Enough: On Emily Jacir."
14. For more on the afforestation projects that have accompanied Israeli state-craft, see Shaul Ephraim Cohen, *The Politics of Planting: Israeli-Palestinian Competition for Control of Land in the Jerusalem Periphery* and Ilan Pappé and Samer Jaber, "Ethnic Cleansing by All Means: The Real Israeli 'Peace' Policy," *Mondoweiss: The War of Ideas in the Middle East*. For more on the connections between past and present uprooting of Palestinian olive trees in the West Bank and Gaza, see Irus Braverman, "Uprooting Identities: The Regulation of Olive Trees in the Occupied West Bank," Raja Shehadeh, "The Plight of the Palestinian Olive Tree," and Samer Abdelnour, Alaa Tartir, and Rami Zurayk, citing Oxfam and Ma'an Development Center, in "Farming Palestine for Freedom: Al-Shabaka Policy Brief."

BIBLIOGRAPHY

Abdelnour, Samer, Alaa Tartir, and Rami Zurayk. 2012. Farming Palestine for Freedom: Al Shabaka Policy Brief. *Al-Shabaka: The Palestinian Policy Network*, July 2. https://al-shabaka.org/briefs/farming-palestine-freedom/. Accessed 16 April 2014.

Allen, Lori. 2013. *The Rise and Fall of Human Rights: Cynicism and Politics in Occupied Palestine*. Stanford, CA: Stanford University Press.

Braverman, Irus. 2009. Uprooting Identities: The Regulation of Olive Trees in the Occupied West Bank. *Political and Legal Anthropology Review* 32(2): 237–264.

Cohen, Shaul Ephraim. 1993. *The Politics of Planting: Israeli-Palestinian Competition for Control of Land in the Jerusalem Periphery*. Chicago, MA: University of Chicago Press.

Cruz, Cynthia. 2014, August 7. Silence is Enough: On Emily Jacir. *Hyperallergic: Sensitive to Arts & Its Discontents*. http://hyperallergic.com/142225/silence-is-enough-on-emily-jacir/. Accessed 1 September 2014.

Danner, Mark. 2004. *Torture and Truth: American, Abu Ghraib, and the War on Terror*. New York: New York Review of Books.

Das, Veena. 2006. *Life and Words: Violence and the Descent into the Ordinary*. Berkeley, CA: University of California Press.

Davidson, Lawrence. 2005. Christian Zionism as a Representation of American Manifest Destiny. *Critique: Critical Middle Eastern Studies* 14(2): 157–169.

Harding, Susan. 2000. *The Book of Jerry Falwell: Fundamentalist Language and Politics*. Princeton, NJ: Princeton University Press.

Hooks, Gregory, and Clayton James Mosher. 2005. Outrages against Personal Dignity: Rationalizing Abuse and Torture in the War on Terror. *Social Forces* 83(4): 1627–1645.

Jaber, Samer, and Ilan Pappé. 2014. Ethnic Cleansing by All Means: The Real Israeli 'Peace' Policy. *Mondoweiss: The War of Ideas in the Middle East*, October 17. http://mondoweiss.net/2014/10/ethnic-cleansing-israeli. Accessed 27 April 2015.

Lampman, Jane. 2004. Mixing Prophecy and Politics. *Christian Science Monitor*, July 7. http://www.csmonitor.com/2004/0707/p15s01-lire.html. Accessed 23 November 2007.

Kelly, Jennifer Lynn. 2016. Asymmetrical Itineraries: Militarism, Tourism, and Solidarity in Occupied Palestine. *American Quarterly*. Special Issue: Tours of Duty/Tours of Leisure, eds. Vernadette Vicuña Gonzalez, Jana K. Lipman, and Teresia Teaiwa 68(3): 723–745.

Khalidi, Rashid. 2014. *Brokers of Deceit: How the U.S. has Undermined Peace in the Middle East*. Boston: Beacon Press.

Makdisi, Saree. 2008. *Palestine Inside Out: An Everyday Occupation*. New York: W.W. Norton Company.

McAlister, Melani. 2003. Prophecy, Politics, and the Popular: The *Left Behind* Series and Christian Fundamentalism's New World Order. *South Atlantic Quarterly* 102(4): 773–798.

Naiman, Robert. 2012. Welcome to Palestine: 'Even Prisoners are Allowed Visits'. *Al Jazeera*, April 14. http://www.aljazeera.com/indepth/opinion/2012/04/201241484657679358.html. Accessed 14 May 2013.

Pappe, Ilan. 2013. More Oslos: The Two-State Solution Died Over a Decade Ago. *The Palestine Chronicle*, September 26. http://www.palestinechronicle.com/more-oslos-the-two-state-solution-died-over-a-decade-ago/#.Ukc3DWRoQ9B. Accessed 26 September 2013.

Said, Edward. 1996. *Peace and its Discontents: Essays on Palestine in the Middle East Peace Process*. New York: Vintage Press.

Shehadeh, Raja. 2007. *Palestinian Walks: Frays into a Vanishing Landscape*. New York: Scribner.

———. 2012. The Plight of the Palestinian Olive Tree. *New York Times*, November 13. http://latitude.blogs.nytimes.com/2012/11/13/the-plight-of-the-palestinian-olivetree/?_r=0

Slavin, Barbara. 2002. Don't Give up 1967 Lands, DeLay Tells Israel Lobby. *USA Today*, April 23. http://www.usatoday.com/news/world/2002/04/24/aipac.htm

Stoler, Ann Laura, and Karen Strassler. 2000. Casting for the Colonial: Memory Work in New Order Java. *Comparative Studies in Society and History* 42(1): 4–48.

CHAPTER 6

Absent Performances: Distant Fieldwork on Social Movement Theater of Algeria and India

Neil Doshi

To work on political theater in Algeria amounts to research marked by absences. Between 1989 and 2000, the country endured a brutal civil war that pit the ruling *Front de Libération Nationale* (National Liberation Front, or FLN) party against insurgent Islamist groups. Many of Algeria's leading intellectuals died or fled into exile, and as the warring factions targeted civilians, the dynamic cultural institutions that had led Algeria to be considered a "laboratory for pluralism" in the 1980s ground to a halt.[1] Memories of violence continue to shape present-day Algerian civil society, and in the cultural domain, the art and theater scenes still seek to recover the vitality that they enjoyed in the two decades following independence in 1962.[2] In this context, the study of both Algerian theater history and postindependence drama illuminates the trajectory of the young nation, making visible the desires of artists invested in imagining alternative, democratic versions of national culture to that which dominated postindependence Algeria.

Efforts to recuperate for analysis the work of major playwrights from the pre–civil war heyday of Algerian theater grate with scholarly conventions of performance studies. As a discipline that privileges the live, performance studies

I thank the *Fondation Abdelkader Alloula* and in particular Raja Alloula for her support as I completed research in Oran. I am grateful to the University of Pittsburgh Department of French and Italian, and the Dietrich School of Arts and Sciences for support received for research in Algeria.

N. Doshi (✉)
Department of French and Italian, University of Pittsburgh, Pittsburgh, USA

S. Puri, D.A. Castillo (eds.), *Theorizing Fieldwork in the Humanities*,
DOI 10.1057/978-1-349-92834-7_6

maintains a bias toward the temporal present; indeed, the fieldwork so integral to performance scholarship is all too often predicated on the simultaneity of performer and spectator in space and time.[3] What forms of performance studies scholarship are possible where there is limited or no live performance? Focusing on the work of the Algerian playwright and director Abdelkader Alloula, this chapter explores how insights drawn from performance studies might be reoriented in the Algerian context and used to both address performances in the past and nuance the reading of theater texts.

In June 2012, I traveled to Algeria to seek out actors who had worked with Alloula and to visit the *Fondation Abdelkader Alloula* (Abdelkader Alloula Foundation), which is dedicated to preserving the memory of his works. Assassinated by radical Islamists at the height of the civil war in 1994, Alloula was the leading Algerian playwright of the late twentieth century, most remembered for devising Algerian performance forms that drew on local popular culture to challenge the conventions of the Algerian stage. Alloula's vision for a decolonized and democratic national theater was importantly shaped by his career-long experience producing open-air community performance, through which he addressed diverse and frequently marginalized nonelite publics.[4] Undocumented and ill-addressed, Alloula's non-proscenium production is an expression of political desire, attention to which illuminates the alternative visions of national community that animated Alloula's practices and represented broad hopes for the independent nation.

Alloula's plays continue to be performed today, but few groups engage in outdoor performance and there are no recordings of his work in open-air settings.[5] Any discussion of Alloula's plays must further contend with an incomplete archive, and the fact that a play or spectacle is a nonrepeatable, unrecoverable event, subject to the specific conditions of its local performance.[6] Bringing archival findings and research conducted in Algeria into dialogue with fieldwork, this chapter rereads Alloula's play *El-Adjouad* (*The Generous Ones*) through both a consideration of the cultural contexts in which Alloula worked and the analysis of popular theater forms. I draw importantly on the study of analogous, popular political theater in India to underscore how performances like Alloula's create spaces for multiple modes of social expression, or sociality.[7] Rereading Alloula's text through this understanding of performance as site of social possibility, I show how the *El-Adjouad*, the text of which was published after numerous stagings, bears the trace of its performance history. Fieldwork sustains, in this analysis, heuristic models of performance that serve to expand our reading of the theater text.

NATIONAL ALLEGORIES OF THE THEATER

Alloula's work in Algeria's prominent playhouses takes center stage in any assessment of late-twentieth-century Algerian theater. He is remembered for his innovative use of popular theatrical elements in mainstream performance and for his ceaseless efforts to render the theater institutions in which he worked accessible to wider audiences. His plays continue to be performed today, but he is remembered less for the radical political potential in his theater than for his adaptation of local performance forms. In a personal interview, Alloula's wife Raja explained that alongside his professional roles, Alloula organized several amateur theater groups that ran independently of the state-sponsored institutions in which he was officially employed.[8] He consistently sought to form links through theater with marginalized publics, and by some estimates, he is said over his career to have performed in front of tens of thousands of spectators in open-air and nontraditional settings such as schoolyards, labor union headquarters, and factories.[9]

Alloula's investment in open-air theater was shaped by aesthetic concerns as much as by activism. Open-air performance enabled him to engage with storytelling forms and served as an inspiration for his production on the stages of Algeria's leading theaters. He adapted the local *halqa* (literally *circle* or *round point*) storytelling form into his practice and, through it, sought to devise performance forms that would break the Aristotelian conventions of classical theater that he saw as hinging on the passive absorption of the spectator. Alloula worked, in short, to develop an art that would simultaneously entertain audiences and inspire broad reflection on the development of democratic national culture in Algeria.[10]

Consideration of Alloula's theater career expands the notion developed by scholars like Bouziane Ben Achour, who have suggested that at their inception, postindependence Algerian theater institutions were seen as a "vector for the protection of the national spirit."[11] Understood through this metonymic relation between theater and nation, Alloula's career tracks not only the central role played by theater in defining the national culture of the new Algeria but also the tensions that arose after independence about who would constitute the national public and, by extension, the national polity. The brief survey of his career that I offer here therefore frames discussion of both the historical conditions that shaped Alloula's interest in open-air theater and the *national* debates to which it responded.

Following a period in which he acted with amateur youth groups and trained with the renowned stage director Jean Vilar at the *Théâtre national populaire* in France, Alloula joined the newly founded *Théâtre national algérien* (National Theater of Algeria, or TNA) in 1963. The first years of the TNA were both productive and marked by internal debate about such issues as the appropriate language of performance (French, Arabic, or dialect) and suitability of French adaptations on Algerian stages. These questions, and the lofty but vague ideals for the edification of the Algerian masses (*le peuple*) that the theater set as its mission, represent the larger social and political discussions that divided the nation at its outset.[12]

In 1972, following the decentralization of the TNA, Alloula was named head of the *Théatre régional d'Oran* (Regional Theater of Oran, or TRO).[13] He arranged theater workshops, invited amateur groups to perform, and, importantly, organized open-air theater performances, notable among which was the play *El-Meïda* (*The Table*, 1972), performed in support of the so-called

Agricultural Revolution, a top-down, state-sponsored initiative to nationalize agricultural production. Alloula devised the play collectively with his actors, and then staged the play numerous times in rural Algeria to rally popular support. Describing the experience in a 1989 interview, Alloula observed:

> We were taken [to rural spaces] to perform in open-air settings, literally on the construction sites of the agricultural cooperatives that were being built. We had left with an immense theater set which we had to progressively lighten as we performed, since the spectators would sit in a *halqa* [in a circle] around the performance area. This led the actors to adapt multidirectional techniques into their method.[14]

Producing *El-Meïda* crucially sparked Alloula's interest in the popular *halqa* form, elements of which he sought to integrate into his stage theater practice. Though *El-Meïda* represented initial support of governmental reform programs under President Houari Boumédiene, subsequent policies enacted by the regime clashed with Alloula's most fundamental beliefs.[15] Though Alloula made few political statements, his subsequent career was in some sense shaped by tensions between his commitment to pluralism and the policies of a state government increasingly intent on promoting a monolithic, Arabo-Muslim vision of national identity.[16]

In 1976, Alloula was promoted to head of the TNA with the mandate to revitalize the increasingly stagnant theater house. Alloula expanded the reach of the theater, arranging in-house public educational programs and workshops, and sending the TNA troupe to surrounding areas to perform on stages at a further remove from the capital. As anecdotally reported, these outreach programs invited participants to work in both local languages and Arabic dialect which, by the mid-1970s, the state sought to suppress as it imposed Modern Standard Arabic as the national language.[17] Only 11 months into his new position, however, Alloula was discharged by the Minister of Culture Taleb Ahmed Ibrahimi. Though the official record remains vague, critics have widely attributed Alloula's dismissal to the incompatibility of his cultural vision with state doctrine.[18]

Returning to Oran, Alloula resumed stage work at the TRO and subsequently produced the plays for which he is most remembered: *El-Agoual* (*The Sayings*, 1980), *El-Adjouad* (*The Generous Ones*, 1985), and *El-Litham* (*The Veil*, 1989). These plays notably allegorize the social tensions and instability that marked the decade, one in which Algeria's steps toward liberalization and multiparty politics foundered as the country grappled with economic stagnation and widespread poverty.[19] In 1989, Alloula founded the independent theater group *Coopérative théâtrale du 1er mai* (May 1 Theater Cooperative), which included both TRO and amateur actors. The group adapted *El-Adjouad*, developing the play through performance in open-air settings and in schools.[20] As political violence escalated through the 1990s, radical Islamists targeted Alloula, assassinating him in 1994.[21]

From Text to Play

Alloula's turn to open-air theater can be said to be motivated by a perceived rift between national institutions and public space, on the one hand, and a disenfranchised, heterogeneous population, on the other. It overlaps with a wave of activity in the 1970s and 1980s focused on non-proscenium political theater and collective production.[22]

Working between outdoor and stage settings, Alloula sought to develop a theater that was both in dialogue with transnational practice and representative of local form, and in this, he broke with the conventions that dominated the Algerian stage through independence. In the essay "La Représentation du type non-Aristotélicien dans l'activité théâtrale en Algérie" ("Non-Aristotelian Representation in the Algerian Theater"), Alloula observes that the plays that dominated the colonial stages through the twentieth century tended to be melodramas, vaudeville acts, and the occasional performance of French classical theater. Such programming, he maintained, was outdated for a modern Algerian stage: for him, colonial European theater was retrograde, and popular forms represented the way forward. This investment in local culture was partially mediated through Alloula's study of avant-garde theater practitioners who figured importantly in the revolutionary canon of writers assimilated by the anticolonial movements of the 1950s and 1960s. Alloula cites the works of such luminaries as Piscator, Meyerhold, and Maïakovski as having been formative for his thinking, but he reserves a special place for Bertolt Brecht, whom he describes in interviews as both his "spiritual father" and "kindred spirit."[23] Through these authors, Alloula began to articulate the potential he saw in local performance forms to devise a practice that would contribute to the *dis-alienation* of the Algerian spectator. This new theater, Alloula declared, would be "[…] guided by a vision aiming to revalue the social function of theater […] a theater where the spectator abandons traditional roles as consumer and observer to occupy a new position as *co-creator*."[24] Such statements reflect Alloula's affinity with Brecht and his critique of the tendency of plays popular on the colonial stage to assume a passive, inactive spectator.

Where Brecht produced theater on proscenium stages for a largely bourgeois public, Alloula's open-air performance addressed marginalized audiences, whose participation Alloula figured as being both physical and intellectual. Performed at the ground level, with the audience surrounding the performance area, Alloula's open-air theater allowed for direct audience participation sustained by moments in performance that allow for actor improvisation and response to the public. But Alloula equally measured participation in terms of the imaginative capacity of the spectator. As he explained it:

> I am working to create a new role for the Algerian spectator…. [I]t is with regard to this that the form of theatricality that I propose is guided by words, by speech, both in the narrative and in the agency of the story. In a particular theatrical mode, I 'offer for listening' [*je 'donne à écouter'*] a ballad or a narrative, and I invite the audience to create, to re-create with us, its own representation during

the performance. In this theater, the simultaneity of the action as speech and speech as action work in the sense of *giving the ear an opportunity to see and the eyes an opportunity to hear* [*donner à l'oreille à voir et aux yeux à entendre*].[25]

The synesthesia of hearing and sight in Alloula's phrasing emphasizes the centrality of the spectator to his thinking, and the importance he accorded to the capacity of the spectator to engage in unencumbered, subjective interpretation. Further, the statement fundamentally captures the modernity of his practice, one that broke with the realist aesthetic of the colonial stage to explore minimalist form. Alloula used the practical limitations of an itinerant, open-air performance that could only sparingly use props and costumes to his advantage, as a means of encouraging his publics to create meaning out of combinations of gesture, language, and silence.

As a local dramatic form, the *halqa* is focused on the interaction between a storyteller (or *goual*) and a responsive public that circulates in and out of an open performance space.[26] Alloula is said to have spent countless days studying performances—observing and conversing with *goualine* (storytellers) in marketplaces, studying popular poetry and the oral stories that *halqa* performers adapted. For Alloula, the *halqa* allegorized a form of democratic practice rather than a tradition, and as such, he would refer to it in his writings interchangeably as a "genre" and "perspective," thereby underlying its value as an attitude rather than as a set of unchanging formal conventions.[27]

But the "point" of open-air theater is its occasion. When bound and delivered for consumption by silent, isolated readers, Alloula's plays read as vignettes that capture glimpses of daily life, with the occasional political allusion. In their printing, they seem to have lost that other life that they had, as a product of social activism that engaged both acting bodies and spectators. How can we open texts like Alloula's to alternative readings? To cite Edward Said, who asked similar questions about theory that travels, how might we better grasp Alloula's drama in the various places and times out of which it emerges, and then measure the subsequent places where it reappears, even as nostalgic evocation of lost political promise?[28]

DISTANT FIELDWORK

Confronted with a *silent* Algerian theater, I reflect on these questions by drawing more broadly upon theater-based fieldwork experience that I conducted in India. I call this "distant fieldwork."

From August 2004 to July 2005, I observed and participated as a member of the theater group the *Jana Natya Manch* (People's Theater Group, or JANAM). Since 1976, JANAM has practiced open-air theater—or "street theater," as it is referred to there—to address marginalized audiences in urban and semirural areas primarily in and around New Delhi. Like Alloula, the group values collective production and grounds its practices in both European avant-garde theater and popular culture. Like Alloula, further, the group has had to contend with extreme violence. Founder Safdar Hashmi was brutally assassinated mid-performance in 1989, and the collective has since been led by Safdar Hashmi's partner Moloyashree and the writer/director/actor Sudhanve Deshpande.

I draw here on my experience observing and briefly training with JANAM to inform my reading of Alloula's texts. In what follows, I juxtapose an analysis of Alloula's play *El-Adjouad* (*The Generous Ones*), refracted through a brief account of the JANAM play *Ākhrī Julūs* (*The Last Strike*), to trace how direct experience of space and audience in performance can shape both notions of textuality and the reading practices that one might bring to the dramatic text. In what ways does the JANAM performance illuminate the reading of Alloula's play, facilitating the imagination of the text's performative possibilities?

Produced in 1984, *El-Adjouad* is unquestionably Alloula's most famous play, and he himself acknowledged it as the one that moved closest to the realization of his vision of modern Algerian performance. First performed in 1985 at the TRO, the play continues to be staged today in both Algeria and France. In outdoor settings, Alloula's May 1 Theater Cooperative developed and performed portions of the play as did the eponymous group *El-Adjouad* in the late 1990s. Texts of the play itself were published posthumously—a French translation in 1995 and Arabic versions in 1997 and 2009. As Lamia Bereksi has noted, the differences between the 1997 and 2009 Arabic texts indicate that the text was edited, indicating lack of an original (authoritative) script.[29] The significance of the observation takes on greater contour when aligned with recent work on the relationship between performance and dramatic text. Commenting on the ways performance studies has construed texts as "archives" in relation to which ephemeral, embodied performance is the "repertoire," William Worthen, for instance, has suggested:

> Theater often treats—or claims to treat—the book as a kind of regulatory reliquary, but it seems fairer to say that it's precisely the practices of the repertoire that intervene, imagining and creating the force of writing as performance. The repertoire materializes the process of transmission [...] that produces both a sense of what the text is, and what we might be capable of saying with and through it in/as performance.[30]

In the context of Alloula's theater, following Worthen's insight, I reverse the tendency to measure performance against the text to ask how the text has itself been imprinted by the different conditions of its staging.

Neither the Arabic nor French text versions of *El-Adjouad* present stage directions, which is wholly consistent with a popular theater performed with minimal décor. Further, one notes through the text that much of the dialogue is arranged as direct discourse quoted in a narrative by storytellers; these discursive shifts are marked in the text by quotation marks in the French and asterisks in the Arabic. In a context with few actors, one can imagine the play being staged with two or three *goualine* performing the roles of the characters they evoke. Conversely, in the sole video recording of *El-Adjouad* that I could find, a copy of a 1985 performance at the TNA that was broadcast on television, I noted a larger group of actors who would, as a *goual* narrated a story, perform the corresponding scene on stage. The play's narrative structure, organized as *a mise en abime* in which dialogues are embedded as direct discourse in the text (i.e. characters narrate dialogues), permits a fluid staging.

Consisting of seven short independent scenes, the structure of the play also lends itself to outdoor settings where spectators might frequently arrive and depart. The analysis here will focus on "Er-Rebouhi," the well-known second scene of the play.[31] The vignette rehearses a comical narrative in which the eponymous hero of the scene, the poor steelworker Er-Rebouhi Habib, takes it upon himself to save the animals of the municipal zoo, who, though under the care of the local government, suffer from neglect and starvation. To remedy the situation and preserve the public space, Er-Rebouhi organizes the youth who live in his neighborhood/district, and together, they collaborate to deliver food to the animals. As Er-Rebouhi makes his nightly feeding visits to the zoo, the creatures cease to accept the substandard fare offered by the zookeepers and are seen as having gone on "strike." The authorities suspect that they have succumbed to a pernicious external influence and work to identify the miscreant who, in their eyes, is corrupting their animals. On one of his late-night escapades, Er-Rebouhi is finally caught by the simple, but honest zoo watchman. The bulk of the scene focuses on their dialogue and the gradually shifting perspective of the watchman, who ultimately declares solidarity with Er-Rebouhi's cause.

Alloula frequently suggested that his work be thought of primarily in terms of "social critique" rather than political engagement. For him, this entailed a theater calling for social transformation, and "[...] the intervention of the masses in social life, in the organization of social life more generally."[32] Criticism has of course recognized the social relevance of Alloula's plays, which, as they celebrate the resourcefulness, guile, and common sense of his popular characters, lampoon the inequities of the bureaucratic state. Critics have equally attended to the language of Alloula's plays, which employ local Arabic dialect that Alloula painstakingly researched.[33] However, importantly, these tendencies are internal to Alloula's plays; one can deduce as much by reading the texts and consulting Alloula's writings and interviews. I use fieldwork conducted with JANAM to ask what modes of reading and understanding one might use such that the lack of performance—or associated traces in the text that gesture toward ways the performance might intervene in its specific contexts—might be keenly felt. I argue that reading for the virtual space of performance entails, in this play specifically, reading for moments of multiplicity, when the language gestures to the contingency of the spectator in creating the performance.

Overlapping historical contexts, thematic considerations, and formal elements ground the comparison of JANAM's and Alloula's production. Both JANAM and Alloula turned to open-air forms in the context of perceived autocratic shifts at the level of state government that narrowed prevailing notions of national community. In such situations, open-air theater represented a means to both affirm a pluralist vision of national belonging and inspire political action. Further, both JANAM's and Alloula's inclusive political agendas evolved in function of their association with trade unions and national communist parties, which, by the 1970s, had become the outposts of radical leftist thought in both countries. While JANAM has, since its inception, maintained an explicit alliance with the Marxist Communist Party of India (CPI-M) and the Central Indian Trade Union (CITU), the link is rather more indirect in the case of Alloula. Though his plays regularly allude to unions or union-like organizations, Alloula remained circumspect about identifying with any political party; this is due, doubtlessly, to the fact that the FLN banned the PCA in 1964 and never recognized its successor, the *Parti d'avant-garde socialiste* (Avant-garde Socialist Party, or PAGS). Anecdotal evidence suggesting that Alloula was a member of both the PCA and PAGS would seem to be borne out by the fact that the name of Er-Rebouhi is a virtual anagram of the first name of Berrahou Mejdoub, a PCA activist remembered for having organized an agricultural trade union in the Tlemcen area (not far from Oran).[34]

Methodologically, JANAM and Alloula draw eclectically from the work of avant-garde thinkers (most prominently Brecht) and local popular performance. This translates formally into the arrangement of the performance at ground level, with the audience in close proximity, frequently surrounding the spectacle. In Alloula's *halqa* and JANAM's street theater, the open performance space is seen as representative of a nonhierarchical, collective public sphere. Crucially, both Alloula's and JANAM's plays draw widely from local forms, conceived of not as a fixed, "folk" repository but rather as an evolving, heterogeneous practice, and in this regard, their plays frequently incorporate storytelling genres.[35] Many of JANAM's plays involve a *sūtradhār* (analogous to the Algerian *goual*) who circulates in and out of the performance, alternately commenting on events, addressing the audience, and playing a role.[36] Further, staged with few props, if any, both the Algerian and South Asian performance rely on gesture and speech to create meaning.

The experience of the JANAM live performance illuminates a reading of Alloula's texts, suggesting performance possibilities in the open-air contexts. Drawing on statements by both JANAM members and Alloula about the key role played by audiences in outdoor performance, this discussion focuses on spectator experience in the outdoor setting. I argue that one of the major features of the type of open-air theater JANAM and Alloula practice is that it produces possibilities for the imagination of autonomous forms of solidarity.[37] Such moments are embedded in Alloula's text and become visible through the consideration of the dynamics of the analogous, South Asian performance.

During my fieldwork period, I had the opportunity to watch JANAM's *Ākhrī Julūs* numerous times. I reflect on these experiences broadly, but focus on one performance, which took place on March 22, 2005, in Mangolpuri, an outlying area of New Delhi.[38] First performed in early 2004, in conjunction with the CPI-M political campaign to defend the right to organized labor protest in India, the play strikingly invokes both the internationalist discourses of the early-twentieth-century labor movement and the anticolonial struggle in its defense of labor protest as right.[39] *Ākhrī Julūs* focuses on two characters: an unnamed Supreme Court judge and his driver/servant, Ramdin, who find their car trapped in a traffic jam caused by a workers' strike, which, as the judge explains, will be India's last labor strike following the Supreme Court ruling. Other characters include the chorus, who appear in the performance as the group of strikers causing the disruption, and the *sūtradhār*, or chorus leader, who steps out of role in the transitions between scenes in the play to narrate events and to provide background information. The play alternates between scenes depicting dialogue between the judge and Ramdin and scenes involving the strikers, the latter of which are notable since, rather than depicting a strike procession, they feature short vignettes enacted by the strikers that are part of the strike itself. Framed by dialogues between the judge and Ramdin, each of the three scenes staged by the chorus draws from labor history to depict precedents for worker protest, thereby justifying the present-day struggle. The experience of participating in the scenes in the rally hardens the judge, but Ramdin emerges transformed and at the conclusion of the play, he himself goes on strike—his defiance rendering invalid the judge's own statement, issued at the beginning of the play, indicating that this would be India's final labor strike.

The proximity of JANAM performers and audiences facilitates moments when the performance engages the spectators. For instance, at the outset of the play, Ramdin describes the strike procession, gesturing in a broad arc that construes the audience as participants in the protest. The action signals in a real sense, the interruption to normal traffic flow that, as an instance of popular mobilization, the street play creates. Such identification is highlighted at the play's conclusion when Ramdin joins the strikers, represented by the chorus, and, as they chant slogans defending labor protest as a right, disperse into the audience, thereby signaling once again possible identification between attending spectators and public protesters. Other moments in the play similarly incorporate the audience to different effect. For instance, in the final short scene staged by the chorus/strikers (in other words, the embedded play), the actors recreate the trial of four of the labor organizers accused of having instigated the 1886 Haymarket riot. The arrangement of the scene, in which the accused face the judge to deliver short monologues indicating the inhumane working conditions leading to the strike, situates the audience as the jury. Whether construing the audience as active strikers or deliberating jury, the play works pedagogically to incite reflection on the principles behind the defense of labor protest rights.

The JANAM performance makes readable moments in Alloula's text where one can similarly imagine meaning arising out of the enactment of the play, supplementing or even supplanting the meaning of the spoken text. Consideration of the spatial arrangement of spectators and JANAM performance transforms, for instance, the reading of Er-Rebouhi's interactions in the zoo. Having entered the zoo at night, Er-Rebouhi delivers a long address as he distributes food to the malnourished animals:

Er-Rebouhi: Hello ... hello my little ones good evening.... Shh! Quiet ... this is secret!

...

Today I've brought you some quinces... If I am not mistaken I would say that the young ones stole them from Monsieur Hadj Brahim's orchard. It's pardon-able ... Pardonable ... Monsieur Hadj Brahim is filthy rich.... He has money growing out of his ears. Here!...[40]

The protagonist's monologue, justifying his actions and expressing affection, runs for two pages in the printed text of the play. Read in terms of the move-ment of JANAM theater, one imagines the actor circulating the perimeter of the stage, facing out as he speaks, addressing the audience, and effectively con-fronting the audience with the possibility they might somehow identify with the creatures subjected to the whims of the state. The frequent ellipses in the printed text indicate the staccato rhythm of his speech, which I interpret as corresponding to his movement between cages and signaling silences for pos-sible audience response. The moment of identification of the audience with the caged creatures is subsequently alluded to in the conversation between Habib and the zoo watchman. In the course of their conversation, and as the watchman realizes that Habib is in fact a well-known figure in the community, Habib observes: "But look how these poor creatures follow the conversation and desire themselves to speak, to give their opinion.... They too demand democracy."[41] Er-Rebouhi's comment sustains the allegory linking audience to creatures as it expresses the relative silencing of Algeria's minority and nonelite populations in the postindependence era.

The watchman's conversation with Er-Rebouhi also allows us to consider the watchman's gaze as a possible proxy for the spectator, and his subsequent alliance with Er-Rebouhi can then be read as serving a pedagogical purpose in the play. Er-Rebouhi frequently alludes to the fact that the youth with whom he colludes are stationed around the park, keeping watch, and prepared to intervene should anyone attempt to interrupt the plan to feed the animals. These statements open yet another interpretive possibility, allowing for the identification of the spectator with the Er-Rebouhi's collaborators.

On the one hand, as with the JANAM play, the political role for the observer is scripted—in the sense that to circulate in the zoo at night and to associate with Er-Rebouhi is an act that the state finds threatening. On the other hand, the *halqa* as an open form encourages circulation, and as such, its function is as much the opening of spaces for dialogue as it is the presentation of a nar-rative. The interpretation of the play—the situation of the audience vis-à-vis the animals and Er-Rebouhi's activist group, and the social implications of the performance—is left open and depends certainly on the place of performance. The one element linking all of these possible interpretations, however, is the notion of an autonomous social organization, represented variously in the rela-tionships that form between Er-Rebouhi, the youth, and the watchman. The agency of all of the characters is predicated on free and voluntary association, independently of structures imposed by the state.

Alloula's vision of democracy hinged on an idea of social practice grounded in a fundamental notion of equality. The idea emerges piecemeal in comments, made in interviews, about both his production methods and politics in Algeria. In a 1979 interview, for instance, Alloula explained his method of alternating between collective production and single authorship of plays. For him, the choice represented less opposing methods than a means to "allow large numbers [of actors] to create while also permitting individuals to thrive. Collective creation, after all, entails the shoring up ... of artistic potential in a framework of exchange and confrontation, in a democratic framework."[42] The insistence that Alloula placed on democratic processes as the basis for theater production finds further iteration in 1985, when he was asked to comment on political theater in Algeria. Alloula suggested that, "[i]t turns out that we don't have great [democratic] traditions to draw from. We are all learning what democracy is. One sees this every day in union meetings for instance."[43] Such comments illustrate how democracy represented for Alloula a horizon of symbolic meanings that evolve out of social practice rather than state institutions.

Reading Alloula's play through the JANAM performance suggests ways one might extend Alloula's discussion of theater composition to outdoor performance itself as a space of negotiation, exchange, and confrontation. At the most simple level, this is visible in terms of the organization of outdoor performance, where audience members are free to circulate; performances interrupt the flow of public life, opening spaces for passersby to become spectators engaged in performance, or to interact with one another. At another level, as plays like *Ākhrī Julūs* illustrate, the arrangement of spectators around a performance area creates openings in which the spectator's attention is called to the act of spectating; whether one is immediately proximate to the performance area or withdrawn with an obstructed view (a view limited by other spectators), one is immediately conscious of those nearby and those facing the performance across the stage. One therefore both hears and sees fellow audience members who, whether or not they participate directly in the performance, at least partly occupy the attention of the attending spectator.

The attention audience members give to each other and their own spectatorship is integral to the performance, and indeed, contributes to meaning. As an illustrative example, I turn to a moment early in the play *Ākhrī Julūs*, when the judge and Ramdin found themselves stopped in the congestion caused by the labor protest. As the judge deliberates how to extricate himself from the traffic jam, Ramdin naively suggests that as an authority figure, the judge should be able to issue an order to disperse the crowd. "What if you just snap your fingers?" he asks. Clearly accustomed to the use of such gestures that serve as a fillip to his decrees, the judge vainly snaps his fingers, much to the amusement of the spectators closest to the stage. From the first moments of the play, the crowd was clearly set up to expect the judge to be little more than a caricature, so the action was unsurprising. What was notable, however, is that spectators at a slight remove from the performance area, where the normal ambient noise was more audible, could not hear the judge snapping his fingers. As I experienced it as well, when behind three or four other spectators, one has an obstructed view of the stage, and not all the movements of actors are visible. In such a situation, the spectator is reliant upon the audible and visible reaction of fellow audience members, which provide cues as to what is transpiring on stage. It was common, moreover, to observe that during moments of particular vociferous audience reaction, spectators at further remove from the performance area would turn to a neighbor to discuss what was understood as having happened.

These processes, in which interaction between performance and audience activates different senses and shapes spectatorial attention, emerge out of the live performance. Though impossible to read definitively in Alloula's play, there are nonetheless ways the text gestures to such dynamics. Consider for instance the moment the watchman confronts Er-Rebouhi. When the latter reveals his name, the watchman refuses to believe that the small disheveled man before him is a figure of local renown. Incredulous, he states: "In truth, I don't know Er-Rebouhi Habib the steelworker.... But they say that he is tall, strong, and hardy ... According to what they say, he has presence...! But you...."[44]

Er-Rebouhi produces his identity card, but the Watchman suggests that as he is unable to read, he cannot verify its holder's identity, but what ultimately convinces the watchman is Er-Rebouhi's suggestion that his final proof would be to call out, so that his collaborators—the youth who keep watch as he feeds the animals—present themselves. Er-Rebouhi's discourse and the suggestion that he is accompanied by members of his community are enough to convince the watchman of his interlocutor's veracity. The watchman responds: "Ah, that's it then! That's why from time to time they [Er-Rebouhi's collaborators] would stop to ask me the time or directions to the train station!... It was to turn my attention elsewhere! It was a strategic move!"[45] If one considers that the watchman and the youth offer two different proxies that channel the audience gaze, this moment marks one in which the watchman symbolically negotiates his understanding of what he sees in terms of the Er-Rebouhis's youth. In this way, Alloula's play figures in its content forms of joint or social spectatorship that are the potential of the live performance.

As the criticism emerging out of the "sonic turn" in performance studies suggests, such experiences are not exclusive to outdoor theater forms.[46] Theater critics are increasingly paying attention to questions about attention as an active process that is shaped jointly by sound, visual stimuli, and the co-presence of spectators. However, I would argue that in the case of a JANAM play or Alloula performance, these experiences are integral to the political practices that the plays represent: in other words, to reuse Alloula's terms, the exchanges and confrontations out of which common political sensibilities are forged hinge on the cues that audience members share. Read through recent work at the nexus of phenomenology and performance studies, moreover, this dynamic is linked to forms of embodiment.[47] Considered as a form of exertion, the act of attending—paying attention—can be understood as inscribing a dialectic between body and the world. Through a physical layout that intensifies the experience of attending audiences, the theater I address here intensifies the embodying effect of attention through the triangulation of performance, individual spectator, and collective audience.

To think of outdoor theater forms like JANAM's and Alloula's as engaged in a politics that involves embodiment takes on even deeper significance when one considers the demographic of their audiences. In the case of Alloula, open-air collective forms began to flourish at the precise moment when minority and, to a significant degree, nonelite populations were written out of the national contract represented by the 1976 constitution.[48] Whether audience members engage the spectacle or simply enter the space of the popular performance—a space where different forms of personal engagement become possible—the JANAM example illustrates the ways audience members become comprehensible to each other as acting, sensing subjects collectively forming an audience. This is not to say that every performance is the same, or that the "success" of any spectacle is measurable. Rather, in a context where the efficacy of genres like street theater are all too often measured in terms of the physical transformation of space and the direct participation of the spectator, JANAM's and Alloula's theater alert us to ways open-air theater is equally or perhaps even more invested in opening spaces for fluid, intersubjective audience relations.

If the JANAM performance renders "readable" certain aspects of Alloula's performance, the space of Oran illuminates the local stakes of Alloula's practices. As Raja Alloula had suggested to me, Alloula devoted his production of open-air theater to the poorest quarters of the city—neighborboods like *Ras El-Aïn* and *Kouchet El Djir* that house *bidonvilles* or slums. As areas the populations of which exploded in the 1970s during a period of heavy migration from rural to urban areas, these neighborboods are within the limits of the city. Zoning and land use legislation hold little sway here, and ongoing municipal efforts have repeatedly sought to relocate residents and demolish these "favelas," as they are sometimes called.[49] These neighborhoods are notable for their relative proximity to the Oran zoo, and in a context where even today these neighborhoods are deprived of basic municipal services, one can imagine the public park as a flashpoint for tensions around public space and accessibility.[50] Alloula's play in fact makes an indirect allusion to these spaces. Speaking to the watchman, Er-Rebouhi suggests:

> Er-Rebouhi: This park is not far from the more popular districts… The well-off don't bring their children to this garden; they take them rather to Europe to see animals and to enjoy distractions that we don't have in this country. We believe that this park is the park of the people, if you will. The park for the children, in any case…."[51]

Er-Rebouhi's mention of domestic economic disparity underscores his shared class position with the watchman, and their shared project becomes the reclamation of national space. There is little record of the condition of the Oranais park when Alloula wrote his play, so I do not know if the preservation of the zoo was indeed an issue. But what the present-day space makes palpable is that, whether or not the performance materially transformed communities or spaces, there is an important political dimension of performance that fosters the emergence of modes of relation in an audience that is otherwise invisible and in an extreme state of dispossession.

CONCLUSION

Much current anthropological work focused on multisite fieldwork considers varying sites within a single cultural field or within the nation-state.[52] In this chapter, I have sought to work across cultural and political boundaries, but without assuming the types of transference and equivalence sustained by theories of universal theater or intercultural theater. To be sure, there is an argument to be made recognizing that there are global discourses of political theater focused on empowering forms of audience interaction. But in this chapter, observations gathered during fieldwork serve less as a basis for the generalization of commonalities across genres than as an illustration of the processes and social dynamics of performance that can be fruitfully applied to readings of Alloula's scripts. In a context where Alloula's texts have tended to be celebrated for either their reference to "authentic" local form or their political commentary, I suggest that live performance signals alternative interpretive possibilities marked by moments of indeterminacy in the text. Put another way, performance fieldwork focused on JANAM both raises questions about the embodiment of Alloula's plays and suggests that the democratic thrust *in performance* hinges as much on the parody of existing power structures as it does on the creation of spaces for alternative modes of sociality. The combination of proximate fieldwork in the strikingly still-present neighborhoods of Alloula's performance with distant fieldwork on JANAM's inspires a nuanced view of Alloua's outdoor performance that recognizes the ways spectacle interrupts daily life to create spaces for the emergence of democratic social relations.

NOTES

1. Luis Martinez, *La guerre civile en Algérie, 1990–1998*, 12. For an assessment of the civil war that attends to the different Islamist factions involved, see Abderrahmane Moussaoui, *De la violence en Algérie: les lois du chaos*.
2. Assia Djebar's compelling memoire *Les Blancs de l'Algérie* narrates the sense of personal and broader cultural loss that accompanied, during the civil war, the passing away of many of Algeria's major cultural figures. See Assia Djebar, *Les Blancs de l'Algérie*. For an assessment of the lasting impact of Algeria's civil war on the nation's social life, see Ahmed Cheniki, "Le Théâtre Politique: l'expérience algérienne," 8–9; and Kamel Daoud, "The Algerian Exception."

3. Regarding this simultaneity, which is sometimes referred to as "liveness," see Henry Bial, "Performance Studies 3.0."

4. In this chapter, I have only addressed Alloula's theater. Readers interested in his work in cinema and his successful acting career may consult Dominique, Bax, *Kateb Yacine & Abdelkader Alloula: du théâtre au cinéma*.

5. Regarding contemporary outdoor performances of Alloula, the exceptions are the performances staged in the late 1990s by the theater group *El-Adjouad*, led by Kheireddine Lardjam.

6. For a useful assessment of performance in terms of "eventness," see Elin Diamond, *Performance and Cultural Politics*.

7. I define "sociality" as a dynamic, malleable relational matrix in which individuals interact. As such, in this definition, sociality indicates less ties or bonds than ongoing, evolving processes of interaction. See Nicholas J. Long and Henrietta L. Moore, eds., *Sociality: New Directions*.

8. "Amateur theater," here, does not imply a qualitative distinction. The expression has been used widely in Algerian theater histories to distinguish full-time professional actors from those who are not—it is a simple shorthand that does not necessarily convey a level of training or capacity for theater work.

9. See Hadj, Dahmane, *Le théâtre algérienalgérie : de l'engagement à la contestation* and Raja Alloula, "Etre artiste, c'est toute une vie," Abdelkader Alloula (blog), January 27, 2007.

10. Alloula, See interview by B.K., "Tête à tête avec Alloula," *Algérie Actualité*, June 1–7, 1969.

11. Ben Achour, *Le théâtre en mouvement Octobre 88 à ce jour*, 29. Unless otherwise indicated, all translations are mine.

12. Articles 1, 5, and 7 of the TNA's founding charter clearly underscore the central but still vague role the theater was to play in the edification of the masses. See Algerian Ministry of Culture, *Décret n° 63–12 du 8 janvier 1963 portant sur l'organisation du théâtre algérien* (1963).

13. For a more detailed account of Alloula's career, see bio-bibliographic entries in Chowki Abdelamir and Association Abdelkader Alloula, *En mémoire du futur: pour Abdelkader Alloula*.

14. Abdelamir, *En mémoire du futur*, 143–4.

15. Houari Boumediène had overthrown Algeria's first president, Ahmed Ben Bella, in 1965. Through his tenure as president, Boumediène consolidated state power through an increasingly technocratic regime. For succinct histories of 1960s Algeria, see Phillip Chiviges Naylor, *France and Algeria: A History of Decolonization and Transformation*; Hugh Roberts, *The Battlefield Algeria, 1988–2002: Studies in a Broken Polity*.

16. As part of a nation-building project, the Boumediene regime sought in the 1970s to pass reform establishing Algeria as a singularly Arabo-Islamic nation with Modern Standard Arabic as its official language. While such policies consolidated state power, they also alienated ethnic and linguistic

minorities in the nation. For more, see essays on politics of language collected in Anne-Emmanuelle Berger, ed., *Algeria in Others' Languages*; Stora and Majumdar, in Margaret A. Majumdar and Mohammed Saad, eds., *Transition and Development in Algeria: Economic, Social and Cultural Challenges*.

17. For a history of language conflict in Algeria, see Mohamed Benrabah, *Language Conflict in Algeria: From Colonialism to Post-independence*.

18. See Raja Alloula, "Etre artiste…" and Ali Hadj, "Alloula au Théâtre National Algérien: Une expérience brisée nette." *Alger-republicain*, http://www.alger-republicain.com/Alloula-au-Theater-National.html.

19. Following Boumediène's death in 1978, Chadli Benjedid assumed the presidency to oversee an Algeria rendered instable by the oil crisis and resistance to both the government liberalization schemes and policies around Arabization. Such factors directly contributed to the rise in popularity of Islamist factions. In 1989, to secure a mandate to govern, and to comply with IMF terms of assistance, Benjedid ratified a new constitution legalizing opposition political parties. Unexpectedly, however, the *Front du Salut Islamique* (*Islamic Salvation Front* or FIS) swept the subsequent elections. Alarmed at the possibility of an Islamic government, civilian and military cadres (loyal to the FLN) overthrew President Benjedid and outlawed the FIS—sliding the country into civil conflict.

20. These interests in public theater are reflected equally in Alloula's last stage play, a free adaptation/translation of Carlo Goldoni's *Harlequin, Servant of Two Masters* (1993) that draws on commedia dell'arte forms.

21. The *Front islamique pour le djihad armé* (*Islamic Front for Armed Djihad*, or FIDA) claimed responsibility for the killing, but the assassins were never fully investigated after the war, since insurgent Islamists were granted amnesty in 2005 to ensure a durable peace. Among the reasons posited for the attack is that at the time of the assassination, Alloula had been working on a modern, Arabic adaptation of Molière's *Tartuffe* (*The Imposter*), which was, of course, the famous eighteenth-century play that lampoons the figure of the religious hypocrite.

22. Alloula's most well-known contemporary was Kateb Yacine, who, after establishing himself as Algeria's leading Francophone author, ceased publishing and dedicated himself to producing forms of political outdoor theater. For more on the open-air theater in Algeria, see Khalid Amine and Marvin Carlson, *The Theatres of Morocco, Algeria and Tunisia: Performance Traditions of the Maghreb*; Hadj Dahmane, *Le théâtre algérien: de l'engagement à la contestation*; and D. Le Boucher and J. Dumont, "L'univers d'Alloula: témoignage de Lakhdar Moktari, comédien," 253–60.

23. Abdelkader Alloula, interview by M'Hamed Djellid, October 1985, "Abdelkader Alloula parle des *Généreux*, du théâtre," transcript, Library of the *Institut du monde arabe*, Paris. Lest one too quickly describe Alloula's work as derivative of European traditions, it should be remembered that

such categorizations are problematic, not least of all since Brecht's own work emerges out of his understanding of Chinese opera. For more on Brecht's genealogy, see Carol J. Martin, "Brecht, Feminism, and Chinese Theater," 77–85.

24. Alloula, "Abdelkader Alloula parle...".

25. Alloula. My emphasis added; the use of quotes is as in the original transcription of the interview.

26. For more on the *halqa* form, see Khalid Amine and Marvin Carlson, *The Theatres of Morocco, Algeria and Tunisia: Performance Traditions of the Maghreb*.

27. Alloula's vision of popular culture as practice might be usefully contrasted with the general concept of "folk." As David Lloyd has suggested: "[T]he fetishization of 'folk culture' as a fixed and primordial expression of a transcendental people is in fact most often itself an idée fixe of official state culture deployed in the monumental rituals and ceremonies that perform the identity of citizen and state. Popular culture continues its complex and partially self-transforming, partially subordinated existence in the shadow of the state." See David Lloyd, "Nationalisms against the State," 189.

28. Edward Said, *The World, the Text, and the Critic*, 242.

29. See Bereksi Meddahi, *Abdelkader Alloula: culture populaire et jeux d'écriture dans l'oeuvre théâtrale*.

30. William B. Worthen, "Antigone's Bones," 12.

31. The scene has in fact frequently been staged as a stand-alone performance—most recently at the time of the writing of this chapter, in March 2015 at the TNA.

32. Mohammed Habib, Samrakandi and J. F. Clément, eds., *Le théâtre arabe au miroir de lui-même et son contact avec les créations des deux rives de la Méditerranée*, 16.

33. Alloula wrote all of his plays in the colloquial, Algerian Arabic, *derija*. For my English translations of his plays, I have referred to the French translation that was prepared for the staging of the play in France in 1995 (translated by Messaoud Benyoucef), and in addition, I have referred to Lamia Bereksi's notes, corrections, and commentary on the published Arabic text and its French translation.

34. For an account of a meeting between Alloula and Mejdoub, see Boualem, Lechlech, "Quelques Souvenirs avec Abdelkader Alloula."

35. As JANAM founder Safdar Hashmi famously suggested, "Tradition is to be found in our lived atmosphere, over living environment; such tradition naturally infuses our work and our experiments." "Pāramparik Rūpoṇ aur Devices ke Savāl," In *The Right to Perform: Selected Writings of Safdar Hashmi*, 57.

36. In the Sanskritic tradition, the *sūtradhār* (*sūtra*: thread; *dhār*: one who holds) is the leader of the chorus. The *sūtradhār* is a narrator of events, a commentator on characters, and one who holds the plot together.

37. I use the term "autonomy" here to refer to forms of moral and political agency in a context where persons are recognized as being socially embedded and shaped by complex social determinants.

38. I choose this particular performance because it represented a performance staged well after the play was devised, at a point when the broad narrative of the play was stable—though small variances could be detected between performances due to environmental factors, the attending audience, sounds, and events particular to the site of performance.

39. In the landmark case *T.K. Rangarajan vs. Government of Tamil Nadu and Others* in August 2003, the Supreme Court of India both ordered striking government workers to end their work stoppage and issued a ruling that denied government workers the right to engage in future organized labor protest. The judgment set worrying precedent and represented a breach of the International Labor Organization (ILO) conventions.

40. Abdelkader Alloula, *Les Généreux: Les Généreux, Les Dires, Le Voile*, trans. Messaoud Benyoucef, 26.

41. Alloula, 33.

42. Alloula, interview by B.K., "Le cœur sur les planches."

43. Kahoua and Saadi eds., *Abdelkader Alloula, vingt ans déjà!*, 25.

44. Alloula, *Les Généreux...*, 30.

45. Alloula, 34.

46. See Jim Drobnick, ed., *Aural Cultures*; Lynne Kendrick and David Roesner, eds., *Theatre Noise: The Sound of Performance*.

47. See George Home-Cook, *Theater and Aural Attention: Stretching Ourselves*.

48. As Jane Goodman has suggested, "It was as if the equality and 'brotherhood' (*fraternité*) of all Algerians—a cherished national value in the aftermath of more than a century of subaltern exclusions—could be fashioned only through a rubric of homogeneity." "The Man behind the Curtain: theatrics of the state in Algeria," 782.

49. See "Les Planteurs, Ras El-Aïn, Kouchet El-Djir: Près De 41.000 Constructions Illicites Recensées."

50. The degree to which spaces like Kouchet El Djir lack services is reflected in the fact that many parts of these neighborhoods are only accessible by foot due to poor roads/lack of clear pathways, and strewn rubbish.

51. Alloula, *Les Généreux...*, 30.

52. See, for instance, Lila Abu-Lughod, "Locating Ethnography," 261–67 and George Marcus, *Ethnography Through Thick and Thin*.

Bibliography

Abdelamir, Chowki, and Association Abdelkader Alloula. 1997. *En mémoire du futur: pour Abdelkader Alloula*. Arles: Sindbad; Actes Sud.

Abu-Lughod, Lila. 2012. Locating Ethnography. *Ethnography* 1(2): 261–267.

Alloula, Abdelkader. 1969. Tête à tête avec Alloula. Interview by B.K. *Algérie Actualité*, June 1–7.

———. 1979. Le cœur sur les planches. Interview by M. Blidi. *Algérie Actualité*, March 3–9.

———. 1985, October. Interview by M'Hamed Djellid. Abdelkader Alloula parle des *Généreux*, du théâtre. Transcript, Library of the *Institut du monde arabe*, Paris.

———. 1995. *Les Généreux: Les Généreux, Les Dires, Le Voile*. Trans. Messaoud Benyoucef. Arles: Actes Sud.

———. 2009. *'Abd al-Qādir 'Allūlah: dīwān a'mālihī al-kāmilah*. Oran: Les 3 Pommes.

Alloula, Raja. 2011. Personal Interview. July 14.

———. 2014. Etre artiste, c'est toute une vie. Abdelkader Alloula Blog. December 29.

Alloula, Raja. n.d. *Abdelkader Alloula* (blog). http://abdelkaderalloula.over-blog.com/

Amine, Khalid, and Marvin Carlson. 2012. *The Theatres of Morocco, Algeria and Tunisia: Performance Traditions of the Maghreb*. New York: Palgrave Macmillan.

Bax, Dominique. 2003. *Kateb Yacine & Abdelkader Alloula: du théâtre au cinéma*. Collection Magic Cinéma Hors-Série. Bobigny: Magic cinéma.

Ben Achour, Bouziane. 2002. *Le théâtre en mouvement Octobre 88 à ce jour*. Oran: Dar el Gharb.

Benrabah, Mohamed. 2013. *Language Conflict in Algeria: From Colonialism to Post-independence*. Bristol: Multilingual Matters.

Bereksi Meddahi, Lamia. 2012. *Abdelkader Alloula: culture populaire et jeux d'écriture dans l'oeuvre théâtrale*. Approches littéraires. Paris: Harmattan.

Berger, Anne-Emmanuelle, ed. 2002. *Algeria in Others' Languages*. Ithaca, NY: Cornell University Press.

Bial, Henry. 2014. Performance Studies 3.0. In *Performance Studies in Motion: International Perspectives and Practices in the Twenty-first Century*, eds. Atay Citron, Sharon Aronson-Lehavi, and David Zerbib, 30–41. London: Bloomsbury.

Cheniki, Ahmed. 2002. *Le théâtre en Algérie: histoire et enjeux*. Edisud: Aix-en-Provence.

———. 2013, December. Le Théâtre Politique: l'expérience algérienne. *Le Soir d'Algérie* 22: 8–9.

Dahmane, Hadj. 2011. *Le théâtre algérien: de l'engagement à la contestation*. Paris: Orizons.

Daoud, Kamel. 2015. The Algerian Exception. *The New York Times*, May 29. http://www.nytimes.com/2015/05/30/opinion/the-algerian-exception.html?_r=0

Diamond, Elin. 1996. *Performance and Cultural Politics*. London: Routledge.

Djebar, Assia. 1995. *Le Blanc de l'Algérie*. Paris: A. Michel.

Drobnick, Jim, ed. 2004. *Aural Cultures*. Toronto: YYZ Books.

Goodman, Jane E. 2013. The Man Behind the Curtain: Theatrics of the State in Algeria. *The Journal of North African Studies* 18(5): 779–795.

Hadj Ali, Smaïl . 2014. Alloula au Théâtre National Algérien: Une expérience brisée nette. *Alger-republicain*. http://www.alger-republicain.com/Alloula-au-Theater-National.html. Accessed 5 September 2014.

Hashmi, Safdar. 1989. Pāramparik Rūpoṇ aur Devices ke Savāl. In *The Right to Perform: Selected Writings of Safdar Hashmi*, ed. Madhu Prasad, 50–60. New Delhi: SAHMAT.

Home-Cook, George. 2015. *Theater and Aural Attention: Stretching Ourselves*. New York: Palgrave Macmillan.

Jana Natya Manch. 2005, March 22. *Ākhrī Julūs*. Performance by the Jana Natya Manch, Mangolpuri, New Delhi, India.

Kaouah, Abdelmadjid, and Nourredine Saadi, eds. 2014. *Abdelkader Alloula, vingt ans déjà!* Algiers: Les Editions Apic.

Kendrick, Lynne, and David Roesner, eds. 2011. *Theatre Noise: The Sound of Performance*. Newcastle upon Tyne: Cambridge Scholars Pub.

Khadda, Jawida, and Naget Khadda. 1994. Abdelkader Alloula. *Annuaire de l'Afrique du Nord* 33: 531–541.

Le Boucher, D., and J. Dumont. 1997. L'univers d'Alloula: témoignage de Lakhdar Moktari, comédien. *Algérie Littérature/Action*. 14: 253–260.

Lechlech, Boualem. 2014. Quelques Souvenirs avec Abdelkader Alloula. *Socialgerie*, June 22. http://www.socialgerie.net/IMG/pdf/Quelques_souvenirs_avec_Abdelkader_Alloula_1_.pdf. Accessed 22 June 2015.

Les Planteurs, Ras El-Aïn, Kouchet El-Djir: Près De 41.000 Constructions Illicites Recensées. 2014. *Le Quotidien D'Oran*, December 2. http://www.lequotidien-oran.com/index.php?news=5206790&archive_date=2014-12-02

Lloyd, David. 1997. Nationalisms Against the State. In *The Politics of Culture in the Shadow of Capital*, eds. Lisa Lowe, and David Lloyd, 173–197. Durham: Duke UP.

Long, Nicholas J., and Henrietta L. Moore, eds. 2013. *Sociality: New Directions*. New York: Berghahn Books.

Majumdar, Margaret A., and Mohammed Saad, eds. 2005. *Transition and Development in Algeria: Economic, Social and Cultural Challenges*. Portland, OR: Intellect.

Marcus, George E. 1998. *Ethnography Through Thick and Thin*. Princeton, NJ: Princeton University Press.

Martin, Carol J. 1999. Brecht, Feminism, and Chinese Theater. *TDR: The Drama Review* 43(4): 77–85.

Martinez, Luis. 1998. *La guerre civile en Algérie, 1990–1998*. Paris: Karthala.

Ministry of Culture, Algeria. 1963. *Décret n° 63-12 du 8 janvier 1963 portant sur l'organisation du théâtre algérien*.

Moussaoui, Abderrahmane. 2006. *De la violence en Algérie: les lois du chaos*. Arles: Actes sud/MMSH.

Naylor, Phillip Chiviges. 2000. *France and Algeria: A History of Decolonization and Transformation*. Gainesville: University Press of Florida.

Roberts, Hugh. 2003. *The Battlefield Algeria, 1988–2002: Studies in a Broken Polity*. London: Verso.

Said, Edward W. 1983. *The World, the Text, and the Critic*. Cambridge, MA: Harvard University Press.

Salah, C. 2011. Des milliers de personnes y vivent dans un danger omniprésent: Ras El-Aïn, Une bombe à retardement. *Le Quotidien D'Oran*, February 27. http://www.lequotidien-oran.com/index.php?news=5149808&archive_date=2011-02-27

Samrakandi, Mohammed Habib, and J.F. Clément, eds. 2008. *Le théâtre arabe au miroir de lui-même et son contact avec les créations des deux rives de la Méditerranée*. Toulouse: Presses universitaires du Mirail.

Worthen, William B. 2008. Antigone's Bones. *TDR: The Drama Review* 52(3): 10–33.

CHAPTER 7

Ethical Dilemmas in Studying Blogging by Favela Residents in Brazil

Tori Holmes

In an early, and influential, ethnographic study of the internet, anthropologist Daniel Miller and sociologist Don Slater argued for the central importance of empirical work for the development of this field of research:

> Social thought has gained little by attempting to generalize about 'cyberspace', 'the Internet', 'virtuality'. It can gain hugely by producing material that will allow us to understand the very different universes of social and technical possibility that have developed around the Internet.[1]

Inspired by this assertion, and taking up Miller and Slater's challenge from a language-based area studies perspective, I reflect on the place and contribution of empirical fieldwork in a research project on digital culture in Brazil, which looked at blogging by Brazilian favela residents. It combined analysis of digital texts with data collected on the practices involved in their production and circulation. Situated within an academic trajectory that has moved from the humanities toward the social sciences, becoming fundamentally interdisciplinary in the process, the research attests to the feasibility and rewards of fieldwork in the humanities, but also highlights some of the key challenges raised by fieldwork in general, and fieldwork on digital culture in particular, to existing humanities ways of working.

Drawing on this example from my practice, I present fieldwork as a process and experience of "in-betweenness," involving the crossing of imagined or real boundaries between humanities and social sciences ways of working, between

T. Holmes (✉)
School of Arts, English, and Languages, Queen's University Belfast,
Belfast, Northern Ireland, UK

© The Author(s) 2016
S. Puri, D.A. Castillo (eds.), *Theorizing Fieldwork in the Humanities*,
DOI 10.1057/978-1-349-92834-7_7

cultural works and the human practices surrounding them, and between encounters on the internet and in person/in place. A hybrid form of field-work, it creates a space for dialogue with both humanities and social science traditions. However, the dual focus on texts and practices in relation to digital culture required me to negotiate complex methodological and ethical issues relating to the status of bloggers as human subjects or authors and to consider the implications for the status of their content in the study. As a result, I argue that humanities scholars should be open to learning and borrowing from disciplines more experienced in fieldwork, but also that the social sciences do not offer all the answers for humanities projects, requiring us to develop our own discourse. I hope to demonstrate, in particular, that there is an urgent need for the humanities to engage with research ethics and to provide models for combining the analysis of textual data with data collected through interviews, interactions, and observations.

Researching Favela Bloggers: Following the Content and Following the People

The last 10 to 15 years have seen the emergence of a range of digital content about Brazilian favelas, for example, photography, audiovisual material, and texts of different types produced by their residents. Reflecting the striking growth in access to digital technologies in Brazil as a whole over this period,[2] self-representational content has become available via blogs, Twitter, profiles and groups on social network sites, photo- and video-sharing platforms, thematic websites, and citizen journalism initiatives, among others. This development has worked against a long-standing and marked tendency for Brazilian mainstream media and cultural production to employ stereotypes when portraying these areas of the city. Such external representations have often failed to grasp and convey the complexity and diversity of favelas, positioning them instead erroneously as homogeneous territories of poverty and violence, and as extraneous and unconnected to the city proper.[3] The representation of place was thus a particular concern of my research on digital local content creation in favelas, with blogs chosen as the primary focus for their more explicitly contestatory stance on this issue, as well as their engagement with potential audiences from outside the favela. However, the study also took into consideration other digital platforms, such as email, and sometimes print formats, as a result of the attention afforded to practices involved in the production and circulation of blog content.

My decision to undertake fieldwork as part of the study was guided by my core research questions, namely, How did residents of a Rio de Janeiro favela represent their neighborhood in public internet content, and what tools did they use for publishing and disseminating this content? Who was the intended audience for these representations, and how did they differ from mainstream representations of the favela? How did content creators "territorially embed" their content?[4] How did they negotiate the translocal visibility afforded by the internet? What was the significance of these user-generated representations for understandings of the city of Rio de Janeiro? My intention was thus not only to analyze and interpret internet content produced by favela residents as "text" but also to develop an understanding of the motivations and practices of those involved in this type of activity and gain access to their own narratives and interpretations of their blogging. While the focus on blogs and associated content means the study can be understood as "paraliterary," the methodological shift goes beyond the type of material analyzed, to the position from which the engagement takes place.

My research led to the development of three in-depth case studies of individual content creators from the Complexo da Maré area of northern Rio de Janeiro. According to the census conducted by a local nongovernmental organization, Centro de Estudos e Ações Solidárias da Maré (CEASM), Maré was home to 132,000 people in 2001,[5] making it one of the largest favela complexes in Rio. It is made up of 16 different communities and was recognized as a formal neighborhood, or *bairro*, in 1994, although it continues to be widely thought of as a favela. Maré is particularly visible in Rio de Janeiro and beyond for its location (on the shores of Guanabara Bay and close to three important expressways, including the main route into the city from the international airport), its historic association with *palafitas* (houses built on stilts over water, now long gone), which led to a widespread and persistent perception of it as a poor area, and its public security situation, with the presence in recent years of a military police battalion, militias and rival drug factions in the area contributing to its marked stigmatization.[6] In March 2014, Maré was occupied by the Brazilian army, in preparation for the future installation of a Pacifying Police Unit (UPP) in the area; the army withdrew in June 2015, when it handed over to the military police (PM) as part of this process, but plans for pacification were suspended in March 2016 due to budgetary constraints. Notably, Maré has given rise to influential NGOs, which have taken a critical stance on the representation of favelas (in particular CEASM, the Observatório de Favelas, and Redes da Maré); it has also been the site of several community media initiatives, individual bloggers and other content creators. The activities of these different actors can be understood as contesting the terms of the area's visibility.

My fieldwork on the work of bloggers from Maré lasted for 13 months in 2009–2010 and involved observation, participant observation, interviews, and textual and visual analysis of content. The overall guiding principle was that of "following the content." This was a responsive and mobile practice, influenced by anthropology, ethnography, new literacy studies, and internet studies,[7] which enabled me to track the circulation and framing of blog texts and to react to and pursue connections arising in the content. In the context of my study, observation meant monitoring blogs and other websites, including those of the mainstream media, through regular visits and really simple syndication (RSS) updates,[8] taking screenshots of new content and design features, following relevant links and recording notes and my thoughts in my online field diary. I did not myself engage in content production as a fieldwork strategy, but positioned the reception of content as an active process and, in Crawford's words, "an embedded part of networked engagement—a necessary corollary to having a 'voice.'"[9] However, as well as following content flows online, the methodology also depended on the development of a rapport with bloggers and interaction with them on the internet and face-to-face, in order to complement my own observations of content framing and circulation with the bloggers' own narratives on their practices. In this way, the "following the content" approach also implied "following the people," in an acknowledgment of the presence of "texts and practices, or content and people" at the heart of the study.[10]

For illustration in this chapter, I focus on the fieldwork relationship developed with one of these Maré bloggers, whom I call A., and the analysis of her texts and practices in response to the research questions outlined above. At the time of the research, A. was a mature student and mother who ran her own literary blog, served as the administrator of a literary community, or group, on the social network site Orkut,[11] and was using different internet channels to promote a collection of short stories recently launched by a small Rio-based publisher, in which one of her own had been included. These were relatively recent activities, and A. was categorical and enthusiastic about the difference the internet had made in her trajectory. She described the difficulties she had faced on returning to education after a 15-year gap, not having a computer to use in carrying out research for her *pré-vestibular* (university entrance) course, and having to physically go to places to fill in forms by hand. When she heard that she had been accepted on a university course, she finally acquired a computer of her own. Laughing, she recalled her happiness at this moment, telling me, "When the computer finally arrived, I said: man, the time has come, the world is mine! And really, that's how it was, more or less like that. It opened up an incredible window."

Having identified the relevance of her digital output to my study (although her literary texts did not explicitly mention Maré, her blog profile information explicitly stated she was a proud resident of the area), I established contact by email; the interaction then developed to include MSN chat sessions, further email exchanges, and the inclusion of my email address in a mailing list of sorts through which A. shared news about print publications, new blog posts, literary competitions, and other relevant information. I also met A. in person on a number of occasions, in Maré and elsewhere, from chatting over a cold drink when I went to the favela to collect my copy of the short story anthology mentioned above, to attendance at launch events for her later self-published books at a cultural center in a suburban area of northern Rio de Janeiro, where I met some of her friends and family. I also conducted an in-depth, recorded interview at her home, part of which happened in front of her computer, looking at her blog. In this way, my interaction with A. took place both in person and via digital technologies, a common blend in contemporary projects.

At the same time, I monitored and took screenshots of the homepages of A.'s blogs and specific posts on them, having informed her I was doing this. Although her literary blog remained my primary focus, I also looked at the other blogs she maintained, as well as other websites and web platforms where her activities and publications were mentioned. I acquired copies of print pub-lications produced by A., maintained notes in my field diary, and collected other digital content sent to me by A. In the analysis and writing-up phase of my research, I corresponded with A., as I did with other research participants; engaged her in a review of relevant fieldwork data, including interview tran-scripts and the discussion of follow-up questions; and consulted her on deci-sions about citation from digital content and communications and the use of screenshots.

The interaction with A. provided me with valuable insights into the circula-tion of digital content, complementing what I was able to observe myself. This applied not only to what A. told me about the reach of her own work, such as her account of contacts established via her blog, and the number of cop-ies of her first self-published book sold (as far afield as Uruguay, Venezuela, and Spain, as well as to readers in the north and northeast of Brazil), which showed her interest in establishing translocal connections via the internet and her investment in affirming her local origins in Maré. My contact with A. also shed light on the circulation of digital content produced and disseminated online by other residents of Maré. On our first face-to-face meeting, we sat in the courtyard of a small shopping complex, discussing the work of local organizations, her university studies, and her plans to encourage the work of other local writers. Her mention of a recent post in the forum of a Maré Orkut community, which included a link to a blog post about a conflict in the favela, revealed how that text was circulating and being noticed locally, complement-ing my own internet-based observations of its trajectory.[12]

Fieldwork thus allowed me to approach digital content dynamically, and to explore the communicative processes which took place around its production and dissemination, particularly its framing through paratexts of various kinds.[13] Although my fieldwork was a mobile practice which did not always involve physical displacement, the observations and interactions carried out in front of a laptop at home in Rio de Janeiro also generated physical trajectories to be fol-lowed in the city, both to the favela of Maré itself and to other locations where I met bloggers or attended events relevant to the research. When writing up the research, I combined observational and interview data and field notes with analysis of digital and sometimes print content. In the case of A.'s content, the focus of the analysis was displaced from her literary texts to consider textual and visual aspects of blog sidebars, headers and footers (including changes in design and layout over time), blurbs, promotional information and prefaces for self-published books, and communication associated with a writing competi-tion developed by A. It was in these paratexts that a relationship to place was most explicitly expressed.

The prominence A. gave in blog profile information to her status as a resi-dent of Maré was striking and constituted an example of what Ramos calls "territorial affirmation,"[14] often involving the naming of specific favelas in song lyrics, on clothing or in other imagery, which has become a feature of the work of some favela residents, organizations and cultural producers precisely as a way of combating discrimination. For a time during fieldwork, the right-hand column of A.'s literary blog included profile information under the heading "Who I am," which clearly situated its author as a favela resident and affirmed her investment in generating her own representations of the favela: "I am proud to call myself a resident of the Maré favela complex and by publishing my texts I want to show that Rio's favelas also produce art, poetry and beauty (and not just criminals [*marginais*])." There was an explicitly contestatory dimension to this statement of intent, in its affirmation of territorial belonging and pride and its attempt to reframe the meaning of a stigmatized neighborhood in the popular imagination of the city.

A.'s pride in coming from Maré was repeated to me in email exchanges and in our interview. I asked her to elaborate on her motivation for so explicitly affirming a territorial identity and for working to establish opportunities to support the work of other writers from similar backgrounds to her own, such as a writing competition for local writers. As A. told me:

> I don't know if the mainstream media has any concern or desire to find out about what we are up to here. That's why with [the writing competition] I think I kind of want to stick it down their throats … I mean, how can I put it, push things a bit so that people see that it's different, you know, that we live differently here.

The tone and scope of existing media coverage of favelas emerged as a compelling motivation and reference for the production and publications of digital content in all three of my blogging case studies, with media representations considered variously shallow, stigmatizing, absent, disinterested or unrepresentative. Bloggers thus sought to combat the negative visibility of favelas with a differential, more nuanced (and sometimes outright positive) visibility, seeking to make available broader and more diverse representations of favelas in general, and Maré in particular.

Blog content itself, and the act of making it available, presented favelas as sites of creativity and voice. In A.'s case, there was an explicit framing of *herself* on the internet and in print as a university student, a teacher and a writer from an area of the city often associated with violence and poverty. She also posted posters and promotional material for events taking place in Maré on her blog, giving a sense of local cultural life. In addition, she made a concerted attempt to extend the recognition and concrete opportunities resulting from her own burgeoning visibility to fellow residents of Maré. As A. explained to me during an interview, she had been inspired by her own success in using the internet to attract attention to her work and wished to facilitate this for others:

> When I started to see that things were working out for me, I thought, gosh, I'm here, I'm a nobody …, and there are so many other nobodies here in my community, in my area. But they are just as talented as me, if not more so, so why not … shine a light on them, why can't these people also be noticed?

While A. put herself forward to exemplify Maré as a site of literary production and cultural capital, she also established connections between the individual and the collective, seeking to multiply the visibility already achieved, bring others into the spotlight, and show that she was not exceptional.

One key difference between the approach adopted in my study and a conventional humanities approach lies in the level and nature of the interaction established with A. and the construction of this as a fieldwork relationship. My inclusion in A.'s communications routine, my detailed following of her blog over a period of time, attendance at relevant events, and the informal and formal interviews I conducted with her provided a broader context for understanding her activities and motivations. This fits with ethnography's "commitment to try and view the object of enquiry through attempting some kind of alignment with the perspective of those who participate in the research."[15] In the humanities, however, this type of alignment is not common. As Amy Bruckman has noted, "Literary scholars and art historians who study famous creative professionals typically do not view what they do as human subjects research, even if they study living authors and artists, collecting data from them directly."[16] Taking a historical perspective, Bruckman notes that the decline in research engagement with authors in the humanities coincided with the emergence of human subjects protocols in the medical and social sciences. Although the advent of cultural studies, and its emphasis on popular culture, has gone some way toward changing this, Bruckman argues that it is the emergence of the internet that has thrown the place of human subjects in humanities research into new relief.[17] As cultural studies scholar Kate Eichhorn has highlighted, the types of material and communicative processes developed on the internet raise fundamental methodological and theoretical questions for a range of scholars:

> Can "texts" that promote ... interactivity and immersion ... as well as some forms of hypertext, continue to be understood as texts? At what point do these "texts" become something entirely different? If so, what do they become, and what might the phenomena in question mean to the ethnographer, the literary theorist, and their respective disciplinary traditions?[18]

In my study on blogging by Brazilian favela residents, I conceived of bloggers such as A. as human subjects from the start, with approval for the project given by the relevant university ethics committee and methodological and ethical guidance sought in the burgeoning literature on internet research. However, it soon became clear that, in line with Eichhorn's comments above, important decisions were also required about the status of blog texts, and that this decision-making could not happen in isolation from fieldwork interactions.

By beginning with focusing on bloggers as people engaged in practices, and then moving to an awareness that the texts they authored were also central to the project, I in fact experienced the opposite of Eichhorn, who planned her research into 'zines as a text-based study, and then became aware that she was researching not just texts, but people. As Eichhorn notes, she had intended "to escape to the *imagined* stability and containability of texts" (emphasis in original) in that piece of research, but from the moment she requested 'zines by post from their authors, she "unintentionally initiated the process of nego-tiating access to a community,"[19] requiring her to develop an ethical stance on her interaction with 'zine creators. In my research on blogging, there was a growing awareness that while the blog texts required attention, a conventional literary studies approach to analyzing those texts would not suffice; an ethical stance was also required toward them. The attempt to include both texts and practices in the research thus positioned it between the conventions, and the methods, of the humanities and the social sciences.

NEGOTIATING THE ETHICS OF VISIBILITY IN DIGITAL CULTURE RESEARCH

Although helpful in many other ways, early methodological writing on inter-net research was largely silent on ethical approaches to the internet under-stood as a site of textual production, in comparison with the attention given to the internet as a site where human subjects interact. A key issue regarding internet texts is whether they can be considered "published" in the traditional sense. Although it may be that some internet content can be considered public enough to study without informed consent, such decision-making is a complex process and one in constant flux, in terms of both the range of internet con-tent available and the different ethical approaches taken by researchers working according to different disciplinary traditions and forging new ones.

Sveningsson Elm proposes that rather than a dichotomy between public content and private content, we should think of internet content in terms of a continuum ranging from public to private, passing through semipublic and semiprivate content, depending on the access settings of particular websites and platforms; Bruckman suggests a similar continuum, from published to semi-published and unpublished.[20] However, Elm confesses her ongoing dif-ficulty in taking "a clear stance" on the issue,[21] drawing attention to the subjec-tive dimensions of this question, for both researchers and creators of content. As she points out, privacy is understood differently in different cultural con-texts, and stances on research ethics depend on researchers' backgrounds and disciplines.[22] Drawing a parallel with debates in literary theory about where the meaning of the text is to be found (in the intention of the author, the text itself or the interpretation of the reader/audience), she suggests, "No content is ever either private or public, but potentially both, depending on who you are asking."[23] The act of asking therefore takes on a central importance, even if the ambiguities outlined above mean that the answer given may only be one piece of the jigsaw for a researcher. Although bloggers such as those who participated in my study are constantly negotiating the risks and opportuni-ties associated with publishing content on the internet, there is a potentially different set of issues involved in deciding—as a researcher working with such material—how best to make it visible (or not) in research write-ups. While the bloggers I interviewed expressed a view on this when asked, saying they were happy for me to cite their content, they also all effectively told me that it was up to me to make the final decision on this matter.

The potential invisibility of internet researchers when observing internet content and practices, compared to similar research in non-mediated settings, is one strong justification for making one's presence known and engaging with content creators in this way. However, even if it does not explicitly involve the seeking of consent, contacting content creators can be problematic for humanities scholars, as it may immediately reposition their research into the human subjects category (rather than the default arts and humanities engagement with published texts), given that it implies some degree of interaction and thus a move toward fieldwork, however limited. Trevisan and Reilly have suggested that "Internet research ethics should remain informed by the disciplinary perspectives of those who study online communities," calling for the development of "discipline-specific frameworks."[24] Such frameworks are sorely needed in the text-based humanities, to complement existing codes of ethics in disciplines more experienced in fieldwork such as anthropology and sociology and to raise awareness of the relevance of research ethics to all the branches of the humanities (not only where research on digital culture is concerned). However, projects without a clear home discipline to serve as a fundamental reference may continue to fall between the cracks, requiring researchers to stitch together their own composite ethical and methodological frameworks—a potentially productive process in itself. For research on digital culture, a major reference is the Ethics Committee of the Association of Internet Researchers, which takes an interdisciplinary and flexible approach in its development of ethical guidelines (rather than a code).[25]

In my study, a composite framework was required to link blog texts to the relationships developed with their authors and the fieldwork process of following the content. Bassett and O'Riordan argue for the relevance of debates in the field of life writing, and, in particular, the feminist oral history work of Katherine Borland, to ethical decision-making in digital culture research.[26] Borland affirms the contribution to be made by researchers in interpreting texts acquired through fieldwork, but also the need to allow for alternative interpretations by the creators of those texts. Researchers can analyze texts based on their "knowledge, experience and concerns" and should not be dependent on the validation of fieldwork participants.[27] Yet Borland also recognizes that there is much to be gained by maintaining an ongoing dialogue with the creators of texts throughout the research process and by providing a space where multiple textual meanings can coexist and be negotiated. In other words, as advocated by Bassett and O'Riordan, Borland provides a strategy for linking texts to people as both authors and human subjects, allowing the researcher to engage directly and critically with texts, while maintaining an awareness of their origins in the life of another person.[28]

The ethics of authorship and interpretation, and the connections between people and texts, are further complicated in digital research by the potential "traceability" of direct citations from the internet if included in publications.

This characteristic of textual material published online, which cannot be considered either negative or positive in itself, argue Beaulieu and Estalella, forces researchers to directly confront issues of "anonymity, visibility, exposure, ownership and authorship"[29] when thinking about how to generate and present data, questions that would not normally arise in the usual humanities engagement with published literary texts. Aside from the convention of citing such texts, the humanities would also traditionally include full bibliographical details to enable readers to locate them for themselves. In the social sciences, on the contrary, where research participants have tended to be understood primarily as human subjects rather than as authors, the standard ethical requirement when writing up research has often been anonymization and the use of pseudonyms to preserve the privacy and "locatability" of participants. The traceability of internet content, and the ethical implications of this, thus potentially poses a challenge to both of these traditions.

The overarching issue here is the relationship between protection and accountability. Amy Bruckman raises the central question faced by many researchers dealing with internet material when she asks: "Should [amateur artists] be treated as vulnerable human subjects whose privacy needs to be protected by hiding their online pseudonyms and real names? Or would that rob them of a legitimate claim to credit for their creative work?"[30] There are complex issues associated with both citation and the decision not to cite. Such decisions should be made based on individual research projects and wherever possible in consultation with research participants.[31] Some scholars, like Hine[32] and Banks and Eble,[33] have pointed out that not citing from internet content on principle would threaten the viability of carrying out, and publishing, research into textual production on the internet. Marianne Franklin, who developed her approach to quotation from internet forums over several years of consultation with research participants, argues that "online texts and their authors demand the same level of courtesy and citation rigor as any other written source."[34] She also notes that she would "'respectfully disagree' with the principle of absolute anonymity as a hard and fast rule for online research scenarios,"[35] again emphasizing the need for researchers to be flexible, responsive and consultative in developing approaches to the thorny issue of citation.

The challenges are particularly marked in projects focusing on textual production on the internet by marginalized groups, which require researchers to grapple with issues associated both with the digital context and the profile of the content creators in question. The degree to which research participants can be considered, or want to be considered, "public figures" varies drastically. This was a factor in decision-making by Trevisan and Reilly, who took a selective approach to citation of digital material in their study of online disability activism, opting largely to avoid direct citation of traceable material, but using quotes "when the identification of the author was not possible or would not cause specific ethical problems," for example in the case of widely circulated memes or when referencing content posted by what they call "core campaigners" rather than "ordinary" users.[36] Nonetheless, both Franklin[37] and Bassett and O'Riordan[38] point to the risk of erasure if protection is prioritized over attribution and accountability. Similarly, Banks and Eble[39] draw attention to the possibility of affording less authorship and agency to blog authors (such as the young gay men they studied) by treating their work differently from that of conventional published authors. One example of this, though not specifically related to digital culture, is Érica Peçanha do Nascimento's observation that critical writing on the work of writers from the Brazilian urban periphery tends to focus primarily on their sociological profiles, rather than the characteristics of their literary work per se.[40] In addition, some content produced by or for marginalized groups can have the explicit goal of achieving greater visibility, in the absence of mainstream media attention, as Bassett and O'Riordan noted of the lesbian website they researched in the UK.[41] The consideration of A.'s attempts to reframe the Maré favela and its residents has shown that these issues certainly had resonance in my own study, where bloggers were seeking to diversify representations of their neighborhood and contest its stigmatization. Nonetheless, this was one factor among several to be weighed up in my ethical decision-making.

Beyond internet research, the anthropological convention of protecting and anonymizing research participants has been questioned, with scholars querying whether anonymity, which prevents research participants from responding to research findings, "[is] truly always only for the purpose of protecting our 'human subjects,' or is it also about protecting ourselves?"[42] In fact, Beaulieu and Estalella argue that the increased traceability of data in internet research could potentially offer new types of protection and accountability to research participants.[43] Where anonymity does remain a pressing concern, due to the characteristics of the material or people under study, scholars like Beaulieu and Estalella, and Ess,[44] have suggested that alternative approaches to disguising field sites and participants may need to be developed in internet research, such as paraphrasing or altering content, self-anonymization of the researcher, or covert research. The idea of intervening in digital texts by editing them to prevent their traceability may be a particularly challenging proposition for humanities scholars, especially for those who wish to engage in analysis of those same texts.

There are also powerful arguments for taking a cautious approach to citation of traceable internet content, based on a different stance toward visibility as produced by digital technologies. The option to preserve visibility, by citing and attributing content, may in fact mean amplifying that visibility, an intervention in the politics of representation that is not neutral. The inclusion of internet content in research publications may disturb the relative anonymity of the internet, where a single post may not stand out, by "potentially *bring[ing]* a readership to a forum which otherwise might not have that readership" (emphasis in original).[45] This could in turn "bring attention to [...] bloggers by those who would not normally know about them and thus possibly create a conflict where none had existed prior to the reporting of the research in print or at conferences."[46] These dynamics may also be affected by the amount of time that has passed between content being posted online and its discussion in research communications. Finally, the growth in access to digital technologies and the ease of internet publishing means that research results are now more widely available to a range of audiences, a positive trend in many ways, but one that can also be unexpected and unpredictable and that requires academics to be particularly sensitive to ethical concerns when writing up their research.

In my study, I employed an informal and conversational approach to ethics and informed consent throughout the research process, asking bloggers (on email, via chat, and in person) for input on issues, including whether or not to quote directly from internet content and how best to identify them. I did not use a formal consent form. Mention of research protocols such as confidentiality and anonymity occasionally prompted general teasing or dismissiveness, as if it implied the bloggers might have something to hide, but I persisted with this. This ongoing and regular consultation, as well as the insights gleaned through fieldwork itself, proved important in decision-making about how to deal with different data types when writing up the research. Overall, I opted to preserve the visibility of the blog content and the place it represented, Maré, thereby respecting the bloggers' desire, and efforts, to change the terms of that place's social and cultural visibility. At the same time, I attempted to mask, to a small degree, the visibility of the individuals in whose lives it originated. As an approach approximating to Bruckman's "light disguise" model, this sought to protect the privacy of the people involved, while attributing the due importance to their content and recognizing the content's place at the heart of the study, alongside practices.

The decision to cite from content was informed by the bloggers' view that their content was in the public domain and that they were directly seeking a nonlocal audience for their representations of their neighborhood. I focused my citations on the blog content itself, and I explicitly sought consent for this in the final stages of the research. This process worked slightly differently in relation to each of the three bloggers. In one case, for example, responding to a request by the blogger in question, I sent a list of blog posts (and specific extracts from them) that I hoped to cite, for agreement and comment, rather than for securing "blanket" consent for citation, which was given in other cases, without the need for detailed negotiation. I only rarely cited from email or Orkut communication with/by bloggers, again requesting explicit consent where this was the case. In the case study about A., quoted material was largely from "framing content" or nonliterary content, based on my understanding of her, in the context of the study, primarily as a creator of local content rather than as a literary author. In many ways, it was coincidence (or the result of the serendipitous process of fieldwork) that one of the three bloggers in the study was engaged in the production of explicitly literary content, as this was not the focus of the study. However, all three bloggers could be understood as "amateur artists" according to Bruckman's terminology. Crucially, it was by avoiding the literary nature of A.'s work and looking at the texts *around* her literary texts that I developed insights about the importance of "framing content" in expressing territorial embeddedness. At the same time, however, the fact that much of A.'s content was literary, and that she was engaged in self-publishing in print as well as on the internet, helped to surface reflections about the need to consider authorship and its attribution in a hybrid study such as this one.

The option to refer to bloggers only by initials, and not to name or provide the addresses of the blogs where they published their work, was based on a judgment that they were not well-known public figures, despite their work being publicly available on the internet and their own negotiation of the opportunities and risks associated with the circulation and potential visibility of that content. For comparison here, albeit drawing on a case not involving digital technologies, it is worth noting the rationale presented by Pandolfi and Grynszpan for naming community leaders from four Rio favelas who contributed oral histories to their book: they were considered by the researchers to be "public personalities who circulate widely and whose voices are recognized."[47] My assessment of the blogs I studied, and their authors, was that they were not widely disseminated or known even in Rio de Janeiro, beyond certain circles, and certainly not to some of the potential audiences for the research, both Portuguese- and English speaking. In fact, A. herself commented on the visibility that the internet offered to amateur artists, when I interviewed her. Talking about the various social network sites where she maintained a presence, she noted that being on MySpace had been good because she had got to know "artists who, like me, do not have space in the mainstream media, but who have become well-known (*notórios*) on the internet, if we can put it like that." Despite my interest in this process, it was not my central focus, and I concluded that it was not my role to amplify that visibility more than necessary, or to draw attention to what might be considered "success stories" of the way the internet was being used by favela residents, in the way that the media, or projects and reports created by NGOs, the state or private foundations might do. As I have pointed out elsewhere, drawing on the work of Silvia Ramos, not all of those engaged in cultural and digital production in favelas are "the celebrities and personalities […] which some favela-based projects cultivate and present to the media" as a way of combating negative stereotypes about people who live in favelas.[48]

There are many potential contradictions in researching digital material designed to afford differential or affirmative visibility to a marginalized social group, and then taking steps to mask that visibility when writing up the research. Nonetheless, these precautions—such as my use of initials, the pseudonyms chosen by Bassett and O'Riordan, and the delinking of blog analysis from fieldwork data by Banks and Eble (something which would be more difficult in a small-scale study such as my own)—can be justified, given the emergent nature of this type of research and associated ethical frameworks, and the ultimately subjective nature of decision-making on these issues. The measures adopted in my study, where connections were established between texts (traceable internet content) and practices (data acquired through interaction) in case studies focusing on individuals, reflect the particularities and emergent ethical dilemmas of digital culture research, discussed above. They were also designed to be faithful to the fieldwork context in which I encountered the bloggers and their texts, and the process of developing rapport and trust, and ultimately of securing their consent to participate in the study. Drawing on interview and observational data and linking it to cited content from blogs contextualizes and adds insights not available to an audience encountering the blogs on their own. The attempt to separate the access given to texts and the access given to people, at the point of reporting on the research, might seem curious, given the earlier account of how these two ways of understanding the object of study intertwined in the fieldwork. However, it also reveals how in a fieldwork-based study of content creation on the internet, texts can indeed become more than just texts, as suggested by Eichhorn. They cannot be detached from the tangle of fieldwork interactions and other data acquired through fieldwork and the responsibilities that these imply.

Conclusion

As this discussion has shown, research into digital culture may increasingly bring humanities scholars into contact with authors (and different types of authors) and require us to acknowledge that these subjects and interlocutors are not just the producers of texts but also human subjects. Some of the challenges that arose in my study were specifically associated with the focus on digital texts, such as the issue of traceability and the subjective dimension of decision-making on the public or private nature of digital content, but others, like the blurring of fieldwork participants' status as authors and human subjects, and the relative lack of models for combining data types associated with different disciplinary traditions in a single study, could arise just as easily in nondigital projects. Rather than offering a framework or model to be followed by other scholars, I have sought to discuss some of the dilemmas that occurred in my own study and how I addressed them.

An informed decision on the relevance of such questions needs to be taken in the context of individual projects and fieldwork experiences, drawing also on relevant ethical codes and frameworks. Wider awareness raising and training are required to equip humanities researchers to make such judgments, but this process need not necessarily be onerous, and it may provide some pleasant surprises. Like Hine, who asked participants in a discussion list she was studying for their permission to quote material from its archives, and gained relevant insights as a result, I found that in my study "[t]he ethical commitment [...] began as a duty and turned into an interesting and useful engagement."[49] Indeed, the fieldwork component was one of the most stimulating aspects of this research project on blogging by favela residents. Although the questions that arose as a result of following the production and circulation of digital content and meeting its creators in person were challenging, they were also compelling, precisely because they provoked me to think intensively and explicitly about my own research processes and associated decision-making. The lack of predetermined answers, in this case, was productive. Through reflection on that fieldwork process, I have shown the gains of complementing the study of texts with data on practices gained through interaction and observation, but also the disciplinary and methodological certainties that can be lost as a result. The ethical confusions and makeshift resolutions that are inevitable in interdisciplinary projects that involve several different standards can be at least partly addressed by sharing experiences and more explicit reflection on ethical challenges in humanities fieldwork.

As I write this, six years have passed since the end of my fieldwork, and four years since the end of the research project on blogging. Since then, I have often reflected on the issues discussed in this chapter, and asked myself if the approach I adopted was the "right" one. There is of course no "right" approach; mine was the one that seemed appropriate, reasonable, and feasible to me, as I carefully weighed up a range of factors and their possible implications. It arose not only from my original disciplinary training, in modern languages, but also from my awareness of the conventions of other disciplines and methods I was engaging with through the research and the "in-between" space I had come to occupy. It was thus an "in-between" solution, as well as one developed in response to a specific time and place and specific fieldwork encounters.

Despite my best efforts, I have had only limited contact with A. since completing the research. However, I have occasionally visited her blogs and observed that she no longer appears to be publishing content in the way she did at the time of my fieldwork. She may have migrated to other platforms, or she may simply be busy with other activities. At the time of my fieldwork, all three of the bloggers involved in my study were extremely busy, combining their blogging work with study and/or work, and it therefore usually took some time, with occasional rescheduling, before we were able to successfully meet in person. Blogging was just one of the things that they did. Digital practices can shift and evolve over time, both in terms of the platforms used and the time one has available for content creation. A whole host of other factors about which a researcher cannot, and should not, even begin to speculate may affect whether or not people are posting content online at any given moment. In retrospect, citing local content without naming its authors or the blogs on which it originated may serve as a strategy to focus the attention of readers of the research on the blog texts and practices and the specific context out of which they arose and in which they were encountered, rather than on the people in whose lives they originated, lives that continued after the fieldwork ended.

NOTES

1. Miller and Slater, *The Internet*, 1.
2. For annual data, see http://www.cetic.br/pesquisa/domicilios/. For an analysis of trends, see Gilda Olinto and Suely Fragoso, "Internet Use in Brazil: Speeding up or Lagging Behind?"

3. For examples, see Janice Perlman, *Favela: Four Decades of Living on the Edge in Rio de Janeiro*; Lorraine Leu, "The Press and the Spectacle of Violence in Contemporary Rio de Janeiro"; Jailson Souza e Silva, and Jorge Luiz Barbosa, *Favela: Alegria e dor na cidade*; Silvia Ramos and Anabela Paiva, *Mídia e violência—Novas tendências na cobertura de criminalidade e segurança no Brasil*; Beatriz Jaguaribe and Kevin Hetherington, "Favela Tours: Indistinct and Mapless Representations of the Real in Rio de Janeiro."

4. The idea of "territorial embeddedness" is borrowed from Hess's work in economic geography, where it conveys "the extent to which an actor is 'anchored' in particular territories or places" (Martin Hess, "'Spatial' Relationships? Towards a Reconceptualization of Embeddedness," 177). The term has been adapted here to refer to the inclusion of explicit visual or textual references to place in digital content, understood as the expression of a relationship to place. For more on this, see Tori Holmes, "The Travelling Texts of Local Content: Following Content Creation, Communication and Dissemination via Internet Platforms in a Brazilian Favela."

5. Sousa Silva, "Censo Maré 2000: Uma experiência de coleta e geração de informações socioculturais e econômicas numa favela da cidade do Rio de Janeiro," 15.

6. Sousa Silva, 15; Souza e Silva, et al., eds. *O que é a favela, afinal?*, 11.

7. For an in-depth discussion of this approach, see Tori Holmes, "Linking Internet Texts and Practices: Challenges and Opportunities of Interdisciplinarity in an Ethnographically Inspired Study of 'Local Content.'"

8. RSS is a technology that allows users to be automatically informed of updates to the content of selected websites, often via what is known as a feed reader.

9. Crawford, "Following You: Disciplines of Listening in Social Media," 527.

10. Holmes, "Linking Internet Texts and Practices," 138.

11. At the time of the fieldwork, Orkut was the most popular social network site in Brazil. It has since been supplanted by Facebook.

12. See Holmes, "The Travelling Texts" for a full discussion.

13. Jonathan Gray draws on Genette's understanding of paratexts as "the thresholds of interpretation" and explains that "paratexts guide our entry to texts, setting up all sorts of meanings and strategies of interpretation, and proposing ways to make sense of what we will find 'inside' the text". Gray notes that the term "paratext" has not yet been widely used in communication, media and cultural studies (Gray, "Television Pre-Views and the Meaning of Hype," 38).

14. Ramos, "Jovens de favelas na produção cultural brasileira dos anos 90."

15. Horst and Miller, *The Cell Phone: An Anthropology of Communication*, 167.

16. Bruckman, "Studying the Amateur Artist," 224.
17. Bruckman, 223–224.
18. Eichhorn, "Sites Unseen," 576.
19. Eichhorn, "Sites Unseen," 569.
20. Sveningsson Elm, "Question Three. How Do Various Notions of Privacy Influence Decisions in Qualitative Internet Research?"; Bruckman, "Studying the Amateur Artist," 227.
21. Sveningsson Elm, 86.
22. Sveningsson Elm, 69, 73.
23. Sveningsson Elm, 82, 84.
24. Trevisan and Reilly, "Ethical Dilemmas in Researching Sensitive Issues Online," 1142, 1132.
25. Association of Internet Researchers Ethics Committee. "Ethical Decision-Making and Internet Research: Recommendations from the AOIR Ethics Committee," 2012.
26. Bassett and O'Riordan, "Ethics of Internet Research."
27. Borland, "That's Not What I Said," 73.
28. We can find echoes of Borland's approach to personal texts in the work of linguistic anthropologist Jan Blommaert, in his study of personal letters whose author (Julien) he never met or interviewed. He defends this form of textual fieldwork which did not include interaction with the author/human subject of the texts, arguing that he mitigates the risk of silencing Julien's voice "by making my own interpretive procedures explicit (like Fabian); and by showing my own subjectivity in these interpretive procedures (like Bourdieu)" (Jan Blommaert, *Grassroots Literacy*, 89). What is common to Borland's work is the the careful separation of source text from the researcher's interpretation of it, and an explicit attempt to avoid conflating conflating text and author, as a way of compensating for the absence of Julien's own interpretation of his text.
29. Beaulieu and Estalella, "Rethinking Research Ethics for Mediated Settings," 32.
30. Bruckman, "Studying the Amateur Artist," 228.
31. Association of Internet Researchers Ethics Committee. "Ethical Decision-Making."
32. Christine Hine, *Virtual Ethnography* (London: Sage, 2000).
33. William P. Banks and Michelle F. Eble, "Digital Spaces, Online Environments and Human Participant Research."
34. Franklin, *Postcolonial Politics, the Internet, and Everyday Life*, 71.
35. Franklin, 203.
36. Trevisan and Reilly, "Ethical Dilemmas," 1139.
37. Franklin, *Postcolonial Politics*, 203.
38. Bassett and O'Riordan, "Ethics of Internet Research," 245.
39. Banks and Eble, "Digital Spaces."
40. Érica Peçanha do Nascimento, *Vozes marginais na literatura*, 80.
41. Bassett and O'Riordan, "Ethics of Internet Research," 243.

42. Shannon May, "Rethinking Anonymity in Anthropology: A Question of Ethics," *Anthropology News* 51, no. 4 (2010): 10.
43. Beaulieu and Estalella, "Rethinking Research Ethics," 36.
44. C. Ess, "Internet Research Ethics," quoted in Wilkinson and Thelwall, "Researching Personal Information on the Public Web," 397.
45. McKee and Porter. *The Ethics of Internet Research*, 106–107.
46. Banks and Eble, "Digital Spaces," 37.
47. Pandolfi and Grynszpan, eds., *A favela fala*, 29.
48. Holmes, "The Travelling Texts," 265.
49. Hine, "Connective Ethnography for the Exploration of E-Science," 623.

BIBLIOGRAPHY

Association of Internet Researchers Ethics Committee. 2012. Ethical Decision-Making and Internet Research: Recommendations from the AOIR Ethics Committee. http://ethics.aoir.org/

Banks, William P., and Michelle F. Eble. 2007. Digital Spaces, Online Environments and Human Participant Research: Interacting with Institutional Review Boards. In *Digital Writing Research: Technologies, Methodologies, and Ethical Issues*, eds. Heidi McKee, and Dànielle Nicole DeVoss, 27–47. Cresskill, NJ: Hampton Press.

Bassett, Elizabeth H., and Kate O'Riordan. 2002. Ethics of Internet Research: Contesting the Human Subjects Model. *Ethics and Information Technology* 4(3): 233–247.

Beaulieu, Anne, and Adolfo Estalella. 2012. Rethinking Research Ethics for Mediated Settings. *Information, Communication & Society* 15(1): 23–42.

Blommaert, Jan. 2008. *Grassroots Literacy: Writing, Identity and Voice in Central Africa*. Abingdon: Routledge.

Borland, Katherine. 1991. 'That's Not What I Said': Interpretive Conflict in Oral Narrative Research. In *Women's Words: The Feminist Practice of Oral History*, eds. Sherna Berger Gluck, and Daphne Patai, 63–75. New York and London: Routledge.

Bruckman, Amy. 2002. Studying the Amateur Artist: A Perspective on Disguising Data Collected in Human Subjects Research on the Internet. *Ethics and Information Technology* 4(3): 217–231.

Crawford, Kate. 2009. Following You: Disciplines of Listening in Social Media. *Continuum: Journal of Media & Cultural Studies* 23(4): 525–535.

Eichhorn, Kate. 2001. Sites Unseen: Ethnographic Research in a Textual Community. *International Journal of Qualitative Studies in Education* 14(4): 565–578.

Franklin, Marianne. 2004. *Postcolonial Politics, the Internet, and Everyday Life: Pacific Traversals Online*. London: Routledge.

Gray, J. 2008. Television Pre-Views and the Meaning of Hype. *International Journal of Cultural Studies* 11(1): 33–49.

Hess, Martin. 2004. 'Spatial' Relationships? Towards a Reconceptualization of Embeddedness. *Progress in Human Geography* 28(2): 165–186.

Hine, Christine. 2000. *Virtual Ethnography*. London: Sage.

———. 2007. Connective Ethnography for the Exploration of E-Science. *Journal of Computer-Mediated Communication* 12(2): 618–634.

Holmes, Tori. 2012. The Travelling Texts of Local Content: Following Content Creation, Communication and Dissemination via Internet Platforms in a Brazilian Favela. *Hispanic Issues Online* 9: 263–288.

———. 2013. Linking Internet Texts and Practices: Challenges and Opportunities of Interdisciplinarity in an Ethnographically Inspired Study of 'Local Content'. *Westminster Papers in Communication and Culture* 9(3): 121–142.

Horst, Heather, and Daniel Miller. 2006. *The Cell Phone: An Anthropology of Communication*. Oxford: Berg.

Jaguaribe, Beatriz, and Kevin Hetherington. 2004. Favela Tours: Indistinct and Mapless Representations of the Real in Rio de Janeiro. In *Tourism Mobilities. Places to Play, Places in Play*, eds. Mimi Sheller, and John Urry, 155–166. New York: Routledge.

Leu, Lorraine. 2004. The Press and the Spectacle of Violence in Contemporary Rio de Janeiro. *Journal of Latin American Cultural Studies* 13(3): 343–355.

May, Shannon. 2010. Rethinking Anonymity in Anthropology: A Question of Ethics. *Anthropology News* 51(4): 10–13.

McKee, Heidi A., and James E Porter. 2009. *The Ethics of Internet Research: A Rhetorical, Case-Based Process*. New York: Peter Lang.

Miller, Daniel, and Don Slater. 2000. *The Internet: An Ethnographic Approach*. Oxford: Berg.

Nascimento, Érica Peçanha do. 2009. *Vozes marginais na literatura*. Rio de Janeiro: Aeroplano.

Olinto, Gilda, and Suely Fragoso. 2011. Internet Use in Brazil: Speeding up or Lagging Behind? *The Journal of Community Informatics* 7(1–2). http://ci-journal.net/index.php/ciej/article/view/835

Perlman, Janice. 2010. *Favela: Four Decades of Living on the Edge in Rio de Janeiro*. Oxford: Oxford University Press.

Ramos, Silvia. 2007. Jovens de favelas na produção cultural brasileira dos anos 90. In *"Por que não?" Rupturas e continuidades da contracultura*, eds. Maria Isabel Mendes de Almeida and Santuza Cambraia Naves, 239–256. Rio de Janeiro: 7Letras.

Ramos, Silvia, and Anabela Paiva. 2007. *Mídia e violência—Novas tendências na cobertura de criminalidade e segurança no Brasil*. Rio de Janeiro: IUPERJ.

Sousa Silva, Eliana. 2002. Censo Maré 2000: Uma experiência de coleta e geração de informações socioculturais e econômicas numa favela da cidade do Rio de Janeiro. *Rio de Janeiro: Trabalho e Sociedade* 2(3): 15–20.

Souza e Silva, Jailson de, and Jorge Luiz Barbosa. 2005. *Favela, alegria e dor na cidade*. Rio de Janeiro: Editora Senac Rio.

Souza e Silva, Jailson de, Jorge Luiz Barbosa, Mariana de Oliveira Biteti, and Fernando Lannes Fernandes, eds. 2009. *O que é a favela, afinal?* Rio de Janeiro: Observatório de Favelas.

Sveningsson Elm, Malin. 2009. Question Three. How Do Various Notions of Privacy Influence Decisions in Qualitative Internet Research? In *Internet Inquiry: Conversations About Method*, eds. A. Markham, and N.K. Baym, 69–87. London: Sage.

Trevisan, Filippo, and Paul Reilly. 2014. Ethical Dilemmas in Researching Sensitive Issues Online: Lessons from the Study of British Disability Dissent Networks. *Information, Communication & Society* 17(9): 1131–1146.

Wilkinson, David, and Mike Thelwall. 2011. Researching Personal Information on the Public Web: Methods and Ethics. *Social Science Computer Review* 29(4): 387–401.

CHAPTER 8

Reading Delhi, Writing Delhi: An Ethnography of Literature

Rashmi Sadana

I am riding the Violet Line of the Delhi Metro with my three-year-old on an elevated section of the train which runs high over the mostly lower lying dwellings, markets, and roads. We are taking the long curve from Nehru Place toward Badarpur, one of the wide expansive views of south Delhi made newly possible because of the Metro. I am explaining and pointing, while she is looking and inquiring when the woman sitting next to us asks me in Hindi if I had always planned to teach my daughter English this early. The question makes perfect sense to me, since middle-class Indian children tend to speak their mother tongues until the age of five or six and only then get immersed in English-medium education. Without missing a beat, I reply to her in Hindi that I grew up in the USA, so I speak to my daughter in English and Hindi at home. But I can sense her slight anxiety. Was this just another way for me to get ahead? In this city of 16 million, language is mobility.

Delhi has been both a place to be and a research problem—in the sense of something needing to be figured out—for some time. I say "problem" rather than "object" since one is part of the city and so part of the place and the problem. The question of "being there" has long been a feature of the anthropological endeavor—even if "being" may have taken precedence of late. I admit I am still caught up in the "there." In this chapter, I outline how "fieldwork"—the gathering of data through interviewing and observation, but also the physical, emotional, and intellectual immersion in people's lives through sets of encounters in a place or set of places—not only enables certain kinds of research but defines the research problem anew.

R. Sadana (✉)
Department of Sociology and Anthropology, George Mason University, Fairfax, USA

© The Author(s) 2016
S. Puri, D.A. Castillo (eds.), *Theorizing Fieldwork in the Humanities*,
DOI 10.1057/978-1-349-92834-7_8

I have been doing fieldwork in Delhi since the late 1990s, first as a graduate student, then as a resident for five years, and now as a junior professor at an American university who goes back and forth. My first project was about literary language and the production of books, basically a humanities project for which I attempted to create an anthropological method. In the process, I ended up detailing the politics of English and Hindi through an ethnography of publishers, booksellers, writers, translators, and literary officials.[1] The second is on the city's new metro rail system, where I observe and participate in the social life on the trains, track new forms of mobility, and analyze the production of urban space. Both projects stem from my curiosity about what I have experienced moving around the city. In both, rather than study discrete communities within a city, as anthropologists are wisely wont to do, I have perhaps less wisely taken on the task of identifying communities and sometimes bringing them into being.

In what follows, I unravel how I came to define my fieldwork experience as I went from being a student of literature, absorbed in textual analysis, to an anthropologist researching the literary. It is through this cross-disciplinary movement that I put into practice a fieldwork-based methodology for studying literature. It is also a story of how the fieldwork itself came to define the research and clarify the problems I was seeking to address. My problem to start with was how to do fieldwork about books?

THE TURN TO FIELDWORK

In the early 1990s, as I was finishing a bachelor's degree in English, the "boom" in Indian fiction was in full swing. Salman Rushdie had won the Booker Prize for *Midnight's Children* in 1981 and Vikram Seth's *A Suitable Boy* was about to be published in 1993. Indian writers were gaining traction on the "global" literary stage. The "boom" was an English-only phenomenon, and that was part of its allure. To be recognized by the Anglo-American literary marketplace, with its major publishing houses in London and New York and its "international" awards such as the Booker Prize, was and still is a defining moment, a coming-of-age, as they like to say.[2] Indians didn't just know English, they had mastered it.

In 1995, this recognition gathered force by the much-mythologized airplane flight that British literary agent David Godwin took from London to Delhi after having read the manuscript of Arundhati Roy's *The God of Small Things*. That novel, which not only won the Booker Prize in 1997 but also became an international bestseller, would go on to help Godwin establish his agency. Godwin now represents over 100 authors, many of whom come from (and write from) South Asia and Africa.

When I interviewed Godwin at the Jaipur Literature Festival in 2009, he told me that there were three things he saw in Roy's manuscript in 1995 that made him take that flight: (1) "The timing was perfect"—it was just before the 50-year anniversary of Indian independence; (2) the author was female, and women, said Godwin, were able to speak to the political and personal better than male writers; and finally, (3) it was a "terrific book."[3] Talking to Godwin, I came to see how that flight he took to Delhi was a dramatization of the selling of the novel itself and a reversal: The "center" was seeking out the "margin." It became a "win-win" situation.

Yet, something is, or at least was, for me, clearly missing from a story like this, of Indian writers' arrival on the global literary stage (writers, whom, I should add, I enjoyed reading myself). I knew from all the time I had spent in Delhi that the languages around me were Hindi, Urdu, and Punjabi. English was there, but in particular places, at particular times, spoken by particular kinds of people. I wanted to find out what got lost—not in translation, but in transnational literary production. Why was India only being represented in English? What was the relationship between Indian texts in English and those in the 22 other official languages (spread across 29 states)? Surely this writing existed in a multilingual context, but looking at how Indian novels in English were read and received in the USA and the UK, one would never know it. Other writers—Gabriel García Márquez comes to mind—made it globally big in translation. Why not a great Hindi or Tamil or Marathi writer?

By this time I was increasingly reading translations of Indian writers (such as Ismat Chugtai, Amrita Pritam, Rajee Seth, Ambai, Baby Kamble, and others), albeit in an academic context. Nevertheless, this reading reminded me of and connected me to what I experienced on Indian streets and in families: a deep and lively multilinguality and, importantly, perspectives on life emanating from a non-English-language worldview. By reading authors originally writing in Urdu, Gujarati, Bengali, Malayalam, Kannada, and Telugu, to name a few of the Indian languages (or *bhashas* as they are often called, to distinguish them from English, which is now also an Indian language), what I thought was familiar—modern Indian experience—became strange, and reading these works had the effect of making me feel out of place. Out of place, and yet also producing different kinds of recognition within me. I suppose that was when I started to hanker for fieldwork—what I would describe as an intellectual longing not merely to "be there," but to connect the dots of the literary landscape in my mind to the geography of the city and the linguistic histories of its residents.[4]

I started to "get there" while in London, working toward a master's degree in South Asia Studies at the School of Oriental and African Studies (SOAS). In the SOAS library's teaching collection, we students from and of Africa, Asia, the Caribbean, and other "outposts" voraciously read postcolonial theory in the heart of the faded imperium. Texts in colonial languages (English, French, Dutch, Portuguese, etc.) somewhat predictably became privileged as sources with which to better understand the colonial project and to critique colonial discourse. However, the texts themselves were often divorced from their political and cultural contexts, or places, in order so that they might be understood in a larger imperial context.

SOAS, of course, had been the linguistic finishing school for many a colonial officer on his way out to "the field." As I absorbed Edward Said on culture and

imperialism and Ngũgĩ wa Thiong'o on language and colonialism, I started
to see the English language itself as being more about "place" than anything
else. By "place" I don't just mean a particular geographic location, but rather a
particular political and cultural context, always in relation to other contexts. It
was around this time that I began to take note of publishers and places of publication with particular interest, and like many book historians, started to frame
the texts I was reading in new ways. I wrote a thesis about *Midnight's Children*;
I thought maybe the answer would be in Rushdie's heteroglossic text, with its
Urdu cadences and Hindi slang. (It wasn't.)

In London, I also interned at the publisher Granta. In the 1980s, *Granta*
magazine had opened the world of international writing to me and had
inspired me to write to the then editor, Bill Buford. When I met Buford at
Granta's Islington office, we agreed that I would read and report on book
manuscripts, but also come in on the occasional Saturday to go over "the slush
pile." In a small way, I had become a participant observer at one of the centers
in the Anglophone publishing world. I recount this episode because without
knowing it then, reading those Granta manuscripts became the beginning of
my fieldwork.

In terms of contemporary literary distinction, *Granta* magazine symbol-
ized the postcolonial literary moment in 1980s Britain in that writers from
Commonwealth nations wanted to publish works in English. After all, the first
chapter of *Midnight's Children* had been published in 1980 in *Granta*, Issue 3:
"The End of the English Novel." In his editorial preface to that issue, Buford
had characterized the emergence of novelists like Rushdie as nonwhite former
colonial subjects, many of whom were now British citizens, who were "writing
back" in a style, language, and with an imaginary scope that seemed to be sur-
passing English (read: white) writing. However, what *Granta* also represented
was a disjuncture between those English-language texts in the slush pile and
the places they were coming from, originating from. And the point here is not
to fetishize place, but to understand it as a complex of linguistic and other
forms of politics.

We all had heard that Salman Rushdie had written *Midnight's Children*, a
postmodern epic of modern Indian history, while sitting in north London—a
quaint footnote highlighting Rushdie's multicultural, hybrid identity. It was
also a politically significant fact in 1980s Thatcherite Britain, when it was
important to see nonwhite writers as fully British. However, those kinds of
circumstances were certainly not representative of the vast majority of English-
writing aspirants from the formerly colonized world. Sifting through the slush
pile at the Granta office, those submissions became part of another exclusively
Anglophone literary sphere, albeit a multi-accented one. And that is what
made being published in *Granta* so special; you had made it in such a distinctive way. It lifted one out of the literary margins and into the center. Which
is not to say that many, if any, slush pile submissions made it to the pages of
Granta. The manuscripts that made it to the pages of the magazine were the
solicited ones, that is to say, work that came via agents and the already-existing

networks between agents and editors. Nevertheless, the desire and belief were pervasive, even palpable (at that time), in the stamped, handwritten envelopes. Postcolonial criticism, meanwhile, was taking all of these Englishes, of known and rising postcolonial authors, and making its own analyses and theories—important ones—about the nature of power, hybridity, mimicry, and resistance in colonial and postcolonial worlds, where centers and margins were clearly set out.

I started to see the English in India in a slightly different way, not as one among many Englishes in the *Granta* slush pile, but rather as one among many literary languages—spoken and written—in India itself. There was the significance of literature in the imperium versus literature in the Indian context. And, simply put, I came to want to understand the place of English in the Indian context. I soon came to see *Granta* as an abstraction and distraction, rather than a text or even context to be analyzed (at least by me).

Fieldwork in Delhi

The first summer I spent in Delhi as a researcher was disorienting. I wasn't sure how to research the literary. I mostly stayed at home at a family friend's apartment, reading novels under the fan and sometimes cooped up in an air-conditioned room. This seemed safe, and I convinced myself that reading in Delhi was the start of my fieldwork. It wasn't really.

By the second summer, I knew I had to get outside. I took more walks, whatever the weather. I went to the places where I felt some "sparks"—bookshops in South Extension, Khan Market, and Connaught Place, which then led me to more interesting ones on Asaf Ali Road, which is technically the dividing line between "old" Delhi and "new" Delhi—the Mughal-era old city and the British-era new one. The question of "old" and "new" has great resonance in a postcolonial capital, with issues of tradition and modernity, precolonial and colonial, seemingly burnished onto place names and urban forms. "Old" Delhi and "new" Delhi are just kilometers apart; on the surface they feel quite different. In "new" Delhi, cars dominate as do roundabouts; you swirl around colonial-era red sandstone buildings, past regal lawns and stately monuments. In "old" Delhi, you walk or take cycle rickshaws, if you can bear to be pulled along by someone else. A net of gullies leads through Chawri Bazaar, past the Jama Masjid through to Chandni Chowk. You experience the density of population as you walk through the lanes, which become so narrow at certain points that if you look up, you can no longer see the sky. On the steps of the Jama Masjid, you look across to Red Fort on one side and Chandni Chowk on the other and still have some sense of the religious-secular-commercial relationship sketched into the urban landscape a few centuries earlier. Now, with the Metro, old Delhi and new Delhi are just two stops apart on the Yellow Line. The ruse of old and new is finally being laid bare.

When I got the chance in 1998 to live in old Delhi, I jumped at it. I started going to the Sunday morning book market in Daryaganj, a historic neighborhood just inside the walls of the old city. I explored the alleyways of Ansari Road and started to take note of all the small publishing houses and book distributors. I watched workers spill out of storefronts, standing in groups near chaat stalls or sitting on buckling concrete steps in front of shops and businesses. I traveled around the city more, at that time, pre-Metro, by bus and auto rickshaw or in a six-wheeled, eight-passenger *phat-phat*. I carefully examined street bookstalls in a variety of markets. What were people selling, how and which books were on display and in which neighborhoods?

This wandering led me to start talking to booksellers and bookshop owners. I then began peeping my head into publishing offices, talking to staff, making appointments to interview owners. This was how I came to meet Ameeta Maheshwari, the wife of one of the city's most important Hindi publishers. I later interviewed him, too, but it was in that first conversation with Ameeta over chai and samosas that she talked to me about being more "in touch" with one language over another at different points in her life. It was a good way to begin thinking about the kind of multilinguality that most Indians experience on a daily basis.

Other times I was shown around tiny offices with editorial staff typing at old computers in attic spaces. This visual understanding of publishing also became important as a way to open up the very idea of a book. I continued these activities and slowly started to see patterns. I would come to see how the story of Ansari Road was linked to the development of post-Independence publishing, and how book publishing went hand in hand with the promotion of Hindi and English as co-official languages. I saw how the area of Daryaganj forged the link between the material requirements of book production, due to its proximity to the plentiful paper and binding markets of the old city and to the distribution networks afforded by the nearby railway station.

I soon recognized Delhi as the site of the major publishing houses in English and Hindi (from Rajkamal Prakashan and Vani Prakashan to Rupa, India Ink, Penguin, Ravi Dayal), and this enabled me to start seeing the city as a literary field. My wanderings started to resemble a method. I went to events at the Sahitya Akademi, India's National Academy of Literature, and a host of other cultural and literary venues. At first, I relied on newspaper listings for events, lectures, and meetings, crunched in extra small type at the bottom of pages in newspapers such as *The Times of India*, the *Hindustan Times* (in Hindi and English), and *The Hindu*. Then, as I got to know people, I got invited to events, or often just had a sense of where to show up or whom to call. As the writer Pankaj Mishra told me in one of my first interviews in 2001, there was no real literary "scene" to speak of in Delhi. In some sense he was right, in terms of there being—and this is what Mishra emphasized—the quality and standards of writing, editing, and publishing that one found elsewhere and were essential to creating an informed reading public leading to that somewhat elusive literary scene. Yet, my sense was that there was something to be found and discerned, even if it might not look the same, or feel the same, as it did elsewhere. I started to see English in relation to the other Indian languages, or *bhashas*, especially when listening to writers who inhabited both worlds, such as Gagan Gill, Nirmal Verma, Geetanjali Shree, and K. Satchidanandan. These writers, who wrote in Hindi or Malayalam, were engrossed in the modernisms and experiments of their own languages, but were also fluent in English. It was often the relationships they had to different languages that became the focal points of our conversations. It became a way for me to understand how English was more than just a colonial language, how these writers, in fact, had helped indigenize the language; and yet I also came to understand how their literary production could only ever be in a language *other* than English, or more precisely, their own mother tongue. These life histories and reflections gave meaning to the ideological debates about English and Hindi that were pervasive in Indian letters precisely because theirs was *not* a crude nationalism or quest for authenticity.

The question of cultural authenticity in particular—which languages could ever be considered truly Indian ones—became linked to what I came to recognize as the multiple hierarchies of language, between English and Hindi as national languages and different manifestations of elites, between English and the other *bhashas*, and between Hindi and the other *bhashas*. There were, of course, hierarchies among the *bhashas* as well, often depending on issues of class, caste, and script at increasingly local levels. This mapping of language hierarchies made me see the field of Indian literature as one of competing authenticities. I came to see literary language as a live wire and the global literary stage as a true fiction.

When I had conversations with publishers such as Ashok Maheshwari or Ravi Dayal, who offered their own linguistic ethnographies of the city, a map of the literary field began to emerge. As I connected my knowledge of texts to places and people, I began not only to read differently but also to see how a variety of literary practitioners were connected to each other and to recurring notions, realities, and moralities of place. Most of all, I started to see how different languages stood for different things to different people, and what was being created emotionally, intellectually, and politically—on the page, in their lives, and in society—because of it. I came to see that my real "object," or rather, what mattered to people most, was their thoughts and feelings about language, what I came to think of as linguistic subjectivities.

I got my first glimpse of this feeling for language as it related to the city and its forms in two novels—Ahmed Ali's *Twilight in Delhi* (1940) and Anita Desai's *In Custody* (1984). These novels were interesting to me because they were laments for the lost Urdu culture of old Delhi, the walled seventeenth-century city known as Shajahanabad. And yet both novels, written 44 years apart, were written originally in English. I found this curious, and it gave me a clue about what I was looking for in my interviews—the complexity of people's sentiments about language, their own contradictory feelings that could play out over a lifetime, and how sentiments related to places they lived or were from or wanted to be in.

I soon moved from the institutional centers of literature to the outskirts of the city, where writers can actually afford to live. I took long auto rickshaw rides across the bridges over the Yamuna River to East Delhi—a trip that I now make by the Delhi Metro. I was drawn to one apartment block in particular that housed several of the most prominent Hindi writers. Why did where they live matter? I knew it did; I just wasn't sure how. I slowly started to piece together linguistic and literary locations in the city. The idea of cultural authenticity that had such an obvious political dimension in literature in English versus the *bhashas* became more complicated when writers spoke of their own sense of place in the literary worlds of which they were part.

The question of linguistic authenticity became more intimate and personal in my conversations with writers such as Geetanjali Shree. I met her many times over several years, always at her home, and we talked about her writing, but also about where she lived and where she was from, the languages she came to know, the ones she discarded, and how she tried to make literary peace each day at her desk with the one she kept.

Shree defined to me her "use of Hindi" by the way in which she writes "up to the limits" of a particular idiom. Her writing, then, is also about, perhaps chiefly about, her own dialogue with the Hindi language, a dialogue that partly occurs in English. When I told Shree that I had read both the Hindi and English versions of her first novel, *Mai*, and found that each gave me a different feeling, she started to describe how English and Hindi offer different emotional registers in her text:

> Many people say the English translation [of *Mai*] is better, that it is light and has a bounce to it that the Hindi doesn't have. When you are saying things like "I love you" in English and compare it to the Hindi—Main tum se pyaar karti houn—the Hindi is heavy in comparison. It depends what you are talking about of course. The Hindi I write in is not a learned Hindi but the Hindi I grew up in, the Hindi I spoke to my mother.[5]

In the case of the English-language editor and publisher Ravi Dayal, I met him at his home in Sujan Singh Park in central Delhi. A neighborhood of stately red-brick buildings, we sat in his English-style drawing room in the English-speaking heart of the city. It's not that people don't speak Hindi there, but it is the orientation of the area that gives it this linguistic bent. What was interesting about Dayal was gleaned in his life history; he was a boy from the hills essentially, and grew up with a double-consciousness, linguistic and cultural. Dayal compared the dexterity of living in multiple languages with the ability to straddle two civilizations: "To be familiar with Indian classical music and Bach and Beethoven at the same time—some would say what happens is that you don't know either culture very well, that it's always surface, a mannerism, but that's not really true." I took this to mean that Dayal did not think of himself as English in taste and Indian in blood. And I also took it to mean that what was "Indian" and what was "English" were not static cultural traits or practices to begin with.[6]

What emerged from my interviews, then, were a series of correspondences between "old" Delhi and "new" Delhi, this side of the Yamuna River and that, north Delhi and south Delhi, Delhi and beyond. The people I interviewed and got to know over several years had their own linguistic and literary geographies; their stories became central to my descriptions of Delhi's literary field.

In my reading of Delhi, my conversations with publishers, writers, and others, and my analysis of texts suggest how the meanings of a language, from the everyday to the ideological, emerge from the places in which language is located and lived through. In this sense, individuals' "feeling for language" is a prism through which I came to analyze contemporary society.

THE ETHNOGRAPHY OF LITERATURE

The kernel of my field research experience that I carried around in my head for several years was what I witnessed at a public translation conference at the Sahitya Akademi. It could be thought of as a "dead fact" that came alive for me during the process of my research.[7] I had been in Delhi, interviewing Hindi and English publishers, writers, booksellers, and others for some time, so I already had a lay of the land. This "lay of the land" was understood not only from the interviews but also from the routes I took to get to those interviews and often what I found along the way. It was about how I came to know that these were the people I should be interviewing, information I often gleaned in casual conversation at various venues and events in town. Those events and venues I discovered by reading newspapers and talking to people—friends, scholars, and booksellers to start with. The "lay of the land" mostly came from encounters I had outside any formal protocols. But those encounters at the same time led me to the formal ones I needed to know about.

When I went to events at the Sahitya Akademi, it often seemed like the public discussions and talks there were a distillation of many of the issues of authenticity and language that were to become central to my project. In this instance, I happened to hear[8] the Bengali translator of Vikram Seth's novel *A Suitable Boy* give a provocative speech whereby she questioned the authenticity of what the Hindi translator had done in *his* translation of the novel. She chided the Hindi translator for having deleted passages from the original in his Hindi version, and because those passages (about the skinning of cows in relation to shoemaking) could be offensive to Hindus, she accused him of pandering to a presumed upper-caste Hindu audience. The debate that ensued became a launching pad for a discussion of the levels of authenticity at play in the Indian literary field and the places that Hindi, English, and Bengali occupied in that field: literary one-upmanship, forms of distinction, and competing levels of authenticity. The Bengali translator was not only giving a professional admonition to a fellow translator but also implicitly commenting on how the Hindi belt has been more prone to communalism and giving in to the forces of it.

I analyzed what transpired at this event, in the heart of Delhi's literary world, at an institution that managed and produced various hierarchies of language; and I juxtaposed those insights with my analysis of the Hindi translation of

A Suitable Boy in light of its English original and the concerns that the Bengali translator had raised. I compared the English and Hindi versions of the texts and found the omissions she had generally referred to in her talk but had not specified. My task was a socially embedded literary analysis whose ultimate goal was to understand how linguistic hierarchies operate through literature and literary discourse in a postcolonial, independent India. I never set out to write about *A Suitable Boy,* but its significance revealed itself in the everyday politics of authenticity that happen in Delhi and are relevant to the national and global literary stages of Indian literature. It also speaks to the everyday literary realities of translation and writing itself. The meaning of English in India is of course infused with its colonial past, and yet, the everyday interactions Indians have with English have much more to do with its relationship to the other languages in its midst (in this case Bengali and Hindi) than any colonial relationship *per se.*

If embarking on fieldwork threw up my idea of which texts to study, it also opened up new arenas of questioning, and eventually, new texts in particular social and political contexts that called out for analysis. The more interviews I did, with publishers, booksellers, and writers, the more I saw connections between the geography of the city and its literary outlets. These connections also illuminated a relationship between public and private spaces that revealed itself in layers, with the most public being bookshops lining Asaf Ali Road, for instance, or in south Delhi markets; the next layer being literary institutions like the Sahitya Akademi or the offices of publishers, which were more private than the bookshops; and the final layer being people's homes, both writers and publishers.

The more research I did, the more my methods adapted to what I was seeing and listening to, and the more I saw how language ideologies existed not only in political realms but also in everyday life. Fieldwork became a method to link concrete lives to the politics of language and the production of literature. Literature reflects and represents, but it is also produced and consumed under particular social and political conditions. I listened to people and conversed with them. I took my presence in the city seriously and became attentive to a range of encounters in literary and nonliterary milieus. My point was never to juxtapose the methods of ethnography with literary analysis for some kind of layering effect, interpretation upon interpretation. Instead, my method was to crosscut between ethnography and the study of literary texts. My aim was to move *across* the literary field, from text to institution to publisher to author or translator, highlighting and expanding on key ethnographic moments and milieus. My ethnographic approach was not only a method, but became a vision and argument for how to understand English in India and how to discern the relationship between literature and politics in the world more generally.

The ethnography of literature, as I was starting to define it, was writing about the places, people, and institutions that produce literature and the connections between them. And it was about the resultant debates over cultural authenticity—questions such as whose language was the real language of the people, which language could or should be used to express Indian social realities—that were alive and central to a larger understanding about national and regional identity formation, as well as India's place in the world.

Rather than fetishize "the field," I argue instead that the process of undertaking fieldwork defined my research problem in ways that would have been impossible if I had focused exclusively on texts and their contexts. In the process of doing fieldwork on postcolonial literature in Delhi, "literature" became publishers, booksellers, writers, translators, and literary officials. I created a new method—the ethnography of literature—that connected texts not only to the contexts of the city's linguistic histories and geographic spaces, but to the linguistic histories and subjectivities of the publishers, writers, booksellers and others who are players and producers of the literary field.

CONCLUSION

The generic term "fieldwork" does not quite do justice to the kinds of life experiences that undergird what historian James Clifford has called "an unusually sensitive method."[9] The experiential aspect of fieldwork—participant observation—has been a hallmark of anthropological fieldwork, and as Clifford writes, it "obliges its practitioners to experience, at a bodily as well as intellectual level, the vicissitudes of translation."[10] Here the researcher's experience of place itself becomes the beginning of an act of translation. Clifford further defines the practice of ethnography as "producing knowledge from an intense, intersubjective engagement." One could also take this to mean: You are your method, and you are part of your research, and yet it is not about you. Instead, you are an instrument or tool that not only enables the fieldwork experience but also defines its parameters, akin to the way an archive might delimit a historian's research object. This dynamic, and personal investment in people and places, has been both the promise and problem of anthropological fieldwork for some time.

In her ethnography of television, *Screening Culture, Viewing Politics* (1998), Purnima Mankekar writes that for her, the purpose of ethnography is not merely to add to the empirical record of places (the old job description of the anthropologist), but rather that ethnography, and by implication its method, is a "strategy." Mankekar explains in her introduction that she not only could analyze television programs but also "must extend to the spaces occupied by television in the daily lives and practices of viewers." Her research objective is to understand how the nationalist narratives found in television programs interact with people, especially women and women's identities vis-à-vis their roles at home, relations with others, and places in society. The spaces where women watch television, and where Mankekar carried out her fieldwork, are, she writes, "the contexts in which texts (television programs) are interpreted." And therefore, she cannot delink text from context.[11]

In my research of Delhi's literary geographies, I was not aiming for an ethnography of readers, of which there is a distinguished tradition in the sociology of literature[12] and even an ethnography of reading.[13] I see my own method as more of an ethnography of literature rather than a sociology of one. In an ethnography of literature, the very production of texts, over time and space, is both anchored and brought to life in a set of people and institutions. Following Mankekar, I see fieldwork itself as a strategy, in my case to excavate the levels of cultural authenticity I saw at play in the debates over Indian literature and identity. It was to see how the everyday politics of language undergirded literary discourse and production in the contemporary world.

In India, it was seeing books being sold on pavements and at stoplights, often by children who could not read, that initially brought me into the realities of language, class, and caste. This reality seemed less abstract than the pages of *Granta*, and yet what I was witnessing was also a kind of abstraction. Capital cities after all are about the projection of power and order. Fieldwork has its own set of illusions, based on how you frame what you see and how you understand your encounters. Now as I ride the Metro, I see the literary map of Delhi I had carefully plotted whiz by me. Places and people are connected more easily and quickly than before. The cultural geography of the city is changing. What keeps me there is the sense of movement and contingency.

NOTES

1. See Rashmi Sadana, *English Heart, Hindi Heartland: The Political Life of Literature in India*.
2. See Sarah Brouillette, *Postcolonial Writers and the Global Literary Marketplace* for a full accounting of postcolonial book prizes.
3. Author interview with David Godwin, January 23, 2009, in Jaipur, India.
4. For more on the concept of "being there" in contemporary debates within anthropology, see John Borneman and Abdellah Hammoudi's edited volume, *Being There: The Fieldwork Encounter and the Making of Truth*, which argues for the experiential encounter of fieldwork over what they see as the rise of textualism in the discipline.
5. Author interview with Geetanjali Shree, February 2001, in Delhi, India.
6. Author interview with Ravi Dayal, February 2001, in Delhi, India.
7. Thanks to Kavita Panjabi for her framing of this part of my research as such.
8. I say "happened to hear," but of course fieldwork is about repetition, being there again and again, when much of the time nothing really striking happens. I had been to countless events at the Sahitya Akademi and heard dozens of lectures before stumbling on to this one. When I did hear this one, I was immediately able to link it to other things people had said in similar forums over the years. I was able to gauge its relevance, worth, and uniqueness in the larger literary discourse.
9. Clifford, "On Ethnographic Authority," 119.
10. Clifford.

11. Mankekar, *Screening Culture, Viewing Politics*, 20.
12. For example, in her comprehensive study of Nigerian novels, Wendy Griswold (*Bearing Witness: Readers, Writers, and the Novel in Nigeria*, 8) writes of the "Nigerian fiction complex-made up of poorly integrated parts, of markets and organization that are simultaneously global and parochial, with people entering and exiting all the time." Griswold neither frames her research as fieldwork nor her study as an ethnography *per se*, but her data includes extensive and multiple interviews with readers, writers, and publishers. At the same time, her focus is not on a single place of production of books and literary discourse. Rather, her invocations of place are through the novels themselves and their representations of Nigeria, long passages that are wonderfully weaved throughout the book and analyzed in juxtaposition to her interviews.
13. See Jonathan Boyarin's edited collection, *The Ethnography of Reading* for a series of articles on anthropologists' engagement with textuality and cultural constructions of reading.

Bibliography

Borneman, John, and Abdellah Hammoudi, eds. 2009. *Being There: The Fieldwork Encounter and the Making of Truth.* Berkeley, CA: University of California Press.

Boyarin, Jonathan, ed. 1992. *The Ethnography of Reading.* Berkeley, CA: University of California Press.

Brouillette, Sarah. 2007. *Postcolonial Writers and the Global Literary Marketplace.* London: Palgrave Macmillan.

Clifford, James. 2007. On Ethnographic Authority. *Representations* 2(Spring): 118–146.

Griswold, Wendy. 2000. *Bearing Witness: Readers, Writers, and the Novel in Nigeria.* Princeton, NJ: Princeton University Press.

Mankekar, Purnima. 1999. *Screening Culture, Viewing Politics: An Ethnography of Television, Womanhood, and Nation in Postcolonial India.* Durham, NC: Duke University Press.

Sadana, Rashmi. 2012. *English Heart, Hindi Heartland: The Political Life of Literature in India.* Berkeley, CA: University of California Press.

PART III

Medium and Form

CHAPTER 9

Daily Life and Digital Reach: Place-based Research and History's Transnational Turn

Lara Putnam

Academic historians are crossing borders as never before—or at least, their narratives are. Researchers are tracking ideas, people, publications, and commodities across territorial boundaries, no longer content to leave "where from?" or "where to?" unasked. Whereas once the topic of many historical studies could be summed up with a single national modifier—French artists, Dutch women, Venezuelan exports, Nicaraguan popular culture—today nationwide coverage and national closure are no longer presumed. Increasingly, we pursue networks, circuits, and connection.

The collective shift has responded in part to critiques of the epistemological errors of "methodological nationalism," in part to ethnographers' and sociologists' accounts of the importance of the transnational fields created by overlapping circuits of migration, communication, and capital in the present day. These interdisciplinary drivers of history's "transnational turn" then received key aid from technological shifts. Indeed, although the theoretical case for transnational history has been under discussion for nearly two decades, most historians' practice remained anchored to subnational study. But in recent years, the linked expansion of source digitization and web-based search has made us radically more able to track connections and flows via written sources regardless of place of publication, catalogued topic, or archive of origin—and median practice has begun to change.

My thanks to George Reid Andrews, Shalini Puri, and Steve J. Stern for discussions and feedback on this chapter.

L. Putnam (✉)
Department of History, University of Pittsburgh, Pittsburgh, USA

S. Puri, D.A. Castillo (eds.), *Theorizing Fieldwork in the Humanities*,
DOI 10.1057/978-1-349-92834-7_9

167

A world of possibility has opened up—but an untheorized-yet-vital tradition of historical fieldwork is at risk. This chapter begins by reviewing the heyday of historical fieldwork: two generations across which techniques of archive-based social historical reconstruction were applied to societies outside the North Atlantic core. Much, although certainly not all, of this work was done by researchers trained in institutions within that North Atlantic core, whatever their birthplace, and thus cross-border transit and intercultural residence were commonplace accompaniments to international archival research. Within US academia, the expansion of social history toward international targets found crucial support in the federally funded area studies paradigm, which across the Cold War era both valued the accumulation of place-specific expertise and provided material support to sustain it, from language training to field research grants to international scholarly exchange.

In the heyday of this overseas expansion of social historical inquiry, the 1980s and 1990s, there was spirited dialogue between anthropologists and historians on multiple issues: hidden disciplinary geopolitics; the risks of teleology, whether Marxian or neoliberal; the proper understandings of class, gender, race, and ethnicity. Yet historians chose not to embrace as relevant to our own practice the debate over the epistemology and implications of fieldwork that was simultaneously under way. The fact that in-depth historical research in notarial archives or parish records required long residence *in place* in the present, as we worked to reconstruct the past, seemed to go without saying and require nothing to be said.

Times have changed and that conversation needs to begin. The changes under way in our discipline are shifting historians' goals and methods in ways that threaten to displace place-based research. By "place-based" I mean two things: research guided by place, in the sense of seeking multidimensional knowledge about a particular society, and research conducted in place, requiring actual residence in the locale under study. The two are distinct, of course, but are frequently synergistic. Each has been central to historians' practice, and each seems poised to become less so.

The drivers of change are external and internal. Area studies infrastructure, hit by the one-two-three punch of left-wing critique, right-wing suspicion, and federal budget crises, is defunded and decaying. Intellectual agendas that cut across traditional "areas"—that highlight connections between Santiago de Chile and Shanghai, say, rather than similarities between Santiago and Buenos Aires—have accelerating cachet. Those agendas demand information gathering at a global scale, which is now feasible as never before. For historians, information means, first and foremost, texts produced in the past. The rapid digitization of a long century of print production from around the world (its chronological bookends set by the spread of printing presses and the horizon of copyright protection) places extraordinary new tools in the hands of historians who seek to trace border-crossing processes. Full-text search of massive web-based holdings, from Google Books to JSTOR and far beyond, can instantly uncover all mentions of a particular individual, phrase, commodity, or town, tracing far-flung webs of connection and communication utterly invisible via analog search.

Our new digital reach means that international presence and international history writing are becoming uncoupled. From one angle, this is an exciting leap forward. From another, it is an unacknowledged return to the past: it replicates a key feature of metropolitan scholars' practice in a bygone imperial era. What risks being lost in this moment of twinned turns? Which choices in regard to research design, method, and scholarly communication may help build those pieces back in? These questions combine ethical with methodological and interpretive dimensions. Do US-based scholars who move—literally or figuratively—through multiple parts of the world in transnational projects need to stop and listen along the way? Do they have an obligation to engage with the scholars for whom those places are a daily reality, their histories a lifelong mission rather than passing interest? When our research follows things on the move, how can we also stay put long enough to report on the impact on those who stay behind? To which "real people" are transnational historians accountable? What spaces and practices can bring those people's priorities into dialogue with academics' agendas?

The examples of area studies research and international social history suggest that *learning about place* and *learning in place*—and through them, being forced to *think critically about your own place*—can provide vital responses to these dilemmas. But will transnational history in a digital age develop a commitment to place-based research? There is no reason that it cannot, but there is no reason it necessarily will. We need to take cognizance of the multiple ways place-based research matters, of how learning of place, learning in place, and learning our own place go hand in hand, in order to ensure that the historical profession's transnational turn does not become, in practice, a neo-imperial whirl.[1]

THE BRIEF HEYDAY OF INTERNATIONAL FIELDWORK IN HISTORY: 1970–2010?

Social history originated with metropolitan scholars studying their own societies: England, France, the USA, Italy. Social historians pursued new questions and pioneered new methods for answering them. Usually the methods required painstaking aggregation of data dispersed across documents, aggregation both quantitative and qualitative. The best work found synergies in combining the two. Pioneering social historians spent long hours in archives compiling grain harvest totals or parish birth and death records. Explanations for previously recognized historical developments, from rural unrest to religious wars to economic growth, had to be rethought in light of those reconstructions.

Before this early- to mid-twentieth-century social historical shift, history had essentially meant the history of state formation, and thus all historical sources sat in metropoles almost by definition. Only powerful and stable states, which had built centralized bureaucracies that curated the documentary record such states required and produced, were understood to have histories worth writing.

"Bottom up" social history embraced a different target field of subjects, one not delimited to a small set of polities. People who had been ruled by unstable states, shifting states, colonial states, or failed states were now recognized as the protagonists of demographic, economic, social, and cultural processes just as worthy of historical investigation, maybe more so. The range of sources that had been made fruitful for metropolitan social history were discovered to have counterparts in many parts of the world. In some cases, such documentation was poorly preserved and partial, in other cases far more copious than any Euro-American example. There were parish records everywhere the Catholic Church had spread, from sixteenth-century Angola to twentieth-century Michoacán. There were notarial archives and local officials' tallies from across vast empires, whether Ottoman, Hapsburg, or Qing. Lands once governed by Islamic or Iberian rulers offered judicial records far more detailed than anything available in the Anglophone common law realm.

The turn to such materials was not everywhere led by external scholars: in some places, quite the contrary. The gathering tide of the social historical turn coincided, for much of the world, with the post–World War II era of decolonization. As new governments were created, intellectuals and leaders within those states embraced the task of writing national histories, often foregrounding trajectories of rule. By the 1960s and 1970s, social histories written of and from West Africa and South Asia and beyond joined those being written of and from Europe, North America, and Latin America (where the new techniques were embraced by local scholars eager to supplant the complacent *historia patria* of that region's postcolonial—nineteenth century, in this case—national elites).

In sum, by the 1980s, metropolitan researchers were routinely applying social historical techniques to reconstruct past processes in faraway places, which meant going there. Meanwhile nonmetropolitan scholars were pursuing similar agendas through similar methods, combining time in local or national archives in the place they were studying (and often were from) with—to the degree funds permitted—time in the archives of former colonial centers. All told, historians were in motion.

Let's pause to consider the modal case: scholars heading off to research the past of places distant from their societies of origin. Neither the complexities nor the generativity of this pattern—that is, of the experiential dimension of international social historical research—drew explicit notice, at least in print form. Historians had some recognition of the need for critical awareness within intercultural/postcolonial research, especially since as anthropology was moving to study the past of the same range of places, the degree of overlap between the disciplines was growing.[2] So as anthropology questioned issues of experience, power, and representation in fieldwork in the 1980s and 1990s, some historians read along. But in general, historians did not treat the quotidian experiences ancillary to archival research as something to be mentioned in footnotes or analyzed as methodology. Oral history indeed saw a boom in fruitful theorization in that era, a time of heightened critical examination of disciplinary truth claims more broadly. Yet the experiential learning that went along with the residence-in-place demanded by international archival research went largely unremarked.

Perhaps it was documentary historians' sense that they were researching a past about whose details and dynamics all living people were equally ignorant that naturalized the lack of debate within the profession over the possible impact of foreign researchers' particular ignorance as they arrived to dive in to the archives. But to an objective eye, the scale of that ignorance was huge. Northern historians heading off to research in the Global South, Western historians heading off to research in the East, Brooklyn-raised researchers heading off to Bremen were outsiders ignorant of many things in the places they landed, quite apart from the ignorance of archival contents that they and local residents shared. A locally raised 30-year-old had 30 years of accumulated knowledge on topics ranging from the subtleties of language and intonation, gesture, and expectation to the basic contours of partisan politics and regional landscapes, labor systems and economic tides. A few years of book learning at a distance offered no substitute, even in regard to the baseline contours, much less in regard to the subtleties.

After six months of research, an outside researcher might well know more about the notarial archives' contents than anyone since the scribes who inscribed them. But what other things had he or she learned along the way? What realms of ignorance remained? And how did that new knowledge and those persistent gaps shape the interpretation of the archival findings that she or he then built? In order to find out, you need to track scholars down and ask, because the importance of this kind of learning—of what we might think of as a kind of "ethnographic dividend" that even non-ethnographers gain from residence in place—was, among historians, rarely mentioned in print. As noted, the disciplines of history and anthropology were intensely in dialogue in the 1980s and 1990s, with generative results. But it was a dialogue about conceptualizations, analytic vocabulary, and disciplinary divisions of labor. It was not about the fact that historians were now increasingly themselves "in the field."[3]

I once asked pioneering social historian Steve Stern whether his experience of living in Peru in the late 1970s had impacted his interpretation of the sixteenth-century notarial sources he explored there, which formed the basis for his landmark 1982 book, *Peru's Indian Peoples and the Challenge of Spanish Conquest: Huamanga to 1640*.[4] What most struck him across those long months in a very new place, he replied, was the way logics of reciprocity structured everyday life, from the largest to the smallest exchange. His months in the field were long, indeed stretching into years, because the methodology he was enacting was painstaking. He sat in the chilly highland archives amid thick tomes of scribe-written *legajos* and copied out longhand the details of transactions over land, tribute, labor obligations. One might note the inefficiencies of this artisanal process: or one might give thanks that it held him in

Lima and Ayacucho long enough for his interpretive practice to benefit from the ethnographic dividend of everyday life. Without the lived experience of the specific, encompassing nature of reciprocity in the highlands, his reading of the dynamics through which sixteenth-century Andean leaders approached the challenges of Spanish rule, and ultimately found themselves transformed by them, would necessarily have been different.

To the extent that technological change enables historians to decouple information gathering from residence in place, such experiential learning is imperiled. Does that matter? Having gained some sense of where international research in history was coming from, let us now look at where it is going. Let us explore the intense and in many ways invaluable impact of web-based access to digitized sources on historians' practice.

Transnational Topics and Digital Reach

In the coming pages you will read nothing about the kinds of cutting-edge projects and innovative methodologies most often referenced under the headings of "digital humanities" or "digital history." Novel applications and skills matter in their own right, of course, but what transforms quotidian practice are technologies that transform quotidian practice. For historians, whose disciplinary epistemology has long been premised on gathering as many contemporary sources as possible linked to a particular topic in the past, and using knowledge gleaned from each additional source to refine critical understanding of the others, mass digitization and web-based search have been game changers. Finding and reading is what we do, with occasional forays into tallying up. We can now find things without knowing where to find them, which has never before been true. Not only is research at a distance increasingly easy, but also tracing things (people, ideas, commodities, publications) across multiple unpredictable locales has gone from extraordinarily difficult to routine.

What are the key affordances of web-based search for historians? Firstly, speed. Web-based search offers near-instantaneous access to an ever-increasing range of secondary sources (sources written by scholars or others about the process of interest) and primary sources (sources generated by the process directly: eyewitness accounts, protagonists' declarations, ships' manifests, birth records). Contrast typing into a search box with the full course of its analog equivalent, in which you go to a library to look in the card catalog to find the name and location of a book that you search out on the shelves to look through the index to find the right pages to look at the footnotes to see which primary source might be useful, before—in the best-case scenario—heading back to the catalog to find the location of copy of that newspaper/volume/document collection before trekking toward different shelves to pull down the first exemplar from a multivolume set and settling in to begin, page by page, to search.

The importance of catalogs and indices in that account underlines the impact of a second characteristic of digital search: granularity. Metadata remain important, indeed, for certain digital humanities projects fundamental. But improvements in optical character recognition software means that the most minor mention of your topic in digitized sources can now be discoverable through full-text search, even if no one would ever have thought to flag it. It is this characteristic that lets us look for things without knowing where to find them and makes it possible for digital sources to reveal transborder connections that no single scholar, however erudite, would ever have thought to attempt to seek out. Of course, the flood of mentions that may be returned from a text search of even a single newspaper database, much less an aggregated database like JSTOR or Google Books or the Digital Public Library of America, is huge. Historians have well-honed techniques for dealing with scant sources, from triangulation to "reading against the grain." We have not yet theorized how to handle overabundance. As literary scholar Ted Underwood observes, "In a database containing millions of sentences, full-text search can turn up twenty examples of anything."[5] How to know how to weigh their significance? Here is another conversation that needs to begin.

All of this would be of little import if digitization were only impacting a narrow chronological or geographical slice of the world's past. It is not. Archives and libraries from across ever more of the globe are posting not just print items but manuscripts, images, maps. The digitization of local newspapers is underway nearly everywhere papers have been printed. Ancestry.com adds birth, marriage, and death records, passenger manifests, and census sheets from across the globe at a dizzying rate. The portal now includes not only tens of thousands of data sets (each one with, routinely, millions of records each) from the USA, Canada, and Europe, but also multiple hundreds of data sets from Oceania, Asia, Africa, and Latin America. Such primary sources are not themselves history, but they are the building blocks of historical inquiry. They offer new ways to answer certain questions historians have long been asking and the potential to answer other questions we had not even dreamed we could.

The speed, granularity, and reach of digitization together mean that national or regional expertise no longer functions as gatekeeper, a requisite or channel for historical research. You do not need to know much about a place to find sources from it, about it, or about things that passed through it. For historians, in whose research practice national archives, national libraries, and national historiographies have always been crucial, this is a fundamental change.

This does not necessarily mean place disappears from our research. On the contrary, digital reach can allow us to engage place in ways both more intentional and more precise. Rather than presuming that national borders reflect the optimal scope of information gathering, or that world regions defined by Cold War calculations reflect the optimal frame for interpretation, we can treat the geographic contours of an investigation as an empirical question, to be answered as the first step of an inquiry and fine-tuned as it progresses. Which locales interacted most closely in a particular era? A study of New Orleans at the dawn of the nineteenth century might be framed along the refugee flows and capital flight that tied the port to Saint Domingue/Haiti and Cuba. A study of New Orleans in the early twentieth century might follow the connections to Panama, Costa Rica, and Jamaica that United Fruit's banana steamers underwrote, while a study of the 1950s would note that the same export and same fleet now tied New Orleans to northern Honduras above all. Indeed some of the most thoughtful theorizations of what can and should characterize "transnational history" point to this: a combination of spatially intentional research design and multiscalar investigation, which seeks to assess linkages between causal dynamics at the local, regional, and supranational levels.[6]

So digital search and attention to place can go hand in hand. But the decoupling of research practice from national/regional expertise on the one hand and physical presence on the other can also allow researchers to remain ignorant of place in unprecedented ways. Indeed, today one can be pretty darn ignorant about somewhere and still accumulate enough facts to write about it. The kinds of contextual knowledge that non-digital search foisted upon us whether we wanted it or not—the contextual knowledge gleaned from reading the headlines on the dozens of newspaper pages that *didn't* contain the information we were looking for, or the dozen books we had to read in order to begin seeking information about one battle, or the dozens of street vendors we passed on the way to the archive—this contextual knowledge, unheralded product of the inefficiencies of analog search, is increasingly stripped away.

Of course, history has not yet become a desk discipline, and archival *bona fides* remain valued enough that it will not do so any time soon. Yet the total time individual researchers spend in individual archives has already shrunk, both because some digitized holdings have been made web available and because documents are now captured so quickly via digital photography. As one colleague at the University of the West Indies in Jamaica reports, only half joking: these days if you see a graduate student from the USA in the archive in Spanish Town, she spends four days photographing documents and then explains, if you happen to ask, that she is leaving for Ceylon tomorrow. *Why the visit at all?* is a reasonable question. Citing archival sources still confers crucial prestige among historians, but this is increasingly a case of collective self-deception: we take such cites to signal a kind of immersive fieldwork experience that everfewer among us can or do make time for.[7]

Implicitly historians are accounting for the new efficiencies when, for ourselves or our students, we promote projects that would have seemed unthinkably ambitious five or ten years ago. But can the knowledge needed to make sense of those documents actually be absorbed any faster than before? Think about the contrast between the speed of information *gathering*—which technology has so accelerated, for primary and secondary sources alike—and the speed of information *processing*. Within quantitative analysis, the latter has also been enormously accelerated by technology. But within qualitative analysis, information processing depends on accumulated understanding that cannot be simply sped in the same way.

Many of the changes above reflect efficiencies generated by decoupling information from its physical form, physical form that required walking along library shelves or reading documents in the archive where they landed. Increasingly, we don't go to information: information comes to us. Yet these same efficiencies bring new disparities. Not everyone has a laptop and wifi. Not everyone has access to JSTOR, to say nothing of for-profit databases. Meanwhile, some of the scholarly practices that previously worked to counteract, or at least make visible, disparities, are being eroded. The real-world friction of seeking information in physical form generates light as well as heat. If we are going to leave that practice behind, we had best think hard about what we are losing.[8]

PLACE-BASED RESEARCH: AWKWARD ENCOUNTERS AND EVERYDAY LIFE

What does daily life in the place under study offer to researchers whose topic of study is not daily life in that place? Many things. Residence "in the field" imposes awareness of a longer chronology. Cities are palimpsests, visibly marked by layers of history. Those studying the present in place cannot ignore that place's past; those studying the past in place cannot ignore that place's present. Study *in situ* also makes us more likely to recognize in-country scholars, who might be invisible on the global stage as seen from Northern institutions. Visiting researchers, if they know what's good for them, show up at local universities and listen to what's going on. They talk to people who have forgotten more about their topics than they will ever know. They present their own research and risk derision, distrust, or disinterest. Each reaction has something to teach.

The same is true of conversations more broadly. As Shalini Puri notes, "When a researcher reads in a library, nobody is reading her back. When one reads in the field, one is constantly being scripted, being made the object of a countergaze, and is thereby forced to confront not only one's geographical but also one's historical location."[9] The experience of being asked to justify your research by people whose story you have assigned yourself the right to tell *should* be awkward. You have in fact overstepped your bounds; you do have some explaining to do. Such encounters make evident the geopolitics of knowledge. They also teach lessons not just ethical, but substantive. Do your interpretations diverge from your interlocutors', your priorities look different from theirs? If you are lucky, people will put into words what they are thinking: why has she come all this way, spending all that money, to study *that*, and yet seem not to care about *this*? The point is not that they are necessarily right. They are not sole owners of their place's multiple truths. But dissonance between their judgment and yours invariably points to something worth knowing.

Corrections are common, and essential. A single crystallizing anecdote can show up your chosen categories of analysis as merely your particular categories of practice.[10] And so if you are going to use nonuniversal analytic terms—as all terms are—perhaps there could be some utility in using terms closer to the society you are studying, even if far downstream from there. Those terms may still mark an improvement. Let's be honest: the privileged insight conferred by total ignorance plus graduate training is likely overstated.

Not long ago, I realized that my first two books both end with a vignette in which I recount being confronted, in a casual conversation, by how far my categories of analysis were from the self-understanding of individuals within the communities I was studying. So critical were those encounters to my understanding of my topic, I see in retrospect, that I felt compelled to break the "fourth wall" of academic history and speak directly about them to my readers.[11]

Those two recorded examples reflect a broader, ongoing, quotidian engagement that was fundamental to my research process—shaping both questions asked and answers heard—yet is nowhere mentioned in my formal discussions of sources or methods. Research in place feeds a kind of untheorized hermeneutic circle through which one continually refines one's awareness of things one might wish to understand, and finds out, by taking lurching baby steps in not-well-planned directions, how far away understanding lies. With some trepidation, I'll give two other examples, so fleeting that they would likely never make it into print except in the present essay.

When I was 15 and learning Spanish for the first time, I lived as an exchange student in Caracas. One day I painted my short fingernails bright red, and my host sister responded with a sniff: "Uñas de cachifa." Servant's nails, she explained; clearly not a compliment. I did my best to learn. But when a few days later I tried to use my new vocabulary word in the kitchen, my host sister's widened eyes warned me to a halt. Never say *cachifa* in front of the maid, she scolded later. My host sister's casual use of the insult, and then urgent correction as to when not to use it, stuck with me. If pushed to analyze the phrase *uñas de cachifa*, I might suggest that it captures both the intersectional construction of class, gender, and respectability by the Venezuelan elite and an embodied practice of resistance to that construct. That *uñas de cachifa* exists as a local category bears witness to the insistence of women with nails broken short by manual labor that they too have a right to feminine display. Or maybe not. It is a fragment of an unfinished mosaic.

Last summer, I was speaking with a gracious Trinidadian matriarch about her experiences as a young widow in the 1970s, when she traveled to Caracas to work as a maid to support her children back home. She recalled with affection a friend ("Negro, like me, but Venezuelan") with whom she ran errands. "'Juana'—she always called me Juana—'*Ven*, quick, *aquí*.'" My interviewee's given name was Juanita, a common one in Trinidad. I was struck by the Afro-Venezuelan woman's insistence on calling her friend Juana, rather than Juanita. Juanita, her actual name, would have sounded to the Venezuelan friend like the Spanish diminutive of "Juana." Perhaps calling a grown woman Juanita—using the condescending diminutive as employers so often do with their maids, maids they also call *cachifas* behind their backs—seemed to this Venezuelan woman and fellow domestic like an insult to the dignity her Trinidadian friend deserved. Again: or maybe not.

These fragmentary anecdotes shape the ear I bring to archival research about gender, labor migration, and race in Venezuela. They are just moments, fleeting and distant; I would be foolish to think they articulate clear questions, much less answers. It feels flatly wrong to fix them here in print. They are not even research, much less research findings. But they pointed me toward dynamics I had not noticed, and set me to listen for things I otherwise might not. To note that quotidian encounters can illuminate one's ignorance in helpful ways does not require romanticizing the knowledge gained. Neither before, during, or after these encounters did I see the world from the subject position of any of the other women involved. The encounters nevertheless increased my understanding of the extent of things I didn't know, and shaped my awareness of the range of things that might matter.

French historian Arlette Farge has described in evocative detail the iterations through which the historian becomes attuned to the subtleties of a particular archive.[12] What she does not stress is how far behind outsiders begin.

In 1915, in Port Limon, Costa Rica, a Chinese immigrant named Po Wo A began courting Theresa D, the 18-year-old daughter of his Afro-Jamaican neighbor. When Theresa became "with child," Po Wo A's older relatives pressured him to break off the relationship. In distress, he wrote her this note.

> Dear friend Miss
> I am know you get to sick now let me sorry very much because I have not time go to see you as soon as I see you to by and by. I am very love you and want marry to you but is time very bad and my business every day very dull I cant manage marry to do so please you must go to look next gentleman and marry to you you must Dont vex and excuse me
> I am yours Dear friends Domio Po Wo A

Furious, Theresa's mother swept downtown to denounce him. Perhaps the threat of legal action helped Po Wo A change his relatives' minds. On October 22, 1915, he and Theresa appeared before the judge to be married.[13]

I cherish love letters from the archives: intimate, highly scripted, mendacious. Into this one I read a story of racial divides that endured in spite of sexual intimacy across boundaries. (Among Chinese immigrants in Limon, men outnumbered women by nearly four to one.) I happened to share the note with a friend, a Jamaican anthropologist, who heard immediately what I had not: the deep *jamaicanness* of Chinese English in Limon, marked by Po Wo A's use of "vex" as intransitive verb. The insight pointed to very different range of questions about serial migration, culture, and connection. Maybe I would have gotten there on my own … eventually … if I had lived in Jamaica rather than Costa Rica. But no amount of text searching or digital photography would have done it.

Above, I described Steve Stern's comments on how the lived experience of Andean reciprocity shaped his reading of sixteenth century notarial archives, as an example of an "ethnographic dividend" that residence in place offers non-ethnographers. I suggest we need to take cognizance of how crucial this experiential dividend has been for historians working from largely textual sources to reconstruct the wide world's past. The experiential dimension of research in place is about developing an ear for local language and cultural cues. It is about hearing what matters to others, and trying to scope your own ignorance. It is about basic knowledge of material fact, and building a broad-based awareness of which questions seem most urgent, to whom, and why.

Fieldwork in this sense seeks the organic accretion of diffuse contextual knowledge. It is not identical to ethnography. Indeed, is it research at all? The Human Subjects "Common Rule" defines research as "a systematic investigation, including research development, testing and evaluation, designed to develop or contribute to generalizable knowledge." What I am attempting to name is the value of *un*systematic, context-specific learning that does not seek the generalizable but instead the place-specific, the particular, the *un*generalizable.

CONCLUSION

We need a full accounting of the knowledge fostered by everyday life in societies under study—which scholars from within have in abundance, and scholars from elsewhere can at least seek to acquire. Absent recognition of the intellectual contribution of informal learning-in-place, digitally accelerated history risks a collective neo-imperial turn. Have critiques of cultural essentialism and origin-based truth claims diverted our attention from the opposite problem— the risks of cultural distance? To the extent that history becomes a desk discipline, researchers will study processes from afar, perhaps never even experience themselves as outsiders to any particular place. But how, then, are they to assess their own gaps in knowledge, and the consequences those gaps might have for the interpretation of the sources before them?

Will historical research after the transnational and digital turns remain place-based in practice? Not unless we insist on it. Look at graduate training. National funding for area studies programs and language training is shrinking, even as we push to expand professional preparation and build in new skills, including digital skills. Meanwhile, time to degree is policed ever more tightly. Who has time to just go somewhere and hang out? Yet if we stay home, or cruise past at top speed, what will push us to note the legacies of the past in the present? How will we see what transnational processes have meant for those who stayed put? If history becomes a desk discipline, if historians based in the Global North become a coterie of adept database divers, if historians based in the Global South have fewer opportunities to confront their far-flung peers with the cosmopolitan truths of local knowledge, surely we all will be the poorer for it?

NOTES

1. In contrast to sometimes facile critiques of area studies, key analyses have underlined the importance of the emplaced expertise it in practice fostered. See Sidney Mintz, "The Localization of Anthropological Practice:

From Area Studies to Transnationalism," 130–131; Karla Slocum and Deborah Thomas, "Rethinking Global and Area Studies: Insights from Caribbeanist Anthropology," 553–565; and Shalini Puri, "Finding the Field: Notes on Caribbean Cultural Criticism, Area Studies, and the Forms of Engagement." 58–73.

2. See Bernard Cohn, "History and Anthropology: The State of Play," 198–221.
3. This failure to connect then intensified over the next decade, as anthropology engaged with "transnationalism" and "globalization" while many historians remained absorbed with internal debates over the cultural/linguistic/discursive turn. Anthropologists' debates, from the late 1990s and early 2000s, over the kinds of "multi-sited ethnography" that might be apt for analyzing systems of long-distance connection raised issues quite similar to those that theorists of "transnational history" would seek to engage ten years later, but the latter rarely reference the former. See note 9 below.
4. See Steve Stern, *Peru's Indian Peoples and the Challenge of Spanish Conquest: Huamanga to 1640.*
5. See Ted Underwood, "Theorizing Research Practices We Forgot to Theorize Twenty Years Ago," 66.
6. See Bernhard Struck, Kate Ferris, and Jacques Revel, "Introduction: Space and Scale in Transnational History," 573–584; Pierre-Yves Saunier, *Transnational History*; and Christian De Vito, "Micro spatial-history of labour." For relevant discussions of research design not explicitly linked to the term "transnational," see Rebecca Scott, "Small-Scale Dynamics of Large-Scale Processes," 472–479; and Lara Putnam, "To Study the Fragments/Whole: Microhistory and the Atlantic World," 615–630.
7. Historian Sumathi Ramaswamy dubs this "archival parachuting."
8. For the parallel concerns raised regarding multisited ethnography a decade ago, and an array of responses, see George Marcus, "Ethnography in/of the World System," 95–117; Matei Candea, "Arbitrary Locations: In Defence of the Bounded Field-Site," 167–184; Mark-Anthony Falzon, ed., *Multi-sited Ethnography: Theory, Praxis and Locality in Contemporary Research*; Simon Coleman and Pauline von Hellermann, eds, *Multi-Sited Ethnography: Problems and Possibilities in the Translocation of Research Methods*; and George Marcus, "Multi-sited Ethnography: Five or Six Things I know about it Now."
9. Puri, "Finding the Field," 69–70. See also Shalini Puri and Debra Castillo, "Theorizing Fieldwork in the Humanities."
10. On the distinction, see Rogers Brubaker and Frederick J. Cooper, "Beyond Identity."
11. Lara Putnam, *The Company They Kept: Migrants and the Politics of Gender in Caribbean Costa Rica, 1870–1960*, 204; and Lara Putnam, *Radical Moves: Caribbean Migrants and the Politics of Race in the Jazz Age*, 239.

12. Arlette Farge, *The Allure of the Archive*.
13. Archivo Nacional de Costa Rica, Serie Judicial, Remesa Limón Juzgado del Crimen 1084 (estupro, 1915).

BIBLIOGRAPHY

Brubaker, Rogers, and Frederick J. Cooper. 2000. Beyond Identity. *Theory and Society* 29: 1–47.

Candea, Matei. 2007. Arbitrary Locations: In Defence of the Bounded Field-Site. *Journal of the Royal Anthropological Institute* 13(1): 167–184.

Cohn, Bernard S. 1980. History and Anthropology: The State of Play. *Comparative Studies in Society and History* 22(2): 198–221.

Coleman, Simon, and Pauline von Hellermann, eds. 2011. *Multi-Sited Ethnography: Problems and Possibilities in the Translocation of Research Methods*. New York: Routledge.

De Vito, Christian. 2014. Micro Spatial-History of Labour. Paper presented at the European Social Science History Conference, Vienna, Austria, April 23–26.

Falzon, Mark-Anthony, ed. 2009. *Multi-Sited Ethnography: Theory, Praxis and Locality in Contemporary Research*. Farnham: Ashgate.

Farge, Arlette. 2013. *The Allure of the Archive*. Trans. Thomas Scott-Railton. New Haven, CT: Yale University Press.

Marcus, George E. 1995. Ethnography in/of the World System: The Emergence of Multi-Sited Ethnography. *Annual Review of Anthropology* 24: 95–117.

——— 2011. Multi-Sited Ethnography: Five or Six Things I know About it Now. In *Multi-Sited Ethnography: Problems and Possibilities in the Translocation of Research Methods*, eds. Simon Coleman, and Pauline von Hellermann, 16–30. New York: Routledge.

Mintz, Sidney W. 1998. The Localization of Anthropological Practice: From Area Studies to Transnationalism. *Critique of Anthropology* 18(2): 117–133.

Puri, Shalini. 2013. Finding the Field: Notes on Caribbean Cultural Criticism, Area Studies, and the Forms of Engagement. *Small Axe* 17(241): 58–73.

Puri, Shalini, and Debra Castillo. 2014. Theorizing Fieldwork in the Humanities. Paper presented at the University of Pittsburgh, Pittsburgh, PA, March 28–29.

Putnam, Lara. 2002. *The Company They Kept: Migrants and the Politics of Gender in Caribbean Costa Rica, 1870–1960*. Chapel Hill, NC: University of North Carolina Press.

———. 2006. To Study the Fragments/Whole: Microhistory and the Atlantic World. *Journal of Social History* 39(3): 615–630.

———. 2012. *Radical Moves: Caribbean Migrants and the Politics of Race in the Jazz Age*. Chapel Hill, NC: University of North Carolina Press.

Saunier, Pierre-Yves. 2013. *Transnational History*. Basingstoke, UK: Palgrave Macmillan.

Scott, Rebecca J. 2000. Small-Scale Dynamics of Large-Scale Processes. *American Historical Review* 105(2): 472–479.

Slocum, Karla, and Deborah Thomas. 2003. Rethinking Global and Area Studies: Insights from Caribbeanist Anthropology. *American Anthropologist* 105(3): 553–565.

Stern, Steve J. 1982. *Peru's Indian Peoples and the Challenge of Spanish Conquest: Huamanga to 1640*. Madison, WI: University of Wisconsin Press.

Struck, Bernhard, Kate Ferris, and Jacques Revel. 2011. Introduction: Space and Scale in Transnational History. *International History Review* 33(4): 573–584.

Underwood, Ted. 2014. Theorizing Research Practices We Forgot to Theorize Twenty Years Ago. *Representations* 127(1): 64–72.

CHAPTER 10

Lessons from the Space Between Languages: Notes on Poetry and Ethnography

Renato Rosaldo

Certain forms of poetry resemble ethnographic inquiry in ways that I have called (in Spanish) *antropoesía* (Rosaldo 2014). To summarize briefly what I've said elsewhere, in poetry and ethnography insight derives more from concrete particulars than from elegant generalizations. In neither case do specifics merely illustrate an already-formulated idea or theory. Both are processes of discovery rather than restatements of the already known. If the poet already knows exactly where her work is going, there is no reason to write further. Similarly, if the ethnographer has decided which theory to apply before examining the data, there is no point in further inquiry. The *antropoeta* and the ethnographer doing thick description dwell in a social context until they apprehend what was not evident in the beginning. Such inquiry requires patience, careful observation, extended conversation, and faith that meanings, though not immediately apparent, will be found.

The work of poetry is to bring into focus its central subject, whether it is sorrow, affliction, joy, or humor. Its task is to bring social life closer and make it tangible. It shows the contours of feeling and explores their shape. It is a space to inhabit and comprehend. It allows the writer and reader to apprehend powerful experiences and make them intelligible and vivid. It allows for the exploration of human subjectivities. The world it investigates is intersubjective rather than a merely subjective one where whimsical understandings abound.

On this occasion, I'd like to explore the ways that implicit cultural referents shape the meanings of what is explicit. "November Twentieth" is taken in Spain, for example, to refer to the date of the fascist dictator Francisco Franco's death in 1975. Nothing more need be said. November Twentieth by itself is a

R. Rosaldo (✉)
Departments of Anthropology and Social and Cultural Analysis, New York University, Brooklyn, USA

© The Author(s) 2016
S. Puri, D.A. Castillo (eds.), *Theorizing Fieldwork in the Humanities*,
DOI 10.1057/978-1-349-92834-7_10

cultural referent a Spaniard can safely assume her compatriots will understand. I learned this the hard way in translating *La alambrada de mi boca* (The Barbed Wire in My Mouth) by Ana Pérez Cañamares (unpublished manuscript), in particular her poem "Veinte de noviembre."[1] She clarified the meaning of "November Twentieth" when she saw that the cultural referent had been lost on me. Her poem begins:

> Te fuiste a morir en la misma fecha
> que aquel que te había jodido la vida;
> nada personal por su parte:
> te la jodió a ti como a tantos otros.
> (You went and died on the same date
> as that guy who fucked up your life;
> it was nothing personal:
> you were one among many.)

I want to speak about translation, about how what happens in the space between languages can be transformative in its social effects. In speaking of translation, I will draw on two examples. One concerns the art of the accessible poem. The other explores the political poem, a form frowned upon, indeed virtually forbidden in the USA. Both examples involve poets I admire, Naomi Shihab Nye and Yusef Komunyakaa. Their work, in my view, is often ethnographic.

It's hard to write accessible prose or poetry, but it's critical in ethnography and antropoesia. It's just plain hard to make it look easy. In writing to be understood, I've sometimes been inspired by what William Butler Yeats, in his poem "Adam's Curse," famously said. "A line will take us hours maybe;/Yet if it does not seem a moment's thought,/Our stitching and unstitching has been naught." In other words, he worked and worked to write lines of poetry that sing with meter and rhyme, yet read as if they were effortlessly dashed off.

Certain readers worry that prose or a poem they can understand is artless, prosaic, merely a good story, certainly not a poem. That readers can be so disconcerted by accessible writing makes one wonder. Do they think poems are beautiful words that can't be understood? What comes to mind for me is what a student said about my lectures in the first course I taught. "Your lectures," she said, "are pure poetry—beautiful. I can't understand a word."

Consider, for example, an accessible prose poem by Naomi Shihab Nye, "Gate A-4,"[2] that recently went viral on the internet (from now on I'll call her Nye for short). I should add that Nye would call her work a short prose piece. I prefer to call it a prose poem because it is so artful and to locate it in the tradition that runs from Arthur Rimbaud to Robert Hass. Her work as published has no line breaks, though the internet versions usually added them. Her carefully crafted prose poem appears chatty, conversational, as if casually told to a friend. Readers posted comments. They agreed that her work was beautiful, but they wondered: Was it poetry? Prose? Or just a good story?

The speaker of the prose poem by Nye begins by saying, "Wandering around the Albuquerque airport Terminal, after learning my flight had been delayed four hours, I heard an announcement, 'If anyone in the vicinity of gate A-4 understands any Arabic, please come to the gate immediately.'"[3] The scene is initially set in the mundane—a delayed flight, though four hours is rather more than usual. Then an announcement in an ominous key: at Gate A-4 Arabic speaker urgently needed. Why the urgency? Terrorism? A profiled passenger in handcuffs requiring interrogation? The reader's imagination, as cocreator of the poem, conjures no end of reasons for the urgency. In her succinct, under-stated, matter-of-fact way, Nye artfully builds dramatic suspense by drawing on her readers' background knowledge of what it means to be a monolingual Arabic speaker in the USA now.

Nye says, "Well—one pauses these days."[4] Indeed.

She then goes to her gate, which happens to be A-4. Once there, she finds "[a]n older woman in full traditional Palestinian embroidered dress, just like my grandma wore, was crumpled to the floor, wailing."[5] A distressed flight ser-vice person pleads with Nye for help. No sooner, she says, had they announced the flight was delayed, than the old woman collapsed into wailing. The mystery in Nye's subtle mini-drama has grown.

The central subject of the poem seamlessly shifts to an interlingual space as Nye speaks with the old woman in her halting, second-generation Arabic. "Shu-dow-a, shu-bid-uck habibti? Stani schway, min fadlick, shu-bit se-wee?"[6] These words, even if accented, are familiar to the old woman who grows calm and stops crying. In talking with the old woman Nye learns that there has been a linguistic breakdown. The old woman (mis)understood that the flight was canceled, not delayed. A canceled flight would have been catastrophic for her. She would have missed her appointment the next day for a necessary medical procedure. Nye phones the old woman's son who was to pick her up at the air-port. They speak English. Nye then phones the old woman's other sons. Other calls follow—for fun, in Arabic—to Nye's father and a few Palestinian poets. Healed by conversing in her native language, the old woman begins laughing and chattering.

Then a homespun epiphany. The old woman "pulled a sack of homemade mamool cookies—little powdered sugar crumbly mounds stuffed with dates and nuts—from her bag and was offering them to all the women at the gate." Nobody refuses. "It was like a sacrament." All the women are covered with powdered sugar. "There is," Nye says, "no better cookie."[7]

The airline joins the ritual process and servers, also sugar covered, pour apple juice and lemonade for all. By now Nye is holding hands with her elder and says, "This is the world I want to live in. The shared world."[8]

And she concludes, "This can still happen anywhere. Not everything is lost."[9]

Nye's art, as I have portrayed it, is to have carefully, in plain-spoken ways, built suspense. The mystery culminates when we readers, looking over the shoulders of the flight agent, see a crumpled old women wailing for no reason.

The mystery dissolves once Nye arrives and speaks Arabic to the old woman. The old woman has been wounded by a lethal mistranslation. When the old woman finds herself in her home language, the mystery dissolves and her mood and that of those around her shifts to joy and communion. Gate A-4 moves from diffuse apprehension through an old woman's severe distress to the joy of her linguistic homecoming and communion with her fellow passengers.

In Naomi Shihab Nye's superb prose poem, the figure of the translator, the bilingual person, is central. That figure is the speaker of the poem, Nye herself. By conversing in her second-generation Arabic, she transforms the social situation from one of mystery and distress to a joyous communion of solidarity. Translation in this case produces healing.

In my second example, I am the translator, the bilingual person. However, I am off stage, not a protagonist in the poem. It began this past June when poet Yusef Komunyakaa sent me an email, asking if I could write a brief preface to the Spanish translation of *Dien Cai Dau* (1988), his classic collection of poems that chronicles his combat experiences during the Vietnam War. I then was contacted by Juan José Vélez Otero, the Spanish poet who was his translator. Let me quote from our email exchanges, beginning with his to me:

> I was given your e-mail by Yusef. I am sure you have talked about the preface.
> I think you speak Spanish, don't you? It would be a good idea if you write the preface in Spanish directly.

Our correspondence from that email on was in Spanish. After starting the preface, I asked to see the translation, and Juanjo wrote saying:

> Te adjunto la traducción del poemario completo, así me haces un favor, y si ves algún error o inexactitud puedes ayudarme y corregírmelo. Ya sabes, no soy bilingüe.
> (I've attached the translation of the entire poetry collection, so if you would, could you do me a favor, and help me by correcting any errors or infelicities you see. As you know, I'm not bilingual.)

In another email, he again asked for corrections to his translation and I found the situation delicate. What if he would be offended by my suggestions? After all, there are people who don't like being told they've made a mistake, even if they have requested corrections.

With trepidation I sent comments on the poem called "Re-creating the Scene," especially the following passage which alludes to the gang rape of a Vietnamese woman:

> The Confederate flag
> flaps from the radio antenna,
> & the woman's clothes
> come apart in their hands.[10]

His translation, "the Confederate flag/la bandera de la confederación," though technically correct, did not make the connection with the fact that the soldiers engaged in the gang rape were from Mississippi and that the Confederate flag invoked a longer history of racism in America.

In response to his translation, I wrote Juanjo the following:

> En Recreando la escena, la bandera de la confederación requiere una nota porque es una provocación fuerte a los soldados norteños y negros. La bandera es de la Guerra Civil de los años 1860s y suele significar que los que ondean la bandera son sureños, racistas y de extrema derecha.
>
> (In "Re-creating the scene," the flag of the Confederacy requires a footnote because the flag is a strong provocation to black and northern soldiers. The flag is from the Civil War of the 1860s and in this context suggests that those who fly it are southern, racist, and right wing extremists.)

Juanjo replied in this way:

> Muchas gracias por tu ayuda. Eran cosas muy, muy importantes, sobre todo la aclaración referente a la bandera de la Confederación.
>
> (Thank you so much for your help. These things are very, very important especially your clarification concerning the flag of the Confederacy.)

I dared not hope he would so welcome my suggested changes. The problem was Juanjo's lack of background knowledge about the meanings of flying a Confederate flag in the USA. What the poet Komunyakaa can reasonably assume an American reader will know is entirely lost on a poet who knows the Spanish rather than the American national context.

Still feeling trepidation I went on, in another email, to suggest changes to the poem "Hanoi Hannah" about a Vietcong propagandist:

> "Hello, Soul Brothers."[11]

The poem goes on to say the following:

> "You know you're dead men,
> don't you? You're dead
> as King today in Memphis."[12]

"Dead as King today" refers, as American readers know, to the assassination of Martin Luther King in Memphis on April 14, 1968. The poem continues in the following manner:

> "Soul brothers, what you dying for?"[13]

My suggestion to Juanjo was as follows:

Aquí por "soul brothers" se entiende que son negros. Diría yo, tal vez, "Hola, hermanos negros" en vez de "hermanos del alma."

(The phrase "Hello, soul brothers" implies that the soldiers being addressed are black. I would say, perhaps, "Hola, hermanos negros/Hello, black brothers," rather than "hermanos del alma/bosom buddies.")

Juanjo responded with the generosity I had found before. He welcomed my suggestions rather than defending his translation. He said:

Muchísimas gracias por las correcciones que me haces. **Son importantísimas.** Le escribo al editor para que sepa que tengo que corregir algo ... Gracias, muchas gracias.

(Thank you so much for the corrections you've given me. **They're extremely important.** I'll write my editor and tell him I have to make corrections ... Thank you, thank you so much.)

He went on to say we should do the best translation we could because Komunyakaa's splendid work deserves no less.

What I learned as I went over the Spanish translations in detail is how deeply raced American English can be. A response Komunyakaa can reasonably expect from an American reader is simply absent for a reader from another—in this case Spanish—national context. When I reflected on this series of mistranslations racism fairly leapt out to me as central to *Dien Cai Dau*. Dictionaries had provided little help. The flag of the confederation, rather than the Confederacy was given by the dictionary. Instead, what was required for the translation was knowledge of implicit cultural referents, the background assumptions about race and racism that are encoded in American English and history. From my valuable collaboration with Juan José Vélez Otero what came into focus was the deep sense in which the poetry in *Dien Cai Dau* is political, profoundly antiracist. Thus, I wrote the following in my preface to the Spanish translation of Komunyakaa's exceptional work:

El poeta nos delinea una óptica anti-racista sobre el conflicto. El racismo estadounidense aparece explícitamente en el poemario de los propagandistas del Vietcong que intentan desanimar a los soldados Africano-Americanos.

(The poet depicts an anti-racist vision of the war. Racism in the United States appears explicitly in the poems through the words of Vietcong propagandists who were trying to discourage the African-American G.I.'s.)[14]

I now see Komunyakaa's poems not only as a chronicle of combat in Vietnam but also as part of the civil rights struggle by other means.

In this chapter, I've conflated the poet, the translator, and the ethnographer. I have done so to call attention to their similarities as mediators between cultural contexts. They work to render one cultural context intelligible to the other. They grapple with verbal texts rewritten in a language other than the original or with verbal texts (whether poems or ethnographies) that try to make a social world, whether their own or another, intelligible. Here, they work with implicit cultural referents that they may draw upon by assuming that their readers share these understandings. These understandings become especially visible in moments of mistranslation. Nye did so by invoking the urgent announcement about the need for an Arabic speaker in the Albuquerque airport. She could assume that her readers would recognize that such an announcement would create apprehension for those who heard it. Komunyakaa also did so by using the commonly understood, among his assumed readers, meanings of flying the Confederate flag and addressing American GIs as "soul brothers."

NOTES

1. Pérez Cañamares, *La alambrada de mi boca*, 18–19.
2. Nye, "Gate A-4," 162.
3. Nye.
4. Nye.
5. Nye.
6. Nye.
7. Nye.
8. Nye.
9. Nye.
10. Komunyakaa, *Dien Cai Dau* (Wesleyan) 19.
11. Komunyakaa, 13.
12. Komunyakaa, 13.
13. Komunyakaa, 13.
14. Komunyakaa, *Dien Cai Dau*, Traducción, prólogo y notas de Juan José Vélez Otero, 11.

BIBLIOGRAPHY

Komunyakaa, Yusef. 1998. *Dien Cai Dau*. Middletown, CT: Wesleyan University Press.
———. 2014. *Dien Cai Dau. Traducción, prólogo y notas de Juan José Vélez Otero*. Granada: Ediciones Valparaíso.
Nye, Naomi Shihab. 2014. Gate A-4. In *Honeybee*, 162. New York: Greenwillow Books.
Pérez Cañamares, Ana. 2007. *La alambrada de mi boca*. Tenerife, Islas Canarias: Ediciones de Baile del sol.
Pérez Cañamares, Ana. n.d. *La alambrada de mi boca*. English Trans. Ana Pérez Cañamares. Unpublished Manuscript.
Rosaldo, Renato. 2014. Notes on Poetry and Ethnograpy. In *The Day of Shelly's Death*, 101–114. Durham, NC: Duke University Press.

PART IV

Institutions, Organizations, Collaborations

CHAPTER 11

Researching the Cultural Politics of Dirt in Urban Africa

Stephanie Newell

This chapter reflects on the intellectual and methodological challenges that arose out of the European Research Council (ERC) research project, "The Cultural Politics of Dirt in Africa, 1880–present."[1] From 2013 to 2015, the project comprised two African teams of early-career researchers who collaborated with a local regional coordinator, me, and one another, in producing research as well as data; after 2015, the project has comprised two Nigerian researchers based at the University of Lagos. Drawing from a rich seam of theoretical discourse in anthropology, critical theory, and cultural studies on the topic of dirt and its associated terms—filth, waste, debris, contamination, disgust, and trash—in global cities, the hypothesis of the project has been that, while dirt permeates everyday life in urban Africa, it is more than an empirical substance: dirt is an idea, carrying with it a complex set of histories and representations that shape local perceptions of community and the body and influence people's attitudes toward urbanization, neighborliness, and inward migration to the city.

Dirt has been a potent category in European encounters with Africans for over a century. European travelers' accounts of the continent from the mid-nineteenth century onward repeatedly describe the "filth" of people who quite clearly do not need to take a bath.[2] Dirt also recurs as a literary trope in a striking number of African novels, including, from West Africa alone, Cyprian Ekwensi's *Jagua Nana* (1961), Ayi Kwei Armah's *The Beautyful Ones Are Not Yet Born* (1968), Sembene Ousmane's *Xala* (1974), Ben Okri's *The Famished Road* (1991), and Veronique Tadjo's *As the Crow Flies* (2001), where it is

S. Newell (✉)
Department of English, Yale University, New Haven, USA

© The Author(s) 2016
S. Puri, D.A. Castillo (eds.), *Theorizing Fieldwork in the Humanities,*
DOI 10.1057/978-1-349-92834-7_11

employed not only to describe urban degradation but to comment on postcolonial political corruption and the rise of antihumanist ideologies. My project
proposal initially arose from a core question raised by these various narratives:
What discursive function does dirt perform if it does not simply signify the
opposite of cleanliness? If dirt is not dirty, what ideological work does it do?

To some extent, this was a genuinely quixotic starting point in which textual theorizations and literary representations of dirt set a hypothesis in place
for a team of researchers to undertake fieldwork with contemporary urban
residents. Cervantes' Don Quixote read so many outdated popular romances
that his perceptions of reality became distorted: convinced that he was a knight
errant of old, that his decrepit horse was a noble steed, and that local women
were damsels in distress, he rode forth to save the world, and in so doing,
offered a comic warning to readers against assuming that the repetition of plots
and character types in printed narratives adds up to anything like an accurate
description of the empirical world. Don Quixote's rational sidekick, Sancho
Panza, runs after his master and repairs the damage, ensures Don Quixote's
survival (and the survival of this targets), and sees the world through a realist lens. While it is tempting to interpret Don Quixote as a comment on the
pitfalls of literary analysis and Sancho Panza as the exemplar of social research,
this chapter will attempt to reconcile any such extremes, showing the value
of fieldwork to textual studies and the value of qualitative textual analysis for
social research into African urban cultures.

Alongside its comic lesson against the misuses of literacy in consuming too
many popular novels, *Don Quixote* (Part I, 1605; Part II, 1615) anticipated, by
nearly 400 years, Edward Said's important understanding that the textual (and
visual) productions of knowledge in contexts of colonial power

> can create not only knowledge but also the very reality they appear to describe.
> In time such knowledge and reality produce a tradition, or what Michel Foucault
> calls a discourse, whose material presence or weight, not the originality of a given
> author, is really responsible for the texts produced out of it.[3]

Whether located in archives or art galleries, on bookshelves, newspaper stands,
film racks, or digital platforms, Said's point is that texts and images are always
mediations of realities, offering a wealth of historically specific information
about people's opinions, perceptions, prejudices, self-understandings, aesthetic
preferences, memories of the past, and dreams for the future. These ordinary
daily texts contribute to people's experiences and help to form the urban imaginaries that underwrite this project.

"Fieldwork" is an alien word to many literary scholars. Terms such as
"fieldwork" and "methodology" come out of a social research framework in
which texts comprise data for content analysis, interviews—whether one-to-
one interviews or focus group discussions (FGDs)—have topic guides, and
may be structured, semi-structured, or open, and content analysis may be
qualitative or quantitative, each with its own careful subdivisions and range of

methods. Even the act of observation has its own strategies (structured, participant, ethnographic, etc.). If social research fieldwork takes place in archives, using manuscripts, reports, digital resources ("e-data"), or published materials, methodological rigor and transparency are ensured through clearly articulated sampling and coding techniques. By contrast, the fieldwork methods employed by literary scholars can be described at best as "close reading" and "random qualitative sampling." I therefore want to bring some of the techniques and tools of African literary studies into contact with other disciplines in the humanities and social sciences, not least ethnography and media and communication studies. In approaching the theme of dirt through literary and cultural mediations, and the theories and conversations such texts generate, I want to ask questions, firstly, about how diverse dirt-related concepts are used in mainstream and social media in and about Africa—with literary narratives treated as a subset of these broader media—and, secondly, about the ways African urban dwellers make use of these mediated interpretations of urban life to report back on and think about their environments.

Key scholars in European cultural studies have transformed our understanding of the history of urban cultures through their attention to the place of filth in Western cities. Georges Bataille's ideas about excess, urbanization, and (post)modernity have had a major impact on discussions of contemporary urban cultures and postmodern theories of waste and public spaces in the West.[4] Similarly, Peter Stallybrass and Allon White's classic study, *The Politics and Poetics of Transgression* (1986), posits dirt and disorder—by which they mean the slum and the sewer—as the starting point for an understanding of "social division and exclusion" in European cultural history.[5] Their book gives dirt (and disgust) a "poetics," enriching and extending Mary Douglas's famous formulation that dirt is "matter out of place."[6] Stallybrass and White examine the dense language surrounding urban dirt in mid-nineteenth-century Britain in order to understand the many binary oppositions—including suburb versus slum, rich versus poor, clean versus dirty, health versus disease—that emerged as the defining features of public health discourse in the Victorian period and after. Such understandings of public health, as parts of this chapter will suggest, provided an influential framework for British urban planners in colonial Africa in the early twentieth century in their reactions to the contagious potentiality of freely circulating "native" bodies, particularly prostitutes, homosexuals, women, and children, in tropical cities such as Nairobi.

Recent publications on the cultural history of dirt in colonial and postcolonial locations break out of conventional "dirt versus cleanliness" molds in new ways, showing how the subject of dirt—in both senses of subject, as a topic and a person—is a great deal more complex and culturally meaningful than suggested by its binary oppositions with bodily cleanliness or moral purity. This work is exemplified by Adeline Masquelier's edited collection, *Dirt, Undress, and Difference* (2005), which contains ethnographic essays on the topic of bodily transgressions through acts of undressing, bathing (or not), and ideas about dirtiness in diverse global settings.[7] In relation to Africa, several localized studies of discourses about dirt have also been published, including Ashleigh Harris's (2008) examination of the Zimbabwean slum clearance policy, "Operation *Murambatsvina*" ("one who detests filth," "drive out rubbish") and Timothy Burke's (1996) outstanding study of the history of soap in Zimbabwe.[8] These publications draw attention to the underlying cultural and historical processes that produce dirt as a classification for cultural encounters and sexual morality, providing models for our understandings of dirt in our project.

After three weeks of intensive teambuilding and research methods training in the UK at the start of the project, the six researchers returned to their respective cities—Lagos and Nairobi—for the pilot period, during which they undertook semi-structured interviews and FGDs using topic guides designed in collaboration with the team. Of particular concern to all of us during this start-up period were the methodological challenges of transcription and translation from local language interviews into English. Given the importance to the project theme of nuanced translation and interpretation, the researchers were encouraged to exchange transcripts with one another and, during our fortnightly conference calls involving all team members, to discuss transcription and translation methods. Such discussions were informed by the large body of published work on translation studies in the context of cultural and postcolonial studies. Given the necessity of translation work across multiple languages, this was not a project in which a "principal investigator" (PI) could prescribe the content or interpret the data produced by the researchers. Indeed, the translation work required for interview transcripts of necessity positioned the researchers as vital interpreters of their data.

As part of the knowledge exchange and reflexive activities of the project—in our fortnightly reports, fortnightly online meetings, and through the project blog—we reflected on the practicalities of our methods in research contexts that were anything but "ideal." While I remained relatively secluded in various colonial archives, researching the histories of dirt in colonial cities, the project researchers faced methodological challenges that often directly countered the strict ethical guidelines prescribed by the European Research Council. In Kenya, for example, Rebeccah Onwong'a and Anne Kirori were forced by necessity to adopt what they termed the "Participant Exchange Focus Group" model in crowded, low-income areas of the city. This model described how a departing focus group participant was spontaneously replaced, over a period of 40 minutes, by a new participant without the say-so of the interviewers. While FGD numbers remained consistent, faces changed as people continuously entered the semi-open spaces in which discussions took place. Private room hire was not possible in these areas, not only because of the lack of local facilities but more significantly because members of the communities concerned—especially women—were unwilling to risk accusations of "secrecy" by fellow community members if they entered closed spaces with the facilitator. Anne Kirori described the situation thus:

On my part I would say "participant exchange" during a Focus Group Discussion has been my remarkable experience. What I mean by this is that: you start an FGD with 10 participants, and after exhausting the first topic, one or two of the participants leave the group and are replaced by another participant who is new and quickly gets absorbed into the discussion. This then means you might end up with different people from the ones you started with. In my case I only had 2 constant participants in an FGD of 13 people. The other 11 kept exchanging and new ones coming. The most interesting bit is that it never affected the quality of data, and the discussion became more exciting as we progressed. The discussion was mainly about current and emerging issues such as Ebola, teenage pregnancy, culture degradation, people's lifestyle changes/behaviors just to mention a few.[9]

Data from FGDs such as these were deemed unusable by the ERC's ethical advisor on the grounds that the introductory statement describing the project and participants' rights in FGDs was not reiterated to each subsequent entrant to the FGD, and informed consent was not therefore obtained from every participant. This is but one example of the many methodologically challenging situations that arose for the researchers in the field, through which the European funder's exemplary ethical standards were impossible to meet in real-life urban contexts.

My own work focused on archival and historical materials relating to the rise of dirt as an interpretative category in nineteenth-century European traders' writings about West African consumers of global commodities. I focused on the journals of Thomas M. Knox, an employee of the soap manufacturer Lever Brothers, who traveled overland from North to Central Africa in the mid-1920s in order to assess the capacity of West African markets to increase their consumption of imported Lever Brothers products and their production of the raw materials, especially palm oil, required for soap manufacture in Britain.[10] Knox's chief objective was to wean local consumers off their own locally manufactured equivalents to Lever Brothers' soaps. This study of colonial travelogues compared Knox's negative responses to the strangeness of others in the 1920s with similar reactions of other British travelers and traders in Africa in the late nineteenth and early twentieth centuries: for Knox, Lagos was "a town of unspeakable squalor … [I]t is the nurse of disease. Filth everywhere."[11] How unique, the project asked, was Knox's identification of the source of the filth: "Everything reeks of dirty natives."[12]

A year before Knox's travels, Percival Christopher Wren, author of the best-selling adventure novel *Beau Geste* (1924), also described Lagos in what had already become a familiar shorthand for the city, referring dismissively to "the rubbish-heap called Lagos, on the Bight of Benin of the wicked West African Coast."[13] In these and other colonial-era accounts, any physical dirt associated with the city is reattached to the body of the "dirty native." Again and again in the archives for West and East Africa, I found that references to filth and dirt were used in travelers' and traders' accounts of the continent to judge people, rather than things, by negative moral standards. Visual observations about the stranger's consumption habits were repeatedly processed by Knox and his peers into meaningful (for readers at home) opinions and projections about the stranger's *habitus*. Drawing from the Victorian tradition of writing about industrial slums in Britain, Knox, Wren, and their compatriots in Africa added race to the category of class, and in so doing, used the category of filth to transform visual perceptions of other cultures, or otherness, into the visceral category of disgust.[14] Knox and his peers were vectors for a distinctive, shared anti-cosmopolitan discourse that, as this chapter will suggest, continues to have global currency in contemporary public discourses about "disgusting" and "unnatural" types of behavior, most especially relating to urban dwellers' sexual morality.

As the researchers on the project begin to code and analyze their media and interview data in the coming months, we expect to extend this network of negative connotations of dirt by adding a layer of positive associations to dirt-related terms, particularly when the broad category of dirt is filtered through the lens of "waste," "trash," and other local terms for what people throw away. For example, project researcher John Uwa has found that when Lagosians reflect on the entrepreneurial work of mobile toilet owners, who install facilities in low-income areas and charge a small fee for use, or on the work of "scavengers," still regarded by some local elites as untouchable human "scum" for picking over the city's municipal and informal trash heaps, the potential for income generation from "dirt" is appreciated by many people, even if they would not personally undertake such work.[15] Whether dirt still remains dirt in this context of economic transformation is a question for further consideration.

"The Cultural Politics of Dirt in Africa" began as a "tale of two cities," proposing a comparative historical study of Nairobi and Lagos as two African cities with structural similarities, including comparable positions in World Bank indicators of poverty ratios, life expectancy, and urban development. Both cities contain a plethora of unplanned spaces in which the majority of residents depend for their survival upon informal networks of financial and social support, as well as highly visible planned urban spaces such as public parks, municipal rubbish dumps, and gated private housing estates. The popular narratives and commentaries generated by these diverse urban spaces give rise to common themes in Kenyan and Nigerian media—shared with many other African cities—such as concerns with people's sexual lifestyles, political corruption, poverty and wealth, immigration, religious toleration, pollution, and the environment.

Three portfolios were developed for the researchers: first, "Public Health and Environment," for which researchers would identify resources and build relationships in the fields of public health, environmental strategy, and waste management. Key areas of their research included interviews with public health users, providers, and NGOs and with users of and residents on or living nearby waste management sites. Second, "Education and Schools," for which researchers would look into the ways children and young people interpreted the connections between urbanization and dirt, urbanization and hygiene, and urbanization and migration. Third, "Media and Communications," for which researchers would focus on cultural production in the public sphere, including newspapers, radio and television documentaries, popular music, popular films, television soap operas, online blogs, local publications, and other popular urban media. For this last portfolio, work included the regular sampling of media materials, in-depth interviews and FGDs with media producers and audiences, and the sampling of newspapers, blogs, and broadcasts.

As the two teams of researchers progressed with their fieldwork in health centers, schools, and media outlets in Lagos and Nairobi, however, with each pair of researchers using shared topic guides, similar research methods, and regular online meetings to ensure the stability of methods for comparative analysis, many of these similarities started to be overshadowed by differences on the ground. Lagos and Nairobi started to populate the topics in different ways, not least because the beginning of fieldwork proper, February 1, 2014, coincided with the outbreak of the Ebola virus in West Africa.[16] From February onward the Nigerian media and public discussion were dominated by Ebola stories, months before the arrival in Lagos of the Liberian-American civil servant, Patrick Sawyer, dubbed in the Nigerian press as "the Liberian weapon of mass destruction" who brought the virus to Lagos in July 2014 and infected a number of health workers.[17]

While Ebola exemplified many themes of the project and focused our minds—along with the rest of West Africa—on the transmission of the virus from one contagious body to another, it had a further distorting effect on the comparative framework. The content of our interviews and FGDs diverged significantly across the continent: in one city, basic urban practices such as handshaking, entering a bank, visiting a barber's shop, and queuing for public transport became sources of extreme interpersonal anxiety, while in the other city life continued as before, with one or two popular songs circulating about the socially disruptive effects of Ebola in the west of the continent.[18] "We couldn't go out to *relate*," reflected one Lagosian focus group participant in January 2015: "There was this risk people would withdraw their hand" during a greeting, causing intense social embarrassment and public humiliation.[19] "You [were led to] assume anybody has Ebola," reflected another Lagosian on urban fears of transmission: "You don't want to know *where* it's coming from. People would not shake hands. People would withdraw hands because of Ebola, they feared they would contract it."[20]

Besides the obvious differences generated by such crises to the stories about urban encounters that residents tell in Lagos and Nairobi, residual differences in the two countries' colonial and postcolonial histories also impact on the shape of present-day urban cultures and the interrelationships of residents. Lagos is a multiethnic coastal city, an African "melting-pot" of religions and peoples with a history of trade and migration closely connected to the trans-Atlantic slave trade and its abolition. With the British colonial annexation of Lagos in the 1850s, and with passenger and cargo ships plying the West African coast well into the twentieth century, the city formed the last port of call in a network of trade ports along the West African littoral, including Freetown, Monrovia, Sekondi-Takoradi, and Accra, bringing visitors and residents from the entire region and as far afield as Syria and Brazil (the "Saro" community of ex-slaves came to Lagos from Brazil via Sierra Leone).[21] Long-established Anglophone elite families with pan-West African surnames moved freely through these migratory networks, building houses according to their cultural identifications, practicing as doctors and lawyers, setting up newspapers and political parties, and marrying across "British West African" territories.[22]

Unlike the historic city of Lagos, Nairobi required no annexation by Europeans. Established in 1896 on swampland owned by the Uganda Railway,[23] it grew from a small inland transport depot, where Europeans and Indian railway workers and traders built stores and houses, with a skeletal provincial government "miserably housed in corrugated iron structures," into a sprawling capital city.[24] From its inception as a residential space, race and the control of land were key structural factors in the organization of trade and town planning in Nairobi. Kenya's status as a settler colony, attractive to European residents who came to farm in the fertile highlands, and to set up businesses in the late nineteenth century, made the city more akin to colonial Harare and the towns of apartheid South Africa than to the "white man's grave" on the other side of the continent, where Europeans rarely settled permanently.[25]

Kenya's centuries-old history of trade and religious exchange focused largely on Mombasa, with its pronounced Arab-Islamic urban influences, and its ancient trading networks with the Indian subcontinent along the famous spice routes. As with Lagos, flows of trade in slaves and ivory in the nineteenth century created a versatile "polyethnic, mercantile and predominantly Islamic People of the Coast," out of which Swahili emerged as the dominant language of urban East Africa.[26] As the settlement of Nairobi grew into a town, and thence a city, these established coastal relationships were reflected in the presence of South Asian and Arab-Islamic populations engaged in trade, the civil service, and the professions, for whom Kenyan languages coexisted with the languages and literatures of the Indian subcontinent.[27]

One key word stands between the easy comparison of postcolonial Kenya and Nigeria: oil. The discovery of "black gold" in eastern Nigeria in the aftermath of the civil war in the early 1970s and the vast oil wealth it generated for the state produced political affects that reverberate into the present.[28] Nigeria's postcolonial history is marked by a rapid succession of military dictatorships in the struggle for control of the oil-rich economy, culminating in the murderous regime of General Sani Abacha (1994–1998), whose list of executions and assassinations included the international author and oil industry antagonist, Ken Saro-Wiwa (1941–1995), who campaigned for ethnic minority rights in the Niger Delta region. The term "kleptocracy" accurately describes the country's postcolonial governments until recently, and fraud and violence have become so embedded that the declared anticorruption measures of the current, democratically elected government of ex-military-dictator Muhammadu Buhari barely touch upon a resolution to these entrenched problems.[29]

While the above offers little more than a snapshot of the two cities' complex political, economic, and cultural histories, the blatant message for a literary scholar entering the field of urban cultural studies is that cities cannot be read like books: one cannot simply compare the opinions and preoccupations of urban dwellers as one might capture and contrast literary characters and themes in texts from diverse cities, even with the sophisticated insights made possible by comparative literature and postcolonial theory, with their attention to the nuances of history, identity, and place. As fieldwork for "The Cultural Politics of Dirt" progressed, what appeared on the surface to be common broad themes in African urban media—such as poverty and wealth, immigration, religious toleration, sexuality and sexual promiscuity, waste and the environment—were found to mask localized differences that generated vital gaps of non-comparison with implications for comparative literary as well as cultural studies. In producing knowledge about Lagos and Nairobi, we required a framework through which difference could be theorized in productive ways.

Towering above all these factors, however, was the obvious drawback of deploying an Anglophone term, "dirt," to support an ambitious multicultural investigation into diverse people's opinions and perceptions about urban experience. The category was useful only as a starting point for conversations about urban experience. In a fieldwork context, "dirt" required immediate (dis)qualification, not least in the polyglossic environments of two large cities where street noise is in Yoruba, Nigerian Pidgin, Hausa, Swahili, Gikuyu, Sheng, Arabic, and a multitude of other African and international languages. While media and interview data were superficially comparable through the shared themes listed above, and through the fact that the media is dominated by English in both countries (although Swahili is an important literary and media language in Kenya), urban dwellers' preoccupations were, unsurprisingly, specific to their cities of residence rather than continent-wide. As the research teams in Nairobi and Lagos analyzed contemporary media discourses, interviewed diverse urban residents, and conducted FGDs, the last thing participants wished to do was compare policy from country to country, to identify shared themes, or to compare themselves with the residents of African cities on the other side of the continent.

While the people of the cities resisted easy comparisons, two premises of the project have remained in place from the outset: first, that the qualitative, interpretative, subjective approach of arts and humanities disciplines can contribute to the social sciences by showing how "texts"—broadly interpreted to mean literature, media, and the stories people tell about themselves and other people—merit close attention for the ways in which they mediate urban relationships and resonate with past ideologies. Cultural representations ("texts") and popular interpretations (by readers/audiences) have a close relationship to people's social and economic experiences, helping to structure and define the ways people think about themselves and others in the city. Whether articulated in the media or in the exchange of opinion, popular representations impact on people's daily lives and help them to reflect on their relationships with others, especially in cosmopolitan urban environments where a scarcity of resources often generates social and cultural networks between strangers. Socioeconomic conditions in both Nairobi and Lagos generate interpersonal understandings and relationships of trust between people of otherwise vastly disconnected backgrounds. In asking about the ways in which African city dwellers understand and represent themselves and their environments through media, films, literature, and the exchange of opinion, therefore, this project insists not only on the relevance of narratives and textual interpretations to urban scholarship but also on their significance in "creat[ing] not only knowledge but also the very reality they appear to describe," helping to shape what scholars of global cities term "urban imaginaries."[30]

A second premise remained in place across these often incomparable urban cultural contexts. A recurrent turn toward the "dirtying" of particular populations in public discourse was observable in the press releases and speeches of politicians and parliamentarians, especially presidents, during the period of the project. On many occasions, their sentiments were reiterated uncritically in the mainstream media, while they were often fiercely debated—both for and against—on social media platforms.[31] In February 2014, during the start-up period of fieldwork, with Ebola dominating the press in West Africa, President Yahya Jammeh of the Gambia was widely reported as describing homosexuals as "vermin" who should be tackled like malarial mosquitoes.[32] Nigeria's Goodluck Jonathan preempted Jammeh's position, signing into law the "Same Sex Marriage (Prohibition) Law" in January 2014, not only banning same-sex marriages with prison sentences of up to 14 years but also criminalizing "shows of same-sex public affection" with up to 10 years' imprisonment and reinforcing colonial-era legislation against sodomy with the promise to "cleanse" and "sanitize" society of what a previous Nigerian president, Olusegun Obasanjo, had already labeled "unnatural" and "un-African."[33] In East Africa at the same time, Uganda's long-standing president, Yoweri Museveni, explained his toughened anti-gay legislation using associations learned directly from the discourse of dirt and bodily contamination discussed earlier in this chapter in relation to colonial discourse, describing gay people as "disgusting" and "abnormal" and strengthening the colonial-era law outlawing sex acts deemed to be "against the order of nature."[34] Kenya's president Uhuru Kenyatta followed suit, criminalizing homosexuality with up to 14 years in prison and introducing controversial anal testing to prove or disprove homosexual activities.[35]

In country after country across the continent at this particular time, colonial-era laws against homosexuality were strengthened, accompanied by substantial public discussion in the media and in churches about acceptable and unacceptable, natural and unnatural, palatable and disgusting sexualities, including considerable public protest, in Kenya at least, against the legislation and the accompanying rise in homophobic violence.[36] Given how often this public discussion revolved around homophobic hate speech, I started to wonder whether such highly charged and politically productive discourses—designed to generate a common enemy, to isolate and target a "not-me" among the majority—stemmed from colonial-era (re)iterations of cultural difference through the supposedly empirical category of dirt. The connections with the archival materials by Knox and his 1920s peers are manifest: in both cases, expressions of disgust and hatred are regarded by those who articulate them as "natural" and instinctive, rather than as ideological, precisely because they involve a set of visceral reactions to the preferences of strangers.[37]

This chapter does not have the scope to examine why African cultures that are renowned historically for their accommodation of diverse sexualities have allowed their politicians and religious leaders to use the public sphere for homophobic statements that remain largely unchallenged by opposition parties. The key seems to lie in the attempts of public figures such as parliamentarians, pastors, and imams to harness the media—the "public sphere"—for political and moral campaigning, over and against the discreet toleration of diverse sexual preferences to be found among numerous ordinary people. To attempt to understand this homogenizing current in the contemporary public sphere, a comparative perspective remains not only feasible but necessary, first, geographically between instances of homophobic hate speech in Nairobi and Lagos, and second, historically, between colonial-era and contemporary expressions of disgust at the behavior of strangers. (The category of strangers here includes foreigners, or locals as encountered by foreigners, but it also includes members of subcultural groups such as LGBTI people who are routinely denied access to public spaces such as conference centers and hotels).

A popular truism about historical research is that it gives access to attitudes and ideologies that have subsequently become outmoded and that, as a consequence, stand out to later generations of scholars in shocking, entertaining, or perplexing ways. For historians of empire, such gaps and differences—especially when exposed in documents in the archives—can enrich our understanding of why particular beliefs and behaviors arose in particular social and political contexts, how they were negotiated between different constituencies, such as the Colonial Office in London and respective colonial governments, if and how they were challenged, and how they ultimately came to pass into policy or disuse. In tension with this idealistic notion of archival transparency, however, are the practical and intellectual challenges of cultural "retrieval" projects, particularly relating to research into the underlying beliefs and prejudices that may have shaped particular policies.[38] Instances of homosexuality and homophobia are particularly difficult simply to identify in the archives. At most, the method best suited to this type of research involves speculative, queer reading in between the lines of documents where insinuations, euphemisms, and adjectives such as "unwholesome" and "unspeakable" appear: these are often the closest a present-day researcher can get to descriptions of diverse local sexualities in the colonial period.[39]

In testing the usefulness of "dirt" as a heuristic for this broad, generalizable anti-cosmopolitanism that connects Lagos to Nairobi, and both contemporary cities to colonial-era discourse, in the larger project from which this chapter is drawn, I also focused on letters, memos, and minutes sent between colonial officials in Nairobi in the early twentieth century on the topic of sanitation and public health in order to identify the continuities, and highlight the gaps, between contemporary homophobic discourse in the public sphere and similar anti-cosmopolitan currents in the colonial period. The starting point for this comparison is the understanding, drawn from the field of hate studies, that a characteristic of dehumanizing discourse is the fear of cross-contamination by other people and that the metaphor of humans as pollutants—waste, trash, dirt, vermin—is one of the chief features of both racism and homophobia.[40]

If hate speech cannot be detached from the history of dirt, not all references to the dirt or dirtiness of others should be categorized as hate speech. On many occasions in the nineteenth and early twentieth centuries, the binary us–them ideology embedded in this use of dirt marks the limits and failures of the traveler's representation of other cultures, but, in addition, European travelers use dirt-related concepts to express fascination for, or befuddlement about, other cultures, rather than "hatred" of the other.[41] Traders in particular could not afford overt hate speech because they wished to transform the consumers of locally manufactured (thus "dirty") products into consumers of imported mass-produced commodities from Europe.[42] The dehumanizing gesture that characterizes hate speech, whereby the other is transformed into vermin or trash for elimination, could not therefore be allowed to dominate the traders' responses to the bodies of potential consumers. Rather, dirt is converted into the expression of a desire to understand, and thence to transform, local communities, and it therefore operates as the mediating category, rather than the stopping point, for the traders' unfamiliar encounters.

The point is that whether expressed as hate speech or, viscerally, as physical revulsion, the category of dirt performs a failure of cross-cultural understanding—and culture, as mentioned earlier, is taken here to include sexual subcultures as well as ethno-linguistic cultures—on the part of the commentator, whose observations about others, when released into the public sphere of print or other media, have the power to dramatically affect a person's future. When viewed as a failure of individual perception, located outside the power structures of the colonial state, the church, or postcolonial governments, the language of filth, applied to others, contains some potential for cross-cultural understanding, at least when the onlooker recognizes the gulf separating himself from his object of interpretation.[43] Again and again in our research, the teams have found homosexual tolerance among small groups and individuals who identify as heterosexual. Such liberalism in small FGDs and one-to-one interviews compares starkly with public discursive spaces such as newspapers and broadcasts.

Outside the Anglophone framework that has dominated the above analysis, and outside the public sphere of print and mass media, one can find countless positive valuations of people's bodily encounters with dirt, including the aesthetic properties of earth as a beautifying substance for people and dwellings, and its long history of uses in masquerade, sculpture, recycling, compost, building, decoration, and leisure. Indeed, if regarded solely as earth, or mud, dirt is removed from the moral, evaluative realm of disgust. Other examples are more relevant: in numerous East African jokes, excreta and the presence of vermin are treated as signifiers of wealth, such as the Sheng jokes in Nairobi about the presence of flies on a person's mouth, or around a person's anus when they fart, being a sign of an enviably rich diet[44]; or the mocking colonial descriptions of Kenyan women for whom the "fine heap of dung by the door-way proclaim[s] her husband's wealth."[45]

Dirt is a catchall interpretive category that includes moral, sanitary, economic, and aesthetic evaluations of other cultures. Part of the reason for its resilience in scholarly discourse is that diverse interpretive categories converge into one resonant category, ranging from missionary understandings of local sexualities and colonialist understandings of domestic hygiene through to contemporary television images of slum life in postcolonial cities. For obvious reasons, therefore, while dirt has been a vital category in epidemiological and environmental research in so-called developing countries, scholars in the global humanities have tended to avoid approaching the topic in the style of Stallybrass and White and their Western counterparts in cultural studies, because of its capacity to perpetuate the very stereotypes about global cities that it is ostensibly utilized to critique.

The physical degradation of Lagos, the largest city in Africa with nearly 18 million inhabitants, has earned it labels such as "mega-city of slums" and "the dirtiest city in Africa." International media attention has remained focused on the rubbish heaps and squalid informal settlements of Africa's sprawling cities.[46] Significant as dirt might be as an anti-cosmopolitan heuristic, questions remain about what social and ideological work it undertakes as a scholarly category. Does it help to produce the very histories in which it is deployed as an explanatory tool? Would our conclusions about the failures of urban sexual tolerance, past and present, be different if we included diverse African languages and a multilayered linguistic approach?

Dirt is a source of fascination for Western publics and scholars alike, as evidenced by the popularity of the Wellcome Collection's exhibition of global artifacts, "Dirt: The Filthy Reality of Everyday Life," in London in 2011, and by the plethora of dirt-related monographs since the turn of the twenty-first century. This raises broader questions about the intellectual validity of a thematic approach to colonial and postcolonial cultural history. Whether one's chosen theme is dirt, cleanliness, sexuality, gender, or another of the multifarious "ways in" to cultural history, the primary methodological challenge for scholars adopting a themed approach is to preserve the cultural complexity of the chosen global cities while also creating space for non-reductive historical and transnational comparisons. Key methodological questions accompany such projects: Are African cities better studied in comparison with one another within an assumed global (or postcolonial) network, or in their specificity as singular cultural entities, incomparable by too many factors for their superficial similarities to be productive? In thinking about a comparative themed approach in global arts and humanities fieldwork, it is necessary to interrogate the benefits of articulating a common topic for analysis (such as dirt) over and against a non-themed approach (such as the study of urban cultures and popular culture).

If social research is to literary studies what Sancho Panza is to Don Quixote, this chapter has attempted to highlight the significance of texts to social history and urban studies. Without ignoring the extreme conditions and conflicts under which the majority of urban Africans live, the fieldwork for this project has focused on the ordinary lives of urban subjects and their responses to contemporary conditions in the domains of material, popular, and textual culture. From this locally situated, individualized perspective, African urban subjects and African urban texts can be studied for the ways they represent and creatively respond to the flows of local and international people, commodities, and resources in their cities.[47] Focusing on the lives of ordinary people—and the stories they read and narrate—alongside institutional and infrastructural issues, the project tries to emphasize the flexibility and improvisation to be found in African urban cultures, as well as how, where, and in what languages, anti-cosmopolitan discourse operates, and to understand the contexts in which such discourse emerged historically in order to draw attention to the plethora of other local connotations of dirt and dirt-related terms that do not have their origins in a history of hate.

NOTES

1. "The Cultural Politics of Dirt in Africa 1880–present" was funded in Lagos and Nairobi by the ERC (AdG 323343) between Sept. 1, 2013, and June 30, 2015; from July 1, 2015, the project in Lagos has received generous funding from the Edward J. and Dorothy Clarke Kempf Memorial Fund and the MacMillan Center for International and Area Studies at Yale University. The researchers on this project were/are: Stephanie Newell (principal investigator); Olutoyosi Tokun, John Uwa, and Jane Nebe at the University of Lagos, with the support of the Regional Coordinator Dr. Patrick Oloko; Anne Kirori, Job Mwaura, and Rebeccah Onwong'a in Nairobi from Feb. 1, 2014, to June 30, 2015. Far more than "research assistants," from the outset the team members wrote regular blogs for the project website and worked on presentations for dissemination at conferences.
2. See Stephanie Newell, "Dirty Whites: 'Ruffian-Writing' in Colonial West Africa," 1–15; Stephanie Newell, "Dirty Familiars: Colonial Encounters in African Cities," 44–64.
3. Said, *Orientalism*, 94.
4. Georges Bataille, *Visions of Excess*. See Julian Pefanis, *Heterology and the Postmodern: Bataille, Baudrillard, Lyotard*; Michael Thompson, *Rubbish Theory: The Creation and Destruction of Value*.
5. Stallybrass and White, *The Politics and Poetics of Transgression*, 126; see also William A. Cohen and Ryan Johnson, eds, *Filth: Dirt, Disgust, and Modern Life*.

6. Mary Douglas, *Purity and Danger: An Analysis of Concepts of Pollution and Taboo.*
7. Adeline Masquelier, ed., *Dirt, Undress, and Difference: Critical Perspectives on the Body's Surface.*
8. Ashleigh Harris, "Discourses of Dirt and Disease in Operation Murambatsvina in Zimbabwe," 40–50; Timothy Burke, *Lifebuoy Men, Lux Women: Commodification, Consumption, and Cleanliness in Modern Zimbabwe.*
9. Anne Kirori, 6 November 2014.
10. Newell, "Dirty Familiars."
11. Knox, "Niger Company Ltd.: Diary of Tour Through the Congo and West Africa," ms. 72.
12. Knox.
13. Wren, *Beau Geste*, 6.
14. Newell, "Dirty Familiars."
15. Between 2005 and 2015, during his term as head of the Lagos Waste Management Authority (LAWMA), Ola Oresanya ran a public relations campaign aimed at transforming people's perceptions of municipal road sweepers and waste disposal employees. Where Lagos sweepers in 2005 were regarded as shameful and unmarriageable, and hid their faces from public view while they worked, Oresanya employed teams of "beautiful ladies" and insisted that they worked with uncovered faces in order to effect cultural change. A careful media management strategy accompanied this process (Interview, 8 January 2016).
16. Ebola started in Guinea in December 2013 and spread to Liberia and Sierra Leone early in 2014. By July 2014, the first case had reached Nigeria. According to World Health Organization (WHO) figures, just over 11,000 people died from the virus, with three times that number infected, but the WHO acknowledges that these figures vastly underestimate the actual numbers.
17. "Ebola: How 50-Year-Old Nurse and Mother of Four Succumbed to Death After Treating Liberian Weapon of Mass Destruction," *This Day Live*, August 10, 2014. http://www.thisdaylive.com/articles/ebola-how-50-year-old-nurse-and-mother-of-four-succumbed-to-death-after-treating-liberian-weapon-of-mass-destruction/185934/.
18. The most popular song was "Ebola! Don't Touch Your Friends," the theme song from *Malaria Ebola* (directed by Evans Orji, Evanix Merchandise Production, 2014. 41 min), one of several Nollywood movies about the virus. An American rap song, "Ebola (La La)" by Rucka Rucka Ali was also popular in Nairobi, with its emphasis on the racism of travel restrictions on black people, including "Don't let the Obamas on the plane."
19. No. 4, FGD Lagos: January 2015 (Informed consent and anonymization procedures have been implemented for all interviews). FGD chaired by John Uwa, Jane Nebe, and Olutoyosi Tokun.

20. No. 5, FGD Lagos: January 2015.
21. Whiteman, *Lagos: A Cultural History* , 14–15.
22. Whiteman, 30; Kristin Mann, *Marrying Well: Marriage, Status and Social Change Among the Educated Elite in Colonial Lagos*; Karin Barber, ed., *Print Culture and the First Yoruba Novel: I. B. Thomas's "Life Story of Me, Segilola" and Other Texts*.
23. Rather like the East India Company (est. 1600) and the notorious British South Africa Company (established by Cecil Rhodes in 1889), the Uganda Railway had its own police force and judiciary.
24. White et al., *Nairobi: Master Plan for a Colonial Capital. A Report Prepared for the Municipal Council of Nairobi*, 11.
25. Colonial debates about the racial segregation of Nairobi revolved not around whether but how to go about the social engineering of the town. As late as 1948 (a date that coincides with the institutionalization of the apartheid policy in South Africa), the lengthy government study, *Nairobi: Master Plan for a Colonial Capital* discussed different forms of racial segregation, with extensive input from a team of white South Africans and inspiration from the model adopted in Southern Rhodesia (HMSO 1948).
26. Simba, "Street Life: The People of Dar es Salaam," 66.
27. Postcolonial migrations into Kenya include South Asian refugees from Idi Amin's expulsions in the 1970s and, since 2003, Darfuri refugees from west Sudan. In Nairobi's changing cultural map, new trade networks are visible with the numerous Chinese restaurants serving Chinese personnel involved in infrastructure projects.
28. Falola and Heaton, *A History of Nigeria*, 181–208.
29. For an outstanding study of corruption in Nigeria, see Smith, 2007. For a commentary on oil politics, see Michael Peel, *A Swamp Full of Dollars* (2011). The discovery in 2012 of crude oil deposits worth $10 billion in northern Kenya generated concerns among some political commentators that an already unequal economy will become less re-distributive and more "Nigerian." See Wolfgang Fengler, "Will Oil Be a Blessing or a Curse for Kenya?" *Africa Can*, Nov. 4 2012, http://blogs.worldbank.org/africacan/will-oil-be-a-blessing-or-a-curse-for-kenya-lessons-from-indonesia-and-the-rest-of-the-world; "What Kenya can learn from Nigeria's Oil Industry," *Afritorial*, March 27, 2012, http://afritorial.com/what-kenya-can-learn-from-nigerias-oil-industry/. The dramatic drop in global crude oil prices has slowed the exploitation of oil in Kenya (Immaculate Karambu, "How Kenya's oil boom went bust," *Daily Nation*, October 6, 2015, http://www.nation.co.ke/lifestyle/smartcompany/How-Kenya-oil-boom-went-bust-/-/1226/2899924/-/14rah82z/-/index.html).
30. Said, *Orientalism*, 94; Christoph Lindner and Miriam Meissner, "Globalization, Garbage, and the Urban Environment," 1–13;

AbdouMaliq Simone, *For the City Yet to Come*: *Changing African Life in Four Cities*.

31. The discursive spaces offered by social media in Lagos and Nairobi, and many other themes in this chapter, will be developed in subsequent publications arising from this project.

32. "Gambia's Jammeh Calls Gays 'Vermin,' Says to Fight Like Malarial Mosquitoes," *Reuters*, February18, 2014. http://www.reuters.com/article/us-gambia-homosexuality-idUSBREA1H1S820140218.

33. Adam Nossiter, "Nigeria Tries to 'Sanitize' Itself of Gays," *New York Times*, February 8, 2014. http://www.nytimes.com/2014/02/09/world/africa/nigeria-uses-law-and-whip-to-sanitize-gays.html?_r=0; "Nigeria Anti-Gay Laws: Fears Over New Legislation," *BBC*. January 14, 2014, http://www.bbc.com/news/world-africa-25728845.

34. E. Landau, Z. Verjee and A. Mortensen, "Uganda President: Homosexuals are 'Disgusting,'" CNN, February 25, 2014. http://edition.cnn.com/2014/02/24/world/africa/uganda-homosexuality-interview/.

35. Jonathan Cooper, "Kenya's anti-gay laws are leaving LGBT community at the mercy of the mob," *The Guardian*, October 8, 2015 http://www.theguardian.com/global-development/2015/oct/08/kenya-anti-gay-laws-lgbt-community-mercy-of-mob.

36. Elsa Buchanan, "LGBT in Kenya: 'Government Needs to Stop Violent Anti-Gay Attacks,'" *International Business Times*, September 28, 2015, http://www.ibtimes.co.uk/lgbt-kenya-government-needs-stop-violent-anti-gay-attacks-1521533.

37. President Obama told President Uhuru Kenyatta on a visit to Kenya in July 2015 that the country's antihomosexuality laws resembled the politics of racial segregation in America's "Jim Crow" era. See Michael Lucchese, "Obama Compares Kenya's Anti-Gay Laws to Jim Crow," *Breitbart*. July 27, 2015. http://www.breitbart.com/national-security/2015/07/27/obama-compares-kenyas-anti-gay-laws-to-jim-crow/).

38. Ann Laura Stoler, *Along the Archival Grain*: *Epistemic Anxieties and Colonial Common Sense*.

39. For a discussion of queer reading in the archives, see Stephanie Newell, *The Forger's Tale*: *The Search for "Odeziaku."*

40. David Livingstone Smith, *Less Than Human*: *Why We Demean, Enslave, and Exterminate Others* .

41. Newell, "Dirty Whites."

42. Newell, "Dirty Familiars."

43. This gender-exclusive category is necessary given the domination of the sources for this chapter by men.

44. See Miriam Maranga-Musonye, "Literary Insurgence in Kenyan Urban Space: Mchongoano and the Popular Art Scene in Nairobi."

45. FCO 141/6436: Arthur M. Champion: "Native Welfare in Kenya," September 1944, item 4.

46. See Michael Davis, *Planet of Slums*.
47. Simone AbdouMaliq, Introduction to *Urban Africa: Changing Contours of Survival in the City*, 1–26; Jennifer Robinson, *Ordinary Cities: Between Modernity and Development*.

Bibliography

Barber, Karin, ed. 2012. *Print Culture and the First Yoruba Novel: I. B. Thomas's "Life Story of Me, Segilola" and Other Texts*. Leiden: Brill.
Barker, Francis, Peter Hulme, and Margaret Iverson, eds. 1998. *Cannibalism and the Colonial World*. Cambridge: Cambridge University Press.
Bataille Georges. 1985. *Visions of Excess*. Trans. Allan Stoekl. Minneapolis, MN: University of Minnesota Press.
Burke, Timothy. 1996. *Lifebuoy Men, Lux Women: Commodification, Consumption, and Cleanliness in Modern Zimbabwe*. Durham, NC: Duke University Press.
Cohen, William A., and Ryan Johnson, eds. 2005. *Filth: Dirt, Disgust, and Modern Life*. Minneapolis, MN: University of Minnesota Press.
Douglas, Mary. 2002. *Purity and Danger: An Analysis of Concepts of Pollution and Taboo*. London: Routledge.
Falola, Toyin, and Matthew M. Heaton. 2008. *A History of Nigeria*. Cambridge: Cambridge University Press.
Harris, Ashleigh. 2008. Discourses of Dirt and Disease in Operation Murambatsvina in Zimbabwe. In *The Hidden Dimensions of Operation Murambatsvina*, ed. Maurice T. Vambe, 40–50. Harare: Weaver Press.
Knox, Thomas M. n.d. Niger Company Ltd.: Diary of Tour Through the Congo and West Africa. United Africa Company. Unilever Archives and Records: 1924–1927, 2/34/4/1/1.
Lindner, Christoph, and Meissner, Miriam. 2015. Globalization, Garbage, and the Urban Environment. In *Global Garbage: Urban Imaginaries of Waste, Excess, and Abandonment*, eds. Christoph Lindner and Miriam Meissner, 1–13. London: Routledge.
Mann, Kristin. 1985. *Marrying Well: Marriage, Status and Social Change Among the Educated Elite in Colonial Lagos*. Cambridge: Cambridge University Press.
Maranga-Musonye, Miriam. 2014. Literary Insurgence in Kenyan Urban Space: Mchongoano and the Popular Art Scene in Nairobi. In *Popular Culture in Africa: The Episteme of the Everyday*, eds. Stephanie Newell, and Onookome Okome. New York: Routledge, Taylor & Francis Group.
Masquelier, Adeline, ed. 2005. *Dirt, Undress, and Difference: Critical Perspectives on the Body's Surface*. Bloomington: Indiana University Press.
Newell, Stephanie. 2006. *The Forger's Tale: The Search for "Odeziaku"*. Athens, OH: Ohio University Press.
———. 2008. Dirty Whites: 'Ruffian-Writing' in Colonial West Africa. *Research in African Literatures* 39(4): 1–15.
———. 2016. Dirty Familiars: Colonial Encounters in African Cities. In *Global Garbage: Excess, Waste and Abandonment in the Contemporary City*, eds. Christoph Lindner, and Miriam Meissner, 44–64. New York and London: Routledge.
Peel, Michael. 2011. *A Swamp Full of Dollars: Pipelines and Paramilitaries at Nigeria's Oil Frontier*. London: I. B. Taurus.

Pefanis, Julian. 1991. *Heterology and the Postmodern: Bataille, Baudrillard, Lyotard*. Durham: Duke University Press.

Said, Edward. 1978. *Orientalism*. London: Penguin.

Simba, Abdu. 2011. Street Life: The People of Dar es Salaam. In *Street Level: A Collection of Drawings and Creative Writing Inspired by Dar es Salaam*. Compiler and Illustrator, Sarah Markes. Dar es Salaam: Mkuku na Nyota.

Simone, AbdouMaliq. 2004. *For the City Yet to Come: Changing African Life in Four Cities*. Durham, NC: Duke University Press.

———. 2005. Introduction. In *Urban Africa: Changing Contours of Survival in the City*, eds. AbdouMaliq Simone, and A. Abouhani, 1–26. Dakar: CODESRIA.

Smith, David Livingstone. 2011. *Less Than Human: Why We Demean, Enslave, and Exterminate Others*. New York: St Martin's Press.

Stallybrass, Peter, and Allon White. 1986. *The Politics and Poetics of Transgression*. Ithaca, NY: Cornell University Press.

Stoler, Ann Laura. 2009. *Along the Archival Grain: Epistemic Anxieties and Colonial Common Sense*. Princeton, NJ: Princeton University Press.

Thompson, Michael. 1979. *Rubbish Theory: The Creation and Destruction of Value*. Oxford: Oxford University Press.

White, L.W.T., et al. 1948. *Nairobi: Master Plan for a Colonial Capital. A Report Prepared for the Municipal Council of Nairobi*. London: H.M. Stationery Office.

Whiteman, Kaye. 2014. *Lagos: A Cultural History*. Northampton, MA: Interlink Books.

Wren, Percival Christopher. 1924. *Beau Geste*. London: John Murray.

CHAPTER 12

Accidental Histories: Fieldwork Among the Maroons of Jamaica

Paul Youngquist

Fieldwork: for those with a scholarly interest in Caribbean plantation cultures, the word conjures unsettling images: cane bills and fresh bundles, millstones, trash piles, and hot vats of sugar. It describes the labor of enslaved Africans, who cut the cane, hauled the trash, and packed the hogsheads of raw muscovado. The plantation's hardest work was fieldwork, and the slaves who did it were valuable assets. Ledgers list them with cattle and livestock in neat columns labeled "Field Negroes." Those days may be gone and with them chattel slavery as a necessary cog in the machinery of mercantilist capitalism. But a whiff of something unpleasant still attends the whole enterprise of fieldwork, at least in the humanities. It's not what we do. Our work occurs in classrooms, libraries, and special collections. Or (with a little luck and funding), it might take us overseas—usually to metropolitan centers of high culture and fine cuisine. Fieldwork is for cultural anthropologists and other obsessives of the *vernacular*—a word whose very derivation calls up slavery (from *verna*, domestic slave). I don't mean to compare the contemporary academy to a sugar plantation. That would be fatuous. But I do mean to suggest that a certain kind of academic labor, especially in the humanities, remains devalued to the point of neglect as a means of producing knowledge. What could fieldwork possibly have to do with writing literary criticism?

P. Youngquist (✉)
Department of English, University of Colorado at Boulder, Boulder, USA

© The Author(s) 2016
S. Puri, D.A. Castillo (eds.), *Theorizing Fieldwork in the Humanities*,
DOI 10.1057/978-1-349-92834-7_12

INTO THE FIELD

That was my attitude for well over a decade after receiving a PhD in English literature—or would have been had I possessed the ability to say so. But I didn't. Fieldwork mattered so little that it would have been pointless to dismiss it. Why would a physicist dismiss astrological calculation? It just doesn't apply to subatomic particles. Similarly, fieldwork just didn't apply to literary texts. That's what I was taught by omission. I received my training as a professional reader and interpreter of literature at a time (the mid- to late 1980s) when the old pieties of New Criticism were giving way to the bold pronouncements of new "theory." The preferred strategy of the New Critics—close reading—sealed off the literary text from outside influence and empowered the trained reader to perform marvelous feats of interpretation through careful, perhaps mandarin, analysis. "Theory"—really theories—came to change all that, liberating the literary text to a panoply of invigorating contexts: psychoanalytical, metalinguistic, historical, economic. Those days felt like a time of upheaval and new beginning, and while it may not have been heaven to be alive in that dawn, it was at least exciting.

My field was British Romanticism. Traditionally, it consisted of poetry written by six male geniuses (as they were called then): all radical (at least culturally), most university educated (nominally anyway), several dead at an early age (by natural causes). It was the perfect field for close reading and formal analysis. But the advent of theory challenged the complacency of those practices, decrying the exclusion of women writers, the fetishizing of form, and the historical amnesia that characterized traditional studies of Romanticism. The latter criticism hit me particularly hard, and I resolved, after a brief flirtation with Heidegger, to take history for my guide and practice literary criticism with a historicist twist. Romanticism, after all, was a thing of the cultural past, a revolutionary literary movement with clear historical antecedents, most obviously the French Revolution. The populist thrust of that upheaval, at least in its initial phase, made critical historiography with its leftist bent attractive, and a close encounter with Foucault taught me how I could move laterally from literature to other kinds of writing (then called discourse) to claim that, for all its Romantic ferment, British culture during the last decade of the eighteenth century was a pretty carceral business, with its expanding war against France, traffic in human chattel, and colonial empire. Historicist criticism allowed me to deploy professional chops as close reader of literature on other kinds of texts: medical, political, diplomatic, economic.

As I did, I came to find those texts as engaging as literature, to the point that I lost interest in maintaining generic distinctions between either them or the kinds of knowledge they purveyed. Discourse drew literature into history. Documents turned history into fodder for a new kind of criticism concerned less with what texts mean than what they might do if assembled in certain ways toward particular ends—maybe progressive ends. Historicist criticism (of a genealogical sort) opened me up to work that New Criticism couldn't approve.

I became enamored of documents, detritus, realia. I went archival. Ten years out of grad school and I felt set for life. Have text will travel.

As Shalini Puri relates in "Finding the Field," silences can be voluble.[1] In my archival wanders, I encountered one that was especially loud and frustrating: the Haitian Revolution. Seven years in a graduate program then ranked tops in the country and not one of my esteemed teachers had mentioned it. Imagine my surprise. Working on a book about deformed bodies in British Romantic culture, I became transfixed—or rather repelled—by William Blake's depiction of tortured Africans in his engravings accompanying John Gabriel Stedman's *Narrative of a Five Year's Expedition Against the Revolted Negroes of Surinam* (1796).[2] These images led me to investigate eighteenth-century black rebellion throughout the Atlantic. Inevitably Haiti reared its hydra head. The only successful slave rebellion in history occurred as Romanticism began to flower—not as a new beginning but as the summation of over a century of black resistance to European slavery. In my search for English accounts of this black dawn, I soon found my way to Marcus Rainsford's *An Historical Account of the Black Empire of Hayti* (1805), an eyewitness account of the Haitian Revolution written by a Captain in His Majesty's Army, specifically the Third West India Regiment.

A *British* eyewitness account of the *Haitian* Revolution? Here I encountered a second silence, blown like a bubble inside the first. Reading Rainsford's book, I learned that the British invaded St. Domingo (as they then called the French colony on the island of Hispaniola) in 1793. I learned they occupied much of its coastal rim until driven from the island by Toussaint L'Ouverture and rebel blacks in 1798. And I learned the eyewitness account containing these revelations had never been republished since its original appearance in 1805. To the silence surrounding Haitian revolution, add the silence surrounding British counterrevolution. These silences were becoming deafening. Someone should edit Rainsford's book, I thought, and let his history speak its piece about black rebellion and white reprisal. Then came a second thought, as compelling as it was daunting: that *someone* should be me. I knew nothing of editing, and I lacked the credentials the book's subject seemed to require, those of a bona fide historian. But I could read anything and I knew my way around the archive. I put together a proposal and soon found myself preparing a scholarly edition of Rainsford's book in the company of a collaborator, Grégory Pierrot.[3]

We began hunting factoids. So little was known about Rainsford, as soldier, author, and, as it turned out, artist, that any information proved invaluable no matter how minute. Our odyssey in pursuit of this mysterious servant of empire and grudging advocate of black soldiery would add a small chapter to the annals of the micro-history of bibliography, but what matters most is the way it affected my work. Thanks to Rainsford and problems posed by editing his book, my sense of field began to shift: from period to place, from Romanticism to the colonial outposts of British culture, specifically Jamaica. Rainsford forced me out of the archive and into the field, confusing my work in ways I have yet to understand fully. Or maybe he vastly multiplied archives, liberating me from a subjection to documents, to text, as the condition of critical engagement. At his behest, or rather that of his book, I traveled to Kingston, Jamaica, to rifle through the manuscript collection at the National Library. My aims were specific. I was looking for documentary evidence that Rainsford had actually been in Haiti—to corroborate his claim to have served as a recruiter of black soldiers. I was looking too for more information about an incident he recorded involving British deployment of bloodhounds against Jamaican Maroons in rebellion. Dogs? Maroons? I wanted to learn more about both than Rainsford's book told me.

And I would, but not the way I expected. I did find documentary record that Rainsford received payment in Port-au-Prince for his service as an officer in His Majesty's Army—at a time when he claims *not* to have been there.[4] Which was interesting. But what I learned of the Maroons was frustrating to say the least. Independent blacks living in Jamaica's all but impenetrable interior, they rebelled in 1795, or rather a particular group of them did, those living in a place called Trelawney Town in the Parish of St. James, northwest of Kingston. The documentary evidence, however, hardly offered a disinterested picture of their rebellion. Little wonder: the British wrote it. By all accounts—letters, histories, journals, records of the Jamaican Assembly—the merciless ferocity of those Maroon savages more than justified the use of weaponized dogs to subdue them. And a notably humane use it was too, given that the troops accompanying their handlers never once gave orders to set them loose. Terror pure and simple—terror inspired by man-eating dogs—brought the Maroon rebellion to a swift, inevitable finish.[5]

The documentary record left me disgusted. Color me innocent, but I expected better of the British, who in theaters other than war at least occasionally seemed capable of acknowledging the humanity of people different from themselves. One sunny afternoon, I left the National Library demoralized about archival work, which seems to reveal only as much as the British, in their imperial literacy, wanted anyone to know. I met up with my friend and colleague Frances Botkin of Towson University's English Department, committed to as many Red Stripes as it took to work through my confusion. She was happy to oblige. I should mention how very much I owe to Fran, maven of the field, who first encouraged me to explore Jamaican archives as a source of material not available in the metropole depositories in London and Kew.

Fran is sitting at the Senior Common Room bar on UWI campus sipping a rum and water when I arrive. We talk for a while, mostly about the con game of archival scholarship, its investment in documents about as disinterested as army ordnance. A tall man wearing an African amulet around his neck and a serious look on his face walks up and begins talking to Fran about things I do not understand—Maroons, an invisible hunter, the cost of buses, an Afro-centric fashion show. Before I know what has happened, or exactly how, I've been recruited to help organize a conference he's conjuring to coincide with the annual Quao Day celebration in Charles Town. Fran's done so before and shares his vision of a gathering of scholars in Charles Town's Asafu Yard. Now it's known as the Annual Charles Town International Maroon Conference. Then it was a leery dream. The tall man dreaming it and charming me into doing likewise was Colonel Frank Lumsden of the Charles Town Maroons.

Near the end of our conversation that bright day, Colonel Frank did something that in retrospect strikes me as magical: he took from his pocket a well-handled document and started methodically to unfold it on one of the black metal tables. "See this?" he asked. "This is a map of Charles Town. It proves Charles Town can never be sold. See all these plots around it? These boundaries and lines? They mark private property. These lots have deeds. They can be sold. But this blank space in the middle is not private property. No deeds to it exist. It's held in common, common Maroon property. Charles Town can't be sold. It's Maroon land. Forever." At the time, I only dimly understood the point of Colonel Frank's lesson in cartography. In retrospect, however, I see it was a bold declaration of indigenous rights, an act of anticolonial counter-mapping that lays claim, not merely to a represented territory but more completely to a whole way of life, grounded in that Maroon common and sustained by collective ownership without deed. Colonel Frank, appearing like some ancestral spirit, offered an antidote to the archive. His account of the Maroon common, a counter-memory to documentary evidence and its legal and cultural legacies, pushed me further into the field. Knowledge about the Maroons should include Maroon knowledge, and fieldwork alone could harvest it. I agreed to help with the Colonel's conference.

COLONEL FRANK DOES THE WEATHER

June in Jamaica that year was wet; the rainy season came early. The conference seemed to be going well. Participants had all arrived on the designated day in Kingston from their various places of origin: Canada, the USA, Suriname, England, Senegal. The Coaster Fran booked to transport them to Goblin Hill, a tired but lovely resort near San Antonio, made its way with slow ease over the Blue Mountains—and through the rain—thanks to the sure hands of the driver Neville, a big man with a quiet smile. He would ferry us back and forth daily from Goblin Hill to Charles Town too.

We convened the conference in the Asafu Yard, the sacred communal space in Charles Town where Maroons gather to dance, deliberate, and, in the old days, study war—an enclosed green about double the size of a vacant lot, the wall rimmed with a short roof of corrugated zinc. A raised platform flanked the far end, decorated for the conference with green creepers, yellow bunting, and a cow's skull nailed to the transom above. A podium twined with philodendron stood to the left of a looming pile of loudspeakers and a badass mixing board. These Maroons were Jamaican, after all. Colonel Frank and his minions had set up chairs beneath a drab canvas field tent, its walls rolled up and roped.

Two early panels of paper presentations seemed to interest the sparse audience, which included three or four Maroons sitting against the far wall, smoking. I talked about bloodhounds, Fran about the notorious outlaw

Three-Fingered Jack. Other participants presented papers on Maroon military practices, Maroons in Dominica, marine Maroons scooting from island to island in canoes. Colonel Frank had opened our ceremonies with a blessing performed in tandem with Solman, a Saramaka Maroon from Suriname: they spoke patwas in unison, part of whose vocabulary they shared (flashes of mutual understanding crossing their faces), punctuated by sprays of white rum sucked up from the calabash each cradled in his hands.

But now the afternoon was dragging on. Lunch seemed long ago, our participants were growing restless. They needed some diversion. The schedule included an outing to Quao's Village, a nearby clearing a few miles up the river, where—even under gray skies—they might enjoy the view of the mountains misted by cloud, or splash a little in the cool water.

But where was the bus? Frank had agreed to provide a bus to transport conference participants to Quao Village. Our man Neville was off on another booking. Our printed program promised a bus. Our people were milling. Our event was on the brink of disorder. Fran was growing impatient: "It's getting late. We'll disappoint them. Do something, say something, will you?"

Clouds churned above the ridge. Colonel Frank stood still staring into them. I tentatively approached him.

"Excuse me. Colonel Frank. We're wondering about the bus. For our conference participants. You know, to Quao Village? You said you arranged a bus?"

Colonel Frank turned his stare on me, into me.

"What bus?"

"Quao Village. The River."

"There is no bus." He pursed his lips, a look of intense gravity on his dark face.

"But how…"

Colonel Frank interrupted, his voice turning staccato. "Look at me. *Look* at me. Tell me this: is it raining today in Jamaica?"

"Yes, Frank, it's raining today in Jamaica."

"Is it raining today in Charles Town?" He raised a hand above his head.

"No, Colonel Frank. It's not raining here. Not yet."

"*I'm doing that.* OK?" He turned away from me with contempt.

Fran, who had observed the exchange, gave me that "what now" look.

"How should I know? We'll make do. Tell them no Quao Village. Or I will."

Colonel Frank kept the rain at bay for another 90 minutes. Then the skies released their burden and we ran for shelter under the tent. Sounds of rain were everywhere.

Ambient Knowledge

Fieldwork takes two forms for me in Jamaica. One is the Charles Town International Maroon Conference, now an annual event that, like an ersatz season, regularly affects the weather of my professional life. The other is harder to identify and describe, partly because it overlaps with the work of the conference. It involves learning about Jamaican Maroons—often from them—in both systematic and unsystematic ways. Systematic study flatters my archival instincts. It requires that I learn all I can from documentary sources treating the Maroons, and where better than in Jamaican archives? I've logged a lot of time in Kingston at the National Library on East Street near the sea. It holds most of the primary printed material pertaining to Maroons: Edward Long's *History of Jamaica* (1774), Bryan Edwards's *The Proceedings of the Governor and Assembly of Jamaica in Regard to the Maroon Negroes* (1796), R.C. Dallas's *The History of the Maroons* (1803), Bryan Edwards's monumental *The History Civil and Commercial of the British Colonies in the West Indies* (three volumes with occasional remarks about Maroons, 1801), *The Journals of the Honourable Assembly of Jamaica*, *The Votes of the Honorable Assembly of Jamaica*, and *The Laws of Jamaica*, to name a few titles. Manuscript material makes interesting reading too, from the letter books of the Jamaican Assembly and its agents to private accounts of Maroons in rebellion to military reports from the field.

The Jamaica Archive in Spanish Town, half an hour on the bus west from Kingston, offers an abundance of related documents. The stuff that most interests me remains in manuscript: hearings from slave courts, assizes, and the King's Bench, rosters from Maroon towns, original patents and deeds, Parish minutes from St. Andrews and St. James, the *Freedman's Book* of Kingston: all the discursive detritus of colonial domination. However biased these documents, they provide an infrastructure for encountering a history that exceeds British colonial history. Jamaican Maroons, even after decades of guerilla harassment in the late seventeenth and early eighteenth centuries, might not have emerged as an independent people without the assent of the Assembly of Jamaica. Their indigeneity bears a British stamp. The archival record illuminates this British bias built into being Maroon—and tests its presumptive authority.

Maroons are creatures of negotiation—literally. Their warrior leaders, Kojo and Quao, each negotiated a treaty with a representative of His Majesty the King of England (in 1738 and 1739, respectively), gaining independence for their people in perpetuity. The treaties' terms are surprisingly simple, if in some ways deeply vexed: a substantial grant of land to be held in common, service to the Crown as the island's police force (returning runaways and squashing rebellions), presence of white superintendents on Maroon land, and certain limits on Maroon legal authority. The British printed the treaties in myriad formats (a transcription of Kojo's appears in Dallas's *History*, for instance), little to the benefit of an illiterate people.[6] No matter: superintendents were required to read them aloud to their Maroon communities three times a year.

The documentary record establishes, with all the empirical force such records traditionally assert, that being Maroon in Jamaica involves inhabiting history—and being inhabited by it—in several constitutive ways, at least from a British perspective: Maroons share a lived relation to a legacy of resistance to colonial domination, to land held in common forever, and to complicity with the very powers they fought against for independence. To say the least, Maroons today have a complicated relationship to this history. The archival material that documents it has given rise to a formidable body of scholarship on Maroon heritage spanning from Mavis Campbell's meticulous examination of the record in *The Maroons of Jamaica 1655–1796: A History of Resistance, Collaboration, and Betrayal* (1988) and *Nova Scotia and the Fighting Maroons: a Documentary History* (1990) to Kathleen Wilson's astute "The Performance of Freedom: Maroons and the Colonial Order in Eighteenth-Century Jamaica and the Atlantic Sound" (2009).[7] Such historical scholarship sustains what passes in the academy as the official institutional memory of the Maroon people. It's how I first came to know them. It's an important resource not only for learning about their heritage but also its willful destruction, most patently in the aftermath of the uprising that became known as the "Second Maroon War," when the Jamaican Assembly called out the dogs, scotched the rebellion, and ultimately transported the entire Maroon population of Trelawney Town off the island to, of all places, Halifax, Nova Scotia. The more I studied archival records, the more interested I became in that underreported incident in the annals of benign genocide as an episode in the larger history of the Jamaican Maroons.

The more I studied the archival record *in Jamaica*, however, the less comfortable I became with its version of events. The problem was not that, when closely examined, such information proved inconsistent or ambiguous. In fact, documentary history wielded an imperious authority—as long as I remained in the archive. After I left the library, however, and started talking about my work to Jamaican *people*—in taxis, buses, bars, markets, rum shops, and on streets, beaches, and conference panels—far different stories began to emerge, fragmentary, incoherent, and allusive, but no less confusing for their vernacularity. Some I barely understood, coming as they did in the unwritten patwa—or rather patwas—that constitute everyday speech for Jamaicans.

Conversations after working hours left me with the sense that history is not the whole story: "Maroons? They were the first Jamaican freedom fighters." "Maroons! Don't talk to me about Maroons. They betrayed us." "I know they independent. They do that festival up there, you know, in Accompong." "My grandmother was a Maroon. I never been to her town, though." "They just bounty hunters. Hunted runaways. Bad people." "Never heard of Trelawney Town." "Dogs? Bloodhounds? Yeah they used them against us slaves." "They have their own land. They're not Jamaicans. They're their own people." "I like Maroons. My mother likes them—they're authentic. They invented jerk." "Killed a lot of slaves, Maroons. Worked for whites. Bacra give them guns." Or this summation, shouted by an elderly Jamaican man named Inus Austin through the gaps in his teeth: "Maroon-dem dead and gone!"

I had not come to Jamaica to conduct fieldwork, but the field nevertheless came to me. Streets outside the archive teemed with bits and pieces of vernacular memory that sometimes corroborated, sometimes contested the official history sanctioned by documentary evidence. What would happen if

I began to listen to those ambient memories, reversed the relation between written and spoken words, and allowed the latter, in all their ambiguity and dubious intentionality, to shape my understanding of the Maroon past? I'd compromise my disinterestedness as an observer of the historical record, of course, by inserting myself into the circuit of its communication. But what I lost in objectivity (a term without much weight for a literary critic anyway), I might gain in multiplicity: the proliferation of perspectives on a past irreducible to a single (documentary and imperial) account. That these perspectives come charged with emotional investment only adds to their force and explanatory power. If as Walter Benjamin suggests, time doesn't pass—it accumulates— then it piles into the present unevenly, in messy heaps or cacophonies of cross talk.[8] Archives were all around me, in the world I walked through on my way to the National Library (across Parade and down King's Street, the smell of piss and blast of dancehall hanging in the air) as much as in the air-conditioned reading room on its second floor.

One form fieldwork has begun to take for me, then, involves the accumulation of an ambient knowledge of Maroon history: myriad counter-histories that drift through the heads and the hearts of everyday Jamaicans, taking flight in the improvisational play of conversation. This is fieldwork without a manual, unconstrained by the disciplinary imperatives of history, anthropology, or various ethnographies. It moves in slow motion, less devoted to verifiable results than more qualitative, fuzzy outcomes: encounter, acknowledgment, exchange. I am interested now to know what *people* know about Maroon history, not in order to create a definitive counter-hegemonic account, but to qualify the official story by the small measure of such persisting if whispered memories. This ambient knowledge accumulates with time over the course of multiple visits to Jamaica and a lot of listening. It's not the kind of knowledge that makes for powerful grant proposals. It nevertheless enriches the work I now do. It vastly multiplies possibilities for intellectual and social engagement with a history as alive as the people who remember it.

This form of fieldwork as I practice it, or perhaps as it practices me, requires acknowledging a few precepts. First, it is immersive: you can't do it without being in the field, which is to say immersed in the place(s) and space(s) of ambient knowledge. I spent many years in documentary archives before discovering that other kinds existed in the open all around me. Indeed, immersion in this *open* is the vital condition of the kind of encounter, acknowledgment, and exchange yielding the many histories that exceed official history. Second, fieldwork is errant: you can't plan its outcomes in advance, partly because you are involved in producing them. Ambient knowledge isn't just *there* like some dusty tome on a bookshelf. It *occurs* as the effect of immersive encounters and exchanges. It *happens*—and it happens to and through you. Errancy names the accidental itinerary comprising your encounters with others, relations—however fleeting—that spark knowledge in the field. Third, fieldwork is multiple: you can't pursue it in a single archive. Fieldwork multiplies your archives. It plays documents against stories against music against dances against rumors against reports against.… It produces ensembles of incommensurable memories, assemblages of contestable claims. By multiplying archival resources, fieldwork aspires to more than its conclusions can ever say. Perhaps it remains less a practice than a poetics of discovery in the sense Édouard Glissant implies in his peculiar use of the word "relation": "Relation, or totality in evolution, whose order is continually in flux and whose disorder one can imagine forever."[9] Fieldwork, or the totality of ambient knowledge in evolution.

TRACKING TRELAWNEYS

I was determined to learn what I could about Trelawney Maroons from the Maroons themselves, any way I could, even if it meant driving on the wrong side of the road. Ethnographers do it all the time, I thought: talk to people and produce *Significant Insights*. I would dive into living history and come out soaked with Maroon memory. What else could I do? The documentary record petered out in the mid-nineteenth century. All it left me was a bunch of names: Mary Brown, Sarah M'Gale, or Mary Ricketts—Maroon women who had returned to Jamaica in 1841 from Sierra Leone, where the Trelawneys had finally been transported by the British after five cold, desolate years in Nova Scotia. I could spend days in the Island Record Office at J$850 an hour to discover only their death certificates. Big deal. They might not even name the right Sarah or Marys. I wanted more. I wanted stories. I wanted Maroon memories of Maroon history—not as the British recorded it, but as Maroon mothers and fathers and grandmothers and grandfathers handled it and polished it and passed it on to coming kin.

Hadn't Kenneth Bilby, the great ethnographer of Jamaican Maroons, done that work already, compiled those memories? Naw, he was after the Afro-creole core of Maroon culture. Even if there were such a core, a guy as white as me wasn't going to get near it. I didn't have time or funding to hang out in Charles Town romancing the elders and establishing cultural cred. On my budget all I'd get was the usual ersatz ritual repackaged for public consumption: a little lecture on the Asafu warrior, a sneak peek at Kromanti Play. I wasn't pursuing primal memories anyway, hushed accounts of "first time" or ancestor fete-men. I was tracking unknown histories of known events, alternative versions of what historians—Edwards and Dallas or Campbell and Grant—thought they knew. I wanted to tap a vein of living memory. It would bleed revelations. All I needed was a car to get out of Kingston and some dim inkling of where to drive.

It was Fran who supplied the latter, sitting at the bar at Red Bones in the hard morning sun. A semester teaching at UWI Mona Campus and researching the exploits of Three-Fingered Jack had, apparently, introduced her to the majority of the island's inhabitants. "Wakefield," she blurted when I asked. "I hear Trelawney Maroons still live around Wakefield. I mean. Descendants. You need to talk to this lady up there named Mama G. She's their racial memory. Ha. Get it?"

I got it. It was all the hint I needed to rent a car. "Wanna come?"

"I wouldn't let you go without me, whitey."

"But who's Mama G?"

"Rasta woman. Also an activist. I heard she lived three years off the grid without money, building shelters for women with nowhere to go, teaching them crafts so they could earn a few J and maybe live independently. She knows all about the Trelawneys." Fran called City Guide for a taxi to Fiesta Rentals on Waterloo.

I completed the necessary paperwork while she palavered with a gorgeous blue grouper hiding in the kelp of the lobby's saltwater aquarium. A smiling attendant brought a small green sedan to a halt out front and stepped out, holding the door open and beckoning. It was a Toyota, its plastic hubcaps zip-tied to the wheels. I slid into the driver's seat on the car's right side. Fran rode shotgun on the left. I looked at the wheel. I looked at Fran. Everything was backward. Where was the key? I groped with my left hand and found it. The car started with a shiver. I coaxed it slowly down the driveway toward the Waterloo as Fran waved the grouper goodbye.

"You gotta navigate," I said. "Make sure I end up in the right lane. I mean the left. The one that won't get us killed."

"My God, watch out!" I slammed the brakes. She turned to me, all teeth. "Just kidding! Let's go."

The first few turns were tricky, like entering a mirror. Cars, busses, trucks, and motorbikes roared toward us in a reversed dream of vehicular homicide. But I adapted.

We took a right on Constant Spring Road and headed up through Stony Hill, winding our way out of Kingston on the A-3. It followed the twisted spine of the Blue Mountains, under a thick shag of palm and breadfruit, along cliffs dropping to misted vales. The traffic was maniacal. Battered Japanese imports whined past us on steep hills and narrow curves. Lumbering Coasters packed with passengers pulled around slow trucks, coming straight at us until, by some heart-pounding miracle, they swerved and missed. My hands fused to the steering wheel as my right foot worried the brakes as we drove: past the jerk places at Junction, past the turnoff to Scott's Hall, past Tapioca Villas, through banana, coconut, and more banana groves as the road leveled toward the sea.

We took a left on the roundabout outside Annotto Bay, heading toward Port Maria on the A-1, the road opening out to something like a highway, speed limit 80 kph. I relaxed and Fran chattered. Next stop Wakefield.

An hour and a half later we were bumping along the deeply potted road from Martha Brae. Route taxis passed like screaming hummingbirds. I refused their invitation to hurry. The land was flat, expansive—plantation land, open to the sun. Occasional stone columns loomed up from brambly creepers, evidence of old sugar estates, long gone. Wooden shacks dotted the road, set back 20 or 30 feet, built above the ground on short stone piles, porch in front, paint fading.

"What do we do once we get to Wakefield? It's just ahead."

Fran thought about it. "Library maybe?" She had the instincts of an archivist.

We bounced by a hand-painted sign, "Wakefield, Trelawny Parish." On the left stood a small plank structure glowing orange in the hard light. Big block letters on its main gable read "Wakefield Library." I pulled in.

It was shuttered tight, doors obviously locked.

"What now?"

"Police station, maybe? Cops know everybody."

More good instincts, even if police made me nervous. We drove straight to what appeared to be Wakefield's town square, gas station on the left side of the road, police station on the right, a faded white-and-blue building behind a chain link fence with a clock tower rising above it, graceful Arabic numerals on the clock face, hands pointing permanently to ten and four.

We stepped onto the plank porch to be greeted with a wave by a policeman in a natty uniform speaking into the receiver of a massive cordless phone—an ancient artifact from the 1970s. He smiled and raised the index finger of his free hand, soliciting our patience. I couldn't make out what he was saying in his burly patwa, but he soon finished, smiled broadly, and held out a hand: "I'm Corporal Palmer of the Wakefield Constabulary. How may I help you?" His striped shirt was authoritatively spotless, his blue trousers were perfectly pressed, and his striped epaulets were peculiarly compelling. Badge 1269.

"We're looking for Trelawney Maroons," Fran said in her frank way. "Know any?"

The question inspired in Corporal Palmer full-body contortions of mental consideration. Fist to chin, he said, "I see. Maroons. Maroons. Who would know about Maroons. To whom could I direct you. I have it!" His finger shot back into the air. "Mr. MacDonald. Yes. He's an old Rasta. If anybody knows about Maroons it would be him."

"How do we find this, uh, Johnson?" Fran was a stickler.

"MacDonald. Take this road straight from here. Five or six miles. The road turns to dirt. You wind past a river, then you come to a fork and you take the left, bear left, and then you go another mile or so. When you come to a crossroads, Dehaney Crossroads, you will see a shop on the right. Someone will be sitting in front. Ask him where is Mr. MacDonald. Tell him the police sent you. You'll find him. Mr. MacDonald lives near there."

We thanked Corporal Palmer heartily. I snapped a picture of Fran standing next to him on the porch, and we were off, bumping between the potholes.

"Tell them the police sent us? That'll inspire trust."

"Yeah," I said. "Obviously he wants us dead. But who said field work was easy?"

Six miles feels like 60 on a rural Jamaican road. Churches outnumbered domiciles: Baptist, Methodist, Church of God, Latter-day Saints. We found the fork and stayed left, and after driving past some thick foliage came suddenly upon a crossroads. Dehaney Crossroads? A shop on the right, festooned with "Rumbar" pennants, stood directly across from an old stone chapel with casement windows, "The United Church of Jamaica and the Cayman Islands" according to a sign in front. I parked next to the shop. Fran got out of the car and approached the guy sitting on a folding chair in the shade.

"Hey. Sir. Do you know a man named Mr. MacDonald? We're looking for Mr. MacDonald." The guy looked confused, like he didn't understand. He stroked his face. He puffed his cheeks. Without saying a word, he rose, turned, and tottered off the shop's raised planks into the bush. Fran turned to me (I was still behind the wheel) and, raising her hands palms up, shrugged.

"What now?" she mouthed.

"We wait," I mouthed back. Which we did.

The guy returned in a few minutes. "Him no home," he said, shaking his head. My heart sank a notch. "Him at him brother."

"Where's that?"

The guy lifted his arm and pointed across the road to a half-finished house, the ground floor painted peach, rebar sprouting like mad antennae where the second floor should be. "Der."

"There? There! Thanks."

I got out of the car. We walked across the road to Mr. MacDonald's brother's house and knocked on the clean white door.

Sounds within: a small crash, a hushed shuffle. The door opened.

"Mr. MacDonald?"

The man was indeed an old Rasta. He wore thick locks neatly tucked into a knit black-and-orange tam. A tattered gray beard dangled in clumps from his weathered face. Reed thin and bare to the waist, he wore a bright purple towel about his nethers and green flip-flops on his feet. His knees were rickety and his toes were gnarled. His face had the fuddled dignity of a man awakened from a deep sleep.

"Ya, maan. I'm MacDonald." We told him of our quest for Trelawney Maroons. We asked him what he knew about them, lore, stories, anything.

He smiled warmly. "Maroons. Maroons." He paused. "I could teach you about Rastafar-I. But Maroons. I don't know so much. I tell you who can tell you. Wait here." Mr. MacDonald shuffled back inside his brother's house.

Rustling within.

He returned a few minutes later clutching something in his fist and shuffled past us into the dirt road. Pointing to the heavens, in a sweet, low voice, he said, "Reception." He began studiously punching numbers into an old cell phone the size of a passport. He put it to his ear, cocked his head, and waited for a connection.

"Hello. Simba? Simba. Listen, maan. I have a couple here wants to know about Maroons. Can you talk to them? OK." Mr. MacDonald thrust the phone at Fran.

She took the device and started shouting into it—about Maroons, about Trelawney Town, about Emporer Haile Selassie, about Maroons again. She used the word Simba several times.

Pregnant pauses and fierce nodding.

"Yes. Yes. OK. Simba, thank you. Many thanks. Zine. Thanks, mon. OK."
She handed the phone back to Mr. MacDonald and thanked him too. He nodded kindly, jiggling the knots of his ragged beard.

"You're welcome. Bless." The cool of his brother's house beckoned. He put the fingers of his two hands together, and with a barely noticeable bow, turned and disappeared inside, tam, towel, and cell phone.

I didn't say a word to Fran until we were back in the car. Then I said one word.

"So?"

"So I know who we need to talk to."

"Who?"

"Mama G."

"Fran, we knew that."

"Yeah. But now we know where she is."

"Great. Finally. Where do we find her? She live nearby?" I was eager.

"Kingston."

"Kingston?"

"Word. Kingston."

Space Is the Place

The second form fieldwork takes for me is the annual Charles Town International Maroon Conference. I call it fieldwork because it takes place in the field and it's a helluva lot of work. The original vision for the conference belongs to Colonel Frank: an academic gathering to coincide with Charles Town's annual Quao Day celebration on June 23, the great warrior's birthday. Two days of panels in the Asafu Yard involving an international array of scholars of marronage and one day of festivities celebrating Maroon culture, history, and identity. First Fran and then I came on board as organizers of the event's academic days. Frank would handle the cultural celebration on Quoa Day. The appeal for me lay in the event's weirdness—a conference about Maroons convened *with* Maroons: on their terms, in their space, toward ends I believed in but didn't really understand. To scholars from abroad it might look like a Jamaican getaway, a three-day junket in the Blue Mountains on the underdeveloped side of the island, away from the tourists and the Rent-a-Dreads and the other detritus of credit card colonialism. To Colonel Frank it provided an occasion to advance a double agenda of associating intellectual integrity with Maroon culture within Jamaica and projecting a progressive image abroad. To Fran and me it offered the opportunity of an extended stay in Kingston for several weeks prior to the event, justifying grant applications for travel support and summer flight from American malaise. Divers are the motives, unpredictable the outcomes.

Organizing the annual Charles Town International Maroon Conference offers rewards that swing between revelation and benign nightmare. None of it could happen without the Fran's energies. Her ability to imagine and sustain the event year after year is nothing short of miraculous. I work with her in my small way to solicit and vet paper proposals, communicate with participants, create panels, print promotional material, coordinate transportation, arrange lodging, provide food and beverage, handle confusion and complaints, and generally troubleshoot—all the administrative splendors that attend conference organization. There's a difference, of course: this conference occurs in Jamaica. We receive no institutional support to run it. Funding comes entirely from conference fees. We work closely with the Charles Town Maroon Council to produce an event that conforms to their expectations and needs. We find ourselves relating to a wide range of people and organizations in Jamaica: the National Library, the Jamaica Institute, the Jamaica Archive, Digicel, the University of the West Indies, its program for Rastafari Studies, the University of Technology in Kingston, Edna Manley College of the Visual and Performing Arts, the Jamaica Union of Travelers Association, the Liguanea Club Hotel, Red Bones Blues Café, Tony's Bar, the Maroon Indigenous Women's Circle, City Guide Taxi Service, even the office of the US Ambassador to Jamaica. This kind of fieldwork involves multiple fields. As a result, it requires multiple border crossings too: between classes, communities, garrisons, parishes, even (not that we always know it) gang territories. It takes imagination, persistence, patience, charm, luck, and a lot of listening to do this work. Patwa would help enormously, but neither Fran nor I have it. So we make do. We get things done. Barely.

We're in a very peculiar, maybe precarious position. We're caught up in a Maroon micro-politics we only dimly understand. When Colonel Frank expresses his wish that the academic event we organize add something serious to the Maroon cause, he's positioning Charles Town and the conference it hosts as a progressive alternative to Accompong, the most prominent of Jamaica's Maroon Towns. Accompong has acquired that reputation by hosting a festival of its own for many years on January 5 commemorating the signing of the treaty with the British. It's made Accompong in a sense the "official" Maroon community of Jamaica. The festival feels like a county fair held in almost impenetrable hills at a high altitude: the crowd, the hustle, the buzz; cheap goods laid out on blankets, pigs' heads on open barbecues, reggae blasting from banks of loudspeakers; dancing, drumming, speeches by Maroon colonels, edifying words from Jamaican government officials. The Accompong Maroon Festival celebrates Maroons in a nationalist context under the banner of unity as Jamaica's first freedom fighters, its independent indigenous people.

Unlike Accompong, situated deep in cockpit country where steep mountains and narrow defiles restrict easy access, Charles Town's location just a few miles inland from Buff Bay always made its borders unusually porous to outside influence. Colonel Frank's vision is frankly and unapologetically international. He views the conference at Charles Town as an opportunity to create a worldwide web of connections in the name of marronage: among scholars from different institutions and countries, among indigenous peoples from all over the globe, and among both those groups and the local Maroons they come to know. He's taking the high ground morally and intellectually in the belief that convening an academic conference in the Asafu Yard in the company of living Maroons will associate Jamaica's first freedom fighters with something more than trinkets, photo opportunities, and political rhetoric. In part, he has succeeded—if bringing scholars and Maroons from around the world to Charles Town constitutes success. The former have come from England, Canada, the USA, Puerto Rico, Suriname, Venezuela, Barbados, Jamaica, Senegal, and Australia. Maroons have visited primarily from Suriname and Canada. During the three days of the conference, Charles Town becomes a center for global inquiry into the history, future, and persistence of marronage. Jamaican indigeneity opens to transnational encounters and cross-cultural exchange. These effects are oddly in keeping with Charles Town's history as a Maroon community. Anthropologists seeking to study "true born" Maroons preferred more isolated communities like Accompong or Moore Town. But this legacy of cultural "contamination" gives Charles Town today its unusual readiness to accept visitors from around the world and tolerate their commentary on Maroon history and tradition. For Colonel Frank, Charles Town provides a platform from which to preach—and cultivate—awareness about Maroons in Jamaica and around the world.

Its porosity makes Charles Town a strange place to practice fieldwork. It doesn't sustain the specificity usually constitutive of "place" in an anthropological sense. The old distinction between place and space, the local and the global, collapses to the point of pointlessness, a quaint heuristic that gets little lasting purchase on everyday life.[10] Charles Town retains a cultural and historical particularity, of course, incommensurable with anywhere else in Jamaica, let alone the globe. It has its rum shops, its customs, its families, its burial ground, its Maroon *traditions* that make it *Charles Town*, a place apart. But perhaps because of the nature of our work in this particular field, Fran and I find it impossible to segregate place from space, even for the purpose of promoting Maroon history and culture.

While the Asafu Yard is indeed a sacred Maroon place, center of communal palaver and organization, I *heard* it first before I saw it, its titanic sound system blasting Burning Spear into the blue mountainsides around us. Ricardo and the guys who run the soundboard play a mix that runs from reggae to rock steady to hip-hop to rock and roll: loud and bone stirring. Digicel has seen to it that nobody with a spare J goes without a cell phone (red and yellow signs are everywhere: "top up here"). Instant access is island wide—once when we were lost in the heart of cockpit country, Fran whipped out her phone and made a dinner reservation in Kingston. Laptops drink up information from around the world and spew it out in the Asafu Yard. And while I wouldn't for a minute understate the privilege that attends my institutionally funded mobility and the agency it enables—especially in the field—I remain aware too that Colonel Frank does a masterly job of directing it toward ends that, in his view, benefit Charles Town in particular and Maroons in general. Place and space interpenetrate, shifting the form and function of both. Maroons dance and drum in the moonlight. Scholars visit, participate, and go. Their encounters produce incremental changes, and in ways I neither fully celebrate nor bemoan. That's part of the outcome of fieldwork as we've been practicing it in Jamaica. Charles Town the place globally *becomes*—as academics, Maroons, and other Jamaicans interact to ponder the persistent freedoms of marronage.

It goes the other way too. Sometimes the field returns to change its workers: the places they inhabit, the things they do. Academic knowledge, for instance, might happen differently than it usually does. Material for publication that Fran and I have been gathering from the Charles Town International Maroon Conference includes work by contributors who might not qualify as scholars in the academic sense but whose contribution has nevertheless been important for all participants, among them Colonel Frank Lumsden of the Charles Town Maroons; Fidelia Graand-Galon, Ambassador Extraordinary and Plenipotentiary of the Republic of Suriname to Trinidad and Tobago; and Gloria Simms of the Maroon Indigenous Women's Circle. Our hope is to produce a published volume mixing scholarly with Maroon knowledge, academic and indigenous voices speaking to and maybe against each other. As fieldwork, the conference promises not definitive conclusions so much as continuing interactions, of which such a book might prove inspiring testimony.

But the conference can have more direct effects also, whose implications may be difficult to gauge. A while ago Fran and I invited Colonel Frank to attend a panel we were part of at the annual convention of the Modern Language Association. To our surprise, he agreed to come. From his conference to ours: this time Colonel Frank would play the global, and we'd host him in Boston, our meeting place for that year's convention. He cut an intriguing figure in his lavender sport coat, sitting behind a long table at the front of a room packed with scholars of British Romanticism, many of whom Fran and I knew. Panelists gave their talks in the usual way, to the usual respectful applause. Then came Colonel Frank's turn. He moved slowly toward the podium, holding his paper in one hand, his other in his jacket pocket. He stopped at the microphone and leaned slightly. "I want to thank you for this opportunity to speak." And then he spoke a few words in patwa that Fran and I have come to associate with sacred occasions. The academics in the audience, some in slacks and some in jeans but all listening politely, watched as a little pint bottle of Wray and Nephew white rum made its way from Colonel Frank's pocket to his lips. It tipped up. He took a long swig. With a slow sweeping motion of his head, bottle held motionless before of him, Colonel Frank spewed an arc of rum over the audience, effectively baptizing the front row. He smiled gently and proceeded to read his paper. His Maroon ancestors loved what they heard.

POSTMODERN GLOBAL JAMAICAN INDIGENE

We finally found Mama G one warm January afternoon sitting in a tent in the yard of 28 Fairbourne Road on Kingston's east side, just past Mountainview and down a block from the police station. The house she inhabited with her extended family was a wreck. It had caught fire several weeks earlier, burning not quite to the ground, but no thanks to the fire brigade. Their trucks showed up with half-empty tanks. When the water ran out, the brigade made the best of a bad situation and got busy looting. Now the house was uninhabitable. Several colorful camping tents made a makeshift shelter out front.

Fran and I arrived with a pineapple and a six-pack of Red Stripe, gifts she insisted we offer out of respect. Mama G sat on a box near a mosquito-net window in a spacious blue tent. She was surrounded by crafts, presumably hers: a partly finished painting of Rastas dancing in front of a distant slave ship, a crown made from coconut skins decorated with cowry shells, a T-shirt embroidered with the words "Roots Uprising," and several strings of red and black beads. A laptop with a blinking stick modem sat open on a battered bar stool.

What little I'd learned about Mama G since our initial pursuit led me to expect a cross between Nanny of the Maroons and Mother Teresa. Her reputation as women's activist was formidable. Two years at the University of the West Indies studying social work were enough to convince her that academic training would be of little help to women subject to the domestic blandishments of white rum and a machete. She quit school and threw herself into activism, traveling the island wherever women needed help—without financial backing, not a Jamaican dollar or penny. Her Maroon Indigenous Women's Circle taught traditional crafts to help Jamaican women achieve and maintain economic independence. She was an outspoken proponent of Maroon culture, a Kumina dancer, and a self-declared Rastafar-I priestess.[11] Her family's reggae band, Roots Uprising (their equipment all lost in the fire), played the full sonic mythos of Rasta culture, truth in riddim, that indomitable backbeat.

Mama G was small and thin. She smiled wearily as we entered her tent, offering her left hand more for us to notice than to take. "Bless," she nodded. "Bless."

Tight locks trailed to her waist. Her ganja eyes were fierce. She wore a loose blue shirt and a long course shift. Her sandals were the color of her feet. "Sit," she said, gesturing to an old office chair and a camp stool. "Tanks for coming."

Fran offered her a Red Stripe, which she took with distant warmth. "Thanks for seeing *us*."

As Mama G rummaged for a bottle opener, a little girl, maybe four years old, entered the tent carrying an oblong object wrapped in tin foil. Beads dotted her braided hair. "This pickney my gran-datta. You go now, Cookie. Leave me talk." The girl handed Mama G the foiled thing, looked long at Fran, and ran out of the tent with a squeal.

Mama G picked up a little paring knife with her right hand and began unwrapping foil with her left, revealing a steaming ear of grilled corn. She cut small chunks for Fran and me. "Eat," she said. "It's good."

So we ate.

And we talked. And we listened.

It would be pointless to transcribe our conversation. I only understood part of what Mama G said anyway. But I had no trouble comprehending that we were in the presence of a woman who was dreadfully alive. Mama G fired away with ballistic precision at the targets of her enmity: Jamaican politricks, the abuse of women, the mistreatment of Rastas, the stupidity of Maroon colonels who refused to recognize her Trelawney heritage. The whole time she stabbed the air with her little blade, a hungry two inches poking between her thumb and knuckle.

Fran asked if she would be interested in attending the conference in Charles Town.

"Charles Town," she said, looking at the floor of the tent. "Charles Town." She launched into a diatribe, best I could tell, denouncing contemporary Maroon governance. All the colonels were men. That made no sense. Granny Nanny, the great guerilla bane of the British and only Maroon national hero, was a woman.[12] Mama G felt excluded from Maroon leadership. Wasn't she Maroon? Wasn't she Trelawney? Trelawney Town should have a colonel too. Maybe a woman colonel. Just because the British transported her people—illegally—to Nova Scotia for resisting downpression, Trelawney Town deserves no voice in Maroon affairs? No representation? No respect? Maroon colonels were no better than the British. The same tricks all over again. Like the treaty. It was a trick.

Mama G looked at us in disgust. She pulled a little Nokia phone out of a skirt pocket and checked her credit. Apparently our interview was over.

"But yes," she said, as if to the phone. "I'll come to the conference in Charles Town. Take a place alongside the Colonels." A faint smile curled her lips. "Make them see me. Make them remember. Not all Trelawney Maroons left Jamaica on those boats to Halifax. Some run into the bush like their ancestors. Some come back from Sierra Leone too. Settled near Wakefield. Blended in."

I suggested that the fate of those returning Maroons was lost to history.

"History?" Mama G snapped her head in my direction. "British write history. They write it wrong. On purpose. Like Flagstaff Mountain. From on top you can see Falmouth. See anybody coming, troops, whatever. Dallas says the British put a gun up there during the Maroon War. It wasn't the British. It was Maroons. Tiefed a cannon and drag it up dat hill. Call Gunsy Hill since den. Still call Gunsy Hill. By dem who rememer. You unnastan?"

Mama G looked me dead in the eye. In English as polished as any King's, she said, "You can do plenty of research, professor, but you need inspiration too. Remember inspiration."

POSTSCRIPT

We would bring Mama G to the conference later that year. Colonel Frank expressed discomfort at the idea of including a Maroon representative from defunct Trelawney Town, let alone a self-appointed female leader. But Mama G crept on stage anyway during opening ceremonies, carrying a bag containing a large wooden ankh, a conch, and a laptop. She blew the conch before reading her paper from the laptop's screen, ankh perched on the podium beside her. She spoke of indigenous women's rights and children's dreams and life and all and I and I. "What is Jamaica today is Nanny's." Fidelia Graand-Galon, Suriname's ambassador to Trinidad and Tobago—and a Maroon—listened intently with the rest of us. "There is no poverty in this world unless you want to accept it." Later, Fidelia would invite Mama G to Suriname to attend a gathering of indigenous women activists. Fran and I helped raised funds to send her by soliciting donations from conference attendees. The meeting of these two Maroon women from Jamaica and Suriname has brought an international dimension to the Maroon Indigenous Women's Circle, which promises to extend its reach even further: to Belize, Canada, Australia, wherever Mama G's indomitable trod leads. Such are the unforeseeable effects of fieldwork in the humanities. It's not the fieldwork that matters most. It's the work the fieldwork makes possible.

Notes

1. Puri, "Finding the Field," 58–73.
2. See Richard Price and Sally Price eds., *Stedman's Surinam: Life in an Eighteenth-Century Slave Society.*
3. The edition eventually saw daylight as Marcus Rainsford, *An Historical Account of the Black Empire of Hayti.*
4. *Account Book of the Deputy Paymaster General, Hispaniola, 1796–97*, MS 237, National Library of Jamaica.
5. See Marcus Rainsford, *An Historical Account of the Black Empire*, 251–256; Bryan Edwards, *The Proceedings of the Governor and Assembly of Jamaica, in regard to the Maroon Negroes; Votes of the Honourable Assembly of Jamaica, 1795*; R. C. Dallas, *History of the Maroons from Their Origin to the Establishment of the Their Chief Tribe at Sierra Leone*, 2 vols., 41–171; "Parliamentary Intelligence: House of Commons; Blood Hounds in Jamaica," *Times* (London), March 22, 1796; as well as various manuscript accounts at the National Library of Jamaica. My interest in this episode led to Paul Youngquist, "The Cujo Effect."
6. For a complete transcription of the two treaties, see *Laws of Jamaica, 1681–1758*, 258 and 278, respectively.
7. Among the growing scholarship devoted to Jamaican Maroon history, see Mavis C. Campbell, *The Maroons of Jamaica: a History of Resistance, Collaboration, and Betrayal, 1655–1796*, and *Nova Scotia and the Fighting Maroons: A Documentary History, Studies in Third World Societies*, Vol. 41; Carey Robinson, *The Fighting Maroons of Jamaica*; Bev Carey, *The Maroon Story: The Authentic and Original History of the Maroons in the History of Jamaica, 1490–1880*; John N. Grant, *The Maroons in Nova Scotia*; Kathleen Wilson, "The Performance of Freedom: Maroons and the Colonial Order in Eighteenth-Century Jamaica and the Atlantic Sound," 45–86; Kenneth

Bilby, *True Born Maroons*; and Werner Zips, *Black Rebels: African Freedom Fighters in Jamaica*.

8. Benjamin filtered through Ian Baucom, *Spectres of the Atlantic: Finance Capital, Slavery, and the Philosophy of History*, 24.
9. Glissant, *Poetics of Relation*, 133.
10. Loosely considered, "place" here refers to local geographies of habitation and memory and opposes "space," which refers to more abstract geographies of international politics, economics, and communications. Jamaica teaches me to see them as inextricably interwoven, however urgent the claims of locality. On the importance of the latter to fieldwork, see Edward Casey, *The Fate of Place: A Philosophical History*, Tim Cresswell, *Place: A Short Introduction*, and in a Caribbean context, Shalini Puri, "Finding the Field." Space roughly equates with the networked world of globalization, as described for instance in Zygmut Bauman, *Globalization: The Human Consequences*.
11. Mama G's assimilation of Rastafari to the lost heritage of the Trelawney Maroons is a canny act of cultural recovery and affirmation. On the origins of Rastafari, see Richard D.E. Burton, *Afro-Creole: Power, Opposition, and Play in the Caribbean*, 90–155. See also Barry Chavannes, *Rastafari and Other African-Caribbean Worldviews* and *Rastafari: Roots and Ideology* for a detailed exposition of belief and practice, as well as Werner Zips, ed., *Rastafari: a Universal Philosophy in the Third Millennium*. Finally, for a full sense of its cultural, political, and spiritual force, see Yasus Afari, *Overstanding Rastafari: "Jamaica's Gift to the World."*
12. On Nanny as a national hero, see Edward Kamau Brathwaite, *Wars of Respect: Nanny, Sam Sharpe and the Struggle for People's Liberation*. Nanny's image appears on the Jamaican 500 dollar bill.

BIBLIOGRAPHY

Account Book of the Deputy Paymaster General, Hispaniola, 1796–97. n.d. National Library of Jamaica, MS 237.
Afari, Yasus. 2007. *Overstanding Rastafari: "Jamaica's Gift to the World".* Jamaica: Senya-Cum.
Baucom, Ian. 2005. *Spectres of the Atlantic: Finance Capital, Slavery, and the Philosophy of History.* Durham: Duke University Press.
Bauman, Zygmut. 1998. *Globalization: The Human Consequences.* New York: Columbia University Press.
Bilby, Kenneth. 2005. *True Born Maroons.* Gainesville, FL: University Press of Florida.
Brathwaite, Edward Kamau. 1977. *Wars of Respect: Nanny, Sam Sharpe and the Struggle for People's Liberation.* Kingston, Jamaica: API.
Burton, Richard D.E. 1997. *Afro-Creole: Power, Opposition, and Play in the Caribbean.* Ithaca, NY: Cornell University Press.
Campbell, Mavis C. 1988. *The Maroons of Jamaica: A History of Resistance, Collaboration, and Betrayal, 1655–1796.* Granby, MA: Bergin & Garvey.

Carey, Bev. 1997. *The Maroon Story: The Authentic and Original History of the Maroons in the History of Jamaica, 1490–1880*. Gordon Town, Jamaica: Agouti Press.

Casey, Edward. 1998. *The Fate of Place: A Philosophical History*. Berkeley, CA: University of California Press.

Chavannes, Barry. 1994. *Rastafari and Other African-Caribbean Worldviews and Rastafari: Roots and Ideology*. Syracuse, NY: Syracuse University Press.

Cresswell, Tim. 2004. *Place: A Short Introduction*. Oxford: Blackwell.

Dallas, R.C. 1803. *History of the Maroons from their Origin to the Establishment of the their Chief Tribe at Sierra Leone*, vol 2. London: Longman and Rees.

Edwards, Bryan. 1796. *The Proceedings of the Governor and Assembly of Jamaica, in regard to the Maroon Negroes*. London: John Stockdale.

Glissant, Édouard. *Poetics of Relation*. Trans. Betsy Wing. Ann Arbor, MI: University of Michigan Press, 1997.

Grant, John N. 2002. *The Maroons in Nova Scotia*. Halifax: Formac.

Laws of Jamaica, 1681–1758. 1795. St. Jago de la Vega, Jamaica: Alexander Aikman.

Nova Scotia and the Fighting Maroons: A Documentary History, Studies in Third World Societies. vol 41. 1990. Williamsburg, NY: Department of Anthropology, College of William and Mary.

Parliamentary Intelligence: House of Commons; Blood Hounds in Jamaica. *Times* (London), March 22, 1796.

Price, Richard, and Sally Price, eds. 1992. *Stedman's Surinam: Life in an Eighteenth-Century Slave Society*. Baltimore, MD: Johns Hopkins University Press.

Puri, Shalini. 2013. Finding the Field: Notes on Caribbean Cultural Criticism, Area Studies, and the Forms of Engagement. *Small Axe* 41: 58–73.

Rainsford, Marcus. 2013. *An Historical Account of the Black Empire of Hayti*. Eds. Paul Youngquist and Grégory Pierrot. Durham: Duke University Press.

Robinson, Carey. 1993. *The Fighting Maroons of Jamaica*. Kingston: Collins and Sangster.

Votes of the Honourable Assembly of Jamaica, 1795. 1795. St. Jago de la Vega, Jamaica: Alexander Aikman.

Wilson, Kathleen. 2009. The Performance of Freedom: Maroons and the Colonial Order in Eighteenth-Century Jamaica and the Atlantic Sound. *William and Mary Quarterly* 66(1): 45–86.

Youngquist, Paul. 2012. The Cujo Effect. In *Gorgeous Beasts: Animal Bodies in Historical Perspective*, eds. Joan B. Landes, Paula Young Lee, and Paul Youngquist, 56–72. University Park, PA: Pennsylvania State University Press.

Zips, Werner. 1999. *Black Rebels: African Freedom Fighters in Jamaica*. Kingston: Ian Randle.

———, ed. 2006. *Rastafari: A Universal Philosophy in the Third Millennium*. Kingston: Ian Randal.

CHAPTER 13

Engagement and Pedagogy: Traveling with Students in Chiapas, Mexico

Debra A. Castillo

If we do not trespass (not necessarily violently), if we do not go beyond our cultural norms ... we can never be free. To free ourselves is to trespass, and to transform... To trespass is to exist. To free ourselves is to exist.

—*Augusto Boal (xxi–ii)*

It's early June and once again I'm in San Cristóbal de las Casas, at the Fortaleza de la Mujer Maya (FOMMA) facility on Avenida Argentina No. 14 in Barrio de Mexicanos (a nice transnational crossing, I've always thought), to watch a performance of *Viva la vida*. It's the rainy season and—fortunately for us—the day is overcast.[1] Too often I've been here with a group of students who have found it hard to concentrate with the heat and light pouring through the skylights onto the theatrical space, splashing over the audience and making us drowsy. This day we're as ready as we can be to appreciate this event.

Last Spring, on campus in Ithaca, New York, I gave them lectures and readings on Mayan theater in Chiapas; in the Spanish section, they've watched the interview with Petrona de la Cruz Cruz and discussed the excerpt on our course website from the play we are about to see; we've had relevant guest lectures by colleagues in El colegio de la frontera sur (ECOSUR) in San Cristóbal as well as ECOSUR in Tapachula via videoconferencing, and have learned from presentations by local Cornell scholars in the fields of nutrition, sociology,

---

[1] Readers can follow up on topics addressed here with key references in the bibliography.

D.A. Castillo (✉)
Department of Comparative Literature, Cornell University, Ithaca, NY, USA

© The Author(s) 2016

S. Puri, D.A. Castillo (eds.), *Theorizing Fieldwork in the Humanities*,
DOI 10.1057/978-1-349-92834-7_13

235

public health, anthropology, and history, among others. Since we arrived in Chiapas, we've met with the dedicated students and faculty at one of the inter-cultural universities, the Centro Maya de Estudios Agropecuarios in Palenque, part of the Universidad Autómona de Chiapas system. We have accompanied them to the field, and have been inspired by the fieldwork-based curriculum and research-team approach to multilingual indigenous tertiary education. We have read and discussed Héctor Sánchez's report on the issues surrounding health care in Chiapas, both before leaving our home campus and with Héctor himself in a generous follow-up meeting the day before. Héctor has also agreed to accompany us to the clinic in San Juan Chamula.

We have with us today in FOMMA a bilingual medical doctor who works in San Andrés Larrainzar, at the intercultural maternal health facility, Snail Ansetik Vokémolol, who will take part in the post-play discussion, and we have already scheduled a visit to her facility to meet the traditional midwives a little later in the week. One of the students, who hopes to do graduate work in public health, will, in fact, be doing her eight-week internship in San Andrés; another, a graduate student in performance studies, had originally hoped to intern with FOMMA itself, but has accepted a position with a local children's theater instead. I expect they will be particularly invested in this performance.

A woman enters the performance space with an incense burner and lights the copal; soon a thick, fragrant smoke fills the area as Mercedes Sosa's "Gracias a la vida" plays (Argentina meets Mexico again, I think to myself). A few inter-national FOMMA interns join us in the audience, along with an indigenous woman and her child, who seemed to just happen in on the performance.

The play opens when Sebastiana, a heavily pregnant woman in traditional indigenous clothing (the particular styles of skirt and *huipil*[2] generally identify their origin, but the women in this group mix costumes from Chamula, San Andrés, Zinancatán, Cancuc, and other communities), comes into the perfor-mance space. She has already been in labor far too long, but in the next few minutes is seen contending with a philandering husband and a well-meaning but too traditional mother, Dominga, who wants her to drink traditional teas to alleviate her pains. A neighbor brings the midwife, who wisely counsels call-ing an ambulance immediately.[3] However, Sebastiana dies in childbirth, leaving her daughter Lunita behind.

Years later, Lunita (who dresses in Western-style clothing) is on the brink of womanhood and the wise elder Tomasita gives her sane and forthright advice about sex and contraception. Her future husband, a supportive young man with whom she falls in love while watching the classic María Félix film, *María Bonita*, brings her to the clinic for regular appointments throughout her preg-nancy, as well as for her childbirth. Lunita gives birth to a healthy child in the local clinic, attended by a doctor in a white lab coat. The play ends with the celebration of life, and the five actors coming to the front of the perfor-mance space, in silence, with signs that read: "*Luchemos por nuestro derecho de vivir*"; "*El embarazo es bonito pero también mortal. Acude al medico*"; "*Nunca Más*"; "*¡Ya basta! No más muerte*"; "*Debemos de llevar el control prenatal libre* *y responsablemente*" (Let's fight for our right to life. Pregnancy is nice but also deadly. Go to the doctor. Never again. Enough! No more death. We must take charge of free, responsible, prenatal care). The talk back begins.

I am in the field, doing fieldwork. I am, moreover, co-teaching Cornell's most venerable fieldwork course, "Experience Latin America." Created in 1967, this yearlong course has been taught continuously since that time, with organized field trips in many different sites around the continent. Currently, we organize it as a spring preparation course, followed by summer fieldwork (divided into two- or ten-week options) and a fall reflection course, leading to either a deeply researched report to the internship organization or a professional paper.[4] Since 2009, we have been focusing on Chiapas, Mexico, as our specific study site.

While originally designed for needs of international agriculture majors and professional master's students, in recent years, the course has been opened (through cross-listing and my collaboration) as an even more multidisciplinary cross-college project. Students come from crop science, tropical agriculture, watershed management, regional planning, nutrition, assorted health careers, hotel administration, government, linguistics, along with a few from literature or performance studies. I am a professor of comparative literature, a Latin Americanist, a Mexicanist, with research interests in performance and border studies. I'm pretty sure I'm an imposter, and am surprised that anyone takes me seriously, but then again, they have to: I'm giving them a grade.[5]

San Cristóbal itself has in the last 20 years enjoyed a significant increase in tourism deriving from international interest in Zapatismo, the indigenous revolutionary movement that exploded on the world scene along with the implementation of the North American Free Trade Agreement, on January 1, 1994. Local Ladino (nonindigenous) authorities are happy to support and commercialize this tourist interest, though nearly 20 years later, their relations with the Zapatista communities still remain prickly. Likewise, performance events in the FOMMA space attract tourists, Western feminists, and international academics. De la Cruz, in one of many interviews,[6] notes that the women of FOMMA have long been aware that their agenda (sexuality education, self-reliance for women) is both familiar and amenable to international audiences; their primary goal, of course, is to speak to and serve the needs of indigenous women.[7] It is a constant balancing act for them to retain the high-paying tourist income while not portraying a "folkloric" version of their traditions or compromising their core mission,[8] and they are profoundly aware of (sometimes articulators of) critiques of well-meaning efforts by past and present government organizations, like earlier projects of the Instituto Nacional Indigenista (INI), which had been promoting theatrical performances in the highlands as a mechanism to address prevention and care of disease since the 1950s.

Thus, the indigenous woman who joined our group for the performance may be here for a sewing or a bread-making or a literacy class. Or she may want to study acting, or mask making. The long-term interns to FOMMA sitting next to us are probably channeled through NYU's Hemispheric Institute (local people know FOMMA by the cofounders, Petrona de la Cruz and Isabel Juárez; on the NYU website, the same space is called "*Centro hemisférico de performance y política en Chiapas*," and it has been supported by significant Ford Foundation[9] and NYU funding). I, of course, am uncomfortably aware that I have commissioned this performance and that my students, for all their background preparation, are the least invested in FOMMA of any of the other audience members. This is something that I know will come out in our class discussion that evening as their worries that they are behaving as, or (even worse, from their perspective) will be perceived as, tourists in this site. Some of them have shaky Spanish; none of us speak Tsotsil.

Most of the articles that I have read in journals dedicated to engaged learning and pedagogies of fieldwork take a similar form. They include anecdotes, lessons from the field learned by both students and faculty, descriptions of learning outcomes and student evaluations, a cautionary aside, and generally a note of self-praise: this is the best course ever, and it has profoundly changed people's lives. So let me get that out of the way: this is a fabulous course, academically sound, field tested with hundreds of students over a nearly 50-year history, a model for other universities, though admittedly difficult to institutionalize and staff because it is a full-year course, taught every year. It changes peoples' lives—the evaluations consistently tell us so.

My current co-instructor and I have intensified the field component—successfully arguing to the Dean of the College of Agriculture and Life Sciences that while a two- or three-week field visit (the standard for most courses of this sort nationally as well as in our home institution) fulfills the minimum requirement of the major, it by no means constitutes "real" field work. Thus, we have created the summer internship/research program, supplementing what is now a two-week overview trip in Chiapas with an eight- or ten-week field experience, matching students to organizations early in the winter semester so that they can arrive in San Cristóbal ready to contribute substantially, whether it is doing community census work, coordinating women's health workshops, making a film, doing soil sampling, building ecological stoves, working with youth theater, or doing master's research or PhD dissertation work.

Few humanities graduate students take the course. Despite the widespread concern about the "crisis" in the humanities, the demoralizing recognition of a weak job market for literary scholars, the vague but general attraction of social justice work, and the widespread discussion of a need to retool our curricula, within my university humanities fieldwork has little purchase among PhD students. Perhaps it's a failure of communication, or of imagination. Kathleen Woodward's comment sounds very familiar to me:

> Despite the repeated calls over the past twenty-five years for a renewal of the civic mission of higher education, professionalization continues to hold tenacious sway and is largely understood to contradict the purposes and practices of public scholarship, which, in turn, is dismissed under the demoralizing rubric of service or the paternalistic rubric of outreach.[10]

The imagined contradiction between the profession and the public as expressed in the uninspiring rhetoric of public service has consequences. Woodward comments:

> I cannot help but remark that some of the conversations about civic engagement, public scholarship, and the public humanities in the United States betray a distinctly anti-intellectual strain ... We find references to the importance of social development, community development, and economic development, but not intellectual development.[11]

She adds, "In fact, I wonder to what extent the very phrase 'civic engagement' is a stumbling block for the idea—and ideal—of the commitment of scholars to larger social purposes and intellectual goods."[12] From this follows the conundrum: we know that we need the kind of revitalization of the humanities implied by substantive and sustainable engagement, such as fieldwork, but find current models uninspiring or intellectually empty.

Part of the challenge of imagining a space for public humanities within our local intellectual dialogues relates to the narrow, engagement-and-outcome language of the kinds of reports we perpetrate in our various administrative roles. Another part of the challenge is locating hermeneutical and methodological structures and strategies from which to think more productively. Yet I would like to believe that if in certain US academic circles the idea of the public intellectual may seem "a soft oxymoron" (Garber), a subject for knowing snickers among the US-centric theory heads, throughout the hemisphere the concept is regaining the immediacy and vitality that had been slowly eroding since the late 1960s in the USA and the heyday of the Zapatista movement in Mexico in the mid-1990s. We might do well to take advantage of opportunities to learn from our colleagues in Latin America who have long histories of serious engagement with the organic and the intellectual public intellectual as central to major policy and intellectual debates. FOMMA cofounder Isabel Juárez comments:

> All women are intelligent, the problem is that we sometimes don't develop our intelligence well ... because we are sometimes scared, fearful about our neighbors, about our family ... but if you think about your personal situation not taking into account the other people around you, you'll find a way out, you'll have to look for it, you'll have to knock on the doors, because nobody will come here knocking at your door and go, like, do you want to do this?[13]

II

Our medical doctor contact has been kind enough to set up the visit to San Andrés Larrainzar, where we will tour both the Western-style and traditional facilities. The focus on maternal health is an explicit key priority in the state, and there are special challenges involved in getting indigenous women to come to clinics. Thus, the bilingual medical practitioners in San Andrés have focused their efforts on reaching out to the traditional midwives, or *parteras*, to provide them with tools that will help them in their distant communities, to open lines of communication in Tsotsil with San Andrés professionals when the *parteras* recognize dangerous childbirths in process, to create a culturally appropriate physical space for local women who need or choose to give birth outside their homes, and to organize *parteras* in shifts of two at a time staffing that space.[14] Colleagues in San Andrés have sponsored workshops and exchanges of information on traditional medicines and traditional childbirth practices; all the *parteras* who have participated in their program have earned badges exactly like those worn by the Western-style practitioners, and wear them proudly over their traditional *huipiles* when they are in the clinic in their regular shifts.

Officials have built a facility to the specifications of the indigenous advisors, including rooms for spiritual cleansing with herbs and copal, a *temazcal* (or steam bath) for new mothers and babies, and a communal kitchen for family celebrations of birth. Snail Ansetik Vokémolol sits side by side with the Western clinic, sharing a wall and a door, offering the opportunity for immediate stabilization care if the mother's or child's life is endangered, and quick ambulance service to San Cristóbal (less than an hour away), if the situation merits. Since so many Western-trained medical practitioners staffing clinics throughout highland Chiapas are young people from distant parts of Mexico—none of whom speak any of the local languages—who are doing their stint of required public service after graduation from medical school, this initiative is extremely exciting to us. It includes local medical professionals who speak Tsotsil, working with respected elders and local assemblies on a collaborative project, breaking down cultural barriers, creating comfortable spaces for women to give birth, while saving lives.

We have been honored to have eight of the *parteras* with us today, rather than the two we expected, women with soft hands, soft voices, and deeply wrinkled faces, who pat us gently while speaking in Tsotsil, explaining how they came to their vocation, their pride in their work, their commitment to this new facility. Some of what they are saying reinforces for the students Victoria Patishtan's comments on how the FOMMA play reflects traditional childbirth practices: how respect for the husband prevents many women from seeking Western medical care, how their fear that their child will be stolen or changed in a clinic paralyzes them. We see the need to accommodate traditional practices such as ritual cleansing with copal, the steam bath for child and mother, the herb and chile tea to encourage letting down milk, the sharing of a soup made from a hen for a girl and from a rooster for a boy.

We are in the midst of a translated conversation with them, drinking coffee they made for us in the kitchen, when the director of the hospital interrupts us, with considerable fanfare, to introduce the regional medical administrator and the local mayor, both *Ladinos* (i.e., nonindigenous). The mayor, wearing a San Andrés *huipil* and a Western pantsuit, has arrived with her publicity team, including a professional photographer. Our class meeting that night is dominated by speculation about how and to what extent our group became sidetracked as an unwitting political player in the upcoming elections.

We know that neither the state nor the federal government is meeting its obligations under international and national law with respect to access to health providers. Marginalization, discrimination, and structural inequalities have all been documented in damning detail, although lack of complete and appropriate census data in Mexico makes a fuller understanding of the depth of the problem more difficult.[15] According to the 2010 Mexican census, there are 112 million Mexicans. The difference between a dominant culture mestizo person and an indigenous person is largely defined by the language they speak, and approximately 12.7 million Mexicans belong to one of the 68 ethnic groups speaking languages other than Spanish as their mother tongue, with a heavy concentration in the south of the country. The 2009 federal law outlining respect for diversity is very indifferently enforced. Chiapas is a young state, with 47 percent of the population under 15 years of age. Almost 50 percent of indigenous women have no formal schooling at all (versus a claimed 88.6 percent for the country as a whole). Stunting, a serious result of prolonged malnutrition, is at a shocking 54.7 percent level in the state. While medical practitioners know that delay in seeking care can result in maternal and child death, which in Chiapas is far above the national norm, the distances, often impassible roads, distrust of Western-trained doctors, and the fear of losing a day's work prevent people from seeking care.[16]

How do I help my students understand the mayor and the *partera*? How do I understand them myself? We scholars in the humanities who are doing fieldwork, who are teaching fieldwork, and who are publishing fieldwork-derived scholarship urgently need to refresh our critical methods. We are all aware that literary work in the humanities academy privileges the solitary genius model and single-authored publications over collaborative projects; the same is still largely true of culture studies, where one would expect more truly interdisciplinary work. We are dissatisfied. There is little space for alternative epistemologies, little recognition that such epistemologies even exist. We find most theoretical and methodological models inadequate to our material. Perhaps, I think, it is more useful for us Latin Americanists, speaking about a Latin American context, to draw from Augusto Boal[17] and Paulo Freire rather than Alain Badiou and Michel Foucault.

The Brazilian philosopher Paulo Freire is best known for his landmark study, *Pedagogy of the Oppressed*, a work that advances his proposal for bringing together scholarship and activism in a practice of critical pedagogy, founded upon true collaboration. He is a theoretician profoundly anchored in practice, a practitioner deeply invested in theory: "I never advocate either a theoretic elitism or a practice ungrounded in theory, but the unity between theory and practice. In order to achieve this unity, one must have an epistemological curiosity."[18] His theoretical work likewise engages an ethics and practice of inquiry, as a form of continual, respectful questioning and dialogue: "For apart from inquiry, apart from the praxis, individuals cannot be truly human. Knowledge emerges only through invention and re-invention, through the restless, impatient, continuing, hopeful inquiry human beings pursue in the world, with the world, and with each other."[19]

There is no doubt that this pedagogical style resonates deeply with our preferred form in literary and cultural studies: the Socratic method of asking questions to provoke critical thinking in our students. For many of us, this discussion format is what distinguishes humanistic inquiry. Furthermore, the most important qualities of our scholarly work also involve the posing of questions that we are likely to be unable to answer, and where the well-formulated inquiry is the ultimate goal of the investigation. Freire takes this method a step further, from the structure of a privileged questioner and her unanswerable questions, into the construction of knowledge through dialogue between individuals who are presumed to have both a stake in and a significant contribution to the knowledge generated. He warns, though:

> In order to understand the meaning of dialogical practice, we have to put aside the simplistic understanding of dialogue as a mere technique ... On the contrary, dialogue characterizes an epistemological relationship. Thus, in this sense, dialogue is a way of knowing and should never be viewed as a mere tactic to involve students in a particular task.[20]

Later, he adds, "Understanding dialogue as a process of learning and knowing establishes a previous requirement that always involves an epistemological curiosity about the very elements of the dialogue."[21]

Freire contrasts the dialogic model most pointedly with what he calls the "banking" concept of education, in which the teacher is imagined as the possessor of knowledge, carefully doled out to the students in palatable doses, whereupon students become the collectors of materials and information deposited in them. Interestingly enough, Freire defines this model at its core as a failure in a certain kind of storytelling:

> A careful analysis of the teacher-student relationship at any level, inside or outside the school, reveals its fundamentally *narrative* character ... The contents, whether values or empirical dimensions of reality, tend in the process of being narrated to become lifeless and petrified. Education is suffering from narration sickness.[22]

In contrast, says Freire, "In problem-posing education, people develop their power to perceive critically *the way they exist* in the world *with which* and *in which* they find themselves; they come to see the world not as a static reality, but as a reality in process, in transformation."[23] This theoretical framework can, of course, be applied to any pedagogical situation. Freire, however, is particularly interested in the hierarchical structures of knowledge that constrain the oppressed, keeping them in an unfree state:

> The central problem is this: How can the oppressed, as divided, unauthentic beings, participate in developing the pedagogy of their liberation? Only as they

discover themselves to be "hosts" of the oppressor can they contribute to the midwifery of their liberating pedagogy. As long as they live in the duality in which *to be* is *to be like*, and *to be like* is *to be like the oppressor*, this contribution is impossible. The pedagogy of the oppressed is an instrument for their critical discovery that both they and their oppressors are manifestations of dehumanization.

Liberation is thus a childbirth, and a painful one.[24] Suddenly, I am back in San Andrés Larrainzar, in our interrupted discussion with the *parteras*, and the way that knowledge passes and does not pass between indigenous people and *Ladinos* in authority, between us and the *parteras*, and think again about the pedagogies of the oppressed and the performance of caring in politics.

In the 2008 preface to his *Theatre of the Oppressed*, fellow Brazilian Augusto Boal reminds us: "When we study Shakespeare we must be conscious that we are not studying the history of the theatre, but learning about the history of humanity. We are discovering ourselves. Above all: we are discovering that we can change ourselves, and change the world" (ix). I am a comparatist, not a political scientist or a medical professional. I'm a literary and performance studies scholar brought up in the USA, so I cannot help but be reminded of Mercutio's famous monologue in Act 1.4 of *Romeo and Juliet*. Romeo worries that he may be dreaming too much, dreaming too close to the truth, and Mercutio tells him to chill out. The monologue begins: "I see Queen Mab hath been with you. /She is the fairies' midwife. ..." Romeo gets annoyed with his friend after he has been going on for a while and interrupts: "Peace, peace, Mercutio, peace!/Thou talk'st of nothing." Mercutio responds: "I talk of dreams..."

III

The devastatingly poor health conditions in Chiapas have been extensively documented, to the shame of the entire country, and this lack of basic health services was explicitly one of the reasons for the Zapatista uprising, better health care one of the movement's key demands. It is striking, though, that the Zapatistas have maintained a very firm line on rejecting all government health programs and initiatives, meaning that the regional clinics in the Zapatista-controlled areas have a very fluctuating access to health care personnel and materials (mostly via donations from abroad, or from local medical practitioners who sympathize with the cause, combined with traditional medical practices).

Visiting the Zapatista *caracol*, or administrative center, in Oventic has always been the absolute highlight of the field trip for our students, for reasons that seem to me both clear and inexplicable. If there is one thing that students in Ithaca, New York, know about Chiapas, it is that it is the site of the world's first postmodern revolution and that revolutionary fervor is kept alive in the *juntas de buen gobierno* (good government councils) of the Zapatista municipalities. Everyone wants to be part of that history. None of my students wants to think very hard about how the revolution has evolved in the almost 20 years since the uprising first came to international notice. No one wants to hear about "Zapa-tourism." They all want to go to Oventic, the site of the big convocations in the early years of the revolution, the ones they've all seen pictures of, and read about in the communiqués, studied in their history and literature and govern-ment classes. They dream of a chance encounter with *subcomandante* Marcos, but, at best, they will meet local Tsotsiles, some of them born after the 1994 revolution, all of them young subsistence farmers from resistant municipalities, raised in the nearly 500-year-old tradition of rejection of outsiders.

I never know how much time to plan for Oventic. It certainly requires a huge effort on our part, and that of our local collaborators, to get in the gate. Someone has to go personally to Oventic over the winding roads up to the isolated administrative site with a letter from us to get preliminary permis-sion. In this way, our participation in the performance of Zapatismo has begun before we even set foot in the state. When we go to Oventic, on the appointed date and time, that performance takes certain ritual forms. We need to bring passports and have them laboriously checked—against the list we sent, against whatever criteria they apply this year; since we don't speak the language, we can only guess what they might be talking about among themselves—and we need to be prepared to wait—a half hour, two hours—until the *junta* decides whether or not we can enter. Most of the time we are allowed in, with the standard warnings: no conversation with anyone, no pictures of people, no pictures at all until the *junta* officially gives their formal approval. We need to stay together as a group and only go where the silent, masked and armed guide allows us to go. Sometimes the guide is bored and rushes us up and down the hill, only delaying at the small shops where we are encouraged to buy souve-nirs. We notice that the prices are higher than in the Santo Domingo market in San Cristóbal, but buy the T-shirts, the handkerchiefs, the DVDs anyway; there are bragging rights involved in giving friends back in Ithaca genuine purchased-in-Oventic articles.

Some of the times we get to meet with the *junta*, who may be more or less patient with us and may or may not answer our students' questions. (One time they asked us to write up all our questions on a single piece of paper, and while we waited outside, they conducted other business and debated how to answer for an hour or so. When we were allowed in the meeting room, the spokesper-son said something like: we will answer questions 1, 3, 10, 18, and 32. Which they did. One sentence each, no follow-up.) Sometimes, only I am allowed in—a huge disappointment to everyone, since I'm generally the one person in the group who has been there many times already. But the authorities ask who is the leader, and as the professor, fluent Spanish speaker, and (probably equally important for the *junta*) group elder, that person has to be me. Once we were allowed to peek into the clinic. Twice we were allowed down into the school complex.

This visit, from my perspective, has been a particularly good one. We only had to wait outside for a half hour or so, and we brought with us from San Cristóbal a brilliant young indigenous anthropologist, a Zapatista student-scholar known to people from the region. He generously provided information and context all day, before arrival and in Oventic itself, answering endless questions. The *junta* was busy with other matters, and decided to receive only me (a severe blow to at least one dedicated young scholar). I tried to console him: the spokesperson for the *junta*, a woman, spoke to me only very briefly—I suspect her Spanish was minimal, one reason among others not to entertain a group of foreign students.[25]

Gregory Jay asks us to think about the question of how humanities can advance social justice goals. He notes that "it is difficult to see how humanities scholarship can advance community cultural development in quite the concrete ways demonstrated by projects in art, theater, and music"; nevertheless, the context of the current paradigm shift in higher education creates a need for humanities scholars to rethink our teaching and research. He contends that "the future of the humanities depends upon … the organized implementation of project-based engaged learning and scholarship." Like Kathleen Woodward, Jay is allergic to the implications of the "outreach" model, with its hierarchical presumptions about academic relations to knowledge, and profoundly in favor of promoting a much more participatory project of learning with and from the community.

Woodward helps us to think about how the methodologies and skills we have already developed in our humanities training can serve us well in field-work projects:

> But in the humanities, communities of inquiry often come into being through the articulating of questions, which are often inchoate in the beginning and can never be definitively answered. Communities are formed around questions; they are communities of the question. In the humanities, inquiry adds context that ever widens and deepens; this is what has been famously called thick description, and to this I would add thick theory. In short, I believe that the work being done in the public humanities can give life to the uninspiring generalities … What is ultimately at stake in the public humanities is a form of scholarship and research, of teaching and learning, that honors commitment and concrete purpose, has a clear and present substance, reduces the distance between the university and life, and offers civic education for all involved, revealing the expansive future of the humanities in the present and in public.[26]

In our class discussion after our visit to Oventic, I resist the temptation to give the students one more lecture about Zapatismo, and push them to more complex articulations of their questions. I remind them that the key concept in the Zapatista educational project, which rejects all federal government–sponsored Education Ministry programs and textbooks, is *acompañamiento* (walking with someone). How can we take this concept seriously as an intellectual proposal and apply it to our own scholarly practice?

IV

Zinacantán is one of my favorite places in Chiapas, and Tonik one of my favorite people. It's a stunningly beautiful town, where most of the men work in the flower industry (greenhouses cover the valley, and the water is profoundly polluted by runoff from the many pesticides and herbicides), and all the women dress in matching elaborately handwoven and embroidered clothing, bursting with flowers, with colors and designs determined annually by the local council. The same local council has instituted a fee for non-Zinacatecs to enter the city limits, turning the entire community into a kind of tourist park.

Tonik is a local weaver, has over the years become a good friend, and I admire her tremendously. She is a shrewd businesswoman, a talented artist, and a force of nature. She was in her mid-twenties when I first met her, and had already innovated how textiles are sold in Zinacantán, by welcoming tourists into her home, inviting people to watch her and her sisters weave, or encouraging them to take a turn at the backstrap loom, offering them tortillas ground from local corn, then inviting them to playact in a typical Zinacatec wedding. She even does catering on the side. Her Spanish is excellent; she is learning some English to better interact with her customers.

Tonik left home very young, fleeing an abusive father, eventually bringing her five sisters and her mother under her roof to live and work with her. She is the matriarch, though her mother and brothers have to be brought in on any official consultations with city council authorities. She sets the agenda for production and decides how the business will be run. She has encouraged all her sisters to finish at least middle school (she has been trying to do so herself, part time in the evenings) and has sacrificed so that they can even go to high school. Several of her sisters are now married, including one who has married a bilingual elementary school teacher, and who is herself very committed to education in Tsotsil. Tonik says, for her part, that she knows she can never marry; men in her town don't like women who are too strong, or too independent, and she crossed the line when she set up her own house, consolidating her undesirability when she had her father put in jail.

We've just come from San Juan Bautista, the famous church in San Juan Chamula, where chickens are regularly slaughtered, and Coca-Cola, along with the local distilled corn alcohol, posh, and multicolored candles help shamans and healers intercede with the saints for their clients' health. We've toured the clinic catty-corner on the main plaza to the church and have spoken with the young doctor there—a woman from Tijuana doing her public service who speaks excellent English. Zinacantán shares a language and culture with Chamula but is perhaps more westernized[27]; as an indication, there is a sign on the church door saying: prohibited to kill chickens in the church.

I ask Tonik what she and her family do when someone gets sick.

Stay in bed and drink teas until I get better, she says.

And if that doesn't make you better?

I call a *curandera* to come with remedies.

And if that doesn't work?

I go to the church and pray.

And if that still doesn't work?

Then I would call a shaman[28] to treat me, since his prayers are stronger than mine.

And then?

Then, I climb the mountain with the shaman, because on the top of the mountain we're closer to God, and he can hear our prayers. Then I'll surely get better.

We've climbed this mountain once, with Tonik leading the way through town and up the narrow and winding path, over drainage pipes and small streams, past farm fields perched precariously on hillsides. Elegant in her purple-and-blue skirt and cape, flip-flops on her feet, she scrambles sure-footedly over roots and up steep muddy inclines, the rocks made slippery by the day's rain. All the way up she talks continuously: about her family and her business, about the times of year and festivals when it is most efficacious to climb to the shrine at the top, about the offerings that one needs to carry with them. The small shrine is a concrete shelter smelling of copal, housing three simple green crosses decked with pine (a syncretic image, I know, with Christian iconography overlaid on the ancient Maya symbol of the *ceiba*, the world tree that unites the heavens and the undergrounds). Here the Zinacatec Tsotsil woman is closest to God; here prayers are answered and people are healed.

At no time does Tonik ever mention going to the clinic.

The view is spectacular.

NOTES

1. The field notes are composites of several years in Chiapas, rather than a report on any single fieldtrip.

2. A *huipil* is the blouse worn as part of a traditional indigenous woman's clothing. It is elaborately embroidered, often handwoven, and the colors, the placement of embroidery, and the images used are specific to a community and often prescribed by the indigenous authorities on an annual basis—thus, local women like Tonik from Zinacantán can tell you not only what community the *huipil* is from, but what year. See also Walter Morris, *Textile Guide to the Highlands of Chiapas.*

3. FOMMA has always been an all-woman troupe, so women take on the male roles. We always watch the performances in Spanish; when they travel to more distant highland communities, the presentations may be in Tsotsil, or mixed Tsotsil, Spanish, and some Tseltal (Isabel Juárez is more comfortable in that language, though most of the other key performers are Tsotsil speakers).

4. This course has served as a model for many other courses of this sort, including the 15-year-old field course to India, and parallel courses for countries ranging from Ecuador to Tanzania to Indonesia, some of them organized by veterans of the Latin America course who have returned to Cornell as faculty members, or who previously served as faculty for the Latin American course.

5. The course has evolved considerably over the nearly 50 years since it was inaugurated, both with respect to the field sites and in terms of professorial

investment and pedagogical styles. In its current form, it is a yearlong course that begins with a spring semester overview course, co-taught by faculty from agriculture and arts and sciences, including an additional discussion section for students who will be participating in the summer field trip/internship options. Students in that course do research papers on a topic of their interest related to Chiapas and develop work plans in collaboration with the organization with which they will be interning. We have been closely collaborating with the Tecnológico de Monterrey in Veracruz for the last couple of years, so some meetings are joint, via live videoconferencing. Students from the two campuses meet in person during the field visits, and each day's activities are concluded by a round table discussion and analysis session. During the following two months, interns meet weekly for small group discussions, facilitated by a TA appointed by the faculty, and write weekly reflection papers posted on a shared Google doc site. In the follow-up course in the fall, students develop final meta-reflections, reports to their hosting institutions, and a final presentation open to the public.

6. See Adriana M. Manago and Patricia M. Greenfield, "The Construction of Independent Values among Maya Women at the Forefront of Social Change: Four Case Studies," 1–29.

7. Petrona de la Cruz mentions that when she first became pregnant, she did not know having sex could result in a baby (Manago 9). María Francisca Oseguera speaks of how powerful the FOMMA workshops were for her in creating a space to speak about women's sexuality and sexual pleasure, something she never experienced with her husband. She now teaches these workshops herself and comments that her audience is not limited to highland women: "One university student has a husband and still she doesn't know what is sexuality…. It surprised me a lot when I spoke to her about the clitoris of a woman, she didn't know" (Manago 20).

8. The mission statement, inscribed on the wall of the facility reads as follows: "*Grupo de mujeres indígenas que imparten talleres creativos, productivos y culturales para mujeres, jovenes y niños (indígenas). El objetivo principal del grupo es el teatro, así como alfabetización y lecto-escritura tsotsil-tseltal. Contamos con servicio de guardería.*" (Indigenous women's group that offers creative, productive, and cultural workshops for indigenous women, youth, and children. The principal objective of the group is the theater, along with alphabetization and reading-writing in Tsotsil and Tseltal. We have childcare service available.) The story of the complex relations among INI, Sna Jtz'ibajom, FOMMA, Harvard, and NYU, as well as ongoing collaborations with the Laughlins, Diana Taylor, Ralph Lee, Amy Trompetter, and other northern performance consultants is well established and need not be rehearsed here.

9. Castro Santana, "Aplicaciones del teatro en la construcción de la identidad Tsotsil: FOMMA," 71.

10. Woodward, "The Future of the Humanities in the Present & in Public," 110.

11. Woodward, 116.
12. Woodward, 117.
13. Manago and Greenfield, "The Construction of Independent Values among Maya Women," 13.
14. There are approximately 5000 *parteras* working in Chiapas, the majority Tsotsil or Tseltal speakers with no formal training. Along with their training, San Andrés *parteras* are all given basic medical instruments, as well as cell phones to communicate at need with the clinic. See Juan Pablo Mayorga, "Parteras, 'los pilares' en la lucha por reducer las muertes maternas."
15. Sánchez Pérez et al., *Excluded People, Eroded Communities*, 5, 51.
16. See Sánchez Pérez, *Excluded People*; the Mexican census bureau, Instituto de Estadística y Geografía. http://www.inegi.org.mx/; Federico Navarrete, *Las relaciones interétnicas en México*.
17. Another thread to follow: Doris Difarnecio, who has been working with FOMMA since 1999, and is now serving as director of the Hemispheric Institute in Chiapas, came to Chiapas originally to direct FOMMA plays, and has given the women training in Boal techniques.
18. Freire and Macedo, "A Dialogue: Culture, Language, and Race," 382.
19. Freire, *Pedagogy of the Oppressed*, 72.
20. Freire and Macedo, "A Dialogue," 379.
21. Freire and Macedo, 382.
22. Freire, *Pedagogy*, 71.
23. Freire, 83.
24. Freire, 48–9.
25. Students who participate in the internships will inevitably have many opportunities to interact with Zapatista as well as non-Zapatista municipalities and individuals, as well as spend more time at Oventic and/or the other caracoles. This is quite different from a few hours during a fieldtrip doing "Zapa-tourism," and both we and our hosts know it.
26. Woodward, "The Future of the Humanities," 117, 123.
27. There is a very rich body of anthropological work on these two communities, sometimes called the most studied towns in Mexico, due to the Harvard Chiapas Project, which under the direction of Evon Vogt, lasted from 1957 to 2000.
28. I'm simplifying here, since there are different words for traditional healers, spiritual healers, elders, and shamans, all of whom have varying degrees of ability and power.

Bibliography

Álvarez, Francisco Q. 2002. El teatro maya: brevísima semblanza histórica, su situación actual y problemática. *Reencuentro* 33: 75–89.
Boal, Augusto. 1979. *Theatre of the Oppressed*. Trans. Emily Fryer. London: Pluto Books.
———. 2006. *Aesthetics of the Oppressed*. Trans. Adrian Jackson. New York: Routledge.

Castro, Carlo Antonio. 2001. Educación indigenista: El Teatro Petul en los años cincuenta. *Tramoya* 67 (April–June): 211–224. http://cdigital.uv.mx/bitstream/123 456789/4686/1/200167211.pdf

Castro Santana, Karina Vanessa. 2012. *Aplicaciones del teatro en la construcción de la identidad Tsotsil: FOMMA*. Mexico: Universidad Veracruzana.

Centro estatal de lenguas, artes y literatura indígenas (CELALI). Government of State of Chiapas. http://www.celali.gob.mx/

Centro hemisférico de performance y política en Chiapas. http://centrohemisferico. wordpress.com/info-2/

Crabtree, Robbin D. 2013. The Intended and Unintended Consequences of International Service-Learning. *Journal of Higher Education Outreach and Engagement* 17(2): 43–65.

Davis-Floyd, Robbie, Stacy Leigh Pigg, and Sheila Cosminsky. 2001. Daughters of Time: The Shifting Identities of Contemporary Midwives. *Journal of Medical Anthropology* 20(2–3): 105–139.

Escobar, Arturo. 2010. Latin America at a Crossroads. *Cultural Studies* 24(1): 1–65.

Experience Latin America (IARD 4010). n.d. http://ip.cals.cornell.edu/courses/ iard4010/

Frank, Andre Gunder, and Marta Fuentes. 1987. Nine Theses on Social Movements. *Economic and Political Weekly* 22(35): 1503–1507, 1509–1510.

Freire, Paulo. 2000. *Pedagogy of the Oppressed*. Trans. Myra Bergman Ramos. New York: Continuum.

Freire, Paulo, and Donaldo Macedo. 1995. A Dialogue: Culture, Language, and Race. *Harvard Educational Review* 65(3): 377–402.

Frischmann, Donald. 1994. New Mayan Theatre in Chiapas: Anthropology, Literacy, and Social Drama. In *Negotiating Performance*, eds. Diana Taylor and Juan Villegas, 213–238. Durham: Duke University Press.

Garber, Marjorie. 2011. After the Humanities. Lecture at Cornell University, Ithaca, New York, November 16.

Global Envision. What Latin America Thinks about Globalization. http://www.globalenvision.org/library/8/1416

Instituto de Estadística y Geografía. http://www.inegi.org.mx/

Jay, Gregory. 2012, June 19. The Engaged Humanities: Principles and Practices for Public Scholarship and Teaching. *Journal of Community Engagement and Scholarship*. http://jces.ua.edu/

Juárez Espinosa, Isabel. 1994. *Cuentos y teatro tzeltales. A'yejetik sok Ta'jimal*. Mexico: Editorial Diana.

Laughlin, Robert L. 2008. *Monkey Business Theatre*. Austin: University of Texas Press.

Lewis, Stephen E. 2011. Modernizing Message, Mystical Messenger: The Teatro Petul in the Chiapas Highlands, 1954–1974. *The Americas* 67(3): 375–397.

Manago, Adriana M., and Patricia M. Greenfield. 2011. The Construction of Independent Values among Maya Women at the Forefront of Social Change: Four Case Studies. *Ethos: Journal for the Society of Psychological Anthropology* 39(1): 1–29.

Mayorga, Juan Pablo. 2012. Parteras, 'los pilares' en la lucha por reducir las muertes maternas. *CNN México*, July 12. http://mexico.cnn.com/nacional/2012/07/12/ parteras-los-pilares-en-la-lucha-por-reducir-las-muertes-maternas

Montemayor, Carlos. 2007. Theater, Which Once Was Dance. In *Words of the True Peoples, Palabras de los Seres Verdaderos—Anthology of Contemporary Mexican*

Indigenous-Language Writers, eds. Carlos Montemayor and David Frischmann, vol. 3: Theatre. Austin, TX: University of Texas Press.

Morris, Walter F. 2012. *Textile Guide to the Highlands of Chiapas*. Loveland, CO: Thrums.

Navarrete, Federico. 2008. *Las relaciones interétnicas en México*. México: UNAM.

Prins, Esther, and Nicole Webster. 2010. Student Identities and the Tourist Gaze in International Service-learning: A University Project in Belize. *Journal of Higher Education Outreach and Engagement* 14(1): 5–32.

Rieger, Ivy Alana. 2007. Performance and Theatricality among the Highland Maya of Chiapas, Mexico, PhD diss., Florida State University.

Rubin, Donald L., and Paul H. Matthews. 2013. Learning Outcomes Assessment: Extrapolating from Study Abroad to International Service-Learning. *Journal of Higher Education Outreach and Engagement* 17(2): 67–86.

Sánchez Blake, Elvira, and Cecilia Chapa. "Literatura y teatro" on Experience Latin America Through Another Lens. Cornell IARD 4010 supplementary website. https://courses.cit.cornell.edu/iard4010/topic9/index.html

Sánchez Pérez, Hector Javier, et al. 2006. *Excluded People, Eroded Communities: Realizing the Right to Health in Chiapas, Mexico*. Report: Physicians for Human Rights, El Colegio de la Frontera Sur, Centro de Capacitación en Ecología y Salud para Campesinos-Defensoría del Derecho a la Salud.

Sesia, Paola. 1997. Women Come Here On Their Own When They Need To: Prenatal Care, Authoritative Knowledge, and Maternal Health in Oaxaca. In *Childbirth and Authoritative Knowledge*, eds. Robbie Davis-Floyd and Carolyn F. Sargent, 397–420. Berkeley: University of California Press.

Sherredan, Margaret, Benjamin J. Lough, and Amy Bopp. 2013. Students Serving Abroad: A Framework for Inquiry. *Journal of Higher Education Outreach and Engagement* 17(2): 7–42.

Simonelli, Jeanne, Duncan Earle, and Elizabeth Story. 2004. Acompañar Obediciendo: Learning to Help in Collaboration with Zapatista Communities. *Michigan Journal of Community Service Learning* 10 (Summer): 43–56.

Steele, Cynthia. 1994. 'A Woman Fell into the River': Negotiating Female Subjects in Contemporary Mayan Theatre. In *Negotiating Performance*, eds. Diana Taylor and Juan Villegas, 236–256. Durham: Duke University Press.

Underiner, Tamara L. 1998. Incidents of Theatre in Chiapas, Tabasco, and Yucatán. *Theatre Journal* 50(3): 349–369.

Woodward, Kathleen. 2009. The Future of the Humanities in the Present & in Public. *Daedalus* 138(Winter): 110–123.

INDEX

Note: Page numbers with "n" denote notes.

© The Author(s) 2016
S. Puri, D.A. Castillo (eds.), *Theorizing Fieldwork in the Humanities*,
DOI 10.1057/978-1-349-92834-7

J

Jaipur Literature Festival, 152
Jamaica. *See* Maroons; Rastafari
  Kingston, 216, 219, 226, 229, 230
James, Marlon, 13
  A Brief History of Seven Killings, 13
JANAM, 15, 114, 115–23, 126n35
Jana Natya Manch (JANAM or *People's Theater Group*)
  Ákhrí Julús (*The Last Strike*), 115, 118
  Deshpande, Sudhanva, 115
  Hashmi, Safdar, 115, 126n35
  Moloyashree, Hashmi, 115
  sútradhár, 117, 118, 126n36
Jay, Gregory, 245
JSTOR, 168, 173, 175
Judeo-Christian, 52

K

Kant, Immanuel, 62, 82
Katharsis, 83
Kelly, Jennifer Lynn, 14, 15, 95–108
Keywords: A Vocabulary of Culture and Society, 11, 20n40. *See also* Williams, Raymond
King Jr., Martin Luther, 63, 187
kinship, 39, 64
Knox, Thomas M., 197, 198, 203, 207n11
Koch, Gertrud, 73–4
Komunyakaa, Yusef, 16, 184–9, 189n10, 189n14
  Dien Cai Dau, 186, 188, 189n10, 189n14
Koné, Kassim, 56, 68n11
Kourouma, Ahmadou, 53, 67n1
  The Suns of Independence, 53, 67n1
Kouyate, Jeli Mori, 56, 58

L

Lagos, 16, 193, 196–203, 205, 206n1, 207n15
Landell, Saul, 8
landscape
  in literature, 153
  poetics of land, 32, 171

learning from below, 5, 7, 9
Lethbridge, Emily, 3
liberation, 45n11, 78, 86, 87, 109, 233n12, 242, 243
life writing, 139
linguistic authenticity, 158–160
literary studies, 76, 133, 137, 206, 241, 242
  African literary studies, 56, 59, 195, 201 (*see also* comparative literature)
  literary criticism, 4, 9, 30, 36, 39, 56, 42, 53, 59, 64, 67n4, 68n17, 68n18, 213, 214
  use of anthropology, 4, 5, 7, 9
  literary theory, 138 (*see also* world literature)
literary fieldwork, 3, 4, 13, 19n12 39, 40, 152–155, 160, 194, 214. *See also* Dayan, Joan (Colin)
  Haiti, History and the Gods, 4 (*see also* Hartman, Saidiya)
  Lose Your Mother: A Journey along the Atlantic Slave Route, 3 (*see also* James, Marlon; Puri, Shalini)
literary reading
  close-reading, 20n35, 31, 40, 195, 214
  New Critical model, 40
literary silences, 31, 32. *See also* archival absences
lived experience, 11, 18, 8n8, 30, 38, 39, 56, 62, 63, 76, 172, 177
lived history, 75, 78–81, 85–87

M

Macaulay, Thomas Babbington, 9, 45n12
Maconi, Lara, 3
Mahila Atma Raksha Samiti (MARS), 73–75, 85, 88n5
mainstream media, 132, 133, 136, 141, 143, 202
Malinké societies, 53, 55, 56, 58, 66, 68n7. *See also* Diabate, Naminata
Malkki, Liisa, 8, 20n32. *See also* Anthropology
Mama, Amina,
  ethics of study, 66